Honor in the Modern World

Honor and Obligation in Liberal Society: Problems and Prospects

Series Editors: Laurie Johnson, Kansas State University, and Dan Demetriou, University of Minnesota, Morris

Liberalism's political, economic, and social benefits are undeniable. However, these benefits come with a price: liberal societies are losing their sense of honor, civic obligation, higher moral purpose, shared values, and community. This series focuses on classical liberalism, honor, and social and civic obligation. More information about the series can be found at lexingtonliberalism.com.

Titles in the Series

Honor in the Modern World: Interdisciplinary Perspectives, edited by Laurie Johnson and Dan Demetriou

Honor in the Modern World

Interdisciplinary Perspectives

Edited by Laurie M. Johnson and
Dan Demetriou

LEXINGTON BOOKS
Lanham • Boulder • New York • London

Published by Lexington Books
An imprint of The Rowman & Littlefield Publishing Group, Inc.
4501 Forbes Boulevard, Suite 200, Lanham, Maryland 20706
www.rowman.com

Unit A, Whitacre Mews, 26-34 Stannary Street, London SE11 4AB

British Library Cataloguing in Publication Information Available

Library of Congress Cataloging-in-Publication Data Available

ISBN: 978-1-4985-0261-0 (cloth: alk. paper)
ISBN: 978-1-4985-0262-7 (electronic)

∞™ The paper used in this publication meets the minimum requirements of American National Standard for Information Sciences Permanence of Paper for Printed Library Materials, ANSI/NISO Z39.48-1992.

Printed in the United States of America

Contents

Acknowledgments

We'd like to thank the Earhart Foundation for supporting a March, 2015, mini-conference for our contributors, which allowed us the invaluable benefit of hearing and discussing each other's ideas early in the process of collaboration. We'd like to thank all of the authors in this volume for their speedy responses to our various requests. Generous travel and research funding was also made available by the University of Minnesota's Imagine Fund and Faculty Research Enhancement Fund programs. We'd also like to express our gratitude to Leyton Gunn, who as a graduate assistant helped with organizing and recording the conference and the early stages of compiling the contents of this book, and to Ciara Chambers, an undergraduate assistant, who helped out at the conference as well and did great service in making sure all the chapters were properly formatted. Thanks also to Brett Sitts, another undergraduate assistant, who helped with technology at the conference as well.

Introduction

Dan Demetriou and Laurie M. Johnson

The idea that honor can be a legitimate moral or political motive was an ideological casualty of the First World War. It took decades for modern social science to take honor seriously again, the interval having rendered honor so quaint that it could be discussed with detachment, especially as most of the analysis was directed at southern Europeans, Africans, and Arabs.[1] Literary scholars started weighing in soon after, reminding Western intellectuals of the honor traditions of northwest Europe and Scandinavia, which struck their readership closer to home.[2] Around this time, historians began to mount a powerful case that the American Founders were fairly obsessed with their honor, and that honor not only helped propel the Revolution, but steadied a new republic teetering toward monarchy.[3] More recently, psychologists have come to find compelling similarities between the logic of violence in Old World and U.S. honor cultures.[4] Finally, political theorists and ethicists, whose purview is evaluative as well as descriptive, have begun to engage honor seriously enough to debate its compatibility with the more-or-less liberal public conscience.[5]

To some degree, each of these research streams is represented in the following chapters, but none more so than the question of whether honor has a place in a modern, democratic, and/or liberal society. In fact, the suggestion that honor is a moral or political value in need of rehabilitation remains highly controversial. This is to be expected: Western intellectuals usually self-identify as "liberal" in some sense of that term, and liberals have always been skeptical of honor. Since a central question of this volume is whether those suspicions are justified, it would be helpful to review briefly some sources of liberal misgiving.

Ambivalence about honor, especially among intellectuals, is driven in no small measure by confusion over what honor is supposed to *be*. Indeed, in English, the word "honor" is not only ambiguous, but contronymic: as with "cleave" and "sanction," "honor" connotes opposite ideas. On the one hand, honor seems based solely on the good opinion of others. The Greek word *time* is translated as "honor," and Aristotle, in his search for the supreme good, rejects honor as a candidate for this status partially because, however much "cultivated" and "political" people might seek it, honor is "too superficial . . . for it seems to depend more on those who honor than on the one honored, whereas we intuitively believe that the good is something of our own and hard to take from us."[6]

Christian moralists taught that true honor is based on God's favor; but even if God's approval would be reliable and unchanging, this instruction nonetheless portrays honor as supervening upon someone else's mental attitudes, and thus again counts as a form of outer honor. Early-modern Europeans cared enough about outer honor to die for it in shocking numbers, despite being perfectly conscious of how unfair and uninformed society can be. Thus Shakespeare's audiences could nod in agreement with *Richard II*'s Mowbray that

> Mine honour [reputation] is my life; both grow in one:
> Take honour from me, and my life is done.[7]

while nonetheless laughing in sympathy to Falstaff's dismissal of honor as a "scutcheon," or heraldic emblem, a glittering but false value useful only for luring men to their deaths.[8] Writers such as Mandeville acknowledged the moral importance of external honor while admitting that it was something any "debauched fellow who runs in every tradesman's debt" could claim—*if*, that is, he was prepared to duel anyone foolish enough to publicly note what everyone privately acknowledged.[9] And even in standard contemporary usage, one cannot "be honored" by "an honor" unless it is openly bestowed by others, and one cannot be "dishonored" but publicly. So it could appear that honor is to us, just as it was to Aristotle, entirely dependent upon the good opinion of others.

On the other hand, the word "honor" has an undeniably internal sense. As with the term "character" (which once denoted nothing more than one's reputation), "honor" and some of its inflections and idiomatic expressions refer to objective, judgment-independent facts about our moral fiber. Plato offered us a theory of the soul divided into three parts: our various appetites, our intellect, and the *thumos*, the last of which is the motivationally weak intellect's natural ally, a "lion" or "white horse" in comparison to our "beastly" or "black horse" appetites, which is naturally dignified, honor-seeking, spirited, but requires victories to gain confidence and dominance over our ignoble drives. There is a sense of "honor" that refers to the inner characteristics that Plato had in mind. For instance, in common parlance, "honorableness" suggests steadfastness and integrity. Or consider how the U.S. military understands honor as "respect, duty, loyalty, selfless service, integrity, and personal courage."[10] The phrases "honor codes" and "codes of honor" also invoke a personal attachment to some ideal. Once a fixture more or less only of Old-South colleges and military academies ("I will not lie, cheat, or steal, or tolerate those who do," runs West Point's honor code), many of even the most left-leaning universities have introduced honor codes in hopes of curbing difficult-to-catch violations such as academic dishonesty and sexual misconduct. And we reserve the phrase "honor system" for any institution whose sustainability relies on our ability to do the right thing even when no one is looking, such as a lending library with an unmonitored sign-out system or an unattended roadside "honor market."[11]

So which is it? Is honor about having a good reputation, which is necessarily built on the shifting sand of fickle opinion? Or is honor about resolute dedication to the soberest of high-minded ideals, which may or may not be appreciated? No other normative term in English has such dramatically bifurcated meanings.

Western liberals also bridle at honor's gendered associations. Admittedly, *justice* has often been administered differently to men and women. But never was there "masculine justice" or "feminine justice" as there was (and still is) masculine and feminine honor. Beginning with women, most traditional cultures predicated a woman's honor on her fecundity and chastity. Biblical literature is rife with examples of women living in shame for being "barren," and until quite recently "spinsterhood" had grave social consequences for women even in advanced Western societies. And whereas shaming unchastity might seem impossible in the "swipe right" era of dating apps, at least five thousand women are nonetheless still being slain every year in honor killings for offenses as slight as chatting with an unrelated male or being "defiled" by rape.[12]

Although we associate these feminine honor norms with Middle Eastern or central Asian tribal traditions, they were until quite recently applauded by male and female Western audiences. For instance, the sixth century B.C. Roman noblewoman Lucretia has been extolled by Western artists and composers for millennia as a model of feminine honorableness, and her story is illuminating on many levels. As Livy tells the tale, Lucretia welcomes the Roman prince Sextus Tarquinius into her home while her menfolk are away at war. Taken by her beauty, Sextus steals into her bedroom in the middle of the night and begs her to sleep with him. Lucretia refuses, even after being threatened with murder. At last, Sextus threatens to kill Lucretia and a male slave, arranging their bodies so that she "might be said to have been put to death in adultery with a man of base condition." As this threat touches Lucretia's reputation, she accedes. After Sextus leaves, "exulting in his conquest of a woman's honour," Lucretia calls her husband and father back from battle, and tearfully tells them how she "lost her honour" to the prince and that they, "if they are men," will avenge her. The men swear to punish Sextus, and they do their best to support Lucretia, assuring her that her honor hasn't been besmirched. But Lucretia is disconsolate, and says, "Though I acquit myself of the sin, I do not absolve myself from punishment; not in time to come shall ever an unchaste woman live through the example of Lucretia." Brandishing a concealed dagger, she proceeds to stab herself to death in front of her horrified family.[13]

On the other side of the ledger, masculine honor has usually been thought to depend on a man's virility, martial valor, and willingness to defend his women and social prerogatives with violence. In the Mediterranean, male sex characteristics are metonyms for masculine honor. "The ideal of the honorable man" in Andalucía, we are told, "is expressed by the word *hombría*, 'manliness,' [. . .] a term which is constantly heard in the pueblo, and the concept is expressed as the physical sexual quintessence of the male (*cojones*)."[14] In a Cretan village, "the intrinsic principles of honor" for men are synonymous with manliness (*andrismos*), which at its most basic means being *barbatos*, or "well endowed with testicles and the strength drawn from them."[15] If provoked, "a Greek Cypriot, a Bedouin and Berber may answer 'I also have a moustache'" as a way of saying that their sense of masculine honor is intact and that they are prepared to defend it.[16]

Physical attributes aside, what really matters for male honor is performance, especially on the battlefield. Patrick Henry's "Give me liberty or give me death!" is a prototypical liberal battle cry: it calls for courageous action in support of political freedom, but doesn't glorify conflict as such—death is better than tyranny, but still bad. Admiral Nelson's "Victory or Westminster Abbey!" is more representative of an honor mindset: it celebrates battle, and sees an honorable death as securing all-important glory just as well as victory. From prehistory to the Battle of the Somme, where the 8th Battalion Royal East Surrey Regiment kicked footballs across no-man's land, battle was frequently an occasion for men to flaunt their courage and martial excellence, often with an audience not only of their fellows on the battlefield but of the entire village. The most romantic expression of masculine honor is champion combat, where two high-ranked equals compete in violent contests so ceremonial and fair-minded that they blur the line between battle and sport.[17]

Masculine honor has often been thought to demand other, unhappier forms of violence. Cattle-raiding appears to be honored in every herding culture we study, and continues to be an important rite of passage for young men in certain parts of East Africa and central Asia.[18] The need to protect one's herd—or one's easily-stolen goods generally—has been offered as a possible explanation for "cultures of honor," distinctive for the way they promote swift and violent retaliation for threats and even mere insults. And when it comes to insult, perhaps the most primal measure of a man's honor is his ability to violently defend, or at least revenge, offenses against women under his protection. As we have seen, Lucretia goads her men to posthumously avenge her by predicating their masculinity upon it. Edmund Burke expected "ten thousand swords to leap from their scabbards" to avenge "even a look that threatened [Marie Antoinette] with insult." Today, some of Al Qaeda's most effective propaganda harangues Muslim men on points of honor. As Abu al-Zarqawi wrote in one communication,

> Has the honor of your women become so trivial in your eyes? Beware. Have you not heard that many of your chaste and pure sisters from among the Sunnis of Tel'afar had their honor desecrated, their chastity slaughtered, and their wombs filled with the sperm of the Crusaders and their brothers? Where is your religion? Moreover, where is your sense of honor, your zeal, and your *manliness*? (emphasis in original)[19]

If honor really is gendered in this way—if these associations aren't cultural accretions, but essential to honor itself—then honor cannot be accepted by modern Western liberals. Liberalism is, so to speak, gender-neutral in that it imagines individuals (as far as their rights and prerogatives go) shorn of their particularities, including their genders and sexes. We are to be valued as "people" or "individuals" and not as men or women. Any requirements placed on us must be those duties common to any bare individual similarly situated or endowed—this is why, for instance, it is the default liberal position that a woman should be allowed to fight if she can satisfy the physical requirements of a soldier. Thus, insofar as liberalism advocates for maximum liberty for the individual consistent with similar liberties for others, the way traditional feminine honor norms limit sexual and reproductive choices are wholly untenable, however valuable they may be for perpetuating the tribe or assuring husbands of their progeny. And insofar as liberalism conceives of justice as the terms of mutually beneficial cooperative schemes, it is necessarily in tension with the importance traditional masculine honor places on the contest, however meaningful these contests may be for men.

Recent scholarly celebrations of our increasingly peaceful world attribute violence's decline in no small part to the demise of masculine honor norms, which have often been said to require men of honor to be dangerous to their fellows and their government.[20] One need only remember the West's centuries-long effort to eradicate dueling to see this dynamic at work. Dueling, an informal and private outgrowth of the trial-by-combat tradition of the middle ages, had been condemned by the Church from at least as early as the ninth century. To Christian authorities, dueling was not only an offense against man, but also against God, whose intercession was being presumed upon in judicial combat.[21] Monarchs and principalities, too, routinely prohibited the duel to monopolize their own claims to violence, forestall the disorder caused by inferior officers challenging their superiors, and preserve the flower of their chivalry from killing each other at a rate of sometimes tens of thousands a year. The strictly liberal case against dueling isn't as obvious, however. Like any state, the liberal state will try to reserve violence for legal punishment and war. But what about the consensual violence we see in boxing—or, one might reason, the duel—violates liberal principles? In the abstract, the duel may in fact pass liberal muster: under the heading of "mutual combat," some U.S. jurisdictions allow citizens to engage in fair and consensual fistfights that don't damage property or bystanders, and extending this allowance to armed participants isn't unthinkable.[22] But in its historical context, it seemed to many liberal reformers that the duel usually wasn't fully consensual, insofar as refusing a challenge could cost a man his private and professional reputation. For instance, an officer in a military that expressly forbade dueling could still be run out of the service for the "ungentlemanly" conduct of declining a legitimate challenge. Add to that the very real prospect that some men were deadly duelists and used manufactured offense to kill their enemies with impunity, and it becomes clear that laws banning the duel, even if they limited our freedom to fight for offenses, were meant to promote the effective freedom of men to go about their daily business without risking their lives.

To dueling's honor-minded advocates, however, surrendering the right to personal violence left them vulnerable to insult without possibility of riposte. Gentleman and backwoodsman alike found it profoundly troubling to contemplate public offense with no recourse but, at most, a legal one. Some societies, such as the Bedouin, acknowledge honor-related injuries in their legal systems.[23] Liberal ones largely do not because liberalism jealously protects free speech and has tended not to see insult as "material harm." Liberals take the slightest financial or physical threat seriously (legally, you can assault someone by merely threatening violence), but even the gravest calumny is usually not actionable in the most liberalized courts, such as those in the United States. For instance, in a recent ruling striking down a law that criminalized misrepresenting oneself as a war hero (*United States v. Alvarez*), the majority of Supreme Court justices found that the "dilution" of actual war heroes' honor wasn't a material enough harm to warrant the law's threat to free speech.

Early modern European thinkers observed, and to some degree encouraged, this divorce between honor and the law. Montaigne noted that

> [in France] there . . . are two sets of laws, the law of honour, and the law of justice, which are strongly opposed in many matters. The first condemns an unavenged accusation of lying, the other condemns revenge. A gentleman who puts up with an insult is, by the laws of arms, stripped of his rank and nobility, [but] one who avenges it incurs capital punishment. If he goes to the law to redress an offence against his honour, he is dishonoured; if he acts independently he is chastised and punished by the Law. [. . .] [O]ne [of these laws] is responsible for peace, the other for war; the first acquires profit, the second, honour; the first, learning; the second, virtue; the first, words, the second, deeds; the first, justice, the second valour; the first reason, the second, fortitude; the first the long gown, the second, the short.[24]

Montaigne's near-contemporary, Hobbes, quite deliberately disparaged honor's concern with reputation and glory-seeking and even its associated virtues of courage and ambition in his mature works, because he couldn't square his justification of the leviathan state with honor psychology. Only people who valued their lives more than they valued their dignity or immortal fame would find it rational, in a state of nature, to give up their right to violence to an absolute monarch.[25] Liberals have, over the centuries, increasingly come to accept the notion that honor's values and virtues are either silly or at best, private ones, and that the less a society sees of them the more peaceful and prosperous it will be.

However, a number of honor theorists maintain that honor is essential to civilizing violence, to transforming (often inevitable) violence into something dignified and ultimately less harmful. As argued by Montesquieu, a capably violent aristocracy may destabilize a state to some extent, but it also serves as an important brake on autocratic tyranny.[26] There can be little doubt that honor permits aggressive wars for status that liberal ethics would prohibit.[27] But the honor ethos also prompts us to eschew atrocity and even to risk our lives in defense of helpless or unprepared foes, and the case has been made that wars honorably conducted reduce the long-term enmity that so often results from total war tactics.[28] It may be that honor in some sense of the term is indispensable for distinguishing the mercenary from citizen soldier, and it is widely appreciated that the best soldiers in liberal societies tend to come from their more honor-driven subcultures whose recreation and identity center on hunting, guns, and athletics.

Also in tension with liberalism is honor's apparent exclusivity and elitism. Liberalism is egalitarian insofar as it assumes we are moral equals, or that we are all equal in the ways that matter most or fundamentally. In contrast, honor, in the sense of prestige or high standing, is necessarily a zero-sum good: some of us must have less for others to have more. Thus, liberals will be disinclined to say that relative prestige—undeniable and pervasive though it be—should matter all that much. Sure, some of us might be famous and some of us obscure, but the gaps in our social status shouldn't warp our basic self-esteem or the equality of our political or legal rights. Honor cultures on the other hand tend to see prestige as a central value and as reflecting our relative qualities, full stop. Cultures with hereditary honor will teach children that they come from higher or lower stock, and honor cultures with meritocratic or broadly competitive prestige distributions will usually say that the excellences allowing winners to win make them better people as well. For example, pre-philosophical Greeks conceived of a virtuous person as nothing other than an excellent one (i.e., as possessing *arête*), and some industrialists of the gilded age concluded from social Darwinism that they were not only richer than, but morally superior to, the rest of society.

More troublesome yet for liberal egalitarianism, honor cultures tend to be exclusive even with regard to who gets to *compete* for prestige. Honor cultures often exhibit the same basic structure. First, we have those who, although not quite honorable, are not dishonorable either, because they weren't expected to have attempted entry into the salient honor group where prestige can be won. For instance, in traditional societies, children are non-honorable, and vis-à-vis academia, non-academics are non-honorable. Once one has proven oneself worthy through passing the relevant honor group's rite of passage (say, by stoically braving adolescent circumcision, successfully raiding your neighbor's cattle, being knighted, earning your PhD, etc.), one becomes honorable. This sort of honor has been termed *horizontal honor* because, unlike the relative or *vertical honor* of prestige, everyone in the relevant honor group has this sort of honor equally and fully.[29] Thus, all professors in good standing in a department will enjoy the same horizontal honor, but a colleague whose work is groundbreaking will have more vertical honor than one whose work is derivative, all other things being equal. Finally, apart from the non-honorable and honorable are the dishonorable. One is dishonored if the honor group feels she has violated the fundamental norms of the honor group, which usually center on competing for prestige correctly and showing/demanding the respect proper to people given their status. For instance, in the honor subculture of academia, professors who plagiarize or falsify data are dishonored because they tried to gain stature by violating the rules of the game.

In an honor culture in the fullest sense, these distinctions between the non-honorable, honorable, and dishonorable are socially decisive. A (modern, urban, Western) dishonored academic, despite being run out of the profession, can still have a social life and count on the full protection of the law. The same is not true of a dishonored villager living in an illiberal society: he is fundamentally contemptible, a fair target for any insult, mockery, or indeed stone that might be hurled his way. To humiliate the very person, not just the persona (qua academic, qua cyclist, etc.), of an individual is morally impossible to the liberal. Liberals understand *all* individuals as possessing an inherent dignity (or at least a right to dignity) that is unearned, inalienable, and equal.[30] "[Liberal] dignity," Peter Berger has argued,

> as against honor, always relates to the intrinsic humanity divested of all socially imposed roles or norms. It pertains to the self as such, to the individual regardless of his position in society. This becomes very clear in the classic formulations of human rights, from the Preamble to the Declaration of Independence to the Universal Declaration of Human Rights of the United Nations. These rights always pertain to the individual "irrespective of race, color or creed"—or, indeed, of sex, age, physical condition or any conceivable social status. There is an implicit sociology and an implicit anthropology here. The implicit sociology views all biological and historical differentiations among men as either downright unreal or essentially irrelevant. The implicit anthropology locates the real self over and beyond all these differentiations.[31]

The ideological underpinnings of liberal equality are under serious assault. The Christian belief that we are all children of a loving God who is no "respecter of persons" made the notion of fundamental, inalienable, and equal dignity comprehensible to gradually liberalizing Westerners. Christian profession is on the decline, however; and even assuming God exists, few thinkers today would want to base our moral worth on God's approval, just as they wouldn't base the moral worth of children upon their parents' affection, however unwavering that may be.

Nor has a plausible secular ground for liberal dignity been forthcoming. For Hobbes, the equality of man was premised upon our supposed ability to slay each other, by guile and confederation if not by individual might. By the time we get to Locke, we learn that we are equally "creatures of the same species and rank, promiscuously born to all the same advantages of nature, and the use of the same faculties" and thus must treat each other as so. Later, Rawls would consider self-respect to be perhaps the most important "primary good" (roughly, a good one wants whatever else she might want)—which sounds very honor-theoretic—but he also felt that justice requires egalitarian respect because everyone would demand an equal share of rights and liberties behind the veil of ignorance.[32] Weaknesses in these arguments for moral equality are obvious. *Pace* Hobbes, the disabled, infirm, elderly, young, and technologically primitive simply do not present a genuine threat to the rest of us. *Pace* Locke, talents are not equally, or even randomly, distributed, not only because of differences in our environment, but also because of heritable traits, including intelligence. And as animal liberationists have pointed out, accounts of human dignity based on veil of ignorance reasoning must explain why this reasoning extends only to humans—why doesn't the veil of ignorance also hide whether we are human or nonhuman, which would result in rationally motivated people assigning equal dignity to nonhumans?[33] What makes a human more worthy of respect than an equally sentient, or (if intelligence is morally relevant) sapient, nonhuman?[34] Thus, because honor is compatible with—although not committed to—the difficult-to-refute position that people have unequal dignity, it is not only liberal heresy, it is a particularly dangerous one.[35]

How soluble these tensions between honor and liberalism are is much the concern of our contributors. They may be based on false or incomplete notions of honor or the values underlying liberalism. Or not—maybe the two systems are truly incompatible. Our contributors represent a variety of positions on these questions.

CHAPTER SUMMARIES

Our volume begins with two origin stories. The first is philosopher Dan Demetriou's "Fighting Together: Civil Discourse and Agonistic Honor," which argues that the norms of agonistic honor are especially important in circumstances where conflict is inevitable. Just as Hobbes attempted to reconcile self-interest with the self-disadvantaging constraints of justice,

Demetriou aims to reconcile self-interest with the self-disadvantaging norms of the ethos of agonistic honor, which conceives of rightness in terms of fair and respectful contests for status. To do this, he patterns his rational reconstruction of honor after Hobbes's rational reconstruction of justice by imagining honor-equivalents of the "rational" individual in the "state of nature." In his thought experiment, Demetriou posits not disinterested and diffident individuals in a lawless state, but rather highly social, prestige-oriented, and competitive individuals locked in hate-fueled conflict. He describes a multistage process that would naturally culminate in honorable contests among a natural aristocracy. Applying Hobbes's strategy to ethical agonism illuminates how agonistic honorableness moderates conflict and builds respect between opponents, not only in war, but also in other arenas, including democratic politics.

In his contribution, "Liberalism and Honor through the Lens of Darwin," political scientist Steven Forde uses a Darwinian account of honor psychology to shed light on two accounts of liberalism and honor's relationship to it. On one interpretation of liberalism that extends from Hobbes, the social contract and the creation of a leviathan state is necessary for eliminating the socially disruptive competitions for preeminence we would see arising in a state of nature, and is desirable because of the material security and prosperity it enables. A second conception of liberalism, which Forde associates with Francis Fukuyama, holds that liberalism solves the problem of honor not by eradicating it or concentrating it in the monarch, but by evenly distributing it among citizens. Liberalism harnesses the spirited aspects of honor psychology to make authoritarianism intolerable, while simultaneously reining in our desire to dominate our fellows. Recent anthropological and primatological research suggests that the competing forces of domination and egalitarianism are as old as our species. As anthropologist Christopher Boehm has argued at length, hunter-gatherer societies are surprisingly antiauthoritarian, and this suggests that for a long stretch of our recent development our ancestors decided that they were better off with a certain but roughly equal share of power than a small chance at great power. This evolutionary theory corroborates Fukuyama's sense that the main impulse of the liberal isn't material security but universal dignity. Forde concludes by suggesting that a successful liberal culture will cultivate a moralized sense of honor, one that that shapes our innate honor impulses so as to provide us with a society that, while extoling nondomination, nonetheless can summon a spirited elite when necessary.

Under the heading of "liberalism and honor" specifically we have four contributions, beginning with one by political scientist Sharon Krause. Any contemporary assessment of honor's compatibility with liberal democracy must respond in one way or another to Krause's seminal *Liberalism with Honor* (2002). Krause's chapter, "Honor and Political Agency from the Old Regime to Democratic Reform," presents her case for the necessity of a sense of honor to democratic reform and renewal. For Krause, the honor-motivated citizen is both self-interested and self-sacrificing: the honorable vigorously resist insult to their dignity and aspire to greatness and fine deeds, and yet their elevated sense of self also leaves them scornful of physical threat, material inducement, and unquestioning obedience to authority. Thus honor activates powerful self-oriented motivations that nonetheless leave us less, rather than more, susceptible to state control. Building on the observations of Montesquieu and Tocqueville, Krause explains how, in the Old Regime, honor was characteristic of the nobility, whose pride and martial prowess worked to limit monarchial pretensions to despotism. In a democracy, the same sense of honor has been seen to animate liberationists such as Fredrick Douglass and Martin Luther King Jr., who, when oppressed by majority tyranny, summoned the steely resolve allowing them to fight for their dignity, whatever the consequences.

In "A Neo-Aristotelian Theory of Political Honor," philosopher Steven Skultety argues that insuperable limitations of liberal political thought are made plain by an Aristotelian analysis of political honor. According to Aristotle, we award political honor to those whom we believe deserve to rule over us: in its tangible form, political honor takes the form of prestigious offices; in its intangible form, it takes the form of respect, praise, and acceptance of power. Candidates in modern democracies, just as they were in Aristotle's Athens, are selected in part because of their perceived honorableness, and political offices are still seen as honors. But liberalism, Skultety finds, is particularly ill-equipped to grapple with the honor-infused sense of political appointment. This is because liberalism was never meant to be a theory of government, but rather a theory of transcendent "political value." On liberalism, regardless of how the government happens to be ordered, the State must prioritize individual liberty in formulating law and policy. Moreover, the political values around which liberalism revolves—equality in rights and liberties—in no way prepares citizens to rank people as better or worse rulers. In short, whereas liberalism answers the question, "How can citizens with different worldviews flourish peacefully together?" the Aristotelian political question is "Who deserves to rule?" Thus political honor not only continues to play a central role in society, but it reminds us of a different set of questions which we should expect a political philosophy to answer.

In his "Putting One's Best Face Forward," philosopher Ryan Rhodes defends honor's concern with public perception against a number of liberal and ethical objections. It is stereotypical for honor-minded individuals to lie to save face (even when the lie is obvious to observers), to privilege their reputation despite destructive consequences to themselves or others, and to regard or disregard criticism depending on the critic's status. Liberalism in contrast purports to care about autonomy, material welfare, equality, and a liberty secured in part between "a sharp separation between public and private interests." Moreover, contemporary approaches to the ethics of argument and moral criticism tend to see it as fallacious to make the weight of a criticism contingent on its source. Rhodes replies that maintaining "face" is an important public virtue when honor is internalized—when one seeks not to be honored so much as to be *worthy* of honor. Honorable people are motivated by a desire to have virtuous qualities recognized, be they one's own or others'. Moreover, disregarding the criticism of the dishonorable isn't necessarily elitist, irrational, or self-serving. The dishonorable critic is hypocritical, exemplifying a disregard for the very values his disparagement is based on. Finally, guarding one's reputation is often essential to one's ability to effect positive change in the world, because it is what enables one's genuine virtue to be viewed as a model for emulation. Those in the modern public sphere, much like knights of old, cannot perform their valuable duties unless they enjoy a certain amount of public trust. Remembering this fact goes a long way to justifying a concern for reputation, both in general and as a remedy for some of liberalism's traditional deficiencies.

Political theorists usually see liberalism as being in tension with communitarianism, and one of the foremost exponents of the communitarian position has been sociologist and political theorist Amitai Etzioni. In his chapter, "Communitarianism and Honor," Etzioni provides a retrospective account and analysis of communitarianism, whose themes and goals resonate with the problem of honor as a motivator for strong communities. Drawing on his involvement with the political branch of communitarianism, Etzioni summarizes the history of communitarianism and how its most prominent ideas relate to honor. These include the communitarian emphasis on promoting the common good, balancing individual rights against social responsibilities, and creating substantive moral dialogues. The chapter closes with a discussion of cultural relativism, according to which communities ought to be the ultimate arbitrators of the good, versus a more universalist stance. The problem of honor in liberal societies is captured in the debate between cultural relativists advocating for particular culturally-based definitions of honor, and those who argue that honor can and should adapt to a universal, liberal, moral code.

In the third section of this book we have three discussions of honor's importance to the citizen and statesman. Philosopher Anthony Cunningham argues that leadership in democratic societies should not be seen as starting at the top, but at the bottom—in the ordinary, daily interactions of citizens. What does it take to lead within our communities, not just at the level of politics, but at the level of civil society? Liberal societies depend upon clear conceptions of citizens' rights and obligations. But in order for any of that to matter, citizens must know what they owe others and what others owe them. In our everyday interactions, citizens depend on the good will and kindness of others who are largely unknown to them, but if they could not generally count upon being treated with respect, kindness, and gratitude, democratic civil society would fall apart. An attitude and an assumption of benevolence is necessary in order for citizens to see each other as human beings to respect, people with whom they can deliberate and conclude for the common good. But, as Cunningham explains, the psychological terrain of benefaction is complex and varied. Any adequate understanding of the ethical intricacies of human benefaction must include a rich depiction of the nature and value of gratitude, because giving and receiving gratitude is essential for building mutual respect and benevolence, and gratitude is best understood against a backdrop of honor. A key psychological force on either end of benefaction, the giving or receiving end, is the firm resolve to make good on the demands of being an excellent person by returning good for good. The debt of gratitude differs from the strict obligation of respecting the rights of others, but a robust sense of gratitude is no less important than respect for our fellow citizens—in fact, one could argue it is an essential ingredient in the resolve to respect others as free and equal persons, without whom true civic participation is impossible.

Another aspect of leadership discussed in this section is more immediately recognizable as a necessary ingredient in the development of honor at the level of politics: that is, honor at the top. Political scientist Mark Griffith's chapter on the character and actions of British Prime Minister Winston Churchill explores the complexities of Churchill's character, and especially his own evolving and very personal sense of honor. Churchill's understanding of honor developed and grew richer over time, demonstrating well how an individual, tested by extremely challenging circumstances, can continue to grow and change in his understanding and modeling of honor throughout a lifetime. Griffith shows that honor in the lives of actual politicians is more complex (and messy) than the idea of honor in theory. To examine and identify the political thought of Churchill and in particular his thoughts about honor, Griffith looks at several sources, including Churchill's writings, speeches, and the practical circumstances of politics and war that he found himself in. Griffith focuses the most on Churchill's speeches and draws from them the rhetorical case for Victorian honor. Most actions by politicians produce mixed results, and Churchill's were no exception to that rule. Churchill is one of the most revered leaders of the twentieth century, and we can learn a great deal about honor in general and his sense of honor in particular by the thorough study that Griffith undertakes. He uncovers the many ways Churchill thought about and demonstrated his sense of honor. In a short speech to students on October 29, 1941, Churchill said, "Never give in, never give in, never, never, never, never—in nothing, great or small, large or petty—never give in except to convictions of honour and good sense." Churchill exemplifies the intersection of the old, aristocratic honor code, with its emphasis on courage and manly spirit, with a likewise spirited defense of liberal democracy.

In his "Life in Death: Democracy and Civic Honor," philosopher Ajume Wingo borrows from traditional African and classical Western thought to offer a conception of citizenship that reconnects it with civic honor. In the West, Wingo diagnoses a diminished sense of what the key civic categories of citizenship, liberty, and personhood amount to: essentially, subjecthood with certain rights. This is paralleled by a degraded sense among Africans of what it means to live or to be a person in the fullest sense: basically, biological survival. Although to some degree modern attempts to extend dignity to marginalized groups are to be applauded, these same efforts "leveled down" citizenship, personhood, and freedom to their lowest common denominators. Instead, Wingo argues, we must maintain with classical Western and traditional African societies that full citizenship requires activity and sacrifice on behalf of the community, that freedom is measured in our ability to shape (not escape) our government, and that life and personhood are not biological categories but honorable achievements. Wingo concludes by offering a spectrum of citizenship (subjecthood, liminal citizenship, citizenship simpliciter, and statespersonship) that makes use of a traditional African distinction between the fates of wastrels ("death in life"), upstanding community members ("life in life"), and "immortals" ("life in death"), whose civic contributions are so transformative that they are thought to live on in the body politic.

How the concept of honor applies to women is particularly problematic, both in Western culture and beyond. In order for honor to be useful in modern liberal societies, its application to women, indeed its whole relationship to sex, must be examined and developed. Is it possible to have different honor codes for men and women in modern liberal societies? Conversely, is it possible to apply a single code to all people, an option that is much more in accord with our prevailing emphasis on equality? In the fourth part of this volume, we have two chapters that deal with women and honor. Historian Andrea Mansker provides a fascinating examination of female honor in postrevolutionary France, a time in which some women were very boldly challenging the idea that honor (except for honor as female chastity) was the exclusive province of males. Mansker examines multiple attempts by women in postrevolutionary France to redefine traditional honor codes to conform to the rise of liberal ideology. Historians of modern France have demonstrated how the exclusive, aristocratic honor culture was retained and democratized by bourgeois men after 1789. The Revolution had proclaimed an end to privilege and ushered in liberal economic and political policies that favored individualism. But scholars have argued that these public codes were the exclusive prerogative of men, a key way of defining masculinity. Very little has been said about women's often successful endeavors to align honor with their own public identities and conceptions of citizenship. Mansker focuses on three prominent female journalists who publicly challenged women or men to duels and sometimes carried them out, Olympe Audouard, Astié de Valsayre, and Arria Ly. Analyzing these conflicts as they unfolded in the press along with these women's writings on the honor culture, Mansker argues that women, like men, used the dominant honor codes to negotiate the transition to liberal democratic society. Yet given the masculine boundaries of the honor culture, women's feminist appropriation fundamentally altered the gendered meanings of both liberalism and honor in the process.

Whereas the women journalists Mansker discusses urged a more active form of honor, traditional honor for women is based on preserving their sexual purity. Psychologists Joe Vandello and Vanessa Hettinger provide us a look into this type of honor and its relationship to male honor, and indeed, male violence. In many honor cultures, purity comprises both a set of qualities girls and women are said to possess and also a set of expectations for proper female behavior. Purity norms require girls to avoid behaviors that might call their reputation into question. They also prescribe loyalty and sacrifice within relationships, sometimes suggesting that women's role is to "tame" men, who are often thought not to possess the inherent moral purity of women. As women are carriers of family honor, purity norms also create expectations for men to "protect" female family members. Vandello and Hettinger review recent research linking purity norms to male partner violence and female disempowerment. Cross-cultural research as well as experiments with U.S. college undergraduates suggests that honor is more central to women's than men's self-concepts and moral judgments. They consider the implications of this empirical research for the broader question of the tension between honor norms and modern, liberal societies, and whether female purity norms are defensible and sustainable.

Honor is most at home, it seems, in discussions of military matters. And yet, perhaps especially here, honor is problematic because it instigates both incredible courage and resolve but also acts of violence that can be morally questionable. Normally we think that the ancient view of honor, which is all about military skill, courage, and frankly, selfish displays of destructive capability, is simply what modern liberalism rejects and escapes in hopes of a more peaceful world. However, the ancients, precisely because of the destructive aspects of this overwhelming desire for honor and glory, critiqued it and grappled with how to control it. An expert in international relations, Richard Ned Lebow provides an account of the development of honor in the context of warfare in a discussion of the ancient Greeks' attempts to moderate the destructive aspects of the desire for honor, power and wealth. In doing so Lebow offers a novel way of looking at questions such as the problem of order at the domestic, regional and international level. How do international orders arise? What sustains them? Why and how do they decay or collapse? What can be done to shore up existing orders and supplant them with more successful arrangements and bring some degree of stability to more chaotic countries and regions of the world? Lebow attempts, not to answer all of these questions, but to provide a novel way of looking at them based on ancient Greek thought about the nature of the individual and political order and their relationship to the concepts of honor and justice. In particular he examines how thinkers like Thucydides, Plato, and Aristotle, proposed to moderate the destructive aspects of the desire for honor, power, and wealth.

Another expert in international relations, Paul Robinson, expresses the misgivings many people have about the place of honor in modern liberal societies and even within the modern military. He examines Canada's controversial Veterans Charter, which comprises a set of benefits and services veterans receive as a result of their service, benefits such as health care, disability services, and ongoing and lump-sum payments. In a current legal case in Canada, military veterans are arguing that the Veterans Charter is inadequate and should be declared unconstitutional because it betrays the "honor of the Crown," a concept previously invoked by aboriginal inhabitants of Canada to try to get the government to honor its commitments and make right its relationship to these groups. Veterans who make this argument consider the "honor of the Crown" to be tied up with a sacred obligation to continue to honor veterans and to provide for their needs in an open-ended way, whereas the Veterans Charter defines and limits what benefits and considerations veterans will receive. Robinson's chapter explores the concept of the "honor of the Crown," and through this, undertakes a broader examination of Western liberal democracies' obligations to their soldiers. The veterans' appeal to the principle of the "honor of the Crown" appears to reflect a common view of civil-military relations, according to which the military and the state have a quasi-feudal relationship in which each is bound to fulfill certain obligations towards the other not by contract but by vaguer ties of honor. Robinson argues that this fits uneasily with a liberal democratic order. The chapter concludes with a look at attempts to entrench such special status in law, such as the "Military Covenant" in the United Kingdom.

Finally, leadership scholar Joe Thomas and philosopher Shannon French tackle similar issues, but from the vantage point of the modern American military. Their chapter explores the varied meanings of honor in the U.S. military, and describes the teaching methods used to encourage and enhance honorable conduct, demonstrating how the military's operationalization of honor serves modern liberal society. Within the military, the concept of honor is rarely seen as harmful or negative. Rather, honorable conduct is an explicit learning outcome in military education. Yet we may be at a turning point in military usage of these terms. Two of the most common uses of honor are as a standard of integrity (a cadet does not lie, cheat, steal, nor tolerate those who do) and an implicit code of moral restraint (honorable treatment of noncombatants, for instance). It is the second conception that is explored in this chapter. How does the concept of honor serve to guide the moral life of service members? Does the concept of "glory" provide an example of a richly meaningful word that has changed dramatically over time? Prior to the twentieth century, glory was a significant part of the objective of fighting, along with defense of home and family. In many ways it was a far more attractive motivator to young men. Today of course the term "glory" is more than passé. It is almost never invoked as a motivation for fighting, and for good reason. The horrors of war (including lasting physical and psychological costs for troops) faced by military personnel do not allow for appeals to glory. Does the future hold the same for "honor" within the military subculture of the United States? Or is the concept of honor more resilient and timeless?

NOTES

1. E.g., J. K. Campbell, *Honour, Family, and Patronage: A Study of Institutions and Moral Values in a Greek Mountain Community* (Oxford: Clarendon, 1964); the essays in ed. J. G. Peristiany, *Honor and Shame: the Values of Mediterranean Society* (Chicago: University of Chicago Press, 1966); and James Henderson Stewart, *Honor* (Chicago: University of Chicago Press, 1994).

2. E.g., George Fenwick Jones, *Honor Bright: Honor in Western Literature* (Savannah, GA: Frederic C. Bell, 2000); William Ian Miller, *Bloodtaking and Peacemaking: Feud, Law, and Society in Saga Iceland* (Chicago: University of Chicago Press, 1990); Alexander Welsh, *What is Honor?* (New Haven, CT: Yale University Press, 2008).

3. Douglass Adair, "Fame and the Founding Fathers," in *Fame and the Founding Fathers: Essays by Douglass Adair*, ed. T. Colbourn, (New York: Norton, 1974), 3–26; Joanne Freeman, *Affairs of Honor: National Politics in the New Republic* (New Haven, CT: Yale University Press, 2002); Garry Willis, *Cincinnatus: George Washington and the Enlightenment* (Garden City, NY: Doubleday, 1984); Gordon Wood, *Revolutionary Characters: What Made the Founders Different* (New York: Penguin, 2006).

4. E.g., Elijah Anderson, *Code of the Street* (New York: Norton, 1999); Richard Nisbett and Dov Cohen, *Culture of Honor: The Psychology of Violence in the South* (Boulder, CO: Westview Press, 1996).

5. See Kwame Anthony Appiah, *Honor: How Moral Revolutions Happen* (New York: Norton, 2010); Geoffrey Brennan and Philip Pettit, *The Economy of Esteem* (New York: Oxford University Press, 2004); Anthony Cunningham, *Modern Honor* (New York: Routledge, 2013); Shannon French, *Code of the Warrior* (Lanham, MD: Rowman & Littlefield, 2003); Sharon Krause, *Liberalism with Honor* (Cambridge, MA: Harvard University Press, 2002); Peter Olsthoorn, *Honor in Political and Moral Philosophy* (Albany, NY: SUNY Press, 2014); Robert Oprisko, *Honor: A Phenomenology* (New York: Routledge, 2012); Lad Sessions, *Honor for Us* (New York: Continuum, 2010); Tamler Sommers, *Relative Justice* (Princeton, NJ: Princeton University Press, 2012).

6. Aristotle, *Nicomachean Ethics*, T. Irwin, trans. (Indianapolis, IN: Hackett, 1999), 1095b25.

7. *Richard II*, I.i.

8. *Henry V*, V.i.

9. Bernard Mandeville, *An Enquiry into the Origin of Honour, and the Usefulness of Christianity in War* (London: Brotherton, 1732), 90.

10. U.S. Army, "Army Values": http://www.army.mil/values/.

11. Jeffrey McPherson, *Honor System Marketing* (Austin, TX: Acres USA, 2011).

12. United Nations Human Rights Council, "Global Violence Against Women in the Name of 'Honour,'" (New York: United Nations General Assembly, 2014).

13. Livy, *History of Rome*, trans. C. Roberts (New York: E. P. Dutton and Co., 1912), I.58.

14. Julian Pitt-Rivers, "Honour and Social Status" in *Honor and Shame: the Values of Mediterranean Society*, ed. J. G. Peristiany (Chicago: University of Chicago Press, 1966), 45.

15. Campbell, *Honour, Family, and Patronage*, 269–70.

16. J. G. Peristiany, introduction to *Honor and Shame: the Values of Mediterranean Society*, ed. J. G. Peristiany (Chicago: University of Chicago Press, 1966), 9.

17. Dan Demetriou, "Honor War Theory: Romance or Reality?" *Philosophical Papers* 42, no. 3 (2013).

18. E.g., Jane Schneider, "Of Vigilance and Virgins: Honor, Shame, and Access to Resources" *Mediterranean Societies Ethnology* 10, no.1 (1971).

19. Mia Bloom, "In Defense of Honor: Women and Terrorist Recruitment on the Internet," *Journal of Postcolonial Cultures and Societies* 4, no.1 (2013), 162.

20. Steven Pinker, *The Better Angels of Our Nature* (New York: Penguin, 2011), ch. 1.

21. Appiah, *Honor Code*, 26ff; Victor Cathrein, "Duel," *The Catholic Encyclopedia* (New York: Robert Appleton Company, 1909).

22. Wikipedia, "Mutual combat."

23. Stewart, *Honor*.

24. Michel de Montaigne, *The Complete Essays*, trans. M. A. Screech (London: Penguin, 1987), 132–33 (punctuation edits for added clarity).

25. Laurie Johnson, *Thomas Hobbes: Turning Point for Honor* (Lanham, MD: Lexington Books, 2009); Laurie Johnson, *Locke and Rousseau: Two Enlightenment Responses to Honor* (Lanham, MD: Lexington Books, 2012).

26. See Krause, *Liberalism with Honor* and Krause, this volume, for an extended discussion.

27. Ned Lebow, *Why Nations Fight* (New York: Cambridge University Press, 2010); Paul Robinson, *Military Honour and the Conduct of War* (Oxford: Oxford University Press, 2006).

28. David Bell, *The First Total War: Napoleon's Europe and the Birth of Warfare as We Know It* (Boston: Houghton Mifflin, 2007).

29. Stewart, *Honor*, first described the vertical/horizontal honor distinction.

30. "The ethos of honor is fundamentally opposed to a universal and formal morality which affirms the equality in dignity of all men and consequently the equality of their rights and duties," writes Pierre Bourdieu in "The Sentiment of Honor in Kabyle Society," in *Honor and Shame: the Values of Mediterranean Society*, ed. J. G. Peristiany, (Chicago: University of Chicago Press, 1966), 228.

31. Peter Berger, "On the Obsolescence of the Concept of Honor" in *Revisions: Changing Perspectives in Moral Philosophy*, S. Hauerwas and A. MacIntyre, eds. (Notre Dame, IN: University of Notre Dame Press, 1983), 176.

32. See discussion in Olsthoorn, *Honor in Political and Moral Philosophy* (Albany, NY: SUNY Press, 2014), 66ff.

33. This point is made in, inter alia, Tom Regan, *Defending Animal Rights* (Urbana-Champaign: University of Illinois Press, 2001), 12.

34. Peter Singer, *Animal Liberation* (New York: Random House, 1975).

35. Jeremy Waldron, *Dignity, Rank, and Rights* (New York, 2009).

Part I

Origin Stories

Honor and the Challenge of Modernity

ONE

Fighting Together

Civil Discourse and Agonistic Honor

Dan Demetriou

In ancient Greece, an *agon* was a public contest meant to reveal excellence. An agon may be a wrestling match between two champions, a poetry competition, an athletic event, or any other forum in which respectable equals are matched up to compete for fame. *Agonism* is just the cultural, psychological, and behavioral syndrome that characterizes these profoundly meaningful struggles between evenly-matched and respectable opponents. Agonistic principles—often spoken of as being "honorable" or a "code of honor"—are obvious enough in athletics and warrior-aristocratic warfare. However, a number of notable political theorists have argued for decades that democracy itself is essentially contestatory and "agonistic."[1]

If democracy is agonistic, or even if (more humbly) it merely has a strong agonistic element, then it would stand to reason that agonistic honorableness would count as a *civic virtue*. And yet it is rarely spoken of in this way. One reason for this may be that discussions of agonistic democracy are often framed in terms of postmodernism, critical theory, and Continental philosophy. Political philosophers leery of those traditions will be disinclined to accept agonism if it means taking on board (what they see as) undesirable theoretical baggage. Another factor militating against categorizing agonistic honorableness as a civic virtue is the widespread (and partially correct) assumption that agonism approaches everything as a fight. To those who think politics and civic debate need be *less*, not *more*, combative, promoting agonistic honorableness will seem like a bad idea.[2] A third criticism of the civic importance of agonism comes from the opposite direction: talk of agonistic honorableness strikes a number of readers as hopelessly romantic: in the real world of dog-eat-dog, combatants (literal and figurative) have no time for chivalric twaddle about fighting fair or respecting one's opponents.[3]

I think the best way to reply to these worries is as a "Hobbes of honor" might. First, a Hobbesian rational reconstruction of agonistic honor on behalf of civility would be perfectly intelligible to readers from any philosophical tradition, be it "analytic," "Continental," or what have you. Second, as we shall see, a Hobbesian reconstruction would have the benefit of explaining how agonistic honor works to quell, not enflame, hostility between disputants. Finally and perhaps most importantly, a Hobbesian reconstruction of honor would explain to our more hardboiled critics why the self-disadvantaging norms of honor are not naïve or unrealistic, but perfectly rational given the agents and conditions involved. So, using Hobbes as my pattern, I begin this chapter by illuminating and justifying the self-disadvantaging principles of agonistic honor by showing how they would emerge from honor's equivalent of "rational" individuals situated in honor's "state of nature."

This Hobbesian exercise makes it easy to appreciate why agnostic honorableness is a civic virtue, especially in spaces (such as pluralistic democracies, universities, courtrooms, etc.) where conflict is inevitable and desirable. Thus, in the second half of this chapter, I apply its principles to the pressing question of civil discourse. In contrast to what might be called the "standard model" of civil discourse, which attempts to neutralize the contestatory nature of public debate, on agonistic honor adversaries are allowed and even encouraged to see each other as status-seeking opponents. Nonetheless, disputants must play by the rules necessary to sustaining the system that allows them to "champion" their causes in the first place.

A HOBBESIAN RECONSTRUCTION OF AGONISTIC HONOR

According to contractarian ethical and political theory, what we are "owed" by justice is determined by cooperative principles. By definition, cooperation is mutually beneficial. But the fact that some scheme is mutually beneficial doesn't mean it is *maximally* beneficial to every individual involved. If I have plenty of chickens but no shoes, and you have no chickens but plenty of shoes, it would be mutually beneficial for us to trade. But it would be even *more* beneficial for you to take my chickens by force, *if* you could do so with impunity. Such an uncooperative act would be patently unjust on contractarian principles, however, because it is coercive. Thus, contractarian justice places constraints on our pursuit of well-being.

What is the value of these contractarian constraints? "The importance of justice itself" does not satisfy the skeptic. Hobbes attempted to answer the skeptical challenge by reconciling justice's constraints with a value the skeptic *does* take for granted: self-interest. Hobbes sought to show that, in certain circumstances, our self-interest is served by respecting the constraints of contractarian justice, and that it is in our self-interest to create such circumstances whenever possible.

Hobbes begins this project by imagining us as completely "rational" on the skeptic's way of seeing things: i.e., as individuals aiming to maximize our own material well-being. He supposes further that we are all equal in the sense that none of us can exert his or her will on others without fear of reprisal. Finally, he assumes a certain amount of material scarcity: we all cannot have as much as we would like, but nonetheless there can be enough for everyone.

If rational agents so conceived and so situated were given total freedom in an ungoverned "state of nature," Hobbes observed, it would be rational for them to be uncooperative. Even if one's neighbors mean to keep their bargains, it makes sense to break faith with them whenever profitable. As a result, cooperative endeavors become impossible, and a "war of all against all" ensues, leaving our imaginary agents without industry, commerce, exploration, or arts, and consigned to lives "solitary, poor, nasty, brutish, and short." To escape this scenario, a law enforcement system must be established that is effective enough to make it irrational for people to violate the terms of their mutually beneficial cooperative arrangements. Since (in Hobbes's view) one mustn't be unjust and yet cannot be obliged to act irrationally, justice itself doesn't come into being until the payoff structure is changed to make it imprudent to break faith.[4]

Turning from justice to honor, it should be noted that Hobbes was also interested in justifying a strong (indeed, totalitarian) government. Hobbes felt that only a powerful state apparatus could enforce covenants and thus enable us to rationally and justly promote our well-being. Aristocrats, however, posed a difficulty for the Hobbesian state since, as Montesquieu would later elaborate upon, they tend to resist totalitarian control.[5] More problematically yet, aristocratic honor-mindedness doesn't square with the psychology Hobbes felt necessary for an orderly society, since honor-mindedness drives its subscribers to fight over trifles, glory, and status. The carrots and sticks of material well-being (life, health, security, etc.) have relatively little sway on the honor-minded, who are moved by considerations of calumny and prestige more than they are physical punishment or material reward. Insofar as people are uninterested in promoting their material or physical well-being, they won't be motivated to construct or obey a leviathan.[6]

Assuming the moral value of material well-being (and the instrumental value of the items conducive to it, such as security or wealth) is important for any apology for justice, since justice is about the cooperative rules governing our pursuit and distribution of these goods. Justice *isn't* suited to managing other sorts of goods, however. It is difficult to imagine how we could create laws redistributing reputation, for example, or how we might collectively increase overall prestige—a zero-sum good that can be gained only by taking an equivalent amount from others—through cooperation. Insofar social status is a good, it is a good justice simply cannot govern, and therefore a good that isn't promoted for oneself by creating a state that enforces our cooperative agreements. Thus, everything would be much easier for Hobbes's political agenda if we agreed that material well-being mattered and social status did not, and that is why Hobbes had to disparage the value of prestige-seeking in his takedown of honor.[7]

Unlike Hobbes, I hold that prestige matters morally, and there are moral constraints on our pursuit of it. Some readers may disagree, but even for skeptics about the moral importance of prestige, it should be interesting to see if the limits agonistic honorableness places on our quest for status can be "reconstructed" in a Hobbesian manner. In other words, would we need to invent agonistic honorableness if we didn't already have it?

Agonistic Honor's "Rational" Agent

We begin by imagining, as Hobbes did, a certain sort of person in a certain sort of circumstance. As noted earlier, to the contractarian Hobbes, rational agents are concerned solely with maximizing their material well-being. In contrast, we imagine agents wholly unconcerned with health, wealth, and security but obsessed with social rank. I stress rank: we are imagining people who wish to be judged as *superior* to their fellows, not just as their equals. Moreover, the sort people we have in mind are highly social, since what they value—social rank—supervenes on the positive opinion of their comrades. In some respects, then, "rational" individuals (insofar as they seek to maximize their "good") in this thought experiment are the polar opposite of "rational" individuals on Hobbes's contractarian picture: they are social (as opposed to individualistic), competitive (as opposed to disinterested), and prestige-oriented (as opposed to prudential).

The puzzle Hobbes hoped to solve is how the restraint justice demands of us could become rational, so he places his prudential agents in a context that makes such restraint irrational for them. For our purposes, we are supposed to be perplexed by how it could be rational for adversaries to obey the constraints of agonistic honor. So we must place our prestige-driven agents in a context that makes the rules of honorable contest superficially irrational for *them*. To make it as challenging as possible for ourselves, imagine our rational agents at war. This war isn't a Hobbesian war of mutually "diffident" (in the archaic sense of "suspicious") disinterested atomic individuals, but a war of two factions—call them the "Reds" and the "Blues"—who utterly abhor each other. Here we have a war not of all against all, but of some against some, and its hellishness is none the lesser for it. For example, the sort of animosity I'm imagining can be found in certain quarters of Israeli-Palestinian conflict, as evidenced by the Palestinian Authority children's show *The Best Home*, which occasionally featured young children reciting poems such as this:

> I lit a fire like volcanoes under their [the Jewish Israelis'] feet
> I refused to be submissive and degraded
> I rejected everything but dying with the honor that will give me life
> From a nation that has forgotten the Muslims' heroism
> Omar ibn al-Khattab and Saladin
> from between the whistles of the bullets I sing:
> "Long live the nation of Fatah and Yasser Arafat"
> Allah's enemies, the sons of pigs
> Destroyed and uprooted the olive and fig trees
> They murdered children with guns, like snakes
> They cut off their limbs with stones and knives
> They raped the women in the city squares
> They defiled Allah's book in front of millions
> Where is the nation of Islam?
> Where are the nation of Islam and the Jihad fighters?
> Where is the fear of Allah in Jerusalem, which has been defiled by the Zionists?[8]

Watching the online video of a young girl reciting such lines is an unsettling and discouraging experience. How could our imaginary Reds and Blues, animated by similar feelings, ever come to treat each other with honorable restraint?

Stage 1: Intramural Ranking

Given the importance of this war for each faction, they will distribute honors and social prerogatives (including, according to anthropologists, mating privileges)[9] to those on their side who do the best job of killing the enemy. We have already assumed that our agents are status-seeking and covet such honors. So the first step in our progression to honorable restraint is an intramural one: although the *fight* is ostensibly against the Reds or the Blues, a *competition* will emerge between comrades.

Examples of intramural ranking abound. Consider, for instance, the culturally widespread practice of taking scalps of the enemy as trophies, a practice old even in the writings of Herodotus, who reports of the Scythian warrior that "he is proud of [his] scalps, and hangs them from his bridle rein . . . the greater the number of such napkins a man can show, the greater he is esteemed among them."[10] Or consider the poem quoted above, which praises "Omar ibn al-Khattab and Saladin," powerful Ottoman caliphs, and admonishes the current generation of Muslims to raise up heroes in their league. Perhaps the most famous example of intramural competition in modern Western culture is found in the rousing conclusion of Winston Churchill's "Finest Hour" address:

> Let us therefore brace ourselves to our duties, and so bear ourselves that, if the British Empire and its Commonwealth last for a thousand years, men will still say, "*This was their finest hour.*"[11]

Although Churchill offered many good reasons for resisting the Nazi threat in his address, these lines—strategically saved for last—activated the anxieties and aspirations of those British citizens who were interested not only in winning the war, but also in surpassing the martial exploits of past and future generations of Britons.

Stage 2: Intermural Ranking

In Stage 1 of our Hobbesian reconstruction of agonistic honor, we saw the first emergence of order from chaos: instead of the Reds and the Blues fighting each other in an egalitarian helter-skelter, we observed each side ranking its combatants according to who does the best job of cutting down enemies. However, each side ranked its fighters based on a crude method that treats every opponent as equal. It's the number of scalps, the number of "w"s in one's "win" column, that counts. But as we all know, not all kills are equally meritorious: defeating a tough foe speaks better of one's prowess than does overmastering a weak one. Thus, those distributing honors in Reds' fight against the Blues must turn their gaze across the battlefield and estimate the relative excellence of individual Blue warriors, and vice versa. If Homer's presentation is any indication, notable warriors of the Greek dark age would seek each other out and risk their lives to strip vanquished equivalents of their armor. In the *Beowulf* epic, Beowulf pursues Grendel precisely *because* Grendel is so fierce, and Beowulf makes it clear to his Danish hosts what the implications would be for their relative prestige if he succeeds where they failed:

> The monster is not afraid of the Danes,
> Of the folk of the Danemen, but fights with pleasure,
> Kills and feasts, expects no contest,
> But he will soon learn to dread the Geats.[12]

In modern militaries, unit citations are given to those who engage in the fiercest combat, and the principle is the same in sports, such as college football, where a team's ranking is determined not just by victories and defeats, but also by strength of schedule. The principle is an old one: "We are known not by our friends, but by our enemies."

Obvious as it seems that we must rank opponents to rank ourselves, judging the quality of our opponents necessitates two significant moral advances. First, evaluating opponents requires us to distinguish among them. No longer are they a faceless mass, a herd of animals to be slaughtered. Now they have identities, even if that distinctiveness is based merely on the quality of the armor they wear or the number of feathers in their hair. Second, ranking our enemies means giving them at least *some* sort of positive appraisal. Evil though they may be in our eyes, at least they manifest an excellence we grudgingly admire—the very same sort of excellence, in fact, we use to rank ourselves.

Stage 3: Intermural Coordination

Even if the Blues and Reds consider the strength of opponents when distributing honors to themselves, no mechanism has been introduced for matching fighters. The inefficiency of this situation is manifest. Combatants ambitious for honors do not want to waste their time, energy, and luck on enemy fighters whose scalps, armor, or standards will earn middling reward. They would much rather find worthier opponents whose defeat would bring greater prestige. On the other hand, fighters motivated to accumulate honor would hesitate to challenge a much higher-ranked foe, since the probability of victory would be so low that, even multiplied by the greater potential payoff, the risk wouldn't be worth it. Thus, in Stage 3, we begin to see fighters in both camps pairing off against their equivalents.

Although an improvement, a mere face-off cannot establish superiority, thanks to problems of incommensurability and vagueness about the rules of engagement. Perhaps the most salient example of this is the battle between David and Goliath.[13] Clearly, agonistic considerations, on both the individual and group level, propel David and Goliath to fight each other as champions. Their combat, however, is problematic as far as fairness is concerned. Goliath's physical advantages are superhuman (on some interpretations, he stands at eleven feet). Absent some offer of handicap, he doesn't seem like a reasonable match for David. On the other hand, ancient slingers like David could kill at ranges over a hundred meters and knock birds out of the sky. The David-meets-Goliath story, then, is hardly one of an underdog standing up to a bully,[14] and the incommensurability of each champion's advantages makes gauging how much honor to award the victor difficult. Was what David did sneaky, within the stated rules but outside the unstated ones, "not quite cricket"? Or was it perfectly fair, considering Goliath's size? Such questions are the warp and woof of Monday morning commentary, but for the champions themselves such questions have existential import, not only for their lives but also their legacies.

Because of incommensurability problems and vagueness about the rules, combatants or their seconds must do more than simply issue challenges—they must actually cross enemy lines and establish rules of combat. In real life, rules limiting battle usually grow organically, by acquired custom, as in the highly ritualized battles described by anthropologists in cultures around the globe. But even in the West and as late as the nineteenth century, we see examples of prearranged combat wherein the terms of battle are set forth as strictly as possible purely for the purpose of making the prestige distribution uncontroversial. Consider, for example, a challenge issued by Captain Broke, Royal Navy, to James Lawrence, U.S. Navy, in the War of 1812.

> Sir, As the [USS] *Chesapeake* appears now ready for sea, I request that you will do me the favour to meet the [HMS] *Shannon* with her, ship to ship, to try the fortune of our respective flags. [. . .] Be assured, sir, that it is not from any doubt I can entertain you of your wishing to close with my proposal, but merely to provide an answer to any objection that might be made, and very reasonably, upon the chance of our receiving unfair support. [. . .] The *Shannon* mounts twenty-four guns upon her broadside, and one light boat-gun—eighteen-pounders upon her maindeck, and thirty-two pound carronades on her quarterdeck and forecastle, and is manned with a complement of 300 men and boys (a large proportion of the latter), besides thirty seamen, boys and passengers, who were taken out of recaptured vessels lately.[15]

Broke's letter goes on to give detailed information—information so specific it would be considered traitorous for a modern officer to divulge—about the *Shannon*'s capabilities, and even offers to escort the *Chesapeake* under flag of truce to a suitable spot for battle. Lawrence never received this letter, but he guessed Broke's intentions correctly and sailed out to meet the *Shannon* in a ship-to-ship duel. The *Chesapeake* was taken, and Lawrence was killed in action (his famous dying words being "Don't give up the ship!") and buried with great honor by the British naval officers in Nova Scotia. For his part, Broke, though severely wounded, survived and was showered with glory, awarded with a baronetcy, and inducted into the Order of the Bath. His challenge to Lawrence was soon published in the newspapers of both countries, and was generally approved of as highly honorable.

Stage 4: Courtesy

Whereas David and Goliath make declarations about how they will feed each other's bits to the birds, Broke and Lawrence—though keen for victory and wholly prepared for death—treated each other with courtesy: had Lawrence survived, naval tradition and probably inclination would have led Broke to host the American captain and his remaining officers to the finest dinner he could provide at sea, and Lawrence would have been paroled with considerable freedom in Canada.

Of course, Broke and Lawrence were cultural cousins. But mutual respect appears to be possible between warriors divided by race, language, and religion. Perhaps this is why some of the most romantic tales of honor are those about Richard I and the above-mentioned Saladin. Richard the Lionheart by all accounts was a phenomenal human specimen and unsurpassed warrior, and as leader of the Third Crusade he inspired awe among both Christians and Muslims. For his part, Saladin was widely credited with being a magnanimous and wise caliph. Although Richard never met Saladin except in literature, we can be fairly confident in reports of their mutual regard. For instance, when Richard fell ill, Saladin sent him fruit, sherbet, and his personal doctor. Richard in turn knighted Saladin's nephew. And in the battle of Jaffa, Saladin sent the unhorsed Richard one of his mounts, remarking that "a king shouldn't have to fight on foot."[16]

Courtesy between champions is predictable for elitist and ludic reasons. As we see in the case of Saladin and Richard ("A *king* shouldn't fight on foot"), elitism can be a powerful bond between antagonists. This is because, after a while, warriors with the highest prestige come to see themselves less as champions *of their sides* and more as *champions* simpliciter, who see war as a platform to prove their superiority. Reasonably, they begin to consider themselves favored by the gods (i.e., lucky) and made of better stuff (good genes), and they value these advantages to such a degree that they would rather their children intermarry with champions of the other side than with commoners on their own side. Perhaps this is why Richard I, in the midst of a religious crusade with strong racist undertones, saw fit to offer his sister in a political marriage to Saladin's brother.

As traditions of extramural coordination strengthen and grow, antagonists inevitably begin to agree to terms that suit their mutual preferences (think of aristocrats delaying battles because of inclement weather). War thus becomes increasingly ludic, a sport to played. At its highest reaches, this sort of combat is pure contest. Gone are thoughts of purging the earth of some defiling enemy, revenging some wrong, or seizing some territory. Fully aristocratic warfare is what John Ruskin called "exercise or play," never to be fought with unwilling conscripts, but only with those of aristocratic leisure—the "proudly idle"—who are kept by circumstance or culture from useful occupation and "thirst for some appointed field for action; and find, in the passion and peril of battle, the only satisfying fulfillment of [their] unoccupied being."[17] This spirit of deadly play is especially evident in the rules of warfare for Kshatriyas, the warrior caste of Hindu society, as outlined in the four-thousand-year-old *Rigveda*:

> Elephants should oppose only elephants; and so the chariots, cavalry, and infantry only their opposite. [. . .] One should strike only after due notice . . . [and never one] who is confiding or unprepared or panic-stricken . . . or [one who is] without armor, or whose weapons are

> rendered useless . . . or [one who is] fatigued and frightened, weeping and unwilling to fight; [or] one who is ill and cries for quarter, or one of tender years or advanced age. [In fact] a Kshatriya should defend even his enemy if entreated with joined hands.[18]

These courtesies continue to pop up in the most unexpected places, including the current Ukrainian conflict. As Paul Robinson (this volume) has told the tale,

> For months, Motorola's [a.k.a. Arseny Pavlov, commander of the Sparta battalion of the rebel Donetsk People's Republic] unit has been attempting to drive the Ukrainians out of Donetsk airport. His men occupy the old terminal, while [Ukrainian Captain] Kupol's occupy the new one. In an unusual development, Motorola this week permitted the Ukrainians to rotate their troops in the new terminal—taking out 48 tired soldiers and bringing in 51 new ones—on condition that they did not bring any heavy weapons in. The rebels inspected the incoming Ukrainians before letting them pass. While the inspection was taking place, Motorola and Kupol met and shook hands.[19]

Thus, we see how, given the initial conditions set forth, it is imaginable that two faceless hordes groaning in their mutual hatred could create a culture of battlefield courtesy and honorable restraint.

As with Hobbes's account of justice, this presentation of honor is mythological: it doesn't accurately represent the actual development of the agonistic ethos, either as a social phenomenon or as an evolved moral instinct.[20] Nonetheless, and in parallel to Hobbes on justice, this reconstruction helps illuminate and justify the value of agonistic honorableness by showing why we would need to invent its constraints if honorableness didn't already call for them. Moreover, this exercise serves to answer the three objections to seeing agonistic honorableness as a civil virtue. First, it allowed us to explain and justify agonistic honorableness without appeal to postmodern, Continental, or critical theory. Second, we have seen that agonistic honorableness, although highly competitive, serves not only to limit conflict but also make it less acrimonious. Finally, a rational reconstruction that begins by positing status-conscious agents every bit as familiar to us as Hobbes's prudential egoists, and illustrated at every stage with nonfictional examples from past and present, should demonstrate that the honorable restraint agonism calls for is hardly an unrealistic ideal.

PRINCIPLES OF HONORABLE CIVIL DISCOURSE

We now turn to the question of whether and how to apply the norms of agonistic honorableness to the problem of civil discourse, which grows ever more urgent. According to a variety of measures, public debate in the United States has reached a level of dysfunction unmatched since

Senator Charles Sumner was caned nearly to death by Representative Preston Brooks in 1856.[21] Universities are currently embroiled in disabling controversies over issues relating to honoring racist founders, addressing racial and gender underrepresentation, and improving campus climates for minorities. Most online news outlets have curtailed their comment boards because of hateful speech. Prominent protest movements seem designed to goad (what they see as) a complacent public more than to garner public support for their causes. Social media feeds are full of outraged commentary and meme-driven rhetoric that heap contempt on positions (on guns, on religion, on immigration, etc.) that wide swaths of the public—indeed, a significant percentage of the typical poster's *own friends*—subscribe to. New injustices and offenses (such as "ableism" and "manspreading") enter mainstream discussion on what seems like a weekly basis; and although some of these new categories of discrimination and wrongdoing are legitimate, the degree of opprobrium aimed at offenders is frequently disproportionate to the level of consensus about the wrongness of these offenses and the degree of real harm they incur. Indeed, even yesterday's well-meaning faux pas has mutated into today's "microaggression."

Possible explanations for the toxic nature of so much public debate include unabashedly partisan cable news channels, the democratization of media by social networking platforms, a troubled and bifurcated economy, increasingly aggressive policing, greater religious and ethnic diversity, and overprotective child-rearing. But whatever the causes, the animus is spilling over into ideological and identity-fueled violence. As I type this, the past few weeks have seen in the United States: a spree shooting at an abortion clinic, a racially motivated shooting of four black protestors, a case of domestic Islamist terrorism, a racially motivated execution-style murder of a white police officer, and a campus closing due to an online threat of racial violence.

One might infer from the raucous nature of the culture wars that its combatants are battle-hardened. Just the opposite is true. Calls for "trigger warnings" are growing frequent, as are the much more problematic demands by some students groups to be exempted from triggering material—discussions of rape, for example, are being curtailed in even our nation's most prominent law schools.[22] Another indication of discourse fragility is the campus "safe space," an area where students triggered by opposing viewpoints can retreat. (In one infamous case, student activists at Brown University—concerned about the psychological trauma that could result from witnessing a formal debate over the widespread claim that colleges are rape cultures—set up a safe space furnished with "cookies, coloring books, Play-Doh, calming music, pillows, blankets, and a video of frolicking puppies."[23]) Thus, it is easy to conclude that political discourse in the United States has grown both more aggressive and more cowardly.

The Standard Model of Civil Discourse

The 2011 Tucson, AZ, shooting that killed six and left Congresswoman Gabby Giffords brain damaged was considered by many at the time to be a signal moment in decline of American civil discourse. At a memorial service for the victims, President Obama called for a renewed commitment to talking our problems out:

> [A]t a time when our discourse has become so sharply polarized—at a time when we are far too eager to lay the blame for all that ails the world at the feet of those who happen to think differently than we do—it's important for us to pause for a moment and make sure that we're talking with each other in a way that heals, not in a way that wounds.[24]

A host of institutes, forums, academic conferences, and news organizations were summoned into existence shortly after President Obama's call to action, and the ethical approach usually assumed in these discussions about the nature and purpose of civil discourse is decidedly non-agonistic.

As reflected by President Obama's remarks, the (what we can call) "standard model" of civil discourse aims at *closing gaps*: on it, the breakdown of civil discourse is explained by ideological polarization, and narrowing the gap between ideologies—either as a precondition of civil discourse[25] or as its goal[26]—is the aim. The standard model's advice on closing those gaps often reads like a crash course in Logic 101 or Introduction to Philosophy. For instance, in an essay for the Association of American Colleges and Universities, Andrea Leskes encourages disputants to "embody open-mindedness" and "use verified information."[27] Another scholar considers civility to require "consideration of diverse viewpoints," an "appreciation for insight offered by those with professional and practical knowledge," and "arguments that avoid manipulation, fallacies or knowingly inaccurate information."[28]

Like any academic, I'd be delighted if citizens had the will and training to weigh the reasoning and empirical evidence for controversial positions. I fully support efforts to improve civil discourse by making citizens more fair- and open-minded, patient, and skeptical. But I feel it would *also* be beneficial if we inculcated virtues of civil discourse that equipped citizens to debate sustainably even when there is no hope of consensus.

Agonistic Civil Discourse

As an approach to civil discourse, agonism denies gap theory. Unlike the standard model, on which adversaries would ideally come to reasoned agreement, agonism requires conflict, and would ideally shape this conflict into respectful and meaningful contest. Whereas the standard model discourages ego and tries to get us to focus on the issues, on agonism disputants are assumed to, even encouraged to, conceive of themselves as "champions" of their causes—a timely feature in our narcissistic cultural moment, where posting a selfie while holding up a sign (often with a hashtag), is a principal form of activism. It may seem counterintuitive to base a philosophy of civil discourse on self-absorption and conflict, but recall that the initial conditions of our Hobbesian reconstruction of honor placed status-hungry combatants in a far more rancorous setting. Status-seeking and conflict are the raw materials from which honorable contest is formed. So although it may be antithetical to the aims of the standard model of civil discourse, it is quite possible, as we have seen, for agonists with utterly different aims to fight respectfully and hold each other in mutual esteem.

Calling for an agonistic approach to civil discourse is not an ivory-tower fancy detached from the grim realities of the political trenches. For instance, former U.S. Congressman and National Endowment for the Humanities president Jim Leach has argued that politics needs more of an agonistic sensibility.

> I really think America needs an "athletic democracy." In the sense of people looking at fairness and the sports mentality. There's no good coach and team in America that doesn't begin with hard work and respecting your opponent. [. . .] After every game you see the two teams put their arms around each other. You don't see that in politics. Sport has come up with a higher ethic than the political ethic. We need to ask ourselves if the vigorous competition in sports can be carried out, shouldn't we expect the same of the political process?[29]

In fact, as we shall see, agonistic ideas are often endorsed in informal discussions about the rules of political and social debate. In what follows, then, I offer a handful of agonistic principles for promoting civil discourse.

Don't find ideological disagreement upsetting, unnatural, or immoral. In the liberal utopian tradition of war ethics, peace is assumed to be good and conflict assumed to be bad, the unquestioned aim of all conflict is conflict-resolution, and conflict itself is evidence of prior moral failure. These assumptions are carried over to political debates—but are they sound? Agreement can be reached on a falsehood or an injustice, after all, and there is little reason to believe that, even if consensus is reached on this or that issue, harmony will reign. There are no decisive debates. Things never seem to settle down. As consensus is reached in one debate, another one takes its place, and the new one appears to be as existentially important as the old one. For pluralistic liberal democracies in particular, it seems that there will never be anything like harmony. We like to speak of "culture warriors," but true culture warriors are not "culture jihadists" or "culture crusaders": they are not pious, regretful fighters yearning for a future when they can beat their swords into plowshares and live in peace with the world, where "peace" is defined by unanimity on some issue, an intellectual landscape purged of evil influence. The sooner we understand that polities such as ours are places of perpetual ideological battle, the sooner politically active citizens can shape themselves into true culture warriors.

Don't expect or desire to convert your ideological opponents. As we have seen, the standard model of civil discourse says that it would be ideal if ideological opponents reached consensus. Common experience suggests that this happens very rarely, even in academic disputes. Giving up on converting your ideological opponents doesn't mean forsaking the hope of making a difference, of course. In parallel to Thomas Kuhn's thoughts on scientific revolutions,[30] it isn't unreasonable to think that real political progress is made by persuading onlookers, not opponents. Agonism psychologically better prepares us for a war of ideas because agonists don't enter the arena in the vain hope that our opponents will toss down their weapons and accede to our points.

Giving up on our opponents as potential converts doesn't mean disrespecting them, nor does it license dishonorable attacks against them or their positions. First, it's worth remembering that fighting honorably for our views, even if doing so disadvantages our positions in the short-term, usually renders our positions more attractive to our audiences over the long haul. And secondly, for agonistic reasons observed above, we are to recognize ourselves in our opponents, and acknowledge the same motives and principled commitments in them that we pride in ourselves. Sure, our ideological opponents would be "better" in some way if they were correct (read: agreed with us) about the issue under dispute—they'd be better scientists, or philosophers, or what have you. But crucially, agreeing with us or even being actually correct *wouldn't make them better warriors*. If they fight honorably, they deserve our respect as culture warriors.

Pick on someone your own size (or slightly bigger). The denotation of the word "bullying" has expanded in recent decades to encompass any form of unwarranted aggression. Traditionally, the aggressor had to be somehow stronger or better-positioned to count as a bully: for a smaller boy to pick a fight with a bigger one on the schoolyard would traditionally be thought of foolish or spirited, but not bullying. Theories of justice have a hard time explaining why the aggressive smaller boy traditionally got a pass—after all, although aggressing on a stronger party is more likely to result in a (poetically just) drubbing than would aggressing on a weaker party, both are equally unjust aggressions. Agonistic honor, on the other hand, does a better job of explaining our old-fashioned conception of bullies. On agonism, competitors must "find their place" in the relevant ranking. This requires a measured sort of ambition according to which one challenges slightly higher-ranked competitors, but never lower-ranked. This makes sense, and is even evident in male-male competition in some nonhuman species (such as among stags), since competing with a lower-ranked party will not elevate one's position whatever the outcome, and competing with a much higher-ranked opponent will almost certainly result in defeat and injury.[31] Bullying on agonism, then, signals weakness or lack of confidence insofar as the bully is interpreted as imagining his hapless victim as a worthy opponent. Bullying also disrupts the ranking by injuring or discouraging a lower-ranked party, thereby violating their honor-right to find their true place in the status competition.

Applied to an agonistic theory of civil discourse, the bully will be someone who chooses a worse-positioned figure for debate or as a target of condemnation. Examples abound. One classic case involves the website *Jezebel*'s reposting of some racist tweets a handful of high school students made about President Obama, deciding not only to publish their names, but also to notify their school administrators about their tweets. Given *Jezebel*'s influence, any web search of these students' names will, in perpetuity, reveal their offensive tweets within the top few results and thus presumably harm their future prospects.[32] More controversial examples of "punching down" include Richard Dawkins's tweets accusing fourteen-year-old Ahmed Mohamed of engineering a publicity stunt with his clock resembling a bomb,[33] and the French satirical newspaper *Charlie Hebdo*'s Mohammed cartoon, which cartoonist Garry Trudeau accused of "punching downward, by attacking a powerless, disenfranchised minority."[34]

Again, on the standard view, it is hard to see why it would be worse to "punch down." Why should the relative status of your interlocutor, or the figure you're calling out, matter, from the perspective of justice? *Do* they do/stand for unjust things, or not? Shouldn't we disregard questions of relative status and power of the parties involved, and focus on *truth* of the accusation or its justification? Presumably so—but the sense that one oughtn't bully persists. Agonism, in contrast, offers us a ready reply: punching down is dishonorable because softer targets are unable to defend themselves or put up a good fight.

As the above examples of "punching down" show, who is higher or lower in the ranking of culture warriors is a point of some dispute. Was *Charlie Hebdo* bullying poor disenfranchised Muslims, or actually standing up to violent Islamists who threaten harmless artists offending against their sacred figures? These debates are being had, and these are the debates that should be had according to an agonistic theory of civil discourse. Generally, however, agonism would take a dim view of professors engaging in (sincere, nonpedagogical) debate with students, public officials denouncing private individuals, and prominent social critics bearing down on relatively obscure ideological opponents. If a better-positioned party wants to address something a weaker culture warrior has said or done, she may do so honorably by diffusing the personal nature of the criticism—say, by taking aim at a general trend that the lower-ranked party exemplifies. Thus, instead of "Obscure person x did bad thing y" it's better for a prominent social critic to say, "I'm noticing some people doing y, and it's bad because of such-and-such reasons." If some more equally-positioned advocate of y defends the practice in response to your criticism, then you may engage them publicly as a representative of the bad practice.

Do not attack noncombatants. Stuck in the early stages of our Hobbesian reconstruction of honor, commonplace ideologues see their counterparts as evil. They expect their champions to have the same uncompromising attitudes and to employ total-war tactics in prosecuting the culture war. Such "true believers"[35] who cross the line should be chastised by their own ideological aristocracy for dishonorable attacks. For instance, CNN anchor Carol Costello was forced to apologize by her own network after encouraging viewers to "sit back and enjoy" a recording of Bristol Palin describing to police an attack she suffered by a stranger in a 2014.[36] Costello's barb violated the time-honored journalistic rule of treating the children of politicians as political noncombatants.

The point applies not only to family of our opponents but also their friends, or those simply too busy, agnostic, or cowardly to speak out one way or another. It is quite common to hear political pundits decry the "silence" or "inaction" from this or that group who fail to denounce some outrage the pundit cares about. In doing so, the pundit is trying to declare the silent, inactive group as a fair target. Now it is perfectly true that the inactivity of the group in question may enable her foes. Nonetheless, their unwillingness to stick their necks out makes them nobodies as far as this fight is concerned, and in the eyes of a warrior, a nobody is a noncombatant because combatants must somehow be engaged in the status competition. They may be cowardly or morally benighted; but until silent supporters actually *do* or *say* anything, they don't deserve (in both senses of the word) to be attacked by culture warriors.

Don't silence opponents by appealing to authorities. In a much-discussed article, sociologists Bradley Campbell and Jason Manning persuasively argue that we are transitioning from a dignity-based culture to an honor-based one based on victimhood. By "dignity" culture the authors mean one that sees everyone as innately endowed with an unearned and inalienable moral worth. On this scheme, our basic moral equality is assumed, assaults on welfare and property are punished by a central authority, and insults are largely disregarded and thus comparatively rare. This regime replaced the traditional honor culture on which some people have more value than others, personal value could be easily lost through shame and insult, and riposte to offense had to be handled personally.[37] According to Campbell and Manning, the new moral culture combines and inverts various aspects of its predecessors. Like a traditional honor culture, victimhood culture is highly stratified, but it elevates *victims* and demotes *nonvictims*, which traditional honor cultures would find bizarre. Also in keeping with honor cultures, victimhood culture is highly sensitive to insult. Nonetheless, on it offenses to dignity are properly handled by authorities, not personally, as if they were "material" attacks on person or property (hence "micro*aggressions*" and not the more accurate "micro-*offenses*").[38]

These appeals to authority result in the demands we are seeing on campuses and in courts for more censorship, more accommodations, lower standards, and tighter limits on speech and inquiry. For instance, the Foundation for Individual Rights in Education (FIRE) has noted a spike in university speakers withdrawing because of official disinvitation and the certain prospect of relentless student heckling.[39] The standard reasons we give against shouting down or censoring our ideological opponents are either Millian (i.e., that debate helps us to discover the truth and keep our moral and political discoveries from becoming "dead dogmas"), or based on the moral/legal rights we have to free speech. However sound these reasons may be, the agonistic perspective adds to them that silencing our opponents through force, intimidation, and threat (not only of violence, but also to careers) is tantamount to refusing to engage them on fair terms.

Don't insult opponents and especially guests. In September of 2007, then-Iranian President Mahmoud Ahmadinejad addressed the campus of Columbia University by invitation of that school's World Leaders Forum. The invitation was vigorously criticized by a wide spectrum of groups, including wealthy donors and lawmakers who control the aid the institution relies on.[40] To his credit, Columbia president Lee Bollinger maintained the invitation. But his introduction of the Iranian leader—clearly aimed to placate his politically powerful critics—was an astonishing six minutes of almost unrelenting insult:

> Mr. President, you exhibit all the signs of a petty and cruel dictator. [. . .] [As a holocaust denier, w]hen you have come to a place like this, this makes you, quite simply, ridiculous. [. . .] [As someone who has threatened to destroy Israel,] do you plan on wiping us off the map too? [. . .] I close with this comment frankly and in all candor, Mr. President. I doubt that you will have the intellectual courage to answer these questions. But your avoiding them will in itself be meaningful to us. I do expect you to exhibit the fanatical mindset that characterizes so much of what you say and do.[41]

Ahmadinejad's response was completely predictable, and warranted from an honor perspective. The Iranian leader contrasted his treatment with his country's tradition, which "requires that when we invite a speaker we actually respect our students and the professors by allowing them to make their own judgment." He went on to say that in

> a university environment we must allow people to speak their mind, to allow everyone to talk so that the truth is eventually revealed by all. Certainly he took more than all the time I was allocated to speak, and

> that's fine with me. We'll just leave that to add up with the claims of respect for freedom and the freedom of speech that's given to us in this country.[42]

Ahmadinejad's complaint about his introduction actually garnered the loudest applause of his speech. Bollinger's dishonorable stridency exposed him to a devastatingly apt lecture on free thought and speech from a dictator of a theocratic regime, and cost him the moral high ground. He would have been better off either not inviting Ahmadinejad or treating him with the respect due an honorable adversary, even if purely as a matter of form.

These agonistic considerations against personal attacks are different but compatible with the reasons given in philosophy classrooms, which stress that personal attacks do not address the strength of an opponent's argument or evidence. The agonistic reason has to do with treating your opponents respectfully and fairly, since they are your moral equals. Of course, many of those we disagree with on ideological matters deserve to be insulted. Agonistic cultures are full of insults, and agonistic ethics holds that insults are often morally required, such as when we must contemn a dishonorable party, or spur a complacent opponent to accept a reasonable challenge. But insults must not be aimed at opponents during debate, since agonists by definition view their adversaries as respectable. This principle is particularly strict when it comes to invited speakers, who are at a disadvantage.

CONCLUSION: AGONISM AS THE LIMITS OF COMMUNITY

Agonistic principles of civil discourse limn the uttermost limits of "sustainable" adversarial speech in a community. Any set of norms more aggressive, hostile, recriminatory, or exclusionary will tear a community apart (even if state coercion forces groups engaging in such ways to remain together politically, their compulsory political entanglements would hardly constitute a community).

Because some communities ought not to be sustained, sometimes *uncivil* discourse will be morally permissible. Sometimes our ideological adversaries simply refuse to play by the rules of either rational inquiry or agonistic debate, and groups that don't even try to govern their speech by reason or honor may be talked to dismissively and derisively, it seems to me. Nonetheless, on the assumption that the conditions of civil discourse are preferable, it is important that we have a good sense of agonistic discourse norms. Precisely because agonistic rules are the most oppositional ones that still count as civil, they are going to be the most psychologically accessible norms for already fractured communities inching back toward toleration of opposing viewpoints.

And because agonistic norms of discourse are the most oppositional of the civil ones, they are the "last, best hope" for sustainable discourse in communities whose partisans are drifting apart. The standard model discourages us from thinking in terms of winning or losing and instead urges us to think of interlocutors as cooperative truth-seekers. This position mirrors the liberal/justice model that promotes cooperation between individuals or states and views conflict as evil. If the first half of this essay is correct, even those inclined to see things this way should admit that it would be beneficial if, when the spirit of cooperation breaks down, adversaries at least fight honorably. Likewise, in the realm of speech, if the cooperative ideal expressed in the standard model is not attainable, agonistically honorable discourse will at least allow us to fight together.

NOTES

1. Among others, see: Hanna Arendt, *The Human Condition* (Chicago: Chicago University Press, 1958); William Connolly, *Identity/Difference: Democratic Negotiations of Political Paradox* (Ithaca, NY: Cornell University Press, 1991); Bonnie Honig, *Political Theory and the Displacement of Politics* (Ithaca, NY: Cornell University Press, 1993); Chantal Mouffe, *Agonistics* (New York: Verso, 2013). See Ed Wingenbach, *Institutionalizing Agonistic Democracy* (Burlington, VT: Ashgate, 2011) for a helpful summary.
2. Steven Pinker, *The Better Angels of Our Nature* (New York: Viking, 2011).
3. Dan Demetriou, "Honor War Theory: Romance or Reality?" *Philosophical Papers* (2013) 42 no. 3, 285–313.
4. Thomas Hobbes, *Leviathan*, ed. Richard Tuck (Cambridge: Cambridge University Press, 1996), chs. 13–15.
5. Charles-Louis Montesquieu, *The Spirit of the Laws*, eds. Anne Cohler, Basia Carolyn Miller, and Harold Stone (Cambridge: Cambridge University Press, 1989).
6. For an extended discussion on these themes, see Laurie Johnson, *Thomas Hobbes: Turning Point for Honor* (Lanham, MD: Lexington Books, 2009).
7. Johnson, *Thomas Hobbes*, ch. 3.
8. "Girl Recites Poem: Jews 'murdered' children. . . ." *Palwatch.org*, March 22, 2013, http://www.palwatch.org/pages/news_archive.aspx?doc_id=8734.
9. Napoleon Chagnon, *Noble Savages: My Life Among Two Dangerous Tribes—the Yanomamo and the Anthropologists* (New York: Simon & Schuster, 2013).
10. Herodotus, *History, Volume III*, trans. George Rawlinson (London: John Murray, 1862).
11. Winston Churchill, "Their Finest Hour," *WinstonChurchill.org*, April 14, 2014, http://www.winstonchurchill.org/resources/speeches/1940-the-finest-hour/their-finest-hour. For more on Churchill's use of honor in his rhetoric, see Mark Griffith's chapter in this volume.
12. Slightly modified from *Beowulf*, trans. Leslie Hall (Boston: D. C. Heath & Co. 1892), bk.10.40.
13. I Samuel 17.
14. Malcolm Gladwell, *David and Goliath: Underdogs, Misfits, and the Art of Battling Giants* (New York: Little, Brown and Company, 2013).
15. Ian Toll, *Six Frigates: The Epic History of the Founding of the U.S. Navy* (New York: Norton, 2006), 406.
16. See Carole Hillenbrand, "The Evolution of the Saladin Legend in the West" in *Mélanges*, ed. Louis Pouzet (Beirut: Dar El-Marchreq, 2006), 1–13; Geoffrey Regan, *Lionhearts: Richard I, Saladin, and the Era of the Third Crusade* (New York: Bloomsbury, 1999).

17. John Ruskin, *Crown of Wild Olive* (Boston: Colonial Press, 2008), 72.

18. Qtd. in Sarva Daman Singh, *Ancient Indian Warfare: With Special Reference to the Vedic Period* (Delhi: Motilal Bararsidass Publishers, 1965), 161–62.

19. Paul Robinson, "The Moral Equality of Combatants," *Irrussianality* (blog), December 17, 2014, https://irrussianality.wordpress.com/2014/12/17/the-moral-equality-of-combatants/

20. For an early attempt at a theory of the evolution of agonism, see Dan Demetriou, "The Ecology of Honor in Humans and Animals," in *Beastly Morality*, ed. Jonathan Crane (New York: Columbia University Press, 2015).

21. Jill Lepore, "Long Division: Measuring the Polarization of American Politics," *New Yorker*, December 2, 2013, http://www.newyorker.com/magazine/2013/12/02/long-division.

22. Jeannie Suk, "The Trouble with Teaching Rape Law," *New Yorker*, Dec 15, 2014, http://www.newyorker.com/news/news-desk/trouble-teaching-rape-law.

23. Judith Shulevitz, "In College and Hiding from Scary Ideas," *New York Times*, March 21, 2015, http://www.nytimes.com/2015/03/22/opinion/sunday/judith-shulevitz-hiding-from-scary-ideas.html.

24. Barack Obama, "Remarks by the President at a Memorial Service for the Victims of the Shooting in Tucson, Arizona," *Whitehouse.gov*, January 12, 2011, https://www.whitehouse.gov/the-press-office/2011/01/12/remarks-president-barack-obama-memorial-service-victims-shooting-tucson

25. E.g., John Rawls, *Political Liberalism* (New York: Columbia University Press, 1993).

26. E.g., Juergen Habermas, *Between Facts and Norms: Contributions to a Discourse Theory of Law and Democracy* (Cambridge, MA: MIT Press, 1996).

27. Andrea Leskes, "A Plea for Civil Discourse: Needed, the Academy's Leadership," *Association of American Colleges and Universities* (2013) 99 no. 4, http://www.aacu.org/liberaleducation/2013/fall/leskes

28. John Gastil, "Good arguments: Modern adventures in the theory and practice of deliberative democracy." Presentation at the National Institute for Civil Discourse, March 8, 2013.

29. Jim Leach "Civility in a Fractured Society" (video), February 18, 2010, https://www.youtube.com/watch?v=J22_iR8bl54&spfreload=1.

30. Thomas Kuhn, *The Structure of Scientific Revolutions: 50th Anniversary Edition* (Chicago: University of Chicago Press, 2012).

31. Demetriou, "The Ecology of Honor in Humans and Animals."

32. Laura Hudson, "Why You Should Think Twice Before Shaming Anyone on Social Media," *Wired*, July 24, 2014, http://www.wired.com/2013/07/ap_argshaming/

33. Matthew Francis, "Rationalist's Irrationality: Why is Richard Dawkins such a Jerk?" *Slate*, Sept 25, 2015, http://www.slate.com/articles/health_and_science/science/2015/09/richard_dawkins_on_social_media_the_author_of_the_selfish_gene_and_meme.html

34. Garry Trudeau, "The Abuse of Satire," *The Atlantic*, April 11, 2015, http://www.theatlantic.com/international/archive/2015/04/the-abuse-of-satire/390312/

35. Eric Hoffer, *The True Believer: Thoughts on the Nature of Mass Movements* (New York: HarperCollins, 2010).

36. Brian Stelter, "Carol Costello Deserved Criticism Over Palin Segment," *CNN*, October 26, 2014, https://www.youtube.com/watch?v=ARI87Ooixj4

37. Vandello and Hettinger, in this volume.

38. Bradley Campbell and Jason Manning, "Microaggression and Moral Cultures," *Comparative Sociology* 3 (2014), 692–726.

39. "Disinvitation Report 2014: A Disturbing 15-Year Trend," *FIRE*, May 28, 2014, http://www.thefire.org/disinvitation-season-report-2014/.

40. Jacob Gershman, "Legislatures May Act on Columbia," *New York Sun*, September 24, 2007, http://www.nysun.com/new-york/legislatures-may-act-on-columbia/63232/.

41. Lee Bollinger, "Introductory Remarks at SIPA-World Leaders Forum with President of Iran Mahmoud Ahmadinejad" (transcript), *Columbianews*, September 24, 2007, http://www.columbia.edu/cu/news/07/09/lcbopeningremarks.html.

42. Mahmoud Ahmadinejad, "Remarks at Columbia University" (transcript), *Washington Post*, September 24, 2007, http://www.washingtonpost.com/wp-dyn/content/article/2007/09/24/AR2007092401042.html.

TWO

Liberalism and Honor through the Lens of Darwin

Steven Forde

To say that liberalism has traditionally been uncomfortable with the notion of honor would seem to many an understatement. Liberalism, the political philosophy of self-interested individualism, is on its face antithetical to honor, a notion redolent of aristocratic pride. Honor represents dedication to something higher, more noble, than self-interest. The man of honor is willing to sacrifice his interest, indeed his life, to honor. This impulse, so irrational from the point of view of material self-interest, may actually be construed as a *threat* to liberalism. Hobbes set the tone when he asserted honor to be an excrescence of the desire for power and thus of self-interest.[1]

Other liberal thinkers were not quite so dismissive of honor, however. John Locke says little about it, but does enlist pride as a key pedagogical tool in his educational treatise, *Some Thoughts Concerning Education*.[2] Hume, Montesquieu, and Rousseau were all more open to the salutary effects of honor.[3] The American Declaration of Independence begins with a ringing endorsement of the liberal philosophy of "life, liberty, and the pursuit of happiness," but concludes with a pledge of the signatories' "sacred Honor."

Were the authors of the Declaration dredging up an archaic concept for merely rhetorical reasons, despite that concept's incompatibility with the principles on which they were acting? The concept of honor does have resonance, however weakened, even among their descendants. I propose tracing two understandings of liberalism that differ from the orthodox Hobbesian view regarding the place of honor in it. First is the neo-Hegelianism that Francis Fukuyama has elaborated, and partially attributed to Alexandre Kojève.[4] The other arises from one strain of contemporary Darwinian (neo-Darwinian) evolutionary theory.[5] These two very different bodies of thought converge on the notion that something like honor—perhaps it is better to speak with Hegel of a desire for "recognition"—is inseparable from human nature and thus must be integrated into liberalism, if liberalism is to be theoretically or practically viable. Both strands of theory fashion an idea of liberalism in which recognition, a universally realizable form of honor, is central, a key to liberalism's desirability, and success. If this represents the truth about liberalism, we gain a great deal by separating ourselves from the straightjacket of the Hobbesian approach, and coming to grips with this more complete understanding of the system in which we live.

LIBERALISM AND HONOR

We must begin with a brief account of Hobbes's view of honor, if only as a backdrop to what follows. *Leviathan*, Hobbes's signature work, takes its name from the book of Job. Hobbes explains that he intended this as an allusion to the Leviathan as the "King of the Proud."[6] It is because of the "pride and other passions" of men that they are compelled to submit to the absolute power of a sovereign.

According to the psychology laid out in the beginning of that work, pride has its roots in the first or deepest impulses of human nature. All of human action is traced to "appetite and aversion," whereby human beings are attracted to certain things, and repulsed by others.[7] From these simple beginnings, according to Hobbes, spring all the passions. Hope, despair, fear, courage, anger, and others, are mere modifications and compoundings of these initial motions. "Glory" and "Vain-Glory" are among these offshoots, which Hobbes describes as "*Joy* arising from imagination of a man's own power," which is "vain" if based on a false estimation of his actual power.[8]

While all human beings might be susceptible to all of these passions, many particular objects of desire are idiosyncratic: some love (have an appetite for) learning, some for luxury.[9] Whatever the object of one's desire, however, there is one thing we must all desire, and that is power, for power is nothing but the ability to fulfill desire.[10] This leads, according to Hobbes, to a universal competition among men, for power. And this leads in turn to a universal competition for honor. For honor reflects the estimate others make of one's power, and much of one's power depends on others' estimate of power (beauty is power, but only if it is recognized as such by others[11]). Since appetite never comes to an end—the satisfaction of one appetite only causes others to rise in its wake—the competition for power, and thus honor, never ends.[12]

Hobbesian honor is a passion or appetite deeply engrained in human nature. It is ineradicable, descending directly from appetite and aversion. It also puts us necessarily at odds with one another, contributing, in the absence of a sovereign power, to the war of all against all.[13] There is no way to reconcile this conflict in the state of nature, for all men have a right to everything, and all appetites are equally legitimate.[14] Each man's desire for honor—for more honor than others have—is legitimate for the same reason. The only resolution Hobbes finds for this situation is for all to lay down their rights to a sovereign, who thereby becomes the possessor of all right. In principle, that means the newly-minted citizens also renounce their rights to power and honor, which also go to the sovereign. Only thus can competition between men be prevented from spiraling into civil war. Of course, the sovereign will allow his subjects to pursue their appetites, to accumulate power and even honor, since these are inseparable from human life. He will confine these pursuits within strict channels, however, knowing the danger they present to social peace. He will even establish a public system of honors, knowing that the desire for honor cannot be simply suppressed.[15] If he does not, we presume, men will do it among themselves, and the sovereign would lose control of honor, with dire consequences.[16]

ISOTHYMIA AT THE END OF HISTORY

If we take this to be the benchmark view of honor for liberalism, we have to ask whether such a view leads to an impoverished or even an ultimately self-destructive politics and culture.[17] But perhaps we should first ask whether Hobbes's view of honor is even true to liberalism itself, at least as liberalism has existed in practice. Francis Fukuyama brought this question to the fore some years ago, with his thesis that Hegel was in some sense correct to hold that modern liberalism represents the "end of history."[18] This is because it best satisfies fundamental human longings. These longings however are not limited to the desire for security and prosperity, or even for freedom. Those are the focal point of the liberalism of Hobbes, Locke, and the English liberals, which has predominated in Anglo-American understandings of liberalism. Fukuyama finds in Hegel, or Alexandre Kojève's interpretation of Hegel, an alternative, and more persuasive, explanation of liberalism's stunning historical triumph. We need not subscribe to the "end of history" thesis to find this explanation compelling as a supplement to Anglo-American liberalism.[19]

The argument that Fukuyama borrows from Hegel revolves around the centrality of *recognition* as a driving force in the advance of liberalism (if not of all human history). Liberalism's success is accounted for by its ability to satisfy the deep human desire for recognition or respect. This impulse stands behind modern man's desire for recognition of his equal dignity among his fellow human beings (democratic recognition) but may also express itself as a desire for exceptional recognition—honor in the aristocratic or traditional sense. In the latter form, it may also become tyrannical. In this understanding, the desire for recognition is the key to the stability, and the justice, of liberal democracy, but is also a potential threat to it.

In Hegel's schematic history of the development of spirit or mind,[20] the initial moment is a struggle to the death between two individuals, or self-consciousnesses.[21] Each sees the other as a challenge to its own independence, and at the same time wishes to demonstrate its own "infinitude," its independence from finite, determinate existence, by risking its life in the struggle. Should one die in the struggle, the winner remains unsatisfied, for self-consciousness does not fully exist for itself, according to Hegel, except by being recognized by another self-consciousness.[22] Self-consciousness is fundamentally a social phenomenon, because of its need to be affirmed by others like itself. Others thus represent both its only path to fulfillment, and a threat to that fulfillment. In the initial struggle, it may happen that one party is overcome by fear of death and submits to the other. This establishes the fateful relationship of master and servant that for Hegel launches the slow development of spirit through history.[23]

In Hegel's analysis, the master-servant relationship is unsatisfactory on both sides: neither party succeeds in gaining the recognition he originally sought. The master is unsatisfied because the servant's "recognition" is coerced, and comes from one he himself has put in the position of an inferior.[24] The servant is paradoxically closer to the attainment of his goal. History, for Hegel, is (among other things) the progressive evolution of social modes of recognition, whose inevitable culmination is the one arrangement that satisfies the longing for recognition, and that is the modern liberal regime. Here, recognition is given to all humanity, since all humanity shares the rationality and self-consciousness that makes it crave, and entitles it to, recognition. Only universal recognition on the basis of fundamental equality is rational, not based on arbitrary or partial categories such as race or class. Only liberalism guarantees recognition to each by conferring inviolable rights on each, and makes each a full participant in the ethical community of the "state."[25]

Hegel's account rests on one postulate in particular that we need to consider. He subsumes classical and aristocratic honor, together with egalitarian mutual respect, under the heading "recognition." The former are both expressions of the latter, with the egalitarian variety being unqualifiedly superior. Hegel is not blind to the magnificence that was sometimes inspired by the classical variety—his account of the unfolding of spirit gives each stage its due—but the liberal solution to the problem of recognition is fundamentally, philosophically, superior. He seems immune to the pangs of nostalgia that Alexis de Tocqueville was to feel for the loss of aristocratic honor.[26] The same can be said even more emphatically about Alexandre Kojève, who affirmed the Hegelian thesis concerning the end of history in the context of twentieth-century European liberal states.[27]

Francis Fukuyama is by no means so sanguine; he worries that the end of history as envisaged by "Hegel-Kojève" might signal the advent of Nietzsche 's "Last Man."[28] Nonetheless, he maintains, the thesis is fundamentally correct: the modern liberal state is history's final stage. Again, in his case, the picture is not quite so sunny as it is for Hegel or Kojève. Liberal democracy is not the final stage because it represents a perfectly harmonious subsuming of all the contradictions that have roiled human history, but because it is the most stable accommodation of all the basic human needs and impulses. Given human nature, no perfectly harmonious resolution of its tensions is possible.[29] The most stable accommodation still must slight some aspects of human nature. Thus the risk that it might breed a contemptible type of human being.

Equally importantly, in contrast to Hegel, Fukuyama does not see this resolution as wholly rational. Whereas for Hegel the end of history was the triumph of rationality in the form of universal rational recognition, Fukuyama sees recognition as an irrational, or at best only partly rational, human impulse. This is indicated by the name he gives to the liberal accommodation: *isothymia*. Its derivation is Greek, referring to *thymos*—spiritedness or heart or pride or anger—the impulse that Plato made one of the three parts of the soul, and the ancient poets attributed to their heroes.[30] Within our context, *thymos* is the impulse for recognition or honor or fame. These are all taken to be manifestations of the same underlying impulse, though only a few might desire fame, the supreme degree of recognition. The desire for great recognition Fukuyama dubs *megalothymia*, *isothymia* being the desire for recognition such as all might share.[31] Contemporary liberalism is the regime of *isothymia*, granting rights to all, and recognizing human dignity in all.

Liberal democracy is the end of history not simply because it grants security and unprecedented material comfort to populations, though these are clearly partial keys to its success. It has triumphed over its rivals because it gratifies the human thirst for recognition. If material goods, or even security, had been the only engines driving the advance of liberal democracy, so many individuals would not have risked life and limb, and been willing to sacrifice every material comfort, in order to bring it about. Fukuyama plausibly argues that every major triumph of the liberal idea, from the American and French Revolutions up to the mostly peaceful uprisings that brought about the collapse of the Soviet empire in 1989, was fueled decisively by the desire for a recognition denied by illiberal regimes.[32] This in itself would be enough to spark a reevaluation of the Anglo-American understanding of the basis of liberalism.

Such a reevaluation leads us to rethink not only what motivated pivotal events such as 1989 (and how we might best advance the cause of liberal democracy in the future), but how we understand the workings of liberal democracy itself, its center of gravity, as it were. It leads us to a different understanding as well of its weaknesses. To begin with, the stability, and the historical irresistibility, of liberal democracy comes not simply from its material benefits, but from its spiritual or psychological ones. The love of freedom and of equality that observers of democracy have noted for millennia is not simply appetitive, but thymotic. So is the resentment people feel when being deprived of these. These facts explain the doggedness of liberal democracy's proponents. The same impulse can be instrumental in righting wrongs within a liberal society, as was witnessed in the American civil rights movement; it can also fuel the less savory "leveling" instinct that has long been seen as a pathology of democracy, where all forms of inequality are seen as an affront to individuals lower on whatever gradient is at issue.[33] Recognition, viewed as the mainspring of liberal democracy, is less predictable, more volatile, than security and prosperity. What human beings will come to regard as the recognition or respect that is due them is not foreordained. It may be that "rational recognition" as Hegel defined it is the proper benchmark, but we have already noted that recognition as it manifests itself at the end of history is not quite so tractable.

These are different problems than one would expect on a security-and-prosperity understanding of liberalism. In that traditional view, the loss of public spirit and the predominance of private over public interest are the principal pathologies of liberalism. The problems brought by unleashing the thirst for recognition are rather different, and have been explored by authors as diverse as William Galston and Charles Taylor.[34] In brief, either "expressive individualism" (Galston) or group-identity multiculturalism (Taylor) come to demand recognition for any expression of "the self," or any manifestation of any subculture within society, "recognition" meaning not only toleration, but respect or affirmation by society at large. These demands could be made by Islamic communities who insist on maintaining illiberal practices, or an urban-gang subculture that regards crime as a legitimate response to social oppression, prison time a badge of honor.

At the same time, recognition properly trained or channeled can be instrumental to the success of liberal democracy. It fuels the vigilance against government overreach and against tyranny that liberal society needs. This is the significance of that final flourish in the Declaration, whereby "sacred Honor" is enlisted in the cause of independence. It was a prickly sense of egalitarian and republican pride, rather than mere security and material comfort, that allowed the Americans of that day to undertake separation from Britain. Laurie Johnson and Sharon Krause have made eloquent cases for bringing a healthy honor into liberal society. Krause sees that an elite sort of honor is needed to foster the leadership that causes like independence or civil rights need, causes that must be championed in liberal society, even at great personal cost.[35] Johnson adds to this the need for codes of honorable behavior among ordinary citizens. The virtue that was to be produced by rational calculation in the social contract tradition is more reliably produced by honor—but only if honor is internalized as "self-recognition," and formed by an appropriately liberal sensibility.[36]

The first part of that formation (or reformation) must be to make honor egalitarian, to get it to embrace *isothymia*. Even those prompted by honor to distinguish themselves, to lead, must do so ultimately in the name of equal rights and freedom, rather than the glory of a Caesar or Alexander. One of Francis Fukuyama's final worries about the end of history is whether the regime of *isothymia* can truly satisfy *thymos*, which is a thirst for distinction, after all. Isothymia is a kind of compromise, whereby we each renounce the exceptional status we all desire, in exchange for not being dominated by the winners that would emerge from a high-stakes competition over honor.

DARWINIAN HONOR

Something like this view has emerged from a strain of modern Darwinian evolutionary theory. According to Darwinism, humans are descended from earlier primates, and we have close relatives in the primate world. As with all living creatures, our attributes are the result of natural selection; these are the traits that prevailed in an eons-long competition for survival and reproduction. Moreover, not only our physical attributes, but key elements of our psychological makeup evolved in this way. If we are inherently competitive, or empathetic, or motivated by a desire for recognition or lust for domination, it is because these are traits that proved their adaptive value over time.[37]

It is notoriously difficult, however, to determine which of the traits we observe in humans today are inherited, and which are the product of culture. The human ability to alter behavior through the development of culture is in fact one of the great achievements of the human genome. Its plasticity has allowed the species to spread over the entire globe, adapting to a wide variety of environments—and to adapt again, on the basis of changes we ourselves make to those environments. Nonetheless, it is clear that there are some very important traits that are inherent in human nature, traits that culture evidently cannot change. These are chronicled in the history and literature of every age. Modern evolutionary researchers attempt to get at these by inference from the behavior of our nearest primate relatives, anthropological studies of the hunter-gatherer societies that still exist and that are presumed to resemble prehistoric human society, psychological studies of human infants presumably uncolored by culture, and carefully designed studies of adults.

Chimpanzees, one of our closest relatives, live in fairly complex social groups, express what look very much like versions of human emotions such as ambition, indignation, and empathy. Chimpanzee bands exhibit limited variations in their "cultures," but all chimpanzee society is male-centered and hierarchical, dominated by a single alpha male. Being the alpha male brings significant feeding and reproductive advantages, and it appears that every male chimpanzee aspires to be the alpha. This ingrained ambition leads to periodic fights over the leading role. It does not lead to a war of all against all; for the most part, chimpanzee society is stable, the alpha male undertaking to calm disputes among other members of his band (the females do the same). When fights for alpha status do occur, they are rarely lethal. Chimpanzees are however killed by other chimpanzees. Chimpanzee bands are territorial, and sometimes execute lethal raids on adjoining bands, in which targeted chimps can be quite brutally killed.

These facts have led some evolutionary psychologists to infer that humans are ambitious, competitive, aggressive, and warlike. Darwinism has been used to justify a realist perspective on international relations, whereby the zero-sum struggle for power among nations is taken to stem directly from unalterable traits of human nature.[38] After all, it is the very essence of Darwinism that lethal struggle, the "survival of the fittest" and the elimination of the less fit, permeates all of biological nature.

Others point out, however, that this same ruthless process has resulted in some supremely cooperative, even altruistic species. There are ants and other social insects, though their relevance to the human case is quite limited. Then there is the Bonobo, the much less violent cousin of the chimpanzee. Bonobo society is much more matriarchal, much less strife-ridden than that of chimpanzees. Notoriously, Bonobos are given to resolving conflict with promiscuous sex, rather than war. Humans are about exactly as close to Bonobos, genetically, as to chimpanzees, which has led to a debate as to which species is the better analogue to humanity. Neither will be a perfect fit; humans are different from either species of *Pan*. The ubiquity of war in human history, alas, forecloses the possibility that we can simply imitate the bonobos. Moreover, it appears that proto-humans split off from the chimpanzee line before the chimpanzee and bonobo lines split. Behaviorally, bonobos seem to be the outliers among the "great apes," our section of the primate lineage.[39] The widespread if not universal competition for status in this lineage, especially among males, points to the same conclusion. Human sexuality is more jealously possessive than that of bonobos; it seems to lead to conflict more often than reconciliation. On the other hand, humans have a knack for cooperation beyond anything seen in these primates. Human societies are capable of organizing cooperation in many different manners, some of them much less hierarchical than chimpanzee society. Chimpanzee bands cannot get larger than about one hundred individuals; humans are capable of cooperation on a much larger scale.[40] Though chimpanzees display empathy, it is much more limited than in humans. Chimpanzees will share food, but only grudgingly; widespread sharing of food is a near-universal human custom. Chimpanzees display what looks like indignation, but it is almost always on behalf of the self; human indignation can be disinterested, on behalf of third parties. It can be mobilized on behalf of culturally variable, or chosen, norms or principles. Humans will bear significant costs to punish those who break the rules, or are seen as taking unfair advantage, even if the punisher is not personally harmed by the violation, a phenomenon known as "altruistic punishment."[41] Anger is often the motivating force for this.

Human nature is cooperative, not simply Hobbesian, then; but cooperation is imperfect, and always prone to collapse, as individuals are tempted to defect whenever occasion presents to do so with impunity. As Hobbes pointed out, humans are incapable of the perfect cooperation seen in beehives or ant colonies, for two separate reasons. First is the tug of individual self-interest, which is not felt among social insects. Second is "competition for honor," which does not exist among bees or ants.[42] Modern anthropological and psychological studies reveal that human beings, behaviorally, are on the one hand norm-driven—they internalize the strictures of their culture—and on the other, they will often take opportunities to violate those norms to their advantage, if they can do so with impunity. Human beings exhibit this bifurcated psychology from a very early age: children need and crave "structure," rules of behavior; but as soon as the rules are in place, they devote themselves to finding ingenious ways around them. Among themselves, they will create elaborate rules for playground games they make up, and be very vigilant against cheaters; yet cheaters there will be. Given the precariousness of rules or norms, mechanisms must be in place to defend them. For this, human beings have evolved both the ability to internalize norms, minimizing infractions through a guilt reflex, and a very refined ability to detect cheaters—as well as an indignant zeal for punishing them once detected. This effect has been found in a number of experimental studies.[43] We all know of it from experience as well, and of course from the literature, theology and philosophy of all ages.

These mechanisms by themselves allow small, tribal societies to function with no written law and little in the way of formal enforcement. The mechanisms are not tied to any particular set of norms or rules, but will attach themselves to whatever rules are culturally dictated. This has given human beings the adaptiveness they have used to spread across the globe. That same adaptiveness has now given us vast, multiethnic states, which require supplemental means of social and political control. It has brought about the possibility of "politics" properly so called, the deliberate and authoritative choice of principles for a community, by that community.

Honor appears from a Darwinian perspective as a descendent of the competitions for status that are seen in a great many species. Hens arrange themselves in a status hierarchy, demonstrated by who can peck whom; male wolves compete for the position of alpha, as do most of the great apes. The penchant to create such "pecking orders" generally indicates that the natural social organization of a species is hierarchical, meaning to say that social cooperation naturally organizes itself around a rank ordering of status. That human beings compete endlessly for status, in public and private life both, is an obvious fact. Yet human political organization has displayed a wide range of forms, from rigid hierarchy (such as ancient Babylon) to militant egalitarianism (such as ancient Athens) to moderately egalitarian (liberal democracy, with its cadre of elite "representatives"). Given the preliminary indication that human society is naturally hierarchical, can we make a case that liberal democracy is a more natural or stable form, that it is in any sense the "end of history" for the species?

Our closest primate relatives are highly hierarchical. This is true of chimpanzees and gorillas, less so of bonobos. Most of human history has passed under rigidly hierarchical political regimes. Yet most aboriginal peoples who have been studied are organized in much more egalitarian fashion. Human social and political development seems to exhibit what one anthropologist has called a "U-shaped" pattern: rigidly hierarchical in our primate prehistory, rigidly hierarchical for most of our history, but largely egalitarian in between, during human prehistory.[44] Yet it was during this prehistory of a hundred thousand years or so that humanity emerged as a species, and during which our genetic endowment received its current form. It would seem then that this intermediate stage reflects the "original" or even "natural" human social formation. Another anthropologist, Christopher Boehm, has argued that, though this stage is most natural in a sense, it must be understood as an invention of culture fully as much as nature, one motivated by, and resting on, the human desire for honor or recognition.

Boehm's argument is that the egalitarian cultures observed in simple societies represent not the absence of hierarchy, but a "reverse-dominance hierarchy"—effectively, status hierarchies turned on their head.[45] The logic is this: Humans emerged from a primate line that is heavily hierarchical (and male-dominated), but in which all males aspire to the role of alpha. Submission is the fate of most males (and all females) within this social structure, but it is not one they accept gladly. There are occasional challenges for the top position; at least in chimpanzee society, challengers (and alphas) build coalitions for the purpose. The decisive change, according to Boehm, came when early humans or protohumans began assembling such coalitions for the purpose of preventing *anyone* from becoming dominant in the full sense, and for reining in the power of any who were given a measure of predominance. A number of innovations were required to make this possible. One is the capacity to build a coalition around a plan, a plan requiring some deliberation concerning a desirable, or preferable, state of affairs. This would seem to require in turn both great intelligence, intelligence of a specifically social and imaginative sort; and language in order to build a consensus around a certain vision of social order, and to perpetuate it culturally. Its perpetuation also requires the ability to discern others' intentions from cues other than language, to discern whether their cooperation is genuine, something we've already run across in humans. Once the reverse-hierarchy was in place, Boehm argues, it provided a man-made environment, as it were, to which evolution itself would further adapt the species—"gene-culture coevolution," in the phrase of the evolutionists.

We are not fully adapted to this sort of egalitarianism, as is shown by the hierarchical societies that succeeded this prehistoric stage. What makes it so common in prehistory, though, and (according to Francis Fukuyama) at the end of history, is the way it gratifies the desire for status, or recognition, of the great majority. Or perhaps better, the way it allows the majority to escape the state of submission, which is the greatest affront to their desire for status or "dignity." Boehm presents the reverse-dominance hierarchy explicitly as a "social contract" in which individuals renounce their (typically slim) chances of becoming alpha, in exchange for ensuring that they do not become subordinate.[46] Students of Plato's *Republic* may recognize this as the social contract among the weak that Glaucon proposes at the beginning of Book 2.[47] The exchange here though seems not to be "renouncing injustice so as not to suffer injustice"—for is the dominance of an alpha chimpanzee "unjust"?—but a human longing for freedom from domination, for autonomy of some sort. That is, the ambition to control others is renounced in order to have control of one's own life as much as possible. Nor does it fit the liberal-contractarian mold, as the goal of the "contract" is not material security so much as a measure of freedom or *isothymia*.

Boehm surveys the anthropological literature to produce a portrait of the typical simple society of hunter-gatherers, the type of society that presumably comes close to matching the first human societies. In such societies, differential status is accepted (best hunter, best planner, shaman), but it is not allowed to become *authority* of any kind. There will typically be an acknowledged leader, but this individual will not have the right to order anyone around; major decisions are made by consensus, often after a common deliberation. Extreme vigilance is maintained against anyone's superior status shading into authority, against "upstartism," as Boehm describes it. The community is very alert to any sign that someone has an ambition to become dominant in anything like the alpha-primate way. In extreme cases, upstarts who threaten to overthrow the balance of equality will be assassinated. Such cases are not uncommon, testifying to both the persistence of the alpha impulse in humans, and the intensity of the social reaction against it.[48] Differentials of wealth are tolerated, but social practices are in place to level it, such as large dowries or other forms of generosity expected of any who have significantly more.[49]

Boehm dubs this the "reverse-dominance hierarchy" because in essence the community collectively dominates the would-be dominators, vigilantly guarding against and aggressively suppressing attempts at individual domination. Boehm postulates that once the reverse-domination hierarchy was in place, it exercised a selective Darwinian pressure of its own (especially if deviants were regularly eliminated). The resulting "gene-culture coevolution," as evolutionary biologists call it, is a uniquely human phenomenon: over time, our evolution has been to some degree been directed by culture, as well as the reverse.[50]

Although human nature has adapted itself to this state of affairs, the adaptation is imperfect. Humans today, in Boehm's view, have a split nature on this score, "highly contradictory behavioral tendencies," a combination, as he says, of Hobbes and Rousseau.[51] That very split might be adaptive, from an evolutionary perspective. Although egalitarian cooperativeness prevails within groups of hunter-gatherers, intergroup violence seems to be endemic even to them. Indeed, it has been argued that only the pressure of lethal intergroup violence, at a fairly high level, could have produced the group-oriented, altruistic or "prosocial" elements that are distinctive to humans.[52] Only if bands of cooperators were able survive while those infected with cheaters were repeatedly wiped out, it seems, can a cooperative profile such as ours come into being.[53] This creates a pressure somewhat counter to that of the reverse-dominance hierarchy, requiring the retention of an element of *megalothymia*, especially among warrior males.

Eventually, human groups grew beyond the size at which the reverse-dominance hierarchy could be sustained by the informal mechanisms of hunter-gatherer life. There seems to have been a sudden spike in settlement sizes around twenty thousand years ago, perhaps enabled by some cultural or genetic breakthrough.[54] Hunter-gatherer bands are generally limited to the size of chimpanzee bands. "Tribes," are one step above hunter-gatherer bands, in anthropological terminology. They tend to exhibit greater hierarchy, and are often significantly more warlike. With war comes the need to unleash more of the alpha-male *thymos*, even to cultivate it.[55] With the advent of systematic agriculture, twelve to ten thousand years ago, societies grew larger still—and more hierarchical.[56] Eventually, kingdoms or states were formed, and human history—that is, recorded history—began.

HONOR REDEEMED?

"Honor" or recognition as used by those who would revive honor today is somewhat different from the anthropological sense I have been employing, though I am arguing that they are closely connected. For primatologists and anthropologists it is simply an observed social phenomenon, whose roots are in the desire to dominate but whose reach, in humans at least, can extend to social systems dedicated to *preventing* domination. Still, we may say its basis (in humans at least) is the individual desire for recognition, which may settle into the desire for individual autonomy, autonomy being that measure of alpha-male dominance that can be shared by many at once. And of course, it is fully compatible with fairly autocratic rule within each male's household.[57]

This seems to bolster Fukuyama's argument that the central nerve of modern liberal culture is not self-interest understood as material security and prosperity, but *isothymia* or universal recognition. What liberalism has added to the egalitarianism bequeathed to us by our most ancient forebears is a measure of individual autonomy vis-à-vis society itself. Whereas preliberal egalitarianism, as in ancient Athens, was rather intolerant of this form of autonomy, liberalism nourishes it. In Athens, *isothymia* meant a share of rule, which lent itself to imperialism, the city playing the alpha-male collectively. Liberal *isothymia* is directed more to a private form of autonomy, but *isothymia* it is nonetheless.

Hobbes saw honor as a mere cipher for motives of self-preservation: honor reflects power, power is instrumental to preservation. On one level, Darwinism agrees. The impulse to honor, like every trait produced under natural selection, established itself in the species because it furthered the survival and reproductive advantages of those who had it. But the logic by which this operates in Darwin is quite different from that seen in Hobbes. First, individuals are not likely to think of their honor-motived actions as devoted to survival or reproduction, but rather as things that simply "must be done."[58] This may make them more difficult to tame. Second, in the Darwinian view, the human sense of honor is descended from a primate dominance-impulse, and will bear some signs of its origin. Natural selection often takes traits designed for one purpose and recruits them for another. It took the skeletal structure of a quadruped and adapted it bit by bit to an erect, bipedal use. The resulting form is an imperfect adaptation, showing signs of its origin. One result is our species-typical knee, back and neck ailments. The same can no doubt be said of our psychic endowment. The human sense of honor has been, or can be, recruited for egalitarian purposes, but it retains more than a few vestiges of its primate past. Its mixed or conflicted character may even be adaptive. Human sociability is more egalitarian than that of other primates, but the species still needs warriors and leaders, and hence some vestige of the old domineering impulse. It would be useful to the species to have a genome capable of producing an array of types, or psychic dispositions that can express themselves in different ways depending on environmental conditions.[59]

The human desire for honor or recognition, like much of our physical and psychological endowment, is remarkably flexible. If (proto-)honor in the great apes is heavily self-centered, the human version can be disinterested, enlisted on behalf of a concrete vision of the common good (a reverse-dominance hierarchy, perhaps), or ideals even more abstract. It is adapted to support a wide variety of culturally variable norms. Some of these we would like to call undesirable, even pathological. What some social scientists call "honor cultures," for example, arise in semi-lawless agricultural or herding societies, or semi-lawless urban environments, where avenging slights or injuries to self or to clan, with violence if necessary, is the norm.[60] In such semi-Hobbesian societies, having a reputation as one whom it is dangerous to cross is useful if not necessary.

We would like to call such cultures, and their understanding of honor, defective or damaged in some way. This is not the honor we seek to revive in this volume. But, against the Darwinian background, are we entitled to make any such moral or normative judgment? Such cultures are adaptive in their circumstances, after all; we might even say that they are *natural* to humans in that environment. This in itself poses no insurmountable difficulty to a normative judgment; all moral theories must account for barbarous cultures. Aristotle would have no hesitation asserting that these represent defective or inferior cultural formations, relying on his teleological view of human nature. For him, human nature can come into its own only under a proper regime of law. Kant would condemn such cultures from the transcendental viewpoint of reason, which stands outside and above brute nature. A classical liberal, finally, might rely on the postulate that certain human impulses, self-preservation above all, have a moral status that makes them the font of right.[61]

Darwin himself believed that nature supported a preference for the sociable over the antisocial impulses in human nature,[62] but it seems to me that Darwinism properly understood poses grave difficulties for any such solution. It is hard to see how Darwinian nature could confer moral status on any creature's desire for preservation, especially when it has at the same time raised up predators for those creatures. The only teleology supported by Darwinian nature, the only purpose it assigns to us, is survival, or rather reproduction. But this is the same imperative given to all creatures, and it is hard to see it as a moral imperative. If I die prematurely, or without offspring, it is difficult to portray this as some kind of failure or miscarriage of nature. Indeed, if our whole species were to die out, it would seem to have no more significance to Darwinian nature than the extinction of countless other species overseen by nature before. Our nature, moreover, human nature, seems not to be a *whole* of the type needed to support teleology, at least not of the Aristotelian type. Like our bipedal structure, it is cobbled together of archaic and new elements, some of which do not mesh perfectly with each other. As to the reason on which Kant so relies, it is the descendent of the more primitive neural faculties seen throughout the animal kingdom. It is capable of abstract moral and philosophic thought, but in moral matters, it appears not to be a moral legislator, but to take its cue from notions of fairness that are engrained in our affect, moral sentiments of a kind.[63]

If we leave it at this, it would seem impossible to prefer one understanding of honor (or of any particular culture or way of life) on moral grounds. It might be possible to say that one alternative produces greater happiness individually or overall (under certain circumstances), that one is productive of a more stable, or wealthier, or more peaceful society, or one more conducive to the flowering of some particular human capacity. But under the view just sketched, none of these would generate a moral imperative. Is it possible, though, that this account does not capture all the relevant factors? It seems that there is a good for the human individual and the human species that goes beyond mere survival and reproduction. These capacities may have evolved to serve merely Darwinian purposes, but they have produced a creature whose richness of experience and capacity for understanding transcends anything else we know of in nature. These capacities are "spandrels," or "emergent qualities," wholes greater than the sum of their parts.[64] The good life they make possible has emerged fortuitously as a purpose for human life, not as nature's intent. Hans Jonas argued that they were goals nature has been striving toward from the beginning. Larry Arnhart argues that all species have a normative "good" peculiar to them, and the human good is just one among them.[65] It seems to me, though, that the human good is unique in nature, being much richer due to the presence of self-consciousness and rationality. Though they emerged from natural processes, they cannot be regarded as the goal of those processes. There is a human perfection, in other words, that arises from nature, but is unplanned by nature. It is "natural," but only fortuitously or indirectly so.

Self-consciousness and rationality have given human beings the unique capacity for deliberative choice, at the individual and collective level, concerning paths of action and ways of life. We can collectively decide that reverse dominance is preferable to dominance, that honor in the form of universal recognition is preferable to the honor of domination. These choices can be grounded in the view that what serves a richer, more complete human happiness is to be preferred. This puts us in the traditional territory of political philosophy, although with an altered understanding of the human reality that serves as our foundation. In the case of honor, we must take account of its evolutionary history, and of the fact that nature does not directly dictate to us what form of honor we should choose. We should choose, then, it seems to me, a form of honor that does justice to our uniquely human character. If cosmic nature does not give us a standard, our human nature can. The standard is ambivalent, though, owing partly to the conflicting impulses that are built into human nature and the human sense for honor. No single regime of honor does justice to them all. Thus, as Tocqueville for example held, aristocratic honor and democratic honor each have much to say for them, just as elitism and egalitarianism may both serve (and disserve) the human good, in different ways. There are, however, forms of honor that we may exclude, such as the honor of gangs, and bands of thieves.

One thing that is distinctive about the human sense of honor is its flexibility. It is capable of supporting not only the desire to dominate, but a moral community of nondomination. It can attach itself to purely abstract ideals, and to a sense of personal integrity linked to those ideals. It is like human reason in that way, which may have originated in mere calculation, but has gained the capacity for purely abstract and disinterested thought. That this sense of honor may be attached to a form of liberal democracy is the argument of many of the authors in this volume.[66] They add that liberal democracy needs this sense of honor in order ultimately to sustain itself. The Darwinian analysis endorses this view, I believe, though for distinctive reasons and with distinct implications. The impulse to some sort of honor is ingrained in human nature; any regime must account for it and, if that regime is to be successful, shape it. Honor's roots are in the alpha impulse, which has been modified or interlaced with less domineering elements, to allow it to serve both elitism and egalitarian autonomy. In neither case, though, has its domineering past been completely effaced. Moreover, "honor cultures" of the pathological type are a natural adaptation to certain types of circumstances. Those circumstances should be prevented from arising. More importantly, culture must be enlisted to nurture the preferred form of honor, and mitigate the undesirable. For our sense of honor is extremely sensitive to cultural cues—more perhaps than to other aspects of the environment. We must attend to cultural formation both for the sake of liberal equality, and for the cultivation of the higher capacities of human nature. These goals do not come from nature, at least not directly so, but whose validity does not depend on mere convention. We may call it "sacred honor" if we wish, so long as it is dedicated to republican honor, rather than the chest-thumping of our remotest past.

NOTES

1. Thomas Hobbes, *Leviathan*, ed. Edwin Curley (Indianapolis: Hackett, 1994), ch. 10. Hereafter, citations to this work will be given in the text, by chapter and section as identified in this edition.

2. §56, 81, 107, 110, 115, 148. See Laurie M. Johnson, *Locke and Rousseau: Two Enlightenment Responses to Honor* (Lanham, MD: Lexington Books, 2012), ch. 2. Locke does discourage fencing, as apt to make one too liable to fight over "points of honor" (§199).

3. These authors may not be considered fully in the liberal fold, but at least the first two were immensely influential in the thought of the American Founders.

4. Fukuyama, *The End of History and the Last Man* (New York: The Free Press, 1992). With apologies to Hegel, I will label this general theory "Hegelian."

5. I will label this "Darwinism," for brevity.

6. *Leviathan* 28.27.

7. 6.2.

8. 6.39.

9. 6.7, 11.3–5.

10. 10.1.

11. 10.13, 6.8.

12. 11.1.2.

13. 13.8.

14. 13.13, 10.

15. 18.15.

16. See Laurie Johnson, *Thomas Hobbes: Turning Point for Honor* (Lanham, MD: Lexington Books, 2009), 36–8.

17. Laurie Johnson and Sharon Krause are two who voice such doubts, and survey the emerging literature on the subject (Johnson, *Thomas Hobbes: Turning Point for Honor; Locke and Rousseau: Two Enlightenment Responses to Honor*; Krause, *Liberalism with Honor* (Cambridge, MA: Harvard University Press, 2002).

18. Fukuyama, *End of History*.

19. Charles Taylor is perhaps most famous for linking modern democracy to dignity, e.g., "The Politics of Recognition," in *Multiculturalism*, ed. Amy Gutmann (Princeton, NJ: Princeton University Press, 1994), 25–74. Jeremy Waldron traces the liberal notion of rights to aristocratic ideas of rank and dignity in "Dignity, Rank, and Rights: The 2009 Tanner Lectures at UC Berkeley." *Public Law and Legal Theory Research Paper No. 09–50* (New York: New York University School of Law, 2009). Josiah Ober does the same in "Democracy's Dignity," *American Political Science Review* 106, no. 4 (2012). Alexis de Tocqueville argues that the American concept of rights is a feudal inheritance. *Democracy in America*, trans. Harvey C. Mansfield and Delba Winthrop (Chicago: University of Chicago Press, 2000), 1.1.2, 29.

20. The German word is *Geist*, which can be translated in various ways.

21. 401ff.

22. 399.

23. Hegel's terms are *Herr* and *Knecht*, which are often rendered as "master and slave." "Servant" is a more correct translation.

24. 406.

25. *Philosophy of Right and Law*, in *The Philosophy of Hegel*, ed. Carl L. Friedrich (New York: Modern Library, 1954, 221–329), 404ff. Hegel uses the term *Staat*, commonly rendered as "state," but Hegel's meaning is closer in some respects to the classical notion of "regime," a meaning within the bounds of the German word.

26. See Tocqueville, *Democracy in America*, trans. and ed. Harvey C. Mansfield and Delba Winthrop (Chicago: University of Chicago Press, 2000.), vol. 2, part 4, ch. 8.

27. See Kojève, *Introduction to the Reading of Hegel*, trans. James H. Nichols, Jr., ed. Allan Bloom (New York: Basic Books, 1969), especially Ch. 2–3.

28. Fukuyama, *The End of History*, 144.

29. Fukuyama *End of History*, especially part V.

30. We see references to this in Plato's *Republic*, particularly Book 4. Also, in the opening section of Book 3 of the Republic, there is a treatment of the poetic tradition.

31. Fukuyama, *End of History*, 182. Both words, though of classical Greek derivation, seem to be of Fukuyama's coinage.

32. *End of History*, ch. 13, 16. See Steven Skultety's suggestion in this volume that equal *esteem* is a lynchpin of liberalism, in "A Neo-Aristotelian Theory of Honor."

33. Tocqueville gives one of the classic accounts of this: *Democracy in America*, 1.1.2, 2.2.1.

34. Galston, *Liberal Purposes: Goods, Virtues, and Diversity in the Liberal State* (Cambridge: Cambridge University Press, 1991), ch. 12, speaks of the "expressive" strain of American individualism, whereby any expression of the self has come to be seen as a matter of right; Taylor, *Multiculturalism and the "Politics of Recognition"* (Princeton, NJ: Princeton University Press, 1992) examines the claims made on behalf of *group* identity.

35. Krause, *Liberalism with Honor* (Cambridge, MA: Harvard University Press, 2002), especially ch. 5, 6.

36. Johnson, *Locke and Rousseau*.

37. Or they could also be indirect consequences of other traits that proved adaptive—so-called "spandrels" of evolution. See S. J. Gould and R. C. Lewontin, "The Spandrels of San Marco and the Panglossian Paradigm: A Critique of the Adaptationist Programme," *Proceedings of the Royal Society of London* B 205: 581–98 (1979).

38. See, e.g., Bradley A. Thayer, *Darwin and International Relations: On the Evolutionary Origins of War and Ethnic Conflict* (Lexington: University Press of Kentucky, 2009).

39. See Christopher Boehm, *Hierarchy in the Forest: the Evolution of Egalitarian Behavior* (Cambridge, MA: Harvard University Press 1999), 150–55, ch. 6; Dale Peterson and Richard Wrangham, *Demonic Males: Apes and the Origins of Human Violence* (New York: Houghton Mifflin, 1996), 151, 181. The "great apes" include gorillas and orangutans, as well as chimpanzees and bonobos.

40. Peterson and Wrangham, *Demonic Males*, 69; Boehm, *Hierarchy*, 24.

41. See, e.g., Marc Bekoff, "Wild Justice and Fair Play: Cooperation, Forgiveness, and Morality in Animals." *Biology and Philosophy* 19 (2004): 489–520; Samuel Bowles and Herbert Gintis, *A Cooperative Species: Human Reciprocity and its Evolution* (Princeton, NJ: Princeton University Press, 2011), 25–38, 106–9, ch. 9; Michael Tomasello, *Why We Cooperate* (Cambridge, MA: MIT Press, 2009), 105–6.

42. Hobbes, *Leviathan* 17.6–8. See also Boehm, *Hierarchy*, 244–5, 254; Richard Dawkins, *The Selfish Gene* (Oxford: Oxford University Press, 1989), 3, 118, 139, 201.

43. See the citations in note 28, above.

44. Bruce M. Knauft, "Violence and Sociality in Human Evolution." *Current Anthropology* 32, no. 4 (1991): 391–428.

45. Boehm, *Hierarchy*, 3, 91, 128.

46. Boehm, *Hierarchy*, 105, 123, 194.

47. *Republic* 358d–359b.

48. Bowles and Gintis, *Cooperative Species*, 108.

49. Boehm, *Hierarchy*, 46–7, 102; Bowles and Gintis, *Cooperative Species*, 112, 117–28.

50. Boehm, *Hierarchy*, 216, 223; see also Bowles and Gintis, *Cooperative Species*, 13–14, 112, 198.

51. Boehm, *Hierarchy*, 3, 15, 149, 173, 197, 207.

52. Steven Pinker has made one of the most extensive arguments for the violent character of early societies: *The Better Angels of Our Nature: Why Violence has Declined* (New York: Penguin, 2012), 40–58. On the role of violence in the evolution of cooperation, see Boehm, *Hierarchy*, 221; Bowles, and Gintis, *Cooperative Species*, 103–6.

53. Bowles and Gintis make this argument at length, using mathematical modeling, in *Cooperative Species*, ch. 6–7. The external pressure could come from, e.g., climate change (which was extreme during the late Pleistocene, when modern humans evolved) as well as from war. There is at least one other way that cooperativeness can be sustained: If all the genes that pass from one generation to the next pass through a single conduit, as with the queens of ants and bees, "cheating" genes can be prevented from infecting the population. This does not apply to humans, however. See Dawkins, *Selfish Gene*, 256.

54. Philip Kitcher, "Ethics and Evolution: How to Get Here from There," in *Primates and Philosophers: How Morality Evolved*, eds. Stephen Macedo and Josiah Ober (Princeton, NJ: Princeton University Press, 2006): 120–39, 137.

55. Boehm, *Hierarchy*, Ch. 5; 140.

56. Boehm, *Hierarchy*, 104; Larry Arnhart, *Darwinian Natural Right: The Biological Ethics of Human Nature* (Albany: SUNY Press, 1998); Tomasello, *Why We Cooperate*, 103

57. See Boehm, *Hierarcy*, 9, 93, 248; Arnhart, *Natural Right*, 62; 137–39.

58. See Richard E. Nisbett and Dov Cohen, *Culture of Honor: The Psychology of Violence in the South* (Boulder, CO: Westview Press, 1996), 3.

59. For the latter, see Boehm, *Hierarchy*, 252; Robert Wright, *The Moral Animal: Evolutionary Psychology and Everyday Life* (New York: Vintage Books, 1994), 80.

60. See, e.g., Nisbett and Cohen, *Culture of Honor*; Tamler Sommers, "The Two Faces of Revenge: Moral Responsibility and the Culture of Honor." *Biology and Philosophy* 24 (2009): 35–50. We might add that semi-lawless urban environments can also fall into this category.

61. I have argued that Locke does not fall into this category, but relies on a divine legislator, precisely because of the amoral character of nature as revealed by modern science. Steven Forde, *Locke, Science, and Politics* (New York: Cambridge University Press, 2013), ch. 2.

62. Darwin, "The Descent of Man and Selection in Relation to Sex," in Darwin, *The Origin of Species by Means of Natural Selection* and *The Descent of Man and Selection in Relation to Sex* (Chicago: Encyclopedia Britannica/Great Books of the Western World, 1952), 253–600, ch. 304–5, 315–17.

63. See, e.g., Jonathan Haidt, "'Dialogue between My Head and My Heart': Affective Influences on Moral Judgment" *Psychological Inquiry* 13, no. 1 (2002): 54–56.

64. Emergent qualities are seen throughout nature. Hydrogen and oxygen combine to produce water, for example, a substance with qualities entirely different from either of its constituents. A strand of DNA not only has properties separate from its parts, but carries *information*, an entirely immaterial thing. See Ernst Mayr, *The Growth of Biological Thought: Diversity, Evolution, and Inheritance* (Cambridge, MA: Harvard University Press, 1982), 54–71; Roger D. Masters, *The Nature of Politics* (New Haven, CT: Yale University Press, 1989), 118; Larry Arnhart, *Darwinian Conservatism* (Charlottesville, VA: Imprint Academic, 2005), 17–20; *Darwinian Natural Right*, 247; Francis Fukuyama, *Our Posthuman Future* (New York: Farrar, Straus and Giroux, 2002), 171.

65. Jonas, *The Phenomenon of Life: Toward a Philosophical Biology* (Evanston, IL: Northwestern University Press, 2001); Larry Arnhart, *Darwinian Natural Right*, 23–27, 236–7.

66. See for example Ryan Rhodes, "Putting One's Best Face Forward;" Anthony Cunningham, "Good Citizens: Gratitude and Honor" and Steven Skultety, "A Neo-Aristotelian Theory of Political Honor," all in this volume.

Part II

Liberalism and Honor

THREE

Liberal Honor

Sharon R. Krause

Why do men and women sometimes risk their necks to defend their liberties? One thinks first of soldiers, who defend the collective liberty against foreign enemies, but in liberal democracies individual liberties sometimes need defense as well—think of Martin Luther King's defense of civil rights for African Americans, Elizabeth Cady Stanton's defense of women's suffrage, or the contemporary movement in support of gay marriage. For all its advantages, democracy is vulnerable to the problem of majority tyranny. Hence democratic peoples must attend to the defense of individual liberties within the polity even as they protect the collective liberty from outside aggression. Both types of defense require robust political agency on the part of citizens. What sustains this robust agency? What inspires the spirited defense of liberty, especially when the risks are high and the benefits are uncertain?

The spirited defense of liberty once was explained as a point of honor, as when the first Americans pledged to defend their independence with "our Lives, our Fortunes, and our sacred Honor."[1] We rarely speak of honor today. It is a word that lost currency soon after the American revolutionaries declared their independence. These days honor seems obsolete or frivolous, if not outright dangerous.[2] Honor always has received mixed reviews, of course—arousing admiration, envy, and contempt all at once—with the result that those receiving honors today are forever in danger of being run out of town tomorrow.[3] And modern democrats even more than others have reason to distrust honor because the distinctions it draws seem to run afoul of democratic equality.

Yet if we rarely speak of honor, and then only with some discomfort, we have reason nonetheless to reconsider it, for honor is a powerful engine of political action. Recent work in political theory and philosophy has begun to recognize the value of honor in this respect, even while acknowledging its limits and potential pathologies.[4] Others have examined honor empirically using the tools of modern sociology and anthropology.[5] Honor has been documented by historians as well, who show both shifts and continuities in honor in different countries and periods.[6] Despite the recent attention, however, honor continues to be marginalized in contemporary political theory, and its importance for liberal democratic politics remains underappreciated.

As described here, honor is a tripartite phenomenon that includes (a) *public honors* in the form of recognition and public distinction; (b) *codes of honor* as in principled rules of conduct; and (c) the *sense of honor* as a quality of character, the ambitious desire to live up to one's code and to be publicly recognized for doing so. The first part of this chapter lays out the meaning and role of old-regime honor in the political theory of Montesquieu, where honor serves as a forceful spring of resistance to encroaching political power. The second part explores honor in a modern democratic context, engaging Tocqueville to illuminate both the tensions between honor and democracy and their need for one another. The third part demonstrates the value of honor for generating political activism, drawing on two figures from the American political tradition, Frederick Douglass and Martin Luther King, Jr. I briefly trace the continuities and differences between the more egalitarian instances of honor and honor in the old regime, and show how democratic honor can inspire robust political agency that supports not only resistance to the abuse of power but progressive political reform as well.

EXCAVATING HONOR: MONTESQUIEU AND THE *HONNÊTE HOMME*

A rich resource for rethinking honor today is Montesquieu, who connected honor to the vigorous political agency that protects individual liberty against the abuse of power. His understanding of honor reflects the tripartite scheme sketched above, which includes public honors, codes of honor, and honor as a quality of character. The substantive content of codes of honor may vary from one political society to another, as do systems for distributing public honors, or recognition.[7] The formal features of honor as a quality of character are more enduring, however. These aspects of honor remain relatively constant in different contexts. They also illuminate the sources of the political agency that supports individual liberty in the face of obvious risks and indeterminate benefits.

Although Montesquieu was not in favor of revolution or even sudden reform,[8] he thought that spirited resistance to the abuse of power was crucial for individual liberty, and he saw honor as the spring of such resistance. For this reason, honor in Montesquieu has been called "openly rebellious toward authority,"[9] a form of "regulated disobedience,"[10] "interference,"[11] and even "anarchy."[12] Montesquieu's *honnête homme,* or man of honor, distinguishes himself though his disobedience, and the politics of distinction and disobedience that characterizes moderate monarchies divides political power and therefore limits it. Honor is difficult to categorize. It cannot be reduced to self-interest, even self-interest well-understood, partly because honor may motivate the sacrifice of one's most fundamental interest (life itself), and partly because honor as a quality of character is always tied to principled codes of conduct. At the same time, honor in Montesquieu should not be confused with civic virtue. If honor sometimes involves personal sacrifice, it does not aim directly for the common good, as civic virtue does. In contrast to civic virtue—and like self-interest—honor is primarily self-serving. Moreover, honor's function is not so much to motivate political participation as an end in itself as to arouse resistance to the abuse of power, thus protecting individual liberty.

Montesquieu's typology of regimes identifies three main species of government, each with its own "nature" and "principle."[13] The nature of a government is "that which makes it what it is, and its principle that which makes it act. The one is its particular structure and the other is the human passions that make it move."[14] The nature of a republic is popular sovereignty, for instance, and its principle is what Montesquieu calls "political virtue." Despotism is the rule of one on the basis of arbitrary will, and its principle is fear. Monarchy is the rule of one according to established laws, and its principle is honor. Each of the three regimes exists only as a "totality," as the unity between its nature and its principle.[15] Despotism, for example, cannot be sustained unless the people are made to fear the ruler, because fearless individuals capable of "esteeming" themselves very highly "would be in a condition to cause revolutions." Therefore, fear must beat down everyone's courage, and extinguish self-respect and even the slightest feeling of ambition.[16] Without the support of fear, the "passion that makes it move," the institutional apparatus of despotism would give way. Similarly, a republic cannot survive without what Montesquieu calls "political virtue." In the absence of a monarch or a despot, a people must do for themselves what a strong central authority otherwise would force them to do. In particular, they must restrain themselves from harming others by loving equality and the laws, and they must defend the interests of the state (through military service, for example) by subordinating their individual interests to the common good.[17] A constant preference for the public interest over one's own, and even "renunciation of oneself," is the essence of republican virtue for Montesquieu.[18] Without this, the institutions of republican government collapse; its nature dissolves without its principle.

Honor finds its home in the government of constitutional monarchy, where it serves the balance of power that is central to this regime. Although monarchy involves the rule of a king, the structure of the regime includes the "intermediary bodies" that stand between the king and his subjects. They include the lords, clergy, nobility, and towns. Each is a power recognized as "independent" that "checks (*arrête*) arbitrary power."[19] The intermediary bodies provide alternative sites of authority from which the king's use of power can be contested.[20] By mediating the will of the king, the intermediary bodies support the rule of law, because without limits on the king's authority, nothing can be fixed and there is no fundamental law. Of these bodies, Montesquieu emphasizes the role of the nobility, saying that "the nobility enters in some fashion into the essence of monarchy, of which the fundamental maxim is: no monarch, no nobility: no nobility, no monarch. Rather one has a despot."[21]

Lawyers, administrators, and military men, the nobility were charged with carrying out the will of the king. As members of the *parlements* they adjudicated and administered his laws, as mayors of local villages they minded his subjects and collected his taxes, and as soldiers they commanded his armies and oversaw his conquests.[22] Although the nobility was charged with taking care of the king's business, this charge also gave them the power to *interfere* in the king's business, and their legislative and judicial prerogatives had the status of constitutional rights.[23] In theory, for example, the courts had only to receive, record, transmit and enforce the king's directives, but in practice the *parlements* prided themselves on the right to delay registration of a questionable law while they presented their objections to the king and awaited his response.[24] This right of remonstrance was supplemented with other forms of "interference" by the nobility at the level of local adjudication, administration, and enforcement.

Every delegation of authority thus resulted in a potential pocket of resistance, so that "just as the sea, which seems to want to cover the whole earth, is checked by the grasses and the smallest bits of gravel on the shore, so monarchs, whose power seems boundless, are checked by the . . . obstacles" represented by the nobility and other intermediary bodies.[25] They mediate the flow of political power and check the exercise of authority, for "in order to form a moderate government, one must combine powers, regulate them, temper them, make them act; give, that is to say, a ballast to one to put it in a position to resist another."[26] Honor is the "spring" that animates these perpetual tumults between the nobility and the king, tumults that serve liberty by dividing power. Because honor sets in motion the division of political power that moderates government and protects individual liberty, it is indispensable to monarchy, just as virtue is indispensable to republican government and fear to despotism. Without honor, the differentiated structure of monarchy would dissolve into the perfect unity of the unopposed will of the king.

The heart of honor in Montesquieu is principled desire, or high ambition (*l'ambition*), defined as "the desire to do great things."[27] Ambition "has good effects in monarchy"[28] because of its enlivening influence on the intermediary bodies. In moderate monarchies, the ambitions of the nobles counteract the ambitions of the king, which is good for individual liberty. Yet as everyone knows, ambition can be low-minded and petty, and countless commentators have faulted Montesquieu for his defense of it.[29] Indeed, honor frequently is interpreted as nothing more than "ambition in idleness, baseness in pride, the desire to enrich oneself without work, aversion to truth, flattery, treachery, perfidy."[30] Readers who take this account of "the wretched character of courtiers"[31] as the sum total of honor have missed a great deal, however.[32] Montesquieu is nothing if not realistic, and he makes no attempt to sweeten honor. The petty vanities of the courtiers are indeed its not-so-distant relation. Yet honor is far more than petty vanity. It is a complex quality of character partly because it includes ambition without being limited to the lowest forms of ambition, such as that of the courtiers.

The story of the Viscount of Orte displays the higher ambitions of honor and its complexity:

> After Saint Bartholomew's Day, Charles IX having written to all the governors to massacre the Huguenots, the Viscount of Orte, who was in command at Bayonne, wrote to the king, "Sire, I have found among the inhabitants and the warriors only good citizens, brave soldiers, and no executioner; thus, they and I together beg your Majesty to use our arms and our lives for things that can be done (*choses faisables*)." This great and generous courage regarded an act of cowardice as an impossible thing (IV.2).[33]

Orte's disobedience parallels the "interference" of the *parlements*, although it is more spectacular. Why did he do it? Not from self-interest or civic virtue, and not because he applied the principle of "universalizibility," as we say today. Instead, the story of Orte's courage must be understood together with Montesquieu's definition of honor as a form of personal ambition, and even as the prejudice (*prejugé*) of each person and each condition for himself and his own.[34] Orte refused the king's command because killing innocents violates an honorable soldier's code of conduct. He thought too much of himself to undertake something so debased. He expects more of himself than to kill innocent people just because someone told him to do so, even his king. He is, so to speak, better than that; he would not stoop so low. He owes it to himself to uphold his code of honor because this is what distinguishes him from a brute, or from one who is simply the instrument of another's will, and he is proud that he is more than just that.

Still, the courage of Orte is not altogether different from the vanities of the courtly air. What distinguishes Orte from the courtiers is not that his motives are purer than theirs, in the sense of being more altruistic or more universal, for he thinks of himself no less than they do. If anything, Orte thinks more of himself. It is his high opinion of himself that turns his self-concern to this brave act of resistance rather than obsequious social climbing, which is the vocation of the courtiers. The courtiers are obsequious because although they think only of themselves, they think too little of themselves, and so they freely debase themselves. They are ambitious, and yet they will put up with anything. Orte's "great and generous courage" reflects his ambition to be someone special. After all, it is no small thing to refuse a king. This ambition is (for us) an unusual mix of self-concern and higher purpose.

The mixed quality of honor explains why Montesquieu says that with honor, "one does not judge the actions of men as good but as fine, not as just but as great; not as reasonable but as extraordinary."[35] What Orte did was "fine" (*belle*) in the sense of being beautiful or admirable. It exceeded average expectations. Honor is something to live *up* to because it is above average. It is wonderful to see, like a beautiful painting, because it reminds us that there is more to being human than just getting by. Honor is an excellence that "elevate[s] the heart."[36] Yet honor is not the same thing as virtue. It yields "fine" actions but not necessarily "good" ones. For "in order to be a good man (*homme de bien*), it is necessary to have the intention of being one and to love the state less for oneself than for itself."[37] The good man or woman has a pure and selfless heart, and does the right thing for the right reason. But that is not Orte, who acted for himself. If he did the Huguenots a good turn, their welfare was not his sole intention. Orte treated the Huguenots not only as ends in themselves but also as the means to his own self-respect, and even his distinction. Their plight was his opportunity, and he made the most of it. Thus one must judge Orte's courage not as good but as fine.

If honor is not necessarily "good," neither is it intrinsically "just."[38] Contemporary accounts of honor very often treat it as a subset of justice, but Montesquieu emphatically distinguishes them.[39] With honor, one judges actions "not as just but as great" because "the virtues we are shown here are always less what one owes others than what one owes oneself; they are not so much what calls us to our fellow citizens as what distinguishes us from them."[40] What one owes others is the province of justice; what one owes oneself is the province of honor. By emphasizing this distinction, Montesquieu reminds us that they do not always coincide. Justice and honor may conflict. In Orte's refusal to massacre innocents they coincided, but this will not always be the case. What I owe to myself may come at the expense of what I owe to you.

Moreover, except where the laws are nonexistent or very bad, it is possible to be just without making much effort. One need only follow the law. By contrast, honor calls forth a certain "greatness of soul"[41] because it cannot be had so easily. Indeed, "the things that honor prohibits are more rigorously prohibited when the laws do not concur in proscribing them, and those things that honor demands are more strongly demanded when the laws do not ask for them."[42] Honorable people such as Orte ask more of themselves than what is minimally required by the laws and by justice. Risk is involved in honor, along with self-assertion and the willingness to undertake something difficult. Honor is an effort even if it is not exactly self-sacrifice.

Finally, one judges honorable actions "not as reasonable but as extraordinary" because they interrupt the ordinary processes and resist the constraints that condition our expectations. In this regard, honor resembles Hannah Arendt's concept of "action," although there are important differences as well. Action, on Arendt's account, means asserting one's capacity for what she calls "natality," or new beginnings, against the "automatic" processes of nature and civilization. Arendt's actions are "interruptions of some natural series of events, of some automatic process, in whose context they constitute the wholly unexpected."[43] They manifest humankind's "sheer capacity to begin," a robust exertion of agency, because they imply a departure from the given. In contrast to Arendt's concept of action, honor is tied to hereditary social codes and fixed laws, but like action, honor cannot be made routine. It is true that Orte's disobedience is in line with, even demanded by, the laws of honor contained in his code. Yet if the laws of honor can be known in advance, individual acts of honor are more difficult to predict. Honorable actions are often risky and difficult. Their unpredictability and unusual vitality make honor extraordinary.

So honor is ambitious and assertive, and it aims high. In addition to defending its codes, honor as a quality of character seeks public recognition. Being seen and acknowledged is important to the *honnête homme.* Those with honor want to be the kinds of people who live up to their principles *and* they want to be *seen* as the kinds of people who live up to their principles. Their ambition has these two sides to it, both an internal and an external dimension.[44] Montesquieu's idea is to channel the desire for esteem in productive ways, to make it serve the division and balance of power in politics, and thereby to protect individual liberty. Although honor leans on public recognition, it cannot, however, be reduced to recognition. The fact that one's honor is tied to one's code and to self-respect gives honor a measure of independence from public recognition. Orte's principles always will be there for him to defend even when no one is looking. And insofar as his code of honor gives him a consistent standard to live up to, it provides a consistent foundation for his self-respect, whatever anybody else may think of him, even when nobody "honors" him.[45]

The pride involved in honor as a quality of character also is relevant here. Those with honor have high opinions of themselves, which means that they have much to live up to, which makes them willing to undertake risky actions. This explains why the desire for distinction (and not merely recognition) is central to honor. Would Orte have stood up to the king if he could have esteemed himself either way? If doing something exceptional had not been necessary to his sense of self-respect, would he have gone to the trouble? Would he have bothered to risk his life? In a well-ordered society, it is true, great acts of resistance to political authority in defense of individual liberties are not often called for. But the rare instances in which they *are* called for can make all the difference.[46] Honor's high and principled ambitions, which animate its extraordinary acts, serve this crucial function.

Honor faces a fundamental dilemma, however. On Montesquieu's account, honor can support the balance of power that sustains individual liberty only in the context of a relatively entrenched social order. The nobility's spirited resistance to the crown is possible because it has an independent base of power, prestige, and wealth. Honor requires equipment, including titles, political offices, established prerogatives, and land.[47] And the independence of the nobility is sustainable only if it is hereditary, as the principle of heredity is needed to protect the nobility from being captured by the crown. The prerogatives of the nobility also must be exclusive, Montesquieu insists, and must not transfer to the people "unless one wants to attack (*choque*) the principle of the government, unless one wants to diminish the force of the nobility and the force of the people."[48] Although the nobility's "demand for preferences and distinctions"[49] can degenerate into empty vanity,[50] Montesquieu sees these social distinctions and political prerogatives as crucial to maintaining the balance of power that protects liberty.

At the same time, however, Montesquieu suggests (paradoxically) that an inflexible social order is antithetical to political liberty on the grounds that "the laws that order each to remain in his profession and to pass it down to his children are and can be useful only in despotic states, where no one can or ought to have rivals."[51] "The political world," and especially a regime of political liberty, "is sustained by the inner desire and restlessness that each one has for leaving the place where he has been put."[52] Suppressing this natural restlessness is despotic. Restlessness can be used to good effect if it is harnessed and directed in such a way as to fuel the rivalries between political powers. By contrast, a hereditary nobility tends toward "ignorance," "laxity," and "scorn for civil government," which undercuts its effectiveness as a rival to the king.[53] This is one reason why Montesquieu advocates venality, the practice of buying offices.[54] Venality supports the rise of the ambitious and the industrious, and so puts political influence into the hands of individuals who are, if not necessarily wiser or more virtuous than others, at least more assertive. The royal appointment of posts or selection by the courtier class gives political prerogatives to persons who are more likely to flatter the king than to offer principled opposition.[55] An overly fixed social order thus works against the separation and balance of powers because it suppresses rivalries and the personal ambitions that sustain them, and it prevents persons of merit from coming to the fore.

Thus the fixity of ranks and orders needed to protect the nobility from manipulative monarchs also invites its degradation, and with it the enervation of honor. This is a difficulty that Montesquieu himself does not resolve. It suggests that for honor to operate effectively, both the social and the political orders must be democratized in the sense of providing more equality of opportunity and plural sites of power. Only when the prerogatives that give individuals leverage in contesting political power are open to ambition and merit rather than closed by lineage can honor reliably animate the tumults between political powers that protect liberty. Paradoxically, old-regime honor needs but cannot tolerate a fixed social order. It simultaneously resists and requires democratization.

HONOR AND DEMOCRACY IN AMERICA

The suggestion that honor must escape the entrenched inequalities of the old regime to preserve itself is unexpected because honor today is most often associated with these very conditions. The contemporary associations are not altogether wrong, since as much as honor needs a regime of opportunity and mobility, these same conditions may undercut it. Yet honor has had a place in American democracy from its inception, when the American revolutionaries pledged to defend their Declaration of Independence with their lives, their fortunes, and their "sacred Honor." No one understood the ambivalent relationship between honor and modern democracy better than Alexis de Tocqueville. Tocqueville illuminates the features of democracy that generate its resistance to honor, but he also shows why democracy needs honor. To support individual liberty against the twin dangers of majority tyranny and "mild" despotism, Tocqueville seeks to inspire in the democratic character qualities tied to old-regime honor. Courage, pride, high and principled ambition, the desires for distinction and self-respect, and the sense of duty to oneself all prove to be as crucial to democratic freedom on Tocqueville's account as they were to liberty in Montesquieu.

Before articulating the tensions between honor and democracy, Tocqueville suggests a measure of compatibility between them. He points out that the traditional honor of feudal society is "only one of its forms."[56] Honor may not be as prominent in democracy as it was in aristocratic societies or in the constitutional monarchy that Montesquieu described, but "honor is found in democratic centuries as well as in aristocratic times."[57] Those who think that honor is inextricably tied to feudalism have mistaken one instance of honor for the whole of it, and so "have given a generic name to what [is] only a species."[58] Honor displays "a different physiognomy" in the new regime because the specific content of the rules by which public esteem is distributed are different there.[59] Yet despite these differences, every society has some notion of honor because "every time men assemble in a particular society, an honor is established among them right away."[60]

Still, Tocqueville goes on to elaborate conflicts between democracy and honor that tend to weaken honor as an influence on individual action. The first difficulty is that honor's injunctions are "less numerous" in democracies than in aristocratic societies.[61] Honor's prescriptions are fewer in democracies because the same set of prescriptions applies to everyone. In fact, if group distinctions were ever to be fully eradicated in a given society, honor would "be limited to a small number of precepts" that would "stray less and less from the moral laws adopted by the community of humanity in general."[62] To the extent that codes of honor move toward universal moral standards applicable to humanity in general, honor loses its distinctive character and is overwhelmed by a more generalized and therefore less robust humanitarianism. Rules of honor also are "less clear" in democracy.[63] In the old regime, Tocqueville says, honor had a "clear and precise form," with codes of honor being "complete and detailed" and giving "a fixed and always visible rule for human actions."[64] By contrast, in modern democratic regimes "where all the citizens are mobile, where society, being modified everyday, changes its opinions with changing needs," the meaning attached to the word "honor" proves difficult to fix with precision.[65] Democratic honor "is necessarily less powerful" because it is less clearly defined, "for it is difficult to apply with certainty and firmness a law that is imperfectly known."[66] The strength and prominence of honor in the old regime owed a great deal to the power of tradition and the fixity of the social order there, even if, paradoxically, a stagnant social order also tends to corrupt honor.

Another reason for the relative weakness of honor in democracy is the obscurity of individuals in mass society. Among aristocratic peoples, "all ranks differ," and consequently "no one can either hope or fear that he will not be seen." No one can, by his obscurity, escape praise or blame.[67] When equality of conditions prevails, persons "are mixed together (*confondues*) in the same crowd."[68] The result is that individuals tend to become similar and can "no longer be distinguished from one another by any characteristic traits."[69] Ironically, the equal recognition that comes with social and political equality tends to make individuals invisible instead of equally distinguished. The obscurity of individuals in democratic societies keeps them from obeying honor's rules by interfering with the public regulation of praise and blame. Where individuals emerge into public view only to fade away again into the crowd of their equally undistinguished fellows, "public opinion has no grip; its object disappears each instance and escapes it."[70] The invisibility of the individual makes for looser adherence to honor's prescriptions. For all these reasons,

Tocqueville concludes that there is a fundamental tension between honor and the equality of conditions found in modern democracy.[71] Although democratic forms of honor exist, they are not likely to have the same power and predominance as honor in aristocratic societies.

Still, Tocqueville hoped to energize modern democrats with some of the qualities of character associated with traditional honor. Such qualities are needed to counter the "habit and passion for well-being"[72] that leads to "a degrading form of servitude"[73] and opens the door to democratic despotism. Along these lines, Tocqueville remarks that "far from believing that it is necessary to recommend humility to our contemporaries, I would like an effort to be made to give them a more vast idea of themselves and of their species; humility is not at all healthy for them; what they most lack in my view is pride."[74] Pride is a powerful spring of action, and it was a central component of the aristocratic honor that "gave an extraordinary force to acts of individual resistance" in the old regime.[75] Those who "dared in isolation to resist the pressure of public authority" were "men who . . . held a high idea of their individual value."[76]

Pride is at odds with democracy insofar as it implies a sense of personal distinction and runs counter to the passion for equality that characterizes the virtuous democrat. Humility, not pride, appears to democrats to be the proper demeanor for their kind, at least in their relations with one another, as Tocqueville reports.[77] Yet the humble man sees himself as nothing special, and he neither claims anything special *for* himself nor asks anything special *of* himself. The democratic citizen on occasion must ask something special of himself. The courage and energy required to resist majority tyranny, or to take a principled stand against public opinion, or to object to the violation of individual liberties, often require extraordinary exertions of individual character and will. A citizen who asks nothing special of himself because he sees himself as nothing special is not likely to meet this challenge. And without at least a few citizens able to meet the challenge when it arises, democratic freedoms are bound to be tenuous.

Pride also is connected to what Tocqueville calls "great ambitions." While virtually everyone in the United States has ambition, Tocqueville says, almost no one has any great ambitions.[78] By removing the artificial obstacles to individual ambition imposed by the fixed hierarchies of aristocratic societies, democracy permits citizens to realize their ambitions to an unprecedented degree. The increased opportunity to realize ambition promotes its spread, as "the desire to raise oneself is born in every heart at the same time, and each man wants to leave his place. Ambition is a universal feeling."[79] At the same time, however, the equality of conditions that makes ambition widespread also lowers its aims. The reason is that virtually everyone must work to live, which leads to a constant preoccupation with obtaining material necessities and comforts. Few have the luxury to concern themselves with greater objectives. Even if they should win this luxury through their material success, the habit of aiming low is likely to persist, having been long ingrained. Consequently, the objects of democratic ambition tend to remain within the "fairly narrow limits" of material prosperity,[80] and "one scarcely encounters an ambition that is proportionate, moderate, and vast."[81] The low ambitions to which self-interested individuals may incline make them sitting ducks for prospective tyrants and democratic factions, however. "I tremble, I confess," Tocqueville says, "that [democratic citizens] may permit themselves to be so fully possessed by a cowardly love of present pleasures that . . . they may prefer to follow feebly the course of their destiny rather than make a sudden energetic effort as needed to set things right."[82]

By distinguishing the fundamental features of honor as a quality of character, which remain relatively constant, from the external dimensions of honor, which vary, Tocqueville makes it possible for us to conceive honor in a democratic context, severed from the social conditions of inequality and immobility associated with the old regime.[83] And despite the real tensions between democracy and honor, Tocqueville insists that such qualities are available to modern democrats, even if they are not the predominant motives of the new regime. Equality of conditions ensures that honor is not a society-wide ideal in democratic societies, but equality does not make occasional instances of honor impossible. The qualities of character that both Montesquieu and Tocqueville associated with honor are as crucial to sustaining political agency in modern democracies as they were in the old regime. By supporting strong exertions of agency, these qualities can help to generate risky and difficult political action.[84] The place to look for them is not so much in the regular operations of government or the daily activities of ordinary citizens but in the occasional, extraordinary instances of resistance in which people stand up—often at great cost to themselves—to contest the abuse of power and defend liberty.

HONOR AND DEMOCRATIC REFORM

By setting in motion extraordinary political action in defense of liberty, honor in the United States has regularly given rise to democratic reform. Along these lines, W. E. B. DuBois invoked honor as a catalyst for black freedom in his 1906 "Resolutions of the Niagara Movement." He called on African Americans "to sacrifice money, reputation, and life itself on the altar of right," and to "reconsecrate ourselves, our honor, and our property to the final emancipation of the race for whose freedom John Brown died."[85] DuBois saw honor much as Montesquieu and Tocqueville had seen it, as a spring of risky but principled action. He invoked honor for the same purpose that they had done, to inspire political agency and the defense of liberty.

Among the predecessors of DuBois in the tradition of African American reformers, no one exemplifies more aspects of honor than Frederick Douglass, a man whom Booker T. Washington once called "the soul of honor."[86] Douglass was born into slavery in Maryland in 1818, escaped to freedom in New York in 1838, and thereafter became a leader in the antislavery movement, an abolitionist lecturer, author, newspaper editor, and the most famous and admired black figure of his time. Today he is regarded as the "prototypical black American hero" and a democratic embodiment of "heroic greatness."[87]

Douglass powerfully exemplifies the resistance to overweening power that is a central feature of honor. His autobiography describes one such act of resistance, which he came to see as the turning point in his life as a slave. In 1834, Douglass was in service to a man named Covey, a "snakish" man who had a penchant for beating his slaves.[88] After one particularly brutal beating, Douglass resolved "to obey every order, however unreasonable, if it were possible," but "if Mr. Covey should then undertake to beat me, to defend and protect myself to the best of my ability."[89] The next day, Covey attacked him again. Douglass later recounted what happened next:

> I now forgot my roots, and remembered my pledge to *stand up in my own defense*. . . . Whence came the daring spirit necessary to grapple with a man who, eight and forty hours before, could, with his slightest word have made me tremble like a leaf in a storm, I do now know; at any rate, *I was resolved to fight*. . . . [At length,] the cowardly tyrant asked if I "meant to persist in my resistance." I told him "I *did mean to resist, come what might*;" that I had been by him treated like a *brute* during the last six months; and that I should stand it *no longer*."[90]

Douglass described the event as "the turning point in *my life as a slave*" because, he said, "it rekindled in my breast the smouldering embers of liberty . . . and revived a sense of my own manhood."[91] The fight "recalled to life my crushed self-respect and my self-confidence, and inspired me with a renewed determination to be a freeman."[92] He spoke of the event in political terms, saying "he only can understand the effect of this combat on my spirit, who has himself incurred something, hazarded something, in repelling the unjust and cruel aggressions of a tyrant."[93] It was an act of resistance not merely to encroaching power but to despotic power, and Douglass regarded it as a mark of "honor."[94] It was a mark of honor in the sense that it made him respectable in his own eyes and in the eyes of "human nature" itself, he said, for "human nature is so constituted, that it cannot *honor* a helpless man, although it can *pity* him."[95]

The connection that Douglass draws between honor and human nature reflects a shift in the meaning of honor outside the old regime. For

Douglass, this honorable act of resistance vindicates his "manhood," or what he calls his "essential dignity" as a human being, rather than his status as a member of a particular class with a specific role. Whereas before the fight "I was *nothing*," he tells us, afterward "I was a man."[96] This reference to human nature and human dignity rather than social roles and status is a feature of democratic honor more generally. Yet like Montesquieu's *honnête homme*, Douglass's sense of honor motivates his spirited resistance and serves liberty. It results in a kind of redemption, through which he became "a freeman in *fact*" even as he remained "a slave in *form*. When a slave cannot be flogged he is more than half free. He has a domain as broad as his own manly heart to defend."[97] Douglass' sense of honor makes him willing to risk even his life for the sake of his self-respect and his freedom. If his honor is rooted in the notion of human dignity rather than social rank, then, it nevertheless preserves the courage, the pride, and the high ambition characteristic of honor in Montesquieu and Tocqueville.

The fight with Covey was the "turning point" in Douglass's life as a slave, but Douglass had another life as well, one that was lived after his escape from bondage. In his post-slavery life, he became a man of politics and society, a leader, and a political reformer. During this later period, the principles contained in the American Constitution and Declaration of Independence came to embody a code of honor for him, one that guided and inspired his political action. Although his first ten years as an abolitionist in the North were lived by the doctrine of the Garrisonian school, which held that "the Constitution was wholly a pro-slavery document, called for the destruction of the American Union, and opposed the use of the ballot against slavery," Douglass revised his views on these points in the early 1850s.[98] By 1853 he had broken with the Garrisonians fully and had come to believe in the American Union's potential for redemption and the power of the American founding documents to help bring this about. Thereafter, he defended the principles articulated in the Declaration and Constitution until he died in 1895. These principles came to constitute the guiding standard of his personal ambitions, articulated in speech after rousing speech, and exemplified in his public actions.[99]

In an 1865 address entitled, "What the Black Man Wants," he advocated the "immediate, unconditional, and universal enfranchisement of the black man, in every State in the Union," and he defended this demand on the basis of the Declaration's principles and promises.[100] Without the right to vote, he said, "[the black man's] liberty is a mockery; without this you might as well almost retain the old name of slavery for his condition; for in fact, if he is not the slave of the individual master, he is the slave of society, and holds his liberty as a privilege, not as a right. He is at the mercy of the mob, and has no means of protecting himself."[101] He appealed to "the American sense of honor" to "see that this war shall not cease until every freedman at the South has the right to vote."[102] On another occasion, he accused white Americans of having "dishonored" the Declaration by "bartering away the eternal principles of right it enunciated."[103] In a speech delivered on the Fourth of July in 1862, he spoke of the connection between his principles and the robust political agency he embodied, saying that one who abandons "honest principles and high purposes" is bound to be passive in the face of circumstance, "swept on as if by the power of fate."[104] The content of his code differed markedly from the content of honor codes in the old regime, but its role in sustaining and guiding robust political action was the same.

Although Douglass won fame over the course of his long life, he was ambivalent about public honors. After the passage of the Thirteenth, Fourteenth, and Fifteenth Amendments, friends urged him to run for Congress from one of the reconstructed states in the South. He finally decided against a run for national office on the grounds that "the idea did not entirely square well with my better judgment and sense of propriety. The thought of going to live among a people in order to gain their votes and acquire official honors was repugnant to my sense of self-respect."[105] Later in life he "never regretted that I did not enter the arena of Congressional honors."[106] In Douglass, the balance between the internal and the external dimensions of honor was weighted in favor of the former. He preferred self-respect to public esteem. Perhaps as a black man, Douglass knew all too well the fickleness of such esteem, which he saw as based on nothing more than "pride and fashion."[107] Public honors are particularly unreliable currency for members of marginalized groups, and they can be dangerous. The suggestion of superiority in a member of a group thought to be naturally inferior frequently is perceived as a special affront by those in the majority, especially the ones who harbor doubts about their own standing or abilities. For a man such as Douglass, public honors were not only undependable but potentially deadly.

Thus Douglass tended to focus more on the internal dimensions of honor, particularly pride and self-respect, than on public esteem. Once when traveling by train he was compelled to sit for several hours in a portion of the freight car because of his race. Booker T. Washington later recounted the story:

> A friend went into the freight car to console him and said to him that he hated to see a man of his intelligence in so humiliating a position. "I am ashamed that they have thus degraded you." But Douglass, straightening himself up in his seat, looked the friend in the face and said, "They cannot degrade Frederick Douglass." And so they cannot degrade a single individual who does not want to be degraded.[108]

Douglass's refusal to draw his sense of personal worth from white society's sense of it reflects the predominance he accorded self-respect over public esteem. The claim of invulnerability implicit in this refusal, and in Washington's later assertion that "nobody can degrade a big man or a big race" against his will, is admittedly a boastful claim. However strong in character an individual may be, a lifetime on the losing end of injustice will take its toll. But the boast is a noble one. It represents an honorable response to the real power of injustice, and it makes conceivable the robust political agency needed to resist injustice.

Booker T. Washington was not amiss when he called Douglass "the soul of honor." The pride and principled ambitions, the courageous resistance to oppressive power, the sense of duty to oneself, and the desire for self-respect all capture crucial features of honor as a quality of character, and in Douglass they made honor an important source of forceful political agency, first in resistance to slavery and later as a political reformer. These same features of honor were on display in the character of Martin Luther King, Jr. a half-century after Douglass died. King was a complex man of mixed and not always transparent motives, and it would be wrong to say that honor was the sole spring of his action. In his public life as a civil rights leader one can detect a variety of motives, including faith, civic virtue, the sense of justice, and self-interest. But honor played a role as well. It is evident in his high and principled ambitions, his pride, his courageous resistance to encroaching power, his desire for self-respect, and his sense of duty to himself. These qualities supported his extraordinary capacity for political agency. King's sense of honor also inspired political agency in others, and the connection between honor and political agency was important for the civil rights movement as a whole.

It may seem strange to speak of honor in conjunction with King, who had a reputation for being a humble man. When *Time* magazine published a feature story on him in February 1957, the reporter characterized King as "personally humble,"[109] and to many observers the whole method of nonviolent resistance he defended gave an impression of humble resoluteness, even "self-effacement."[110] Yet King's effort to recall America to its principles and simultaneously to radically reform it was anything but humble. He had what Montesquieu and Tocqueville called *grandes ambitions*, and these ambitions were at least as visible as his humility to those who knew him well. "He has a sense of humility and awe at what has happened to him, but he also has a sense of destiny," remarked a Montgomery friend.[111] His extraordinary ambitions were inspiring to some of his fellows but resented by others. Many in Atlanta's old guard "viewed him as an aggrandizing upstart—and a sanctimonious one at that."[112] Members of the NAACP accused him of "laboring under a messiah complex,"[113] and the student leaders of the Student Nonviolent Coordinating Committee (SNCC) took to calling him "de Lawd," complaining that he had a tendency to seize "all the publicity and the glory."[114] One organizational head in Montgomery told him reproachfully, "Don't talk with me through no secy-tary. I'm as big as you are, King."[115] What one historian refers to as King's "reluctance to call attention to his own ambition"[116] did not conceal this ambition from his associates, even if it largely has concealed his ambition from posterity.

The principles that guided King's ambition derived from a variety of sources, including the Bible and the civil disobedience doctrines of Gandhi and Thoreau. His "Letter from Birmingham City Jail" quoted Augustine, Aquinas, Martin Buber, Paul Tillich, Martin Luther, John Bunyan, Thomas Jefferson, and T. S. Eliot, and invoked the models of Socrates and Jesus—all to defend the moral legitimacy of civil disobedience to unjust laws. But the letter concluded with a direct appeal to America's founding principles, which had a special place in guiding his action:

> One day the South will know that when these disinherited children of God sat down at lunch counters they were in reality standing up for the best in the American dream and the most sacred values in our Judeo-Christian heritage, and thusly, carrying our whole nation back to those great wells of democracy which were dug deep by the Founding Fathers in the formulation of the Constitution and the Declaration of Independence.[117]

He noted on another occasion that the nation had begun in civil protest, and he named the Boston Tea Party and the Revolution itself as examples. He concluded that civil rights protesters were "standing up for the highest and the best in the American tradition."[118] In effect, the American principles of liberty and justice for all constituted King's code of honor. That code animated his extraordinary ambition, and he risked—and finally sacrificed—his life on behalf of it. And as with Frederick Douglass, King's spirited defense of his code produced not only resistance to encroaching power but substantial political reform.

In addition to modeling the sense of honor, King sought to cultivate it among movement participants as a way of generating collective action. Along with courage, the movement emphasized "a sense of self-respect and pride," all core features of honor as a quality of character.[119] In the past, King told a crowd after the victory of the bus boycott in Montgomery, "we have sat in the back of the buses, and this had indicated a basic lack of self-respect. It shows that we thought of ourselves as less than men."[120] King's objective was for African Americans to be able to "say to ourselves and the world, 'I am somebody. I am a person. I am a man with dignity and honor.'"[121] He wanted American blacks to remember Frederick Douglass and Booker T. Washington and Roland Hayes and Marian Anderson and Leontyne Price and Langston Hughes and the many other black men and women who "have shown us that, despite our lack of complete freedom, we can make contributions here and now."[122] As he saw it, black people owed it to themselves to remember these outstanding individuals, and to live up to the examples they set. Dignity, honor, and political agency went together and made the spirited defense—or assertion—of liberty possible. For this reason, King and other leaders promulgated the idea that going to jail as a result of protest activity was a badge of honor.[123] They reversed "the traditionally negative connotations of jail" as a "place of shame" and dishonor.[124] Jail became a badge of honor for civil rights activists because for them going to jail was poof of one's principled ambition and one's courage, and a vindication of one's "human dignity," as Douglass had said. This badge of honor also provided public recognition, at least among supporters of the movement, an external reward that complemented the internal prize of self-respect.

The qualities associated with honor that one sees in King and in the civil rights movement as a whole—high and principled ambition, pride, the desires for self-respect and public recognition, courageous resistance to encroaching power, the sense of duty to oneself—represent continuities between democratic honor and honor in the old regime. The content of the codes was different, as were the terms for distributing public recognition. Yet honor as a quality of character remains recognizable across these very different contexts. The honor of King and his fellow activists was not the sole spring of their action, but it was a central component of their uncommon capacity for political agency, their willingness to risk everything to make freedom and progressive reform real.

CONCLUSIONS

Honor is often overlooked in the contemporary study of politics, but it is a powerful engine of political agency and a potent source of freedom and political reform. It combines a proud sense of what one owes to oneself with high and principled ambition. It disrupts the familiar dichotomy between self-interest and self-sacrifice. Indeed, honor's power as a source of extraordinary action lies largely in the fact that it is a mixed motive. As a duty to oneself, honor builds on the particular attachments and private desires that make us who we are and move us to act. It channels and directs personal ambitions rather than suppressing them in the name of a comprehensive common good or a self-sacrificing civic virtue. Indeed, in pluralistic democracies, honor can serve diverse codes.[125] Yet honor always aims high. Honor's principled ambitions motivate risky and difficulty actions that self-interest alone could never sustain. Honor reminds us of liberal democracy's occasional need for extraordinary exertions of agency and the uncommon qualities of character that sustain them. For although liberal democracy normally can get by with good citizens, every once in a while it needs great ones. Like every form of political authority, democratic authority sometimes overreaches its legitimate limits. When this happens, neither self-interest, nor civic virtue, nor the sense of justice, nor reason itself always can be relied upon to motivate principled opposition. Until the day when democracy is no longer vulnerable to majority tyranny and the abuse of power, Americans will continue to rely on the honor of those who occasionally stand up to resist, men and women who are willing to risk their necks to defend their liberties.

NOTES

Portions of this chapter are reprinted by permission of the publisher from *Liberalism with Honor* by Sharon R. Krause, Cambridge, MA: Harvard University Press, copyright © 2002 by the President and Fellows of Harvard College.

1. *Declaration of Independence.*

2. See Peter Berger, "On the Obsolescence of the Concept of Honor," in *Liberalism and its Critics*, ed. Michael J. Sandel (New York: New York University Press, 1984), 149–58.

3. On the practice of running exceptional individuals out of town, see Aristotle's discussion of the use of ostracism in democracies, in his *Politics*, trans. Carnes Lord (Chicago: University of Chicago Press, 1984), 1284al17–34.

4. As in the frivolous violence of duels, or the senseless "honor killings" in some parts of the world of women thought to have shamed their families. For recent treatments of honor, see Kwame Anthony Appiah, *The Honor Code: How Moral Revolutions Happen* (New York: W. W. Norton, 2010); Rachel Bayefsky, "Dignity, Honour, and Human Rights: Kant's Perspective," *Political Theory* 41, no. 6 (2013): 809–37; Jan H. Blits, "Redeeming Lost Honor: Shakespeare's *Rape of Lucrece*," *The Review of Politics* 71 (2009): 411–27; James Bowman, *Honor: A History* (New York: Encounter, 2006); Daniel George Demetriou, *Honor Among Theories* (Ann Arbor: Proquest UMI Dissertation Publishing, 2011); Laurie Johnson, *Thomas Hobbes: Turning Point for Honor* (Lanham, MD: Lexington Books, 2009) and *Locke and Rousseau: Two Enlightenment Responses to Honor* (Lanham, MD: Lexington Books, 2013); Mika Lavaque-Manty, "Dueling for Equality: Masculine Honor and the Modern Politics of Dignity," *Political Theory* 34, no. 6 (2006): 715–40; Christopher Scott McClure, "War, Madness, and Death: The Paradox of Honor in Hobbes's *Leviathan*," *The Journal of Politics* 76, no. 1 (2014): 114–25; and Peter Olsthoorn, "Honour, Face, and Reputation in Political Theory," *European Journal of Political Theory* 7, no. 4 (2008): 472–91.

5. See, for example, J. G. Peristiany, ed., *Honor and Shame* (Chicago: University of Chicago Press, 1966); Frank Henderson Stewart, *Honor* (Chicago: University of Chicago Press, 1994); and Lyman L. Johnson and Sonya Lipsett-Rivera, *The Faces of Honor: Sex, Shame, and Violence in Colonial Latin America* (Albuquerque: University of New Mexico Press, 1998).

6. Guy Chaussinand-Nogaret, *La noblesse au XVIIIe siècle: De la féodalité aux lumières* (Paris: Librairie Hachette, 1976); Jean Meyer, *La noblesse française à l'époque moderne (XVIe-XVIIIe siècle)* (Paris: Presses Universitaires de France, 1991); Léopold Genicot, *La noblesse dans l'occident medieval* (London: Variorum Reprints, 1982); Jonathan Dewald, *The European Nobility, 1400–1800* (Cambridge: Cambridge University Press, 1996); M. L. Bush, *Noble Privilege* (Manchester, UK: Manchester University Press, 1983); and Jean-Pierre Labatut, *Les noblesses européennes de la fin du XVe siècle à la fin du XVIIIe siècle* (Paris: Presses Universitaires de France, 1978).

7. As Steven Forde points out in this volume, "the human desire for honor . . . is remarkably flexible," and it can be "adapted to support a wide variety of culturally-variable norms." These can include "not only the desire to dominate, but a moral community of nondomination."

8. Montesquieu, *The Spirit of the Laws*, preface, in *Oeuvres complètes de Montesquieu*, ed. Roger Caillois (Paris: Pléiade, 1949–51), vol II. Translations are my own, although I have borrowed occasionally from *The Spirit of the Laws*, translated by Anne M. Cohler, Basia Carolyn Miller and Harold Samuel Stone (Cambridge: Cambridge University Press, 1989). Hereafter references to *The Spirit of the Laws* will be inserted parenthetical-

ly into the text with capital roman numerals indicating book and arabic numerals indicating chapter.

9. Michael A. Mosher, "The Particulars of a Universal Politics: Hegel's Adaptation of Montesquieu's Typology, "*American Political Science Review*, 78, no. 1 (1984): 180; Corrado Rosso, *Montesquieu moraliste* (Bordeaux, FR: Ducros, 1971), 100; and David W. Carrithers, "Montesquieu's Philosophy of History," *Journal of the History of Ideas* 47, no. 1 (1986): 76.

10. Louis Althusser, *Politics and History: Montesquieu, Rousseau, Marx,* trans. Ben Brewster (London: Verso, 1983), 80; Mark Hulliung, *Montesquieu and the Old Regime* (Berkeley: University of California Press, 1976), 179.

11. Franklin Ford, *Robe and Sword: The Regrouping of the French Aristocracy after Louis XIV* (Cambridge, MA: Harvard University Press, 1953), 20.

12. Rosso, *Montesquieu moraliste,* 100.

13. III.1.

14. III.1.

15. Althusser, *Politics and History,* 46.

16. III.9.

17. V.3.

18. IV.5.

19. II.4.

20. See Ford, *Robe and Sword,* 7.

21. II.4. Although Montesquieu emphasizes the role of the nobility, he also thought the clergy—and religion more generally—could be a crucial check on political power: "One will forsake one's father, even kill him, if the prince orders it, but one will not drink wine if the prince wants it and orders it. The laws of religion are of a superior precept, because they are given to the prince as to the subjects" (*The Spirit of the Laws,* III.10).

22. For further discussion of the privileges, prerogatives, and duties of the French nobility up to the eighteenth century, see, for example, Chaussinand-Nogaret, *La noblesse au XVIIIe siècle*; Meyer, *La noblesse française*; Genicot, *La noblesse dans l'occident medieval*; Dewald, *The European Nobility*; David D. Bien, "Old Regime Origins of Democratic Liberty," in *The French Idea of Freedom: The Old Regime and the Declaration of the Rights of 1789*, ed. Dale Van Kley (Stanford, CA: Stanford University Press, 1994); Bush, *Noble Privilege*; Labatut, *Les noblesses européennes*; and Kinneging, *Aristocracy, Antiquity and History: Classicism in Political Thought* (New Brunswick, NJ: Transaction Publishers, 1997) especially 50–55.

23. There was a sizable literature in the early eighteenth century on the constitutional standing of the French nobility and the status of its legislative and judicial rights. Books XXVIII and XXX–XXXI of *The Spirit of the Laws* comprise Montesquieu's contribution to these debates. For further discussion, see Keith Michael Baker, *The Old Regime and The French Revolution* (Chicago: University of Chicago Press, 1987); Iris Cox, *Montesquieu and the History of French Laws* (Oxford: Voltaire Foundation, 1983); Kingsley Martin, *French Liberal Thought in the Eighteenth Century* (London: Turnstile Press, Ltd., 1954); and Ford, *Robe and Sword.*

24. Ford, *Robe and Sword,* 80. And note *The Spirit of the Laws,* V.10: "The bodies that are the depository of the laws never obey better than when they act slowly and bring into the affairs of the prince the reflectiveness that one can scarcely expect given the lack of enlightenment in the court about the laws of the state and the haste of the prince's councilors. . . . What would have become of even the finest monarchy in the world if the magistrates, by their slowness, their complaints, and their prayers, had not checked the course of even the virtues of its kings." In this volume, Dan Demetriou also notes the importance of the sense of honor in motivating aristocratic resist monarchical control in Montesquieu's analysis.

25. II.4.

26. V.14.

27. Montesquieu, *Mes pensées,* in *Oeuvres complètes,* vol. I, no. 549[30], 1060.

28. III.7.
29. See, for example, Condorcet, in Destutt de Tracy and Antoine Louis Claude, *Commentary and Review of Montesquieu's* The Spirit of the Laws, trans. Thomas Jefferson (New York: Burt Franklin, 1969), 286f; and G. W. F. Hegel, *Philosophy of Right,* trans. T. M. Knox (Oxford: Oxford University Press, 1967), 178.
30. III.5.
31. III.5.
32. For example, Judith Shklar thinks that Montesquieu "deplores" honor. See Shklar, *Ordinary Vices* (Cambridge, MA: Harvard University Press, 1984), 219. Similarly, Hulliung argues that for Montesquieu honor "withers before virtue" in *Montesquieu and the Old Regime,* 29
33. The Viscount of Orte was Adrien d'Aspremont, vicomte d'Orthe, gouverneur de Bayonne.
34. III.6.
35. IV.2.
36. IV.3.
37. III.6.
38. Although it may be either good or just, or both. The point is that honor is not simply a subset of either "the good" or "the just." It is also worth noting that Montesquieu's effort to distinguish honor from justice is not meant to suggest that justice is irrelevant to monarchical government. Indeed, Montesquieu argues that the administration of justice in monarchy must be scrupulous (*The Spirit of the Laws,* VI.1). But honor cannot be reduced to a form of justice.
39. See, for example, Rawls, *A Theory of Justice* (Cambridge, MA: Harvard University Press, 1971), especially 178f, 440ff and 544ff; and Michael Walzer, *Spheres of Justice* (New York: Basic Books, 1983), chapter 11.
40. IV.2.
41. V.12.
42. IV.2.
43. "Human life, placed on the earth, is surrounded by automatic processes—by the natural processes of the earth, which, in turn, are surrounded by cosmic processes, and we ourselves are driven by similar forces insofar as we too are a part of organic nature. Our political life, moreover . . . also takes place in the midst of processes which we call historical and which tend to become as automatic as natural or cosmic processes, although they were started by men." Hannah Arendt, *The Human Condition* (Chicago: University of Chicago Press, 1958), 168f.
44. In this volume, Ryan Rhodes argues persuasively for the value of the "concern for appearances in honor," noting that an "emphasis on how one is perceived need not . . . be narcissistic, deliberatively heteronymous, nor concerned with appearnaces over reality." Instead, it can motivate forceful action.
45. These features of honor distinguish it from recognition as conceived in the contemporary "politics of recognition" literature, the sole basis of which is public esteem. See Charles Taylor, "The Politics of Recognition," in *Multiculturalism,* ed. Amy Gutmann (Princeton, NJ: Princeton University Press, 1994). In a similar way, Appiah's recent treatment of honor in *The Honor Code* too often collapses honor into the mere quest for reputation. On his telling, for instance, the end of footbinding in China happened because of what came to be a widespread worry about its effects on China's reputation abroad (60). Appiah says virtually nothing about a principled code of conduct or the self-respect that comes from living up to it. Likewise, the honor that Appiah thinks helped end the British slave trade is largely portrayed as a one-dimensional concern with public recognition or the respect of others. See Krause, "Review of *The Honor Code," Ethics and International Affairs* 25, no. 4 (2011): 475–78.
46. It is true that the acts of resistance that Montesquieu associates with honor are not revolutionary. Indeed, one might say that the resistance honor prompts in Montesquieu is better characterized as forms of *inaction* than activism. Thus Montesquieu says that "if honor has been offended it permits or requires one to withdraw to one's

home" (*The Spirit of the Laws*, IV.2). Yet some forms of political inaction can be powerfully activist in effect. Montesquieu capitalizes on this fact, which allows him to defend forms of (in)action that have the effect of checking the overbearing power of the monarch without appearing to attack him. An example is his assertion that the *parlements* "never obey better than when they go slowly" and bring "reflectiveness" into the affairs of the prince (V.10). The *parlements* never obey better than when they resist. And they resist not by attacking the king, but by doing "nothing."

47. V.9.
48. V.9.
49. III.7.
50. VIII.7.
51. XX.22.
52. Montesquieu, *Mes pensées*, no. 69[5], 993.
53. II.4.
54. V.19.
55. V.19.
56. Alexis de Tocqueville, *La démocratie en Amérique* in *Oeuvres complètes d'Alexis de Tocqueville*, ed. J. P. Mayer, 13 vols. (Paris: Gallimard, 1951), vol. I. Hereafter references to *Democracy in America* will be inserted in the text.
57. II.3.8, p. 245.
58. II.3.8, p. 245.
59. II.3.8, p. 245.
60. II.3.8, p. 242–43.
61. II.3.8, p. 246.
62. II.3.8, p. 246.
63. II.3.8, p. 246.
64. II.3.8, p. 247.
65. II.3.8, p. 246.
66. II.3.8, p. 247.
67. II.3.8, p. 248.
68. II.3.8, p. 248
69. II.3.8, p. 249.
70. II.3.8, p. 248.
71. II.3.8, p. 248–49 and 247.
72. II.3.8, p. 290.
73. Tocqueville, *L'ancien régime et la révolution* in *Oeuvres complètes*, vol. II.11, 176.
74. II.3.19, p. 255.
75. I.2.9, p. 328.
76. I.2.9, p. 328.
77. One might say that the dogma of the sovereignty of the people generalizes personal pride to the nation or even the species. Democratic peoples retain their pride *vis-à-vis* other peoples, but among themselves Tocqueville worries that they have too fully adopted the mantle of humility.
78. II.3.19, p. 250.
79. II.3.19, p. 251.
80. II.3.19, p. 251.
81. II.3.19, p. 254.
82. II.3.21, p. 269.
83. Forde also notes in this volume that the value of linking honor to democratic norms so that it can support "equal rights and freedom, rather than the glory of a Caesar or Alexander."
84. In this volume, Demetriou similarly insists that "agonistic honorableness" is an important "civic virtue" for pluralistic democracies (2), especially in terms of its capacity to support civil discourse.

85. W. E. B. DuBois, "Resolutions of the Niagara Movement," in *African-American Social & Political Thought*, ed. Howard Brotz (New Brunswick, NJ: Transaction Publishers, 1995), 539.

86. Booker T. Washington, "Early Problems of Freedom," in *African-American Social & Political Thought*, 388f.

87. Waldo E. Martin, Jr., *The Mind of Frederick Douglass* (Chapel Hill: University of North Carolina Press, 1984), 253, 277.

88. Frederick Douglass, *My Bondage and My Freedom* (New York: Dover, 1969), 251.

89. Douglass, *My Bondage*, 241.

90. Douglass, *My Bondage*, 241–46. Emphasis in the original.

91. Douglass, *My Bondage*, 246.

92. Douglass, *My Bondage*, 246f.

93. Douglass, *My Bondage*, 247.

94. Douglass, *My Bondage*, 247.

95. Douglass, *My Bondage*, 247.

96. Douglass, *My Bondage*, 247.

97. Douglass, *My Bondage*, 247.

98. Philip S. Foner, "Introduction" to *My Bondage and My Freedom*, x. For more on Frederick Douglass's relation to and break with the Garrisonian school, see David E. Schrader, "Natural Law in the Constitutional Thought of Frederick Douglass" in *Frederick Douglass: A Critical Reader*, 86; Charles W. Mills, "Whose Fourth of July? Frederick Douglass and 'Original Intent'" in *Frederick Douglass: A Critical Reader*, 104; Diana Schaub, "Frederick Douglass's Constitution," *The American Experiment: Essays on the Theory and Practice of Liberty*, ed. Peter Augustine Lawler and Robert Martin Schaefer (Lanham, MD: Rowman & Littlefield, 1994); Herbert Storing, "Frederick Douglass," *American Political Thought*, ed. Morton Frisch and Richard Stevens (Itasca, IL: F. E. Peacock, 1983); and David W. Blight, *Frederick Douglass' Civil War: Keeping Faith in Jubilee* (Baton Rouge: Louisiana State University Press, 1989), 32f.

99. See Kelly Miller, "Radicals and Conservatives," in *Critical Essays on Frederick Douglass* ed. William L. Andrews (Boston: G. K. Hall, 1991), 36.

100. Douglass, "What the Black Man Wants," in *African-American Social & Political Thought*, 278.

101. Douglass, "What the Black Man Wants," 278.

102. Douglass, "What the Black Man Wants," 282.

103. Douglass, "The Slaveholders' Rebellion," in *Selected Speeches and Writings*, 500.

104. Douglass, "The Slaveholders' Rebellion," 499–500.

105. Douglass, *My Bondage*, 395f.

106. Douglass, *My Bondage*, 396.

107. Douglass, *My Bondage*, 405.

108. Washington, "On Making our Race Life Count in the Life of the Nation," in *African-American Social & Political Thought*, 382.

109. *Time*, 18 February, 1957. Quoted in Stephen B. Oates, *Let the Trumpet Sound: A Life of Martin Luther King, Jr.* (New York: Harper Perennial, 1982), 115.

110. David L. Lewis, *King: A Critical Biography* (New York: Praeger, 1970), x.

111. Quoted in Oates, *Trumpet*, 127.

112. Oates, *Trumpet*, 150.

113. Oates, *Trumpet*, 157.

114. Oates, *Trumpet*, 308, 352. David Garrow reports that some thought King "took too many bows and enjoyed them," and that he tended to forget the movement was a collective effort. David J. Garrow, *Bearing the Cross* (New York: Quill, 1986), 89.

115. Quoted in Oates, *Trumpet*, 127.

116. For this reason, one biographer has spoken of the "alternately dominant strains in his personality—grandiosity and common sense" (Lewis, *King*, 60). See also Richard H. King, *Civil Rights and the Idea of Freedom*, 93; and Lewis, *King*, 109. Miroff also refers to King's "opposing tendencies—to grandiosity and humility." Bruce Miroff, *Icons of Democracy* (Lawrence: University of Kansas Press, 2000), 308, 314.

117. Martin Luther King, Jr., "Letter from Birmingham City Jail," in *Testament of Hope: The Essential Writings and Speeches of Martin Luther King, Jr.*, ed. James M. Washington (New York: HarperCollins, 1986), 302.
118. Quoted in Oates, *Trumpet*, 167.
119. King, *Civil Rights*, 14.
120. Oates, *Trumpet*, 104.
121. Quoted in Oates, *Trumpet*, 424.
122. Quoted in Oates, *Trumpet*, 426.
123. Oates, *Trumpet*, 209, 218; and King, *Civil Rights*, 43.
124. King, *Civil Rights*, 43.
125. Rhodes notes in this volume that "a liberal society at its best would be a marketplace of honor, where differing viewpoints contend with each other in the public arena to inspire us to" diverse conceptions of the good.

FOUR

A Neo-Aristotelian Theory of Political Honor

Steven C. Skultety

It is well known that Aristotle believes human beings to be political animals. What is rarely recognized is that Aristotle also takes political lives to be anchored in honor. For him, honor is not just one value among many which a given people might choose to cherish and praise, or ignore and discourage. On the contrary, Aristotelian honor is the warp intertwined with the woof of power that helps to explain both the order and legitimacy possessed by those who rule.

In this chapter, I'd like to revisit Aristotle's way of thinking about honor, offer a few reasons for thinking that honor continues to be relevant in liberal democratic societies, and also explore whether liberalism can readily accommodate political honor into its theory of politics.

ARISTOTLE'S CONCEPTION OF POLITICAL HONOR

Aristotelian honor is esteem bestowed by rational agents, offered on the basis of someone's value to a community, expressed as a reward. Merely receiving positive attention from others falls well short of honor: after all, nonrational animals can bestow affection, but honor is something distributed in human communities built on perceptions of justice and the good.[1] Second, not only is honor bestowed rationally, but it is bestowed for certain sorts of reasons. Those who "enjoy being honored by powerful people because they expect to get whatever they need from them" do not correctly understand honor, unlike virtuous people who "want honor from decent people with knowledge."[2] The latter understand that genuine honor tracks excellence in a community, and this is why they "pursue honor to convince themselves that they are good; at any rate, they seek to be honored by prudent people, among people who know them, and for virtue."[3] Finally, honor must be expressed: silent esteem or well-wishing isn't honor, because honor is something that is bestowed by a giver to a recipient.[4]

Because honor reflects value to a community, and because there are different kinds of communities, there are also different kinds of honor. For example, there is honor due a spouse, the honor due elders, and even honor due to the gods with whom humans take themselves to have some communion through their rites and rituals.[5] Of particular interest for this essay is the honor that exists among people who dwell together in cities [*poleis*]. These people do not form city communities merely to ensure a more efficient satisfaction of their basic needs; rather, they live in a city for the opportunity to live well and exercise human virtue.[6]

In his ethical works, Aristotle characterizes the special sort of honor that is unique to city life as a noninstrumental good that is valuable for the soul and which is pleasurable in its own right.[7] Honor is certainly less valuable than the highest human good, happiness; moreover, unlike virtue, honor is a mere external good. Nevertheless, while not highest, Aristotle believes that honor deserves a privileged place in our ethical deliberations. For honor is one of those rare and highly desirable goods that we choose simply for its own sake: "Honor, pleasure, and understanding, and every virtue we certainly choose because of themselves, since we would choose each of them even if it had no further result."[8] Moreover, besides being good in its own right, honor is also the *greatest* external good because it is the uniquely proper response to anyone who, objectively, has truly achieved superiority in something good.[9]

Because Aristotle believes honor to be the proper reward for superiority, and because he thinks that exercising rational virtue over the course of one's life is the supreme achievement, it then makes sense that we find Aristotle attributing honor to the two sorts of lives he considers genuinely flourishing—those successfully leading a political life in the interpersonal world of the *polis*, and those practicing philosophy. For example: "it is evident that almost all of those, past or present, with the greatest love for the honor accorded to virtue have chosen between these two lives (I mean the political life and the philosophic one)."[10] The honor for philosophers is based on the contemplative and scientific excellence that they achieve while living in the city, and honors of the political life are appropriate for those who exercise ethical virtues among their fellow citizens. These political honors might be given, for example, to those fighting bravely in war, or to those spending magnificently on civic festivals and activities.[11]

However interesting it would be to investigate the honors due philosophers, I want to focus here on how Aristotle thinks about the honors of the political life, and the very first point that needs to be made is that a political community is one that exists only among human beings who are equal in nature to one another.[12] Unlike the communities of master/slave and household—both of which Aristotle takes to be organized by natural superiors ruling over natural inferiors—a political community is one composed of people who all have the natural ability to deliberate rationally without impediment. The honor found in the political life is thus an honor won among equals.

The natural equality of those in genuine political communities not only makes it distinct among communities, but it also greatly complicates the question of who should rule in political communities. Everyone, Aristotle thinks, will agree to the abstract meritocratic principle that political decision making should be distributed according to merit.[13] The problem, however, is that different people have different conceptions of merit, and merely citing nature will not settle the debate among these competing conceptions. Nature tells us only that, all other things being equal, natural equals are equally deserving of power, and thus naturally fit to rule and be ruled in turn. But in real-world political communities, all other things are *not* equal since cities are made of different sociological parts like the rich, the poor, farmers, soldiers, priests, etc., and each group thinks it possesses some meritorious trait that underwrites a claim to rule.[14]

This is why Aristotle feels compelled to enter the great debate about who should rule political communities: realizing that nature does not provide enough guidance to end debate, he endorses the view that rule should be proportioned to ethical virtue (a trait that does not arise naturally and which cannot be explained only in terms of nature[15]), thinking that this is a far better candidate for merit than, say, how much money and property a person possesses, or whether one was born to certain parents, or whether an inhabitant has simply been labeled as meritorious by those in positions of power.[16]

Now Aristotle is quite pessimistic about political life in most cities, and he certainly does not expect that his own conception of merit will be widely accepted. Indeed, he thinks that his conception of merit would only be taken seriously in a city that is blessed with remarkably fortuitous natural and human resources. But regardless of which group ends up in charge of any given city's decision making, note that Aristotle's way of conceptualizing civic rule is very similar to his way of thinking about honor. Just as genuine honor is given only to a few people who are superior in some way, so too only some inhabitants will belong to the group of decision makers. Just as honor is awarded to those who are rationally esteemed for their value to the community, so too are positions of political rule awarded on the basis of merit.

In fact, there is a great deal of textual evidence suggesting that Aristotle not only thinks of political rule and honor playing similar roles in the community, but that he thinks of the positions of political authority *to be* honors. For example, consider how Aristotle describes the diverse political offices whose number and organization characterizes a constitution. One of the two Greek words [*archē, timē*] that Aristotle uses to refer to these political office is the very same word that he uses when discussing honor [*timē*], and he often speaks of these specific offices as honors. For example, at one point he recommends that democracies try to appease honor-loving aristocrats by creating additional offices in the constitution for them.[17] The clear implication is that everyone understands such offices to be honors.

The clearest identification of honor and ruling power, however, can be found in Aristotle's discussion of the most powerful civic office—the ruling position held by the group that makes the ultimate decisions for the entire city. Aristotle believes that this group, the *politeuma, is* the city's constitution,[18] and it is this group's approach to decision making as democrats, oligarchs, or aristocrats, etc., that will fix the form of the constitution as a democracy, oligarchy, or aristocracy. Aristotle clearly thinks of this seat of ultimate power as being a great honor. For example, consider the way he expresses his concern about installing a small group of virtuous people as leaders in an average city:

> But should decent people rule and have authority over everything? In that case, everyone else must be deprived of honors by being excluded from political office. For offices are positions of honor, we say, and when the same people always rule, the rest must necessarily be deprived of honors. But is it better that the one who is best should rule? But this is even more oligarchic, since those deprived of honors are more numerous.[19]

Note that Aristotle is not here associating honor with how one *performs* in office; on the contrary, the idea is that the offices and positions of authority *are* honors.

Another sign that Aristotle identifies honor with the positions of rule in a city can be seen in his consistent criticisms of those who disassociate politics and honor. Most people, Aristotle thinks, correctly believe that serving in political office is toilsome labor, and they also correctly realize that someone who serves should be compensated. But what most people do not understand is that simply holding office is payment because "this is honor and privilege."[20] Unable to appreciate the honor of office, most people falsely assume that an office holder needs be compensated with that other major external good, money. But that, Aristotle insists, is a mistake: "it is impossible both to make money off the community and to receive honor from it at the same time."[21]

This idea has rather extraordinary implications. If political office is an honor, and it is impossible to simultaneously make money and receive honor while possessing such an office, then it follows that anyone using political power for profit is really no longer holding *political* office. Their rule has gone from being political to something else—and this seems to be just what Aristotle himself thinks: "The people who are not satisfied with these rewards [of honor] are the ones who become tyrants."[22] Indeed, trouble starts not only when rulers think of office as requiring monetary compensation, but when those who are ruled begin to think this way as well. Consider, for example, Aristotle's description of how farmers think about politics:

> [T]hey find working more pleasant than engaging in politics and holding office, where no great profit is to be had from office, since the many seek money more than honor. Evidence of this is that they even put up with the ancient tyrannies, and continue to put up with oligarchies, so long as no one prevents them from working or takes anything away from them. For in no time some of them become rich, while the others at least escape poverty. Besides, having authority over the election and inspection of officials will give them what they need, if they do have any love of honor.[23]

According to the first three sentences in this quotation, most people do not understand the honor of political office, and then view government service as an uncompensated waste of time and energy that does not deserve their attention. As a result, they also do not believe anything of value is being lost when opportunities for office are restricted (as happens in oligarchy) or eliminated (as happens in a tyranny). So long as the officials of the constitution (regardless of their number or order) stay out of their business, they are content. By contrast, consider the last sentence in this quotation: if there are any farmers who care about honor, then they will want to be involved in ruling—even if their participation only takes the form of voting in competitive elections or being involved in the auditing of decision makers.

Because Aristotle thinks of political rule as being political honor, we can make sense of the rather extraordinary claim that honor "is more or less the end [*telos*] of the political life."[24] Honor not only acts as a *telos* because it is an appropriate capstone for the highest expressions of interpersonal virtue in city life, but also because the very shape of a political community—the city's constitution—is a network reflecting an honor system of who esteems whom. Again, we can now appreciate why Aristotle accounts for the lack of leisure in virtuous political life this way: "apart from political activities themselves, those actions seek positions of power and honors, or at least they seek happiness for the politician himself and of his fellow citizens."[25] A proper political life is one spent exercising power for the happiness of citizens—and, as we have seen, this means possessing "positions of power" that in a political society are "honors."

So conceived, Aristotelian political honor is not simply a patina of goodwill, or merely a prize one receives, after the fact, for a job well done. Such honor would be a kind of metahonor, distinguishable from the honor one receives simply as a participant in the network of esteem that structures the political life of natural equals.

LIBERALISM AND ARISTOTELIAN POLITICAL HONOR

Throughout the twentieth century, many have criticized liberal political theory for being too focused on rights, individuals, and the bare essentials of constitutionalism, and for neglecting the other aspects of social and political life upon which healthy communities depend. Communitarians and civic republicans, for example, charged that liberalism permitted an unsustainable level of civic apathy and argued that it needed to be replaced with a different political philosophy.[26] Many liberals, responding to this critique, also came to believe that there was a need for a theory of "citizenship" that could enrich liberalism. Members of all these groups not infrequently championed Aristotle: as opposed to liberal "atomism," Aristotle understood the "thick" connections that exist among community members; as opposed to liberal focus on privacy and rights, Aristotle understood the virtues and obligations of active citizenship needed for successful political order. In short, Aristotle entered the political discussion as a kind of critical ideal that could be used to highlight some perceived shortcoming of liberalism.

Following in those footsteps, I could attempt to argue that Aristotle's notion of political honor continues to be relevant in contemporary liberal societies because it belongs to this critical ideal. For example, I might try arguing that honor is an intrinsic good, the possession of which would make living in liberal societies more meaningful, or argue that honor is instrumentally valuable for the common good, and insist that liberalism must take honor seriously to avoid some sort of social problem.[27]

In this chapter, however, I'd like to take a different tack because political honor seems to possess two rather remarkable features lacked by many of the other "thick" elements like friendship or community within the familiar Aristotelian critical ideal. First, as I will argue in the last section below, political honor is far from being a missing element in contemporary life that needs resuscitating. On the contrary, it seems to me that liberal democratic societies are shot through with political honor and—even more remarkably—are becoming *more* honorcentric over time. Second, political honor has not merely fallen through the cracks of contemporary political thought: during the early stages of the development of liberalism, Hobbes and Locke explicitly attacked political honor, and, as I will argue below, made a point of excluding it from the domain of political theory. So the fact that political honor does not play a role in liberal thought may not be a matter of benign neglect: it may well be that contemporary thinkers have adopted a view of politics that takes honor to have been killed dead by the basic theoretical commitments of liberalism.

Thus, rather than merely pointing out that Aristotle emphasizes political honor in a way that many liberal theories do not—which I doubt would be much of a surprise to anyone—I'd like to ask what I think will be a more helpful and interesting question: even if Aristotelian honor has yet to play a role in liberal thought, is there anything *preventing* it from doing so? Can the concepts which define a liberal theory as such be extended to include Aristotelian political honor in any meaningful way?

A FEW LEADS THAT CANNOT BE FOLLOWED

Before trying to answer this question in a general way, I think it is helpful to grasp why we will not be able to follow the tactics other scholars have used to reconcile honor with liberalism when trying to incorporate Aristotle's notion of political honor into liberal theory.

Consider the work of Michael Sandel. Sandel, a "citizenship theorist" sympathetic to liberalism, has long been a critic of Rawls's neo-Kantian theory of justice, and has championed Aristotle's desert-based theory of justice as offering a more satisfying account. Especially relevant for us, one of Sandel's reasons for preferring Aristotelian justice is that it supports an intuition that someone who is best with respect to some function or role deserves the *honor* accompanying this superiority.[28]

Inspired by this line of thought, we might incorporate political honor into liberal theory in the following way: liberalism can maintain that political honor belongs to those who best serve the role of implementing justice in the political community. Justice provides rules for a liberal society, and honor belongs to those who make these rules into political reality. This way of incorporating honor into liberal theory seems like a quick and easy fix.

The problem, however, is that this brand of liberal honor would not be Aristotelian, for Aristotle insists that honor must transcend "qualified uses" of virtue:

> For example, in the case of just actions, just retributions and punishments spring from virtue, but are necessary uses of it, and are noble only in a necessary way, since it would be more choiceworthy if no individual or city-state needed such things. On the other hand, just actions that aim at honors and prosperity are unqualifiedly noblest. The former involve choosing something that is somehow bad, whereas the latter are the opposite: they construct and generate goods. To be sure, an excellent man will deal with poverty, disease, and other sorts

> of bad luck in a noble way. But blessed happiness requires their opposites.[29]

Ending injustices, righting wrongs, and working to make society just are all acts of virtue—but they are not actions oriented around the pursuit of honor. While honor cannot be won without correct "proportional" justice—the magnitude of a genuine honor must be proportional to the worthiness of the recipient—honor is not merely the face of such justice.[30] Of course nothing prevents us from developing an anti-Aristotelian theory that conceives of honor in this way, but that would be a different inquiry from the one undertaken here.

Sharon Krause's chapter in this volume suggests another tactic we might use: she points out that liberal democracies can only be successful when citizens are ready to defend their liberty, and then argues that mounting such a defense requires (at least some) citizens to possess honor, understood as a special character trait that inspires people to take risks and act with proper ambition.

While I certainly agree with Krause's thesis, we will not be able to follow this route if we hope to show that Aristotelian political honor can be captured by liberal theory. First, it doesn't seem to me that there is anything particularly *liberal* about the character trait that she is celebrating. In general, protecting, establishing, or changing a political order will require some number of people to be willing to stand in the breach where political affairs are unsettled or contested, and ambitiously assert themselves. Liberal societies certainly need citizens who will take risks to shore up the liberal order, but, then again, Plato too thought that his (clearly illiberal) *kallipolis* would need competitive and honor-loving citizen warriors who would undertake risky action in the face of threats.

More to the point of this essay, however, the specific type of honor that Krause ends up celebrating—that needed to defend liberty in the face of (monarchical or majoritarian) tyranny—need not involve participation in government, or even what she calls "public honors" or the "external dimensions of honor."[31] The honor diagnosed by Krause is something outstanding citizens can possess in or out of office, in the public realm, or as actors in civil society. Her way of reconciling honor to liberalism thus sets aside any connection between honor and the political hierarchy of esteem we saw at work in Aristotle's thought.

For similar reasons, I do not think that we could easily find a home for Aristotelian political honor within liberal theory by following the argument that Steven Forde sets out in part I of this book.[32] Forde argues that the desire for honor may have (at least in part) its origins in evolutionary biology, and that the success of liberalism can be explained by its ability to satisfy this desire through its commitment to universal recognition and autonomy. The problem of reconciling Aristotle to this brand of liberal honor is not so much that an evolutionary grounding of honor is incompatible with Aristotelian teleology,[33] but rather that this conception of honor is explicitly *opposed* to possessing "a share of rule" in governance. Forde stresses that liberal honor can be enjoyed equally by everyone in society; by contrast, here we are seeking a type of liberalism that will help us understand the hierarchy of esteem among those who govern.

THE PRIORITIZATION PROBLEM

The fact that we cannot make use of these specific tactics to insert Aristotelian honor into liberal theory suggests to me that there is some basic conceptual impediment that stands in the way of achieving reconciliation.

One reason to guess that liberal theory will struggle to incorporate political honor is that it gives default priority to liberty as an overarching political value, rather than any number of other competing values that might take that position instead (e.g., equality, nondomination, community, aggregate pleasure). Liberals can disagree with one another over the meaning of the liberty they prioritize, and they can also disagree about how frequently liberty can be trumped by other considerations and still be said to have priority. Nevertheless, all such debates take place within the family of theories that take freedom, rather than some other value, to be of paramount political value.

Taking our cue from socialists, we might very well wonder whether a political philosophy oriented around freedom can plausibly accommodate political honor. Socialists, with a firm commitment to equality, have always worried that the liberal defense of freedom, bringing with it some strong protection of individual property rights, necessarily sanctions unacceptable and unsustainable levels of inequality. There simply is no credible way, the socialist critique maintains, to incorporate successfully substantive equality into a philosophy that prioritizes freedom. So, with this criticism in mind, we might ask the following: if the liberal prioritization of liberty brings with it a strong commitment to protecting the rights of speech, assembly, and property, does this not inevitably mean that citizens will ignore honor at their convenience, and that this, in turn, will lead to political honor playing no significant role in society at large?

Some liberals of a libertarian persuasion respond to the egalitarian critique by biting the bullet and insisting that freedom is so important a good that any resulting inequality, however unfortunate, is ethically acceptable and politically feasible. The more common and influential liberal response, however, has been to embrace a commitment to equality or fairness in basic social goods, and then to argue that these are enabling conditions for any meaningful exercise of freedom. With that strategy, liberty still retains its default priority among political values, but now equality is successfully incorporated into the theory in a robust manner.

Could liberalism deploy a similar strategy to incorporate political honor? It seems plausible to me that liberal theory could accommodate honor in the form of basic social esteem. For example, liberalism could argue that any meaningful exercise of freedom not only requires a minimal amount of basic life goods like food and housing, but also requires the opportunity to lead a life wherein one is generally honored by society, or, at the very least, not treated dishonorably. After all, even if people are protected by a fair, rights-based legal system, and also have adequate resources to take advantage of many opportunities, it seems hard to believe that they will take themselves to be free in any meaningful sense if they are regularly humiliated and shamed by their peers as they exercise those opportunities.

But making sure that everyone experiences minimal social esteem is a far cry from the sort of Aristotelian *political* honor I described in the first section, and I doubt a liberal theory of politics could accommodate this honor by conceptualizing it as a basic good that conditions the possibility of freedom.

First, could liberal theory accept the proposition that serving in political office is a good that *enables* the exercise of liberties? I doubt it. Liberalism would never claim that for any given citizen to exercise liberty, she must serve in office. Besides, unlike money or property, political honor is not the sort of good that can be distributed equally throughout a society to all of its members. As we saw earlier, Aristotelian honor is a good bestowed to someone who has superiority vis-à-vis other inhabitants. If an honor-friendly liberalism attempted to accommodate Aristotelian honor by making it an ennabling condition for the meaningful exercise of freedom, it would end up claiming that freedom belongs only to the subset of inhabitants who have the good fortune of occupying political office.

Now, in the history of political philosophy, we do find types of political philosophy that follow that path. Indeed, if we take citizenship *itself* to be a political office that is required for freedom, and so conceptualize citizenship as a reward for some sort of superiority, then we have indeed incorporated political honor into our theory in a robust way. Aristotle himself would surely be sympathetic to this sort of accommodation since he thinks citizenship is best understood as participation in office:

> It is evident from these considerations, therefore, that there are several kinds of citizens, and that the one who participates in the offices is particularly said to be a citizen, as Homer too implied when he wrote: "like some disenfranchised alien." For people who do not participate in the offices are like resident aliens. When this is concealed, it is for the sake of deceiving coinhabitants.[34]

The problem with this solution, however, is that we have transformed what was supposed to be a kind of liberalism into something else. In fact, this kind of political philosophy looks much less like liberalism and more like republicanism.

So let us try a different strategy. Instead of making political honor a basic good or an ennabling condition for freedom, perhaps we could incorporate political honor into liberal theory by using a version of Rawls's difference principle. We could argue that inequalities in political honor are acceptable for liberal society precisely because they work to the betterment of the least well-off. Just as citizens can live in a free and fair liberal society that exhibits great disparities in wealth, so too they can live in a free and fair liberal society that displays great inequalities of political honor. In both cases, we could argue, these inequalities are acceptable for liberalism because they are allowed only on the condition that they enable all citizens to exercise a meaningful kind of freedom.

While this strategy has some appeal, and seems more promising than that which would make political office necessary for freedom, I still do not think that it incorporates political honor into liberal theory in a convincing manner. First, as far as accommodations go, this seems incredibly weak. Consider, for example, whether we say that liberalism is *incorporating* wealth inequalities into its political theory by using this strategy. Liberalism, as liberalism, does not promote economic inequality, nor does it attempt to explain why economic inequality happens, nor does it advance a theory of how wealth inequalities should be distributed and why they should be distributed that way. Of course, nothing would stop someone who is liberal from also developing an economic theory that explains such things; but that kind of economic knowledge would not thereby count as an aspect of liberal theory.

Similarly, liberalism, as liberalism, does not promote or celebrate inequalities of political honor, nor does it offer a theory of how to distribute unequal honors. Again, someone who is liberal could also study government, political science, and the distributions of power within constitutions—but none of that knowledge would thereby end up being a part of liberalism per se. In short, using the Rawlsian difference principle isn't so much a strategy for incorporating political honor into liberal theory, as much as it is a way of showing that the theory of liberalism is compatible with the distinct theory of how political honors are distributed.

But another consideration suggests that even this conclusion is too optimistic. For it is one thing to suggest that liberalism can permit inequalities in political *power* so long as this helps those who are the worst off and who possess the least amount of power. But, as we have seen, Aristotelian political honor is not mere power: it is a reward for the esteem of being *good* or *virtuous*. Could liberalism adopt the view that it is acceptable for some people to be recognized as ethically superior to others as long as this helped the worst off? Would liberalism accept the proposal that serving in government office is a reward for ethical superiority? It is difficult to see how liberalism could subscribe to such views:

giving freedom priority value certainly gives us no reason to value government service over any other kind of job, nor does it suggest that some citizens are ethically superior to one another. Of course it may turn out that some people are more ethical than others, but it isn't a liberal theory of politics that makes such evaluations. It thus seems that this strategy for reconciling Aristotelian political honor to liberalism fails.

I do not want to suggest that these stumbling blocks prove that it is impossible to incorporate political honor into a political philosophy that prioritizes freedom. Perhaps, instead of treating the possession of political honor as an enabling condition for freedom, or thinking of it as a tactic for helping the least well off so that they, too, can be free, we could find some alternative conceptual strategy for linking political honor to the concept of freedom. Nevertheless, like any political theory that prioritizes some values at the expense of others, liberalism will have to accept trade-offs. It will inevitably demote values that would play a greater role in rival political theories. At first pass, it seems that political honor, unlike equality or general social esteem, is one of those values that must be pushed aside.

ALL HONOR TO THE UMPIRE

These reasons for doubting whether liberalism can accommodate political honor rest upon the role freedom plays in liberal theory. But additional reasons to doubt whether liberalism can accommodate political honor arise when we consider the problem to which liberalism is a solution: to which rules will rational, free, and equal people submit if they are to live together in a political community? Any kind of liberalism will answer (at a minimum) that such people will insist upon (1) rules that maximize the liberty of each to the greatest extent possible, and (2) rules that are applied impartially and universally to all.

What will be the content and scope of these laws? Since liberalism is committed to maximal possible liberty, the only acceptable laws will be those that address truly unacceptable problems. If people find themselves confronted with a myriad of catastrophic problems and threats, then they will rationally allow stronger and broader laws; if they find themselves presented with only a few trivial nuisances, then they will only allow laws that are weaker and narrower in scope. Liberalism demands this proportionality of law and problems: anything else would suggest that some other value, other than liberty, is being prioritized.

Hobbes, of course, gives one of the most memorable accounts of this dialectic: given that free and (relatively) equal humans would, outside of any community, find themselves in a state of total war, they will rationally accept a powerful government with sweeping laws: anything less would be a failure to solve the problem and a return to war. Locke, by contrast, does not imagine the state of nature as total war; he believes that rational beings will accept government to make sure that war, when it is threatening, is be avoided. As a result, because the problems are somewhat narrower, so too is the scope of the Lockean government that will meet them.

What, however, is the "war" that both of these early liberal thinkers have in mind? The word suggests violent and existential conflict, but both Hobbes and Locke mean something broader than the kind of physical violence that we normally associate with that word. First, as Hobbes points out, one can be in a state war even though there is no battle actually afoot: "For War consisteth not in battle only, or the act of fighting, but in a tract of time, wherein the will to contend by battle is sufficiently known."[35] But, more remarkably, Hobbes sees the "will to contend" rearing its head every time two people cannot share something they both desire: "And therefore if any two men desire the same thing, which nevertheless they cannot both enjoy, they become enemies; and in the way to their end (which is principally their own conservation, and sometimes their delectation only) endeavor to destroy or subdue one another."[36] Clashing desires lead to an endeavor to destroy, and this endeavor creates a condition of war. The *problem* of war, then, extends far beyond the appearance of violent conflict: it extends all the way to conflicting desires.

We might, at first, think that Locke has a far narrower conception of the problem of war: "Want of a common judge with authority, puts all men in a state of nature: force without right, upon a man's person, makes a state of war, both where there is, and is not, a common judge."[37] Here the problem of "war" appears to be limited to the use of violent force. But as the *Second Treatise* proceeds, Locke begins to sound more like Hobbes:

> Those who are united into one body, and have a common established law and judicature to appeal to, with authority to decide controversies between them, and punish offenders, are in civil society one with another: but those who have no such common appeal, I mean on earth, are still in the state of nature, each being, where there is no other, judge for himself, and executioner; which is, as I have before shown it, the perfect state of nature.[38]

The language of violence has disappeared, and we now find that human beings join together in a commonwealth not simply to avoid violent death, but to ensure that their "controversies" would be adjudicated. Later, Locke broadens the point:

> Civil society being a state of peace, among those who are of it, from whom the state of war is excluded by the umpirage, which they have provided in their legislative, for the ending all differences that may arise among any of them, it is in their legislative, that the members of a

> common wealth are united, and combined together into one coherent living body.[39]

We have traveled from conflict of "force," to "controversies," and now to "all differences." There are certainly profound differences between Hobbes and Locke. But it seems that both of these thinkers see the problem of war as the far broader problem of conflict without umpires—not just the problem of what to do when swords are drawn.

The fact that Hobbes and Locke conceive of the problem of war in this expansive way has ramifications for how they understand the conditions under which free and equal people should agree to live with one another. Such contractors will not simply want a political body to save them from violent confrontations; rather, they will want a Sovereign power to prevent a broad class of conflicts wherein someone who is stronger, smarter, quicker, etc. could simply take something from them without their rational consent. They will want to continue to be as free as possible, but they will also want to have all the nonconsensual vicissitudes of conflict replaced by consensual contracts or adjudicated disputes. Both Hobbes and Locke agree that this is the central problem for which the State is the solution.

Yet this marks a profound change in the subject matter of political philosophy. Consider competition. A competition is an event that determines winners and losers *without* the rational consent of the competitors: in any competition, someone who is stronger, smarter, more agile, etc. takes something from us without our consent. Of course any competition has rules and requires an umpire—without those it would be a melee—but that does not change the fact that the substance of what goes on *inside* a competition, though within the rules, is not governed, predicted, or determined by those rules. The strategy for winning a game of baseball cannot be deduced from a careful reading of the rules of the game, any more than a Chopin etude can be deduced from careful study of a manual on caring for a piano. Moreover, rationally admitting defeat in a competition is distinguishable from rationally choosing the outcome that your opponent wins.

How will the Sovereign of Hobbes or the Commonwealth of Locke deal with competitive conflict? Because war is so expansively conceptualized, it seems that they both must think of competition as the sort of problem to which the State offers a solution. But only two solutions will be possible: *ban* the competition outright as a form of incipient war, or act *only* as impartial umpire among those who have agreed to enter the competition, remaining silent about the substance of who will win and lose. These are the only two options compatible with its mandate.

This all seems quite reasonable, but note that, with little fanfare, the human struggle that takes place within any sort of competition, large or small, has been neatly severed from the official project of political philosophy. And, to our point in this essay, it also means that Aristotelian political honor has been quietly disassociated from the concern of political philosophy—for such honor is essentially the reward in a competition for communal esteem. The Sovereign of Hobbes and Locke has a function that transcends the tedious questions of who is more superior to whom, who is more or less honorable, or even how many honors there will be. The function of the Sovereign is to erase conflict or ensure that it is overseen by an umpire—that is all.

But if the thesis for which I argued in the first part of this chapter is correct, and Aristotelian political honor is political office, then it will also follow that the Sovereign of Hobbes and Locke does not concern itself with the humane architecture of esteem that organizes the political life of government. That sort of thing, which Aristotle thinks of as the political relations of citizens, would reside down within the substance of competitions that people have with one another, not up at the level of the Sovereign umpire.

Interestingly, both Hobbes and Locke follow this very line of thought: for them, the organization of offices, officials, and government is not so much a concern for political theory as much as it is a matter of prudence. Hobbes, for example, tells us that if not by natural force, Sovereignty is attained "when men agree amongst themselves to submit to some man, or assembly of men, voluntarily, on confidence to be protected by him against all others;"[40] conceptually, nothing depends on whether government is made of one man or many. Hobbes later makes the point explicitly: "The difference between these three kinds of commonwealth [monarchy, aristocracy, democracy] consisteth not in the difference of power, but in the difference of convenience or aptitude to produce the peace and security of the people, which end they were instituted."[41] Similarly, after explaining how the majority, once united into a society, may set up government as a democracy, oligarchy, monarchy, hereditary monarchy, elective monarchy, or "make compounded and mixed forms of government, as they think good," Locke declares that "By 'commonwealth,' I must be understood all along to mean, not a democracy, *or any form of government*, but any independent community."[42] Once again, the shape within government—the architecture of esteem that Aristotle thinks of as political honor—plays no crucial conceptual role in the solution to the major problem of war.

What is perhaps even more remarkable than the transcendence of Sovereignty over and above the realm of political honor, however, is that the very meaning of honor ends up being transvalued in the process. Aristotelian political honor is not merely superseded, but more or less demoted.

The first sign of the transformation is that both Hobbes and Locke disassociate honor from the notion of superiority in a *good*, and instead endorse the view that honor is little more than the face of raw power.

Hobbes announces this in a straightforward way: "Honourable is whatsoever possession, action, or quality is an argument and sign of power."[43] It does not matter if that power is ethical or unethical, just or unjust: "Nor does it alter the case of honour whether an action (so it be great and difficult and consequently a sign of much power) be just or unjust, for honour consisteth only in the opinion of power."[44] Aristotle, recall, thought of honor as one of those goods which we "choose because of themselves." For Hobbes, honor possess only instrumental value as it is nothing but the symptom of instrumental power.

The transformation is completed when we conjoin this new conception of honor with the idea that Sovereignty transcends government. If honor tracks superiority in power, how shall we think of any Aristotelian honor that resides down within the bowels of government, a mere prudential arrangement of the State? Compared to the awe-inspiring power of a Leviathan, the power of any given official in government will be nugatory. Indeed, because the Sovereign has a complete monopoly on power, and so any power possessed by an official must have been bequeathed by the Leviathan, it follows that the Sovereign is the sole source of honor in the political community. Hobbes memorably makes this very point:

> And as the power, so also the honour of the sovereign ought to be greater than that of any or all the subjects. For in the sovereignty is the fountain of honour. The dignities of lord, earl, duke, and prince are his creatures. As in the presence of the master the servants are equal and without any honour at all, so are the subjects in the presence of the sovereign. And though they shine some more, some less, when they are out of his sight; yet in his presence they shine no more than the stars in the presence of the sun.[45]

In the presence of Sovereignty, mere Aristotelian honor is not only surpassed, but dissolved. Every possessor of the honor of office is now but a "creature" in service to the Sovereign. All honor belongs to the umpire, not to any of the human beings who jockey with one another in a competition for esteem.

POLITICAL HONOR AND CONTEMPORARY DEMOCRACY

Should anyone care that liberalism, as a theory of politics, seems at odds with Aristotelian political honor? Liberalism has thrived, has dominated political discussion and debate, and continues to define the aspirations of every major Western nation-state in the contemporary world. If liberalism does not include some conception of Aristotelian honor, and if I am correct that it would have a difficult time incorporating this notion into its theory, why shouldn't we simply shrug our shoulders, admit that some ideas are meant to die in the march of history, and then write the obituary for Aristotle's way of thinking about political honor?[46]

The odd thing about political honor, however, is that, unlike traditional chivalric honor that was often linked to fixed estates, families of long lineage, and aristocratic pedigree,[47] it is very much alive in contemporary democracy. Indeed, it seems to me that the core functions of contemporary democracy are essentially Aristotelian honor systems.

First, consider democracy. "Democracy" means rule by the people who are natural equals: any system that is democratic must, in some sense, allow the great bulk of inhabitants to participate equally in political decision making. In contemporary nation-states, the sense in which the people participate is that they cast votes in competitive elections. Rather than pick their representatives by lot, contemporary nation-states create a power market which measures voters' esteem for one choice vis-à-vis another.

Second, contemporary nation-states do not merely offer a market of *policies* among which voters chose. We can imagine a system wherein a group of councilors regularly constructs ballots with major and minor policy options, and then citizens vote upon those policy options. No contemporary democratic system works this way. On the contrary, the voters pick *people*, not mere policies. This means that when citizens vote, they are not only evaluating political ideas, but candidates' character, personality, and competence as well. Thus we find that the political process in democratic nation-states involves personality evaluation just as much as it does policy evaluation. Candidates do not simply submit white papers for the voters' review; rather, they are tested in debates, in interviews, in town hall meetings, in shadow (donor) primaries, in large primaries, in small primaries, and a hundred other venues meant to push and prod not only *what* candidates believe, but also *who* they are.

Third, the number of people who win competitive elections and thus serve in elective office is very small.

Fourth, winning an election and having the opportunity to serve in elective office is considered an honor. Politicians are expected to realize that holding office is an honor and they make a point of describing it this way. Politicians who are perceived to use their office merely for compensation are looked down upon—even if they are judged to be highly effective and competent. Furthermore, it is considered a dishonor to be forced from office, and a dishonor to lose an election because of perceived character weaknesses. Note, too, that during competitive campaigns, contestants do not simply disagree with one another: they seek to portray themselves as honorable and virtuous, and deliberately cast their opponent(s) as being less so. They argue that while they are worthy of office, their opponents are not. Discussing character issues in elections, and using techniques of honoring and shaming, is not some nefarious development. On the contrary, it is required by the logic of competition among human beings (rather than policies) for positions of honor (rather than brute power).[48]

All four of these familiar aspects of our own, contemporary political system should remind us of Aristotle's conception of political honor. Like us, Aristotle believes that political esteem is bestowed by natural equals. Like us, Aristotle thinks of political office as a hierarchical network of esteem, atop of which sits the highest honors—honors that are reserved for a small number of inhabitants who win office as a reward for their perceived character virtue. Again, like us, Aristotle is deeply critical of those who cannot understand the honor of office, and who think of political office as nothing but a job for compensation, oblivious to the high esteem they hold. Clearly many aspects of Aristotle's political thought have no place in the contemporary world—but it seems that political honor is not one of them. Rather than being an archaic value worthy of pursuit only by a Don Quixote, this is a value that animates contemporary political life, even if it does not animate discussions in contemporary liberalism.

Of course, in one sense, there should be no surprise in the claim that liberalism, as a theory of politics, does not incorporate the honor (and shaming) aspects of democracy. After all, anyone who uses the phrase "liberal democracy" to describe contemporary society, and who believes that this phrase is not redundant, tacitly admits that liberalism is not a complete theory of the political world. But if this phrase is taken to mean only that a society aims at freedom and equality, then we cannot assume that "liberal democracy" recognizes (let alone sanctions) an honor regime. In that case, Aristotelian honor, though it may be alive and well in the core features of our political lives, goes on unannounced, underdiscussed, and unanalyzed.

I suppose that some may still think that this is no great loss. Perhaps a philosopher of politics will simply shrug his or her shoulders, admit that honor is part of real-world contemporary democracy, and then dispatch the study of the hurly-burly of who gets which office, and how, to political scientists.

That reaction would be misguided. Aristotle took honor to be the greatest of external goods, a good in itself, and the object of an ethical virtue that deserved to be called an "adornment of the virtues."[49] Isn't philosophy the proper discipline in which to study ethics, virtue, and the good? Besides, consider that Aristotle offers an account of civil war [*stasis*] that attributes its outbreak to both perceived misallocations of money and honor: "Besides, people resort to faction because of inequality not only of property but also of honors."[50] Perhaps philosophers can turn to economics, rather than their own political theories, to determine which levels of perceived misallocations of money are acceptable and still conducive to the general welfare. But it would be astonishing if *political* philosophers had to turn away from their own theories for help understanding the dangers of politics.

NOTES

1. Aristotle, *Politics*, I.2 1253a14–18; Aristotle, *Nicomachean Ethics*, V.2 1130b2. Hereafter I will refer to these works as *Pol.* and *NE*. All citations refer to book, chapter, and Bekker pagination as found in the editions of I. Bywater, *Ethica Nicomachea* (Oxford: Oxford University Press, 1894) and W. D. Ross, *Politica* (Oxford: Oxford University Press, 1957). I will also here use the translations by Terence Irwin, *Nicomachean Ethics*, 2nd ed. (Indianapolis: Hackett, 2000), and C. D. C. Reeve, *Politics* (Indianapolis: Hackett, 1998).
2. Aristotle, *NE* VIII.8 1159a18–21.
3. Aristotle, *NE* I.5 1095b26–29; Aristotle would very much agree with Ryan Rhodes in his chapter in this volume, "Putting One's Best Face Forward," that for a virtuous person, "reputation is important . . . in the sense that one takes pride in being the sort of person that other people can respect, for the right reasons, and where the other people are themselves worthy of respect for those same reasons."
4. Aristotle, *NE* VIII.14 1163b1–14.
5. Aristotle, *NE* IX.2 1165a21–33.
6. Aristotle, *Pol.* III.6 1278b20–25; *Pol.* III.9 1280a31–34.
7. Aristotle, *NE* I.6 96b16–19; *NE* III.10 1117b28–31; *NE* VII.4 1147b29–31.
8. Aristotle, *NE* I.7 97b2–4.
9. Aristotle, *NE* IV.3 1123b17–21.
10. Aristotle, *Pol.* VII.2 24a29–32.
11. Aristotle, *NE* III.6 1115a31–32; *NE* IV.2 1122b19–23.
12. Aristotle, *Pol.* III.4 1277b7–9.
13. Aristotle, *NE* V.3 1131a25–7; *Pol.* III.17 1288a20; *Pol.* V.1 1302b35.
14. Aristotle, *Pol.* IV.4 1290b39–91b2.
15. Aristotle, *NE* II.1 1103a18-b1; *Pol.* VII.13 1332a38–b8.
16. Aristotle, *Pol.* III.9.
17. Aristotle, *Pol.* VI.4 1318b27–19a3.
18. Aristotle, *Pol.* III.6 1278b11.
19. Aristotle, *Pol.* III.10 1281a28–34.
20. Aristotle, *NE* V.6 1134b7.
21. Aristotle, *NE* VIII.14 1163b8–9.
22. Aristotle, *NE* V.6 1134b7–8.
23. Aristotle, *Pol.*VI.4 1318b14–22.
24. Aristotle, *NE* I.5 1095b23.
25. Aristotle, *NE* X.7 1177b12–15.
26. For a succinct overview of these criticisms, see Amitai Etzioni, "Communitarianism and Honor," in this volume.
27. Although they are not focusing on Aristotle, two good examples of such arguments can be found in this volume. See Anthony Cunningham's "Good Citizens: Gratitude and Honor" and Ryan Rhodes's "Putting One's Best Face Forward," in this volume.
28. Michael Sandel, *Justice* (New York: Farrar, Straus and Giroux, 2009), 186–88.
29. Aristotle, *Pol.* VII.13 1332a11–21.
30. Aristotle thus *does* believe that honor is the kind of good that should be distributed according to (proportional) justice: the more worthy the person, the greater the honor she deserves. Note that this is quite different from the way justice is conceived in the Hobbesian-inspired political tradition. Consider, for example, how in this volume Demetriou describes the relationship between this notion of justice and honor in his essay for this anthology: "Justice isn't suited to managing other sorts of goods [like

honor], however. It is difficult to imagine how we could create laws redistributing reputation, for example, or how we might collectively increase overall competitive prestige (a zero-sum good that can be gained only by taking an equivalent amount from others) through cooperation. Insofar as social status is a good, it is a good justice simply cannot govern, and therefore a good that isn't promoted for oneself by creating a state that enforces our cooperative agreements."

31. Sharon R. Krause, "Liberal Honor," in this volume.

32. Steven Forde, "Liberalism and Honor through the Lens of Darwin," in this volume.

33. In my opinion, Forde underestimates the extent to which Aristotle's thought is amenable to the Darwinian view because he casts Aristotle in too Platonic a light, attributing to him an "external" rather than "internal" teleology. For a helpful introduction to this issue, see James Lennox, "Teleology," in *Keywords in Evolutionary Biology*, ed. E. F. Keller and E. A. Lloyd (Cambridge, MA: Harvard University Press 1992), 324–33.

34. Aristotle, *Pol.* III.5 1278a34–40.

35. Thomas Hobbes, *Leviathan*, ed. A. P. Martinich and Brian Battiste (Toronto: Broadview, 2011), 125.

36. Hobbes, *Leviathan*, 124.

37. John Locke, *The Second Treatise of Civil Government*, ed. J. W. Gough (Oxford: Basil Blackwell, 1946), 11–12.

38. John Locke, *Second Treatise*, 43.

39. John Locke, *Second Treatise*, 104.

40. Hobbes, *Leviathan*, 161.

41. Hobbes, *Leviathan*, 173.

42. John Locke, *Second Treatise*, 65, with italics added.

43. Hobbes, *Leviathan*, 100.

44. Hobbes, *Leviathan*, 101.

45. Hobbes, *Leviathan*, 170.

46. For a well-formulated argument that honor has no place in the liberal State and should thus be jettisoned, see Paul Robinson's "'The Honour of the Crown': The State and Its Soldiers" in this volume.

47. See Peter Berger, "The Obsolescence of the Concept of Honour," *European Journal of Sociology* 11, no.2 (November 1970), for the argument that honor based on fixed social hierarchies was abolished by the rise of industrial capitalism and international trade.

48. For a helpful theory of how we might conceive of political competition as embodying an honor ethic, see Demetriou's "Fighting Together" in this volume. I completely agree with Demetriou that an honor ethic would be more helpful in improving political discussions than non-agonistic theories; all the specific principles he identifies as corollaries to this ethic would indeed promote a more healthy "athletic democracy." Nevertheless, I do think that politics is a competition that is necessarily hurtful in a way that no athletic competition can be. At the end of the day, when deciding who should rule over us, we *rank* candidates based on judgments about their intellect, character, trustworthiness, and everything else that makes them upstanding humans. There is thus a species of character assassination that simply cannot be taken out of political competition given the nature of the prize for which the contestants are fighting. What differentiates contestants is only whether they assassinate elegantly or brutishly.

49. Aristotle, *NE* IV.3 1124a1–2.

50. Aristotle, *Pol.* II.7 1266b38–39; cf. *Pol.* V.2 1302a31–32.

FIVE

Putting One's Best Face Forward

Why Liberalism Needs Honor

Ryan Rhodes

A major objection to honor-based ethics is that it places too much importance on how one is perceived. Members of honor groups, it is argued, are concerned with the appearance of "face" to the exclusion of various moral realities. On one hand, they care too much about other people and their perceptions, to the detriment of their own virtue and authenticity. On the other hand, they care too much about themselves and their standing, to the detriment of others' welfare. Hence honor seems to be objectionably illiberal in terms of individual autonomy and social equality, paradoxically focusing both too much and too little on other people. Nevertheless, I argue that this seemingly problematic aspect of honor is actually an advantage rather than a detriment. After giving a number of examples to illustrate the initial objection, I argue for the positive moral effects of concern for appearance in honor, and sketch how the highly visible nature of honor-based ethics serve as a remedy to some of the failings of modern liberalism.

THE FACE OF THE PROBLEM

Consider the following historical encounter between an English knight and a French squire, Nicholas Clifford and John Boucmel.[1] The two men had many times prior spoken of a jousting match between them, but as of yet had been unable to follow through. On the occasion in question, Clifford was traveling with a group of knights through France on their way to Cherbourg, and they stopped at an inn to rest for the night. As it happened, John Boucmel was with a group of knights lodged at the nearby castle of Vannes, who came to the inn to greet the visiting English. When he saw that Nicholas Clifford was among them, he approached Clifford about their past discussions, saying that since they at last had the opportunity to perform their joust, "I therefore demand from you three courses with a lance."[2] The joust does take place eventually, but not before Clifford three times attempts to refuse. He says first that he is not in a position to stay for a joust, because the other knights with whom he is traveling cannot wait for him. Boucmel counters by offering to escort him to his destination himself. Secondly, Clifford notes that his company is traveling without weapons and armor, to which Boucmel replies that he has many arms at his disposal, and still further, will allow Clifford the first choice of which to use. At this point, "it became quite clear to Nicholas that it would not be honorable to refuse the request, so passionately was it made, and especially since the other knights had heard the entire conversation."[3] Nevertheless, he notes that it may not be possible for him to joust if the senior knights he is with do not allow it. Thus he offers, if such should be the case, to joust with Boucmel as soon as possible after the completion of his current journey. However, as historian Alan Baker relates:

> Boucmel would not yield an inch, and replied: "Seek not for excuses: I have offered you such handsome proposals that you cannot in honor depart without running a tilt with me, according to the demand I make." Nicholas now grew angry at the young squire's manner of speaking to him; the lad had clearly overstepped the mark, for although he himself had considered that it would be dishonorable to refuse the request, for the younger man himself to make such an assertion was another thing entirely.[4]

The next morning, Boucmel and Clifford indeed had their joust, and Boucmel died tragically when a piece of Clifford's lance pierced his neck. While Clifford was distraught over this turn of events, the rest of the knights, including Boucmel's lord, assured him that he had done nothing wrong, and had conducted himself as he must in jousting with Boucmel, despite its unfortunate ending.

Of particular interest in this account is the role played by the witness of the other knights. Both Clifford and Boucmel seem to accept that, at least after his first two reasons for refusing are addressed, honor demands that Clifford accept Boucmel's challenge. However, Clifford also judges that the fact that the other knights had *heard* the request gives the situation additional gravity. The implication is that Clifford's reputation plays a role in determining his moral obligations. More generally, if the "demands" of honor are the demands of *morality*, what one ought to do in the moral sense depends at least in part on how one will be judged by other people if one engages in, or refrains from, some behavior. To a large degree, this idea is likely foreign or distasteful to thinkers in modern times. For many of us, our thoughts on this topic would first recall Book I of the *Nicomachean Ethics*. Praise and reputation depend upon others and their perception of us, while our moral worth would seem to depend instead on our own character and actions.[5] Honor seems rather to embroil us in what Kant would call "heteronomy"—founding our motivations on the potential or actual esteem of other people, instead of our own individual judgment. Furthermore, this type of others-based judgment seems also to give rise to additional objections, located within two main clusters of issues: those relating to one's appearance (both in itself and as contrasted with reality), and those relating to matters of an individual's worth and status (both in one's own case and in the relative worth and status of others).

For example, the bushido guide *Hagakure* relates a story of "The Loyal Samurai Cook" who helped preserve his lord's reputation:

> When Lord Katsushige entertained his guest with some dishes of crane, Kichizaemon Fukuchi acted in the following manner:
>
> A guest said: "Your honorable host, I hear that you can taste the difference between white cranes and black cranes, etc. Is this true?"
>
> The lord replied, "It is true."
>
> The guest went on, "Then, how have you tasted the present dish?"
>
> Katsushige answered, "That was a white-naped crane."
>
> The guest replied: "I don't understand how you can tell the difference. Please send for the cook, I want to ask him."
>
> "Let Kichizaemon Fukuchi come," the Lord said.
>
> Kichizaemon, who had overheard the discussion, quickly went into the kitchen and drank, in succession, several big bowls of sake (rice wine). He was repeatedly requested to come (before the Lord). After some time, he went into the presence (of the Lord and guest). Then the guest repeated his question. Kichizaemon's tongue tripped and he lisped in a foolish manner: "White-black crane, nay, pure-white crane or black crane."
>
> The Lord scolded him, "You are drunk. Get out of my sight." (Thus the Lord's face was saved.)[6]

Katsushige's reputation is upheld, but in an undeserved way—his claim is clearly nonsense and puffery. While Kichizaemon is portrayed positively for his loyalty, the result is not really the well-being of the clan or some sort of greater good, but merely his lord's aggrandizement.

Similarly, much of the action in *The Iliad* is driven by status and complaints about it. Agamemnon's worry that his own worth is diminished if he returns his prize leads him to dishonor Achilles, who in turn refuses to fight and so nearly dooms the Greek expedition. Just after their confrontation, a common soldier named Thersites similarly denounces Agamemnon's behavior. While he was well known as an unruly troublemaker who would insult the officers to spark a laugh from the troops, in this case his criticism appears to be both accurate and just. But despite the fact that Achilles had leveled almost exactly the same charge as Thersites did (even using some of the same phrases), Odysseus rebukes and strikes him for his words, seemingly on the basis of his low rank:

> Thersites! Railer!—peace. Think not thyself, / Although thus eloquent, alone exempt / From obligation not to slander Kings. I deem thee most contemptible, the worst / Of Agamemnon's followers to the war; / Presume not then to take the names revered / Of Sovereigns on thy sordid lips, to asperse / Their sacred character. . . .[7]

Hence Thersites's words are scorned because of his inferior reputation. In this instance, at least, his (lack of) worth is seemingly preestablished and taken as given, regardless of any merit to what he has said.

Arthurian legend, too, depicts honor in ways that seem to be quite problematic. An encounter between Sir Lancelot and a knight named Sir Pedivere appears particularly egregious:

> And as he rode through a valley, among many wild ways, he saw a knight, with a drawn sword, chasing a lady to slay her. And seeing Sir Lancelot, she cried and prayed to him to come and rescue her.
>
> At that he went up, saying, "Fie on thee, knight! Why wilt thou slay this lady? Thou doest shame to thyself and all knights."
>
> "What hast thou to do between me and my wife?" replied the knight. "I will slay her in spite of thee."
>
> "Thou shalt not harm her," said Sir Lancelot, "till we have first fought together."
>
> "Sir," answered the knight, "thou doest ill, for this lady hast betrayed me."
>
> "He speaketh falsely," said the lady, "for he is jealous of me without cause, as I shall answer before Heaven; but as thou art named the most worshipful knight in the world, I pray thee of thy true knighthood to save me, for he is without mercy."
>
> "Be of good cheer," said Sir Lancelot, "it shall not lie within his power to harm thee."
>
> "Sir," said the knight, "I will be ruled as ye will have me."
>
> So Sir Lancelot rode between the knight and the lady. And when they had ridden awhile, the knight cried out suddenly to Sir Lancelot to turn and see what men they were who came riding after them; and while Sir Lancelot, thinking not of treason, turned to look, the knight, with one great stroke, smote off the lady's head.
>
> Then was Sir Lancelot passing wroth, and cried, "Thou traitor! Thou hast shamed me forever!"[8]

While he does send the wicked knight to Camelot to be punished, the fact that Lancelot's *first* reaction involves his own reputation, and not the slain damsel herself, at the very least suggests a skewed sense of priorities. While failing in his promise to protect her may indeed reflect badly on him as a knight, one cannot help but feel that the primary motivation for outrage really ought to be the fact of the lady's murder.

An emphasis on pride and reputation, then, seems liable to engender moral failings in a number of significant ways. By caring too much about appearance, one may value illusion over truth, preestablished status over actual merit, popular opinion to reasoned judgment, and reputation over people's welfare. An additional worry is that a strong sense of one's reputation may leave one compelled to engage in destructive—even *self-destructive*—courses of action, which otherwise one would not undertake. A fascinating and tragic illustration of this last problem may reside in Saddam Hussein and the war in Iraq. James Bowman argues that were it not for the former's concern for appearance, and the West's failure to recognize that concern, the war might possibly have been avoided altogether. For by Bowman's lights, President Bush honestly believed that there were weapons of mass destruction (WMDs). If he had known all along that there were not, then going to war could only serve to expose the deception. Additionally, it was not only the United States, but France, Germany, and Russia that affirmed belief in the WMDs.[9] Thus, the natural question arises: Why didn't Hussein comply with weapons inspectors? After all, as Dick Cheney argued on *Meet the Press*, doing so would have been to his benefit—if he had shown that he didn't have them, he would have had sanctions lifted, earned billions more in oil revenue, and remained in power. Therefore, he (and others) concluded, "the reason he didn't was because obviously he couldn't comply and wouldn't comply with the U.N. resolutions demanding that he give up his WMD."[10] As we know, however, there truly weren't any WMDs. What must be recognized is that Cheney's reasoning is warranted only if the potential gains of "coming clean" were not offset by what Hussein would consider to be other, unacceptable losses. Thus, the explanation for how Western intelligence was so faulty in this case

> lies in the Western inability to understand the Arab honor culture and in particular the "tyranny of the face." Simply put, Saddam Hussein lied because he was part of an honor culture that demanded he lie. [. . .] A better understanding of this honor culture might or might not have made American intelligence analysts more alert to what turned out to be the reality of the situation, namely that Saddam was far more likely to keep hidden the fact that he didn't have WMDs than that he did, but there can be little doubt that the failure to understand just this was responsible for the West's mistake.[11]

If Bowman is right, then this example would seem to illustrate everything that is *wrong* with an ethics that gives a strong amount of weight to how one is perceived. Aside from the fact that it is embodied here not by a putatively noble warrior but a wicked dictator, we have someone who cares so much about how he appears to others that not only does he act against his own self-interest, but doing so leads to wide-scale destruction and loss of life which easily could have been avoided.

THE LIBERAL ALTERNATIVE

These, then, are some of the evils from which liberalism is said to save us. Honor is seen as a fundamentally flawed relic of history, well abandoned in favor of modernity. Instead of a highly stratified social arrangement which privileges status and how one is perceived, liberalism seeks to secure our well-being through a commitment to individual autonomy, equality, and a sharp separation between public and private interests. Given the seemingly undesirable features of honor described above, and the contrasting promise of rights for all, peace, and freedom of choice, liberalism would seem to represent a welcome type of moral and political progress.

Nevertheless, a number of problems remain. While liberalism strives to promote an environment in which multiple ways of life can flourish, it is in some ways intrinsically at odds with this aim. Its overt commitments to neutrality and tolerance are all too conducive not only to an unacceptable kind of relativism, but also, ironically, to a de facto exclusion of certain kinds of values. As regards the former, liberalism is generally taken to endorse, and perhaps be necessitated by, a strong sense of pluralism—the standpoint that there are a multiplicity of values among which we cannot objectively adjudicate. However, this is problematic in two ways. Matthew J. Moore argues that the kind of pluralism in question inevitably leads to relativism if it is taken seriously, and that, further, it is ultimately inconsistent with liberalism. Attempting to justify or derive liberalism from a presumption of pluralism cannot succeed unless we "implicitly violate the premise of value pluralism by assuming that some value or combination of values can be treated as supremely important and therefore capable of rank-ordering value systems."[12] By privileging individualism, autonomy, equality, and the like, liberalism cannot claim to be truly value-neutral. Even beyond this point, however, some types of value systems which theoretically retain a place in liberalism may yet be excluded in a practical sense. R. J. Leland and Han van Wietmarschen, from what they posit as "a sympathetic investigation of what political liberalism must require," describe a method whereby "sectarian" views are, and should be, barred from the realm of political deliberation.[13] A full discussion of the process they recommend is beyond the scope of this chapter. In brief, however, the claim is that in deliberating upon political decisions which are to apply to the population as a whole, each citizen must appeal only to considerations which she could reasonably expect other citizens to accept as well. More specifically, citizens must *not* appeal in their deliberations to matters of personal conscience upon which other persons could rationally disagree.

As an example of how this criterion would work, Leland and van Wietmarschen offer the case of "Sarah," who opposes abortion based on her view that ensoulment takes place at conception. Under political liberalism, they claim, this view does not factor into Sarah's deliberations:

> If Sarah conforms to our conception of reasonableness, she believes that her nonpublic views, including No Abortion, are rejected by some of the most competent judges on the issues under consideration. If she were to appeal to No Abortion, she would be willing to make fundamental political decisions by appeal to a consideration she recognizes that the most competent judges disagree about. Such willingness is straightforwardly at odds with the requirement that fundamental political decisions should be justifiable to all reasonable citizens. [. . .] [T]he ideal of mutual justifiability and the ideal of treating one's fellows as free and equal persons give reasonable citizens a plausible motivation for refraining from appeal to their nonpublic views, on our conception of reasonableness.[14]

They note that the recommended position may be a difficult one, in that "From Sarah's perspective, the restriction that rules out appeal to No Abortion is likely to result in a decision to legitimize murder."[15] Nevertheless, under the liberal state that perspective would be inoperant; Sarah and other citizens would ignore their personal moral, religious, or philosophical convictions in political deliberation, to ensure that no such contested values restrict the free choices of those who do not hold them.

Now, I think we should be extremely skeptical of this proposed state of affairs. Whatever one's actual view on abortion, the idea that good citizenship should compel one to accept what she views as legitimized murder ought to strike us as repugnant. Beyond this specific case, however, is the broader framework that sectarian concerns should play no role in the construction of society. While ostensibly making room for the values of all, in practice this would seem simply to bar people of certain stripes from meaningful participation. Political society, conceived as a *community of seekers after the good*, cannot persist upon the grounds that one's most dearly-held values and conceptions of that good are, from the outset, barred from consideration. It is as if to say: "Your most fundamental commitments regarding the worth of a well-lived life must play no active role in forming the larger society within which that life takes place." As Raymond Geuss notes, "Liberalism has for a long time seemed to lack much inspirational potential; it is good at dissolving traditional modes of life and their associated values, but less obviously good at replacing them with anything particularly distinctive or admirable."[16] He goes on to speculate that while we are seemingly stuck with liberalism for the time being, it is likely that

> changes in the world around us, in our politics, our social arrangements, our economic circumstances, or perhaps simply an improvement in our powers of theoretical imagination, will sooner or later dissolve liberalism and render it as irrelevant to us as feudalism or theories of morality based on honour.[17]

In contrast, I argue that a return to honor is in fact the remedy for many of the deficiencies of liberalism. Most significant, and the subject on which I wish to focus, is that the sort of objections to honor described above in many ways misunderstand honor's character. Once we recognize that fact, it is possible to describe a sense of honor which is not only morally valuable in itself, but which can in some important ways be synthesized with liberalism, providing the latter with the missing and much-needed potential of admirability. While the concept of "face" may seem initially problematic, it is justified as a component of public virtue. An ethics of honor recognizes the legitimate importance of how one is perceived to the cultivation of both individual and social well-being.

VIRTUE AND THE REGARD OF OTHERS

One way in which we can see the truth of this claim is to view the connection from the opposite direction; that is, in terms of one's own regard for other people insofar as they likewise embody ways of being which are worthy of respect. That is, their approval or disapproval is valuable not *simpliciter* or for mere esteem, but because it reflects an assessment of oneself in terms of what is taken to be truly noble and worthwhile. Jonathan Lear describes this phenomenon as it pertains to the Crow Indians.[18] Initially, a young man will be assigned a "personal joker" to ridicule him away from shameful behavior. But this is simply a part of his moral instruction:

> By the time a courageous person emerges in the society, the standards of courage have become standards of *self*-regulation. The courageous Crow warrior didn't avoid shameful acts because he was afraid of getting caught and shamed by his fellow tribesman. He avoided them because they were shameful. Part of what it is to be a courageous person is to have an internal sense of what is shameful—and to rule out such acts as impossible. [. . .] This is one's second nature: the ability to recognize the shameful, find it repulsive, and rule it out as impossible helps to constitute what it is to be a courageous person.[19]

This internalization of the standards of pride and shame, then, points to the value placed on actually being *worthy* of honor, rather than a focus on appearance as such. What matters is that one's life expresses what is fine, and that those who might observe one—whether actually or hypothetically—would be *correct* in their favorable assessment. The failure to understand this relationship lies behind what Bernard Williams categorizes as a "silly mistake" in analyzing pride and shame:

> Suppose someone invites us to believe that the Homeric Achilles, if assured he could get away with it, might have crept out at night and helped himself to the treasure that he had refused when it was offered by the embassy: then he has sadly misunderstood Achilles's character. . . . If everything depended on the fear of discovery, the motivations of shame would not be internalised at all. No one would have a character, in effect, and, moreover, the very idea of there being a shame *culture,* a coherent system for the regulation of conduct, would be unintelligible.[20]

Achilles *must* refuse the embassy, because material loss or gain was never what was at issue. The true stakes were much higher, because at its core the conflict between Agamemnon and Achilles concerned matters of personal worth.

We can see this clearly, in three stages. First, in Agamemnon's complaint over his perceived loss of status in returning Chryseis to her father while others retain their spoils. Second, in his boasting and threats that he will commandeer Achilles's or another warrior's prize to demonstrate his superiority. And finally in Achilles's many invectives against him, in which he decries Agamemnon's lack of desert compared to the ones who do the real fighting.[21] Achilles portrays Agamemnon as a coward and a bully who fails to give other men their proper due. That this assessment is probably accurate is made more likely by the fact that, initially, Achilles was objecting not to Agamemnon's treatment toward *him,* but was actually speaking on behalf of others:

> Atrides, glorious above all in rank, / And as intent on gain as thou art great, / Whence shall the Grecians give a prize to thee? / The general stock is poor; the spoil of towns / Which we have taken, hath already passed / In distribution, and it were unjust / To gather it from all the Greeks again. / But send thou back this Virgin to her God, / And when Jove's favor shall have given us Troy, / A threefold, fourfold share shall then be thine.[22]

Agamemnon subsequently takes his anger out on Achilles, but this was in response to Achilles's defending the need to maintain the status of the "all the Greeks." Thus, while he does personally wrong Achilles in particular, there is a deeper divide in terms of what it means to be worthy of honor, and the recognition or lack of recognition accorded to one's compatriots. Agamemnon plays at being greater than he is, and his further willingness to ignore or sacrifice the deserved status of others is what leads Achilles to rightly describe him as a "Shameless Wolf."[23] A true sense of shame ought to have prevented him from dishonoring others, and two features of the conflict and his eventual attempt to regain Achilles's favor are worth noting in this regard. First is that in trying to pay off Achilles with bounty, Agamemnon is essentially offering the same bargain that he himself had earlier refused. As quoted above, Achilles offered on behalf of the army to repay Agamemnon three or four times over for his loss, once Troy was sacked and there was new treasure to allot. Secondly, this parallel is *dis*similar in that no *man* was responsible for depriving Agamemnon of his prize; giving her up was necessary to appease Apollo and save the army from its plague.[24] Thus, Agamemnon's offer is implicitly another assertion of Achilles's inferiority; he deemed such a proposal beneath himself, but it is supposed to be good enough for Achilles. Add to this the fact that Agamemnon committed an outrage against Achilles and the army specifically, whereas Achilles had not initially sought to dishonor Agamemnon, and it is clear that for Achilles to accept the offer would be unthinkable. To do so would be to place a price on his own self-worth. Achilles's refusal to accept Agamemnon's attempted peace offering of gold and treasure, then, constitutes a certain kind of integrity. Its relationship to how one is perceived by others also serves to vindicate the other dimension of this aspect of honor; the nature of pride. For viewed in terms not of an individual contrasted with others, but as an example of excellence within a community, its operations become expressive not of a self-centeredness antagonistic to morality, but the insistence on proper respect for what is truly deserving of value.

In this way the concern for one's reputation, and the essence of one's pride, springs from the reality of who and what one is. For instance, what our aforementioned Crow warrior cares about is not to be thought courageous whether in fact he is or not, nor a baseless regard which is unattached from his own being. His aim is to be a good member of his community; to exercise the *virtues of a Crow*. In Aristotelian terms, there is no difference between the function of a Crow and the function of a *good* Crow, and he strives to be a model of the shared conception of that kind of excellence. One's reputation is important here in the sense that one takes pride in being the sort of person that other people can respect, for the right reasons, and where the other people are themselves worthy of respect for those same reasons. The specification that the other people are themselves respectable is significant, and further justifies the place of reputation in moral deliberation. Part of the objection to considering the view of others morally relevant depends on the notion that it represents a basically unqualified popularity. But Williams rightly points out the importance of who the "others" are:

> Hector was indeed afraid that someone inferior to him would be able to criticize him, but that was because he thought the criticism would be true, and the fact that such a person could make it would only make things worse. The mere fact that such a person had something hostile to say would not in itself necessarily concern him. Similarly, on the Greek

> side of the war the opinions of Nestor carried weight, and those of Thersites did not.[25]

This observation has brought us back to one of the problems raised earlier, but with an added wrinkle. It seems entirely reasonable that if someone reprehensible scoffs at my behavior, it may well be a cause for pride, let alone not productive of shame. If I strive toward excellence, it is the regard of the excellent that counts. That being said, however, could not a hero and a villain both assess me in the same way? Whether in theory or in practice, if each makes the same claim, then it must be equally accurate or inaccurate whichever one happens to convey it. This was the point of the earlier example of Achilles and Thersites. If we take the same criticism of Agamemnon seriously when uttered by the former, but dismiss it when heard from the latter, is this not to commit the genetic fallacy? How can we reconcile this worry with the seemingly correct notion that in terms of shame, the identity and worth of the one who praises or disparages me ought to matter?

I think the answer lies in certain features of hypocrisy. Discussing the nature of that vice, Christine McKinnon notes that part of its perniciousness lies in its implicit perversion of the idea that it matters how we live. By pretending to argue from values he does not really accept, the hypocrite expresses both disdain for the good of which those values are constitutive, as well as contempt toward the moral community as a whole.[26] All this is indeed true of Thersites, who as aforementioned was a frequent instigator of mockery and dissension within the army's ranks. Still, we may ask, does that matter? That is, should not his assessment of Agamemnon stand or fall on its own merits? In an important sense, however, his and Achilles's criticisms are *not* really the same. When Achilles confronts Agamemnon, it is as one who shares a conception of excellence for a warrior, and he convicts Agamemnon of not living up to standards that putatively, at least, they both accept. His motivations concern worth and recognition, according to shared ideals that both men take seriously. Thersites, on the other hand, is motivated only by the desire to cause trouble, create chaos, and get a laugh. He is not an ally of Achilles, a champion for anyone's deserved recognition, nor even concerned as a soldier. Thus, he is not really insulting Agamemnon, or more precisely, he is not insulting *only* Agamemnon, and not for the reasons he professes. Rather, his actions display contempt for the entire Greek army, and serve not only to undermine its cohesion as a unit, but to denigrate the values its members stand for. When Achilles rages at Agamemnon it is motivated by a respect for martial virtues, whereas Thersites's own remarks trade on their disparagement. On this last point, then, when Odysseus describes Thersites as the "most contemptible, the worst of Agamemnon's followers to the war," we can see the true significance of his words.[27] What Odysseus rejected was not the justified outrage of a sincere but low-ranking soldier, but an attempt to sow discord and insubordination from a man who disgraced the station of warrior and tried to incite others to do likewise.

In similar fashion we may also find Lancelot in the earlier example to be less blameworthy than he initially appeared. I noted before the seemingly skewed priorities involved in his concern for his own shame as compared to the fact of the slain damsel. Nevertheless, it should be remembered that Lancelot's initial rebuke concerned not his own honor per se, but that of knights in general. His claim is that by attempting to kill the lady, "thou doest shame *to thyself and all knights*," (italics added) and we might be curious how this is meant to be so. Why should the actions of some other knight reflect badly on Lancelot, let alone all knights everywhere? The reason becomes clear once we understand the two men as embodying a certain role, with specific duties and goals related to the well-being of the larger society. Felicia Ackerman describes how in addition to fighting for their lords and king, knights of the Round Table were

> quasi policemen and keepers of the peace, who prevent and investigate crimes, rescue victims and potential victims, pacify rebels, and (unlike policemen in our society) lawfully sometimes mete out summary, even capital punishment. [. . .] The goals of upholding the kingdom, doing justice with honor and without brutality, and protecting the vulnerable are vitally important.[28]

As essential as those duties are, the knights' role takes on an even greater importance with the understanding that they were obligated not only to *enforce* justice, but in a sense to actually *create* it:

> Nowadays we are apt to take for granted our modern system of criminal justice, where the guilt or innocence of someone is determined by presenting evidence to an impartial jury of his peers. In Arthur's kingdom, however, guilt or innocence is determined in a trial by battle between the accuser (or a knight fighting on his behalf) and the accused (or a knight fighting on his behalf). In a sense, the judge is God, who is expected to "speed the right" by providing victory to the side of the accused if he is innocent and to the side of the accuser if the accused is guilty.[29]

She notes, however, that while it was generally expected that God would indeed speed the right, such was by no means a foregone conclusion, nor did any delusion prevail that it was one. Constance Bouchard similarly states of both history and fiction that everyone knew that the wrong man might indeed win such a contest. Thus the church ceased its support for trial by battle in the thirteenth century, and romances like the *Song of Roland* portrayed the threat of a villain having to be undeservedly freed. Nevertheless:

> in spite of the doubts raised both in literature and in real judicial discussions, there was a sense throughout the late Middle Ages that he

> who won must have right and probably God on his side, not just his strength and his sword.[30]

For a knight to knowingly fight on the wrong side, then, is more than a personal failing. It is in effect a subversion of all truth and righteousness, as a knight's strength of arms is supposed to be not only the instrument but the guarantor of goodness, justice, and God's will on Earth. Hence, one who forsakes or ignores this responsibility instigates villainy which is not merely local, but systemic and far-reaching.

As such, it begins to become clear why a knight's individual action bears implications for the status and abilities of both other knights and the citizenry at large. Knights must have a reputation for both fairness and strength. Unless they are seen, as a class, to possess both the good faith of acting for what is right and the power to enforce it, then the community cannot depend on the provision of justice or order, and the fabric of society breaks down. Hence, Sir Pedivere's disgraceful actions have consequences for knights in general and Lancelot specifically. Given the nature of a knight's duties, the confidence of the populace in counting on their deeds and abiding by their words is an essential condition of the excellence particular to their role.

In that sense, what Lancelot tries to evoke in Sir Pedivere is the realization that his rage-born action is fundamentally incompatible with who and what he is. (Sharon Krause, in contribution to this volume, describes a similar sentiment in the historical case of the Viscount of Orte, who refuses to massacre Huguenots on the grounds that such would be unworthy of good citizens and brave soldiers.) In the same way, Pedivere is—or at least, can and should be—something better than that; one whose power is wielded in service of justice and prosperity, not as a means to overpower the defenseless. Even were he right about his wife's lack of fidelity (and while the text is compatible with that possibility, it seems we are meant to believe that he is not) he would still be in the wrong by seeking to slay her himself. He was clearly beyond the point of caring whether it was wrong to kill his wife, as evidenced by the fact that he was trying to kill her at all. But he might yet have been brought back to his senses by the notion that he was doing something shameful in general. Hence, Lancelot's focus on the disgraceful nature of Pedivere's activities, and even the fact that the latter has wronged him personally, need not be indicative of self-centeredness. Nor does it constitute a lack of regard for the lady—the crime against her is what *makes* Pedivere's actions shameful. Lancelot attempts to induce Pedivere to view himself in the larger context of what knighthood represents: first to inspire him to give up his unworthy course of action, and later in response to an outrage committed against more than just his intended victim. Pedivere had violated the ideals of knighthood almost as completely as possible, and the story ends with him no longer a knight but doing penance as a hermit instead. As

Lancelot declares, "In a shameful hour wert thou born," for Pedivere had utterly failed to live up to what he should have been, the excellence for both self and society embodied by his former role.[31]

CONCLUSION

What the preceding discussion makes clear is that an ethics which places emphasis on how one is perceived need not for that reason be narcissistic, deliberatively heteronymous, nor concerned with appearance over reality. While these may be real dangers, they arise contingently, and not as an inevitable component of honor. Further to that point, the problematic aspects of "face" depend upon a context of *concealment*—but a genuine ethics of honor is instead committed to *visibility*. One who cares not for moral excellence to begin with will of course want to hide his wickedness beneath a veneer of acclaim, exhibiting the vices described. By contrast, the truly honorable person's public persona is an expression of his actual character; he wants other people to recognize the genuine virtues that his life displays. He cares about being viewed favorably, both in terms of his own good, and because he cares about the values his life stands for and their relation to the good of society. This conceptual connection—between integrity, the good, and how one is perceived by others—helps both to explain and to justify the place of appearance in honor.

In this way, we can further see why the person of honor rightly rejects the claim that his or her personal convictions should play no role in political deliberations. The honorable person is unwilling to hide, or to separate her views of what is most important in life from what may enter the public discourse. This is because it *matters* how we live. A liberalism that would exclude from the outset some kinds of values and ways of living from political relevance, however, must either implicitly deny this fact, or prejudicially decide against some values in the name of making room for all. While that process is quite effective at maintaining a status quo and partisan entrenchment, it is poor indeed at fostering actual dialogue and exploration of what is worth living for. As such, the proper response to a multiplicity of values is not insulation, but an agonism of the sort Dan Demetriou advocates in this volume. A liberal society at its best will be a marketplace of honor, where differing viewpoints contend with each other in the public arena to inspire us toward what is truly good. When one is honorable, she conceives of her life as a conscious statement about what it means to be admirable. Her goals, values, and actions serve as a call upon others to emulate her insofar as she is judged to express genuine virtue—and significantly, she recognizes that same call in the life of others. When we truly care about living honorably, we seek not to separate our community and its values from others, but to interact with them, to the benefit of all parties involved. The recognition that a life well-lived is one in which we strive toward a true conception of human excellence, is one that of necessity acknowledges the possibility of imperfections in that endeavor, yet seeks to reform and strengthen itself through the example of other aspirants to that virtue. In effect, we put our best face forward—not to hide our true selves and values, but to express them—striving as we do with other seekers of the good, to communally embody standards and ways of living which are genuinely worthy of admiration.

NOTES

1. Alan Baker, *The Knight: An Introduction to the Most Admired Warriors in History* (Barnes & Noble Books, 2005), 13–17.
2. Baker, *The Knight*, 14.
3. Baker, *The Knight*, 15.
4. Baker, *The Knight*, 15.
5. *Nicomachean Ethics*, trans. Terence Irwin (Indianapolis, Hackett Publishing Co., 1985), 1095b24–25.
6. Yamamoto Tsunetomo, *Bushido: The Way of the Samurai*, trans. Minoru Tanaka, ed. Justin F. Stone (New York: Square One Publishers, 2002), 74–75.
7. *The Iliad of Homer*, trans. William Cowper, ed. Robert Southey, with notes by M. A. Dwight. (New York: D. Appleton & Co., 1849). Accessed through Project Gutenberg, www.gutenberg.org. Bk. II, 298–305.
8. Sir James Knowles, *King Arthur and His Knights* (New York: Children's Classics, 1986), 180.
9. James Bowman, *Honor: A History* (New York: Encounter Books, 2006), 28.
10. Bowman, *Honor*, 30.
11. Bowman, *Honor*, 28, 30.
12. Matthew J. Moore, "Pluralism, Relativism, and Liberalism." *Political Research Quarterly* 62, no. 2 (2009): 245.
13. R. J. Leland, and Han van Wietmarschen, "Reasonableness, Intellectual Modesty, and Reciprocity in Political Justification," *Ethics* 122, no. 4 (2012): 723.
14. Leland and van Wietmarschen, "Reasonableness," 735–36.
15. Leland and van Wietmarschen, "Reasonableness," 737.
16. Raymond Geuss, "Liberalism and its Discontents," *Political Theory* 30, no. 3 (2002): 320–21.
17. Geuss, "Liberalism," 321.
18. I follow Lear in using the term "Indian" rather than "Native American," which he states to be in accordance with the preference of the Crow themselves (n. 1).
19. Jonathan Lear, *Radical Hope: Ethics in the Face of Cultural Devastation* (Cambridge, MA: Harvard University Press, 2006), 84–85.
20. Bernard Williams, *Shame and Necessity* (Oakland, CA: University of California Press, Ltd., 1993), 81.
21. *Iliad*, Bk. I, 123–287.
22. *Iliad*, Bk. II, 150–59.
23. *Iliad*, Bk. I, 195.
24. *Iliad*, Bk. I, 10–122.
25. Williams, *Shame and Necessity*, 82.
26. Christine McKinnon, "Hypocrisy, with a Note on Integrity," *American Philosophical Quarterly* 28, no. 4 (1991): 327.
27. *Iliad*, Bk. II, 301–2.

28. Felicia Ackerman, "'Never to Do Outrageously or Murder': The World of Malory's *Morte D'arthur,*" in Shannon French, *The Code of the Warrior* (Lanham, MD: Rowman & Littlefield, 2004), 119.

29. Ackerman, "Never to Do . . . ," 118.

30. Constance Brittain Bouchard, *"Strong of Body, Brave and Noble": Chivalry and Society in Medieval France* (Ithaca, NY: Cornell University Press, 1998), 129.

31. Knowles, *King Arthur and His Knights,* 181.

SIX

Communitarianism and Honor

Amitai Etzioni

Communitarianism is one of the smallest philosophical schools, as indicated by the very small number of scholars who consider themselves as communitarians, the relatively small number of academic articles and books published that employ this term each year, and the number of citations. Communitarian ideas, however, have a long history, are found in different civilizations and bodies of religions, and are very widely followed. One finds, for example, strong communitarian elements in many modern and historical political and religious belief systems. They make appearances in both the Hebrew Bible (Old Testament) and the Christian New Testament such as in Acts where it is written that "the whole group of those who believed were of one heart and soul, and no one claimed private ownership of any possessions, but everything they owned was held in common."[1] Similarly, one sees communitarian ideas expressed in the early Islamic concept of *shūrā* ("consultation"); in Confucianism; in Roman Catholic social thought (the papal encyclical *Rerum Novarum*, 1891, as well as the emphasis on the Church as community); in moderate conservatism (e.g., Burke's edict that "To be attached to the subdivision, to love the little platoon we belong to in society, is the first principle . . . of public affections"[2]); and in social democracy, especially Fabianism. Likewise, it is reflected in the scholarship of the authors in this volume who are concerned with issues of honor and obligation in liberal societies.[3]

This chapter reviews developments in the philosophical treatment of communitarian ideas since 1990 from one limited viewpoint, that of one scholar's journey, the author of the essay, looking back at it as it is ending.

THE 1980s

The term "communitarianism" was first used in 1841 by John Goodwyn Barmby, founder of the Universal Communitarian Association, and referred to the public philosophy of those concerned with the development of intentional and experimental communities.[4] After that, it was rarely employed until the 1980s when it was used to refer to the works of Michael Sandel, Charles Taylor, and Michael Walzer. Michael Sandel, particularly, was associated with the communitarian criticism of liberalism, the main theme of which was that there must be common formulations of the good rather than leaving it to be determined by each individual by him or herself.[5] Communitarianism hence holds that the state cannot be neutral.

A telling case in point is marriage. The state can limit it to marriage between a man and a woman or include marriage between two people of the same gender—but in either case it takes a position in that some particular set of arrangements are included within the scope of the term while others, such as marriage among three, are excluded. To those who argue that a true liberal state may remain neutral by refraining from issuing marriage licenses—and, thus, leaving it to religious and other civilian authorities to conduct marriages—communitarians respond that, by staying neutral on this issue but not on others (e.g., by definition what constitutes a crime) the state is nevertheless taking a normative position, namely that marriage is not of significant moral import.[6]

All three communitarian scholars held that one cannot deal with people abstracted from their particularistic attributes and put them behind a veil of ignorance and let them choose the principles on which to found the liberal state. As Joseph de Maistre put it, "In my lifetime I have seen Frenchmen, Italians, [and] Russians. . . . But as for 'man,' I declare that I have never in my life met him."[7] Similarly, Michael Sandel argues against the liberal notion of the "unencumbered self," noting that "To imagine a person incapable of constitutive attachments . . . is not to conceive an ideally free and rational agent, but to imagine a person wholly without character, without moral depth. For to have character is to know that I move in a history that I neither summon nor command, which carries consequences nonetheless for my choices and conduct."[8]

The debate about these two core points and related issues ranged during the 1980s and somewhat beyond, involving on the communitarian side, Charles Taylor,[9] Michael Walzer,[10] Michael Sandel,[11] Avner de-Shalit,[12] Shlomo Avineri,[13] Seyla Benhabib,[14] and Alasdair MacIntyre[15] and on the contemporary liberal side John Rawls,[16] T.M Scanlon,[17] Jürgen Habermas,[18] Will Kymlicka,[19] Robert Nozick, Thomas Nagel, and Ronald Dworkin.[20] In representing the liberal position, Dworkin, for example, argues that "political decisions must be, so far as possible, independent of any particular conception of the good life, or what gives value to life."[21] John Rawls writes that "In a well-ordered society . . . persons are left free to determine their good, the view of others being counted as merely advisory."[22] Since then, the debate has largely died down, leaving in its wake what according to some is a compromise. Liberals shy away from normative claims "founded exclusively on the moral argumentation and political experience of Western liberal societies," that are said to be centered around liberty and individual rights. Communitarians concede that most nonliberal societies, such as those grounded in fascism or caste systems, are according much too high a standing to their conceptions of the common good.[23]

Most of the academics involved were political theorists or philosophers. They were not affected by—nor did they cite—a long and rich sociological tradition of studying related issues that reaches back to Emile Durkheim and Ferdinand Tönnies, and was developed since by scores of works including those of Robert Nisbet,[24] William Kornhauser,[25] Philip Selznick,[26] Robert E. Park,[27] and Georg Simmel[28] among others.

THE 1990s

Most disciplines reflect a tension between basic and applied works. Actually they often benefit from each other. Basic work seems to be at the foundation of applied work and protects its integrity. Applied work seems to encourage "basic" thinkers to consider matters they have not previously reflected on, at least to sharpen and elaborate their considerations. For example, the rise of medical ethics, an applied field, has been credited with helping move the field of ethics beyond a the stalemate that had developed between different ethical camps (as well as between moral realists and antirealists), as it required that ethicists move beyond their preoccupation with general principles to address particular cases, that often called for drawing on more than one set of principles.[29] Thus, bioethics developed from a strong focus on autonomy to include concerns for beneficence, nonmaleficence, justice, and, in some cases, even considerations of the common good.[30]

A similar development took place in the beginning of the 1990s when several communitarians applied this "basic" communitarian philosophy to the political condition of the time.

Nineteen-ninety marks the end of the Reagan and Thatcher era, one built on laissez-faire conservative ideas and policies. Societies seem to suffer from poor cybernetic capacity (or guidance systems).[31] Their policy makers hence tend to oversteer in one direction, which tends to lead to reactions—often overreactions—in the opposite direction. In the United States, President Reagan's drive to scale back the government (on the ideological level) and unfetter the market forces reflected a conservative reaction to a very extensive introduction of liberal programs during the Great Society, during the Kennedy era, and especially during the Johnson era.

In the United Kingdom, the Thatcher era reflected a reaction to the strong left policies and powerful unions that favored nationalization of most industries and financial institutions.[32] Both of these periods in which laissez-faire conservative ideas were extolled, were held to have tilted the British and in particular American society too far toward radical individualism. Particularly telling was a study by Robert Bellah and his associates that found that when what they called utilitarian individualism (defined as a form of individualism wherein people are viewed as self-interested maximizers along the lines of what is now called *Homo economicus*) was added to expressive individualism (defined as the freedom to express oneself, emphasizing the liberation of the individual and participation in profound experience and emotion), that was a sign that society was coming apart.[33]

The Spirit of Community[34] seems to be the first communitarian book aimed at a nonacademic readership. Its main thesis was the next correction ought to be not pulling the society in the opposite direction to rampant individualism—but toward a middle ground of balance between individual and communal concerns, between rights and the common good. It was followed by the issuance of a platform. Its drafters and initial endorsers included James Fishkin, William A. Galston, Mary Ann Glendon, Philip Selznick, Thomas A. Spragens, Jr., and Amitai Etzioni. It was initially endorsed by close to one hundred American and other scholars and public intellectuals from a wide political spectrum that struck a similar position.[35] And in response came scores of articles in the popular press, and radio and TV appearances.

In the 1990s these communitarian ideas received a measure of public support and several public leaders in several Western democracies wove such ideas into their campaign, including Tony Blair,[36] Bill Clinton,[37] Dutch Prime Minister Jan Peter Balkenende,[38] and Barack Obama.[39] These ideas also paralleled or resonated with those embraced by the New Democrats in the United States, Germany's Neue Mitee party, and New Labour in the United Kingdom,[40] as well as many Scandinavian parties, particularly in Sweden and Denmark.[41] A considerable number of voluntary associations revised their respective bill of rights to become a bill of rights and responsibilities.[42] And—a group of thirty former heads of states attempted to complement the UNUDH with a Universal Declaration of Human Responsibilities.[43]

Several scholars were rather critical of these popular communitarian ideas and the authors they referred to as "political communitarians." Elizabeth Frazer dedicated a whole book to show that the core term of communitarianism, "community," was so vague, it defied definition and urged it to be dropped.[44] Other scholars argued that the new communitarian position was undermining the support for individualism and rights[45]—and others that it was insufficiently attentive to the common good and especially to authority as a mainstay of a solid society.[46]

Particularly damaging was the association of communitarian positions with philosophical and ideological positions struck by scholars and public leaders who supported authoritarian regimes such as Park Chung Hee,[47] Bilahari Kausikan,[48] Lee Kuan Yew,[49] Mahathir Bin Mohamad,[50] and Russell A. Fox.[51] They extolled social obligations and the importance of the common good and accorded much less weight to autonomy and rights, viewing individuals as more or less interchangeable cells who find meaning in their contribution to the social whole rather than as free agents. The association of the term "communitarianism" with these authoritarian communitarians was so strong that the three leading academic scholars of the 1980s systematically refrained from using the term at all. This resulted with the odd consequence that those scholars most often cited as communitarians distanced themselves from this approach, although they rarely explained their reason for this distance.[52] The "political" communitarians tried to deal with the same challenges by adding an adjective to their communitarianism, calling it "responsive"[53] or "liberal."[54]

AUTONOMY AND THE COMMON GOOD

The New Golden Rule, published in 1996, attempted to provide a systematic, scholarly foundation to the responsive communitarian position. Its main thesis is that, contrary to both philosophical liberals, whose normative commitments tend to privilege liberty and individual rights, and conservatives who tend to privilege social order and authority, the design of a good society requires drawing on (a) multiple normative principles, (b) principles that conflict with each other at least in part, and (c) a careful balancing of these principles, (d) whose point of equilibrium changes as the historical conditions change. These conditions require some elaboration.

Libertarianism illustrates a philosophical commitment to a single sort of normative values. It not merely privileges liberty over all other considerations, including any concept of honor or obligation at the societal level, but treats alternative values as negative hindrances that may have to be overcome or tolerated. Thus, libertarians are quick to deny that there is a "common good"—a good whose promotion might compete with the imperative to respect individual rights. Generally this denial takes the form of a two-step whose first premise is that there can be a "common good" only if there exists some metaphysical entity who is the beneficiary of that good. The existence of such an entity is then denied, with the entailed conclusion being that there can be no such common good. For example, Robert Nozick argued that "[T]here is no *social entity* with a good that undergoes some sacrifice for its own good. There are only individual people, different individual people, with their own individual lives."[55] Similarly, Ayn Rand argues that "there is no such entity as 'the tribe' or 'the public'; the tribe (or the public or society) is only a number of individual men. Nothing can be good for the tribe as such; 'good' and 'value' pertain only to a living organism—to an individual living organism—not to a disembodied aggregate of relationships."[56] And, Margaret Thatcher, while not quite making it to the normative conclusion, famously affirmed the metaphysical claim, stating ". . . who is society? There is no such thing! There are individual men and women and there are families. . . ."[57] That is, to the extent that such libertarians recognize some form of social good, they do so only in reductive terms whereby that social good is understood strictly as an aggregation of individual goods.[58]

The communitarian response to this objection is to deny the starting premise, namely that the existence of the common good depends upon the existence of some collective metaphysical entity, who is the *beneficiary* of that good.

One account of the common good is that it is some benefit done for the sake of helping others with no regard for who those people are in particular beyond their membership in some community, including future generations. That is, the person acting to further the common good is unable to determine who will be the beneficiary of their actions. They do so because of the value the particular good in its own right. For example, basic research, protecting the environment, preventing climate change, and developing sustainable energy sources are all costly projects that will only pay off over the longer run, and then only to unknown, unpredictable beneficiaries. The common good also includes developing and nurturing and preserving goods that belong to the community but no particular person, including the archeological and historical sites and documents (e.g., the text of the Constitution) and the democratic political process.

BALANCING, WITHIN HISTORY

Given that the communitarian position draws on the recognition of several core values as equal in their standings, as basic foundations of the good society, none of which is privileged a priori—the question arises how these core values relate to one another. Autonomy and the common good are two such core values that need to be balanced. The relationship between the two is not strictly zero-sum. Rather, the two stand in a relation of "inverting symbiosis" whereby the two values enhance each other up to a point beyond which they begin to exhibit something closer to zero-sum behavior. For example, when public safety is restored in a community with a very low level of social order, both rights and the common good benefit. This can be seen in Moscow, following the very high crime rates in the early 1990s, and earlier—in several major American cities. However, once basic order is established, the two core values tend to come into conflict and require balancing. This is highlighted by the debate over whether stop-and-frisk is justified and whether the Patriot Act tilts too far in favor of security, undermining rights.

Communitarianism holds that there is no one set balance point that can be found in all societies. Rather, the particular balance between rights and responsibilities, or rights and the common good, will vary with the cultural and historical context, across societies and over time.[59] The fact that communitarianism is open to both universal values and cultural and historical context makes it a particularly useful approach to those seeking to find a place for honor, as its origins are in the cultural and historical particulars, but we seek to make it compatible with the universalism of liberalism.

Communitarians note that societies constantly adjust the balance between rights and the common good as internal and environmental conditions change. Moreover, they often overcompensate by moving too far toward one value when another one was or seemed underserved. They often tend to oversteer. Thus, one might imagine this movement within dedication to core values as akin to a marble moving in a bowl that is subject to outside forces. Though the marble will swing back and forth over the center of the bowl (the metaphorical optimal balance point), there is a risk that the marble will shoot up over the lip of the bowl, making a return to the bowl's nadir impossible. This metaphorical event stands in for the society that dissolves into irreparable chaos (e.g., Syria in 2011–2013) or breakup (e.g., the former Yugoslavia).

Although critics have challenged the very concept of balance,[60] and advocates often champion one core value over all others, the courts of democratic societies and their legislatures are clearly balancing, and very much in the communitarian way, without being aware of this philosophy or at least its terminology.

Both the Fourth and Fifth Amendments of the U.S. Constitution illustrate this point. Unlike the First Amendment, which states "Congress shall make no law" and is, hence, quite absolute, centering on one core value, the Fourth Amendment states that people's rights are only protected "against unreasonable searches and seizures," with the implication being that there is a whole category of searches that *are* allowed, e.g., when there is "compelling public interest"—a legal term for the common good. Similarly, the Fifth Amendment balances individual property rights with the common good, decreeing that the seizing of property is not necessarily forbidden, but must involve compensation paid to the original owner.

COMMUNITY, THE THIRD SECTOR, AND "SOFT" COMMUNITARIANISM

Much of the public debate about basic principles concerning societal design has focused for the last two centuries on the role of the coercive sources of societal organization (the state)—versus that of voluntary transactions and exchanges (the economy). In this realm as well strong advocates struck positions that centered on one principle ("That government is best which governs least," versus encompassing nationalization and central planning) while in effect all societies draw on some kind of balancing of the two or they become high dysfunctional.

Communitarianism leapfrogged this debate by pointing out that it overlooks the importance of the third sector, composed of families, local communities, voluntary associations, religious organizations, and numerous social groupings including racial, ethnic, professional/vocational, and others. A very large volume of social transactions take place in the third sector, and these heed different principles than either the state or the government. Recognizing this third sector makes communitarianism an attractive perspective for those concerned with honor, as honor codes are mainly formulated and enforced by these smaller, cohesive groups.

To understand these principles one must take into account that individuals are not freestanding agents who make independent choices based upon rational deliberations that led them to what will best serve their self-interest. That is, they are not *Homo economicus*, a concept that was applied well beyond the economic realm to describe the world of politics (assuming the voters are rational agents out to serve their self-interest) and even in social life (including crime, sex, and religious life).[61]

Communitarianism, drawing on sociology and social psychology, pointed out that individuals are, as Aristotle put it, social animals. That meant that they have bonds with others (e.g., family and community members) which affect their preferences and choices in two major ways: the original formation of these preferences during socialization, when the values of their particular communities became part of their selves. Hence they come to view what the community prescribes, including particular honor codes, as lines of actions they freely chose! Second, the bonds serve as a source of continuous subconscious signals that use approbation and social censure to establish preferences or reformulate them. These key observations, communitarians warned, should not be interpreted to mean that people have no degrees of freedom, are fully socially determined, but that the range of these choices is limited by people's social bonds. (Academics, public intellectuals, and "bohemians"—those who live in the Village, Castro, or Left Bank—have unusually high degree of freedom because of the social structure of their sociological environment, but should not project those on others).

Many consequences follow from the understanding of the social nature of individuals. Of particular interest to communitarianism is (a) that people often act in groupings rather than as individuals (hence the great importance of social movements such as the civil rights movement in societal change) and (b) the social bonding provides a major and distinct source of social order, a "soft" one.[62] The reason is that when people abide by norms due to informal social controls, to gain approbation of others to whom they are bonded, or avoid their censure, these "control" mechanisms—leave the ultimate choice to the person in contrast to outright coercion. (Compare the sign "Do not even think about parking here—hospital fire lane!" to a steel barrier or a tow truck).

One ought to further note that informal social controls, including codes of honor and their social enforcement, are essential because the volume of transactions in a modern society is so large that there never can be enough accountants, inspectors, border guards, custom officials, and police to limit antisocial behavior to a level a free society can tolerate. Moreover, these official enforcers themselves need to be policed, as has long been captured in the refrain, "Who Will Guard the Guardians?" Hence the only way a desired level of civility can be attained is if (a) a large number of the members of society (including the law enforcement personnel) will "behave" because they believe that it is their civil or moral duty and (b) a good part of the enforcement will be left to informal social controls, which, to reiterate, draw on limited privacy.

MORAL DIALOGUES VS. REASONING

Given the special import communitarianism attributes to the social nature of people and hence informal social controls and communities, in maintaining noncoercive sources of social order—two major questions arise regarding the substance of the norms that guide behavior. Are they morally acceptable or unacceptable? And who will judge their standing? These questions arise because informal social controls, the foundations of communal order, are not merely based on communal pressure—on granting and withholding social approbations and censure—but also rely on sorting out what the community considers morally appropriate. That is, the particular content whose dictates the communal pressures seek to suppress or uphold. The pressures are like pipelines: the stronger they are, the more volume they can carry. The social norms, behavioral specifications of values, are what flows through these pipelines.

The answer to the twin questions centers around two key concepts: moral dialogues and deontological values. The normative content of communal pressures is constantly edited, formulated, and reformulated, through discussions among members of the community over the dinner table, in places of worship, at the water cooler or coffee pot at places of work, at community pools, and during other social gatherings. Recent examples in the United States include gay marriages, deficits, and gun control.

These moral dialogues should not be confused with the kind of reasoned deliberation political theory and philosophy often explore, the idealized give-and-take of the agora or town hall meeting. These are viewed as deliberations based on reason, ideally evidence-driven, cool, and logical. For instance, consider the debates over the death penalty. In such a discussion, one would focus on the empirical question of whether or not the death penalty is effective at deterring crime. By contrast, moral dialogues engage values, asking, in this case, whether it is ever appropriate for the state to deliberately take a human life.

Note that the precept of moral dialogues is distinct from Habermas's conception of communicative action. For Habermas, the primary challenge of society is how to integrate people who are increasingly alienated from past social institutions and traditions ("disenchanted") and who have different ends, beliefs, and cultural presuppositions.[63] His solution is to call upon social institutions to facilitate what he calls "communicative action"—a form of communication wherein people forego appealing to one another's self-interest (as per coercive threats or market transactions) and, instead, attempt to arrive at some sort of shared end which provides them shared reason to pursue a given course of action.[64] To use Habermas's language, the reasoning process might express itself purely in terms of technical-pragmatic claims rather than in rightness claims or authenticity claims.

More importantly, Habermas calls for neutral proceduralism which communitarians hold does not suffice, and hence the need for moral dialogues to sort out shared formulations of the good. Thus, Habermas holds that participants must follow basic rules such as staying on topic and responding directly to objections and arguments, an improved set of Roberts's Rules of Order. More generally, Habermas suggests that the extent to which one can have faith in the validity of an argument depends upon the extent to which that argument has been rigorously tested, e.g., subjected to a battery of counterexamples and thought experiments, exposed to a variety of counterarguments and objections, etc. Thus, it is not enough that participants follow basic argumentative procedures. Rather, the entire discussion must be structured in accordance with rules that allow for rigorous testing of arguments. Habermas therefore argues that (a) all relevant voices are included in the debate, (b) each participant is given an equal opportunity to participate in the debate, (c) each participant speaks honestly such that they deceive neither themselves nor others, and (d) the participants are free from any sort of coercion as they participate in the process. In this way, Habermas avoids questions of normative value and, instead, frames deliberations as a set of neutral procedures and rules.[65]

Communitarians show that contrary to a widely held belief that moral dialogues lead to prolonged confrontations without resolutions (e.g., about abortion), most moral dialogues do lead to new shared moral understandings, which in turn change behavior, as they are undergirded by informal social controls. Examples include the changed attitudes toward minorities, women, people of different sexual orientations, and the environment.

POST NATIONALISM

To the contemporary ear, it may seem difficult to sustain the argument that nationalism, as a public philosophy that accords a strong emotional and ideological standing to one's own community over all others, is deeply associated with the value of liberty. Nationalism these days tends to bring to mind blind loyalty to the state, xenophobia, and subjugation to demagogues. Historically, though, nationalism largely (far from exclusively) was associated with the breaking up of empires and colonial regimes, allowing major ethnic groups to gain self-determination rather than being governed by others. It was the ideological force that nurtured the social movements that led to the formation of the various Balkan states out of the Austro-Hungarian Empire; the Latin American nations out of the Spanish, Portuguese, and other empires; and many nations of Africa and Asia. Today this kind of nationalism can be observed on the West Bank, where the Palestinians seek to govern themselves in a nation of their own.

In much of the rest of the world, though, nationalism, as at least this communitarian sees it, has become hindrance to a government that will truly serve the people. The main reason is that technological and economic forces are increasingly transnational while the institutions of governance and of bonds remain largely national. As a result, all but the most powerful nations are buffeted by forces beyond their control, and even those considered superpowers cannot effectively manage their economies, security, and environment (climate included). There seems to be a need to form communities, the basis of soft order and source of legitimacy for the state, and develop a layer that is coextensive with the scope of the technological and economic forces. (I write a layer, because just as lower level communities do not disappear, nor the need for them, when nations are formed, so nations may well continue but need to be encased in overarching communities). The EU is a well-known regional attempt to form such a supranational community, and one that is hindered by nationalism. Other examples of attempts to form such communities all failed.[66] Nationalism is on the rise, so are anti-immigration sentiments and anti-EU feelings. Nationalism is also on the rise in Japan and China and elsewhere. Liberalism long sought to focus on universal ideals, especially individual, human rights. How to complement with them with a sense of the common good that encompasses the global community is the challenge for communitarians—as long as they accept that there can be layers upon layers of communal bonding, rather than treating particularistic, local (or national) communities as ultimate.[67]

HONOR AS A COMMUNITARIAN CONCEPT

All societies have a concept of honor, although they use different words or labels to express that which they honor. Honoring serves to highlight which element of character and behavior the community holds in specially high regard, is keen to encourage, and appreciates by paying homage. The values that are flagged in this way are sorted out by moral dialogues (discussed above). They are introduced by educational means at home and in schools, and they are fostered through informal social controls. These controls show respect to those who live up to honorable codes of conduct and disapprove of those who try, but fail, even more than of those who never set out to excel in this way.

While all societies have a concept of honor, they differ a great deal from each other and over time in what they considerable honorable. For some it is poetry (especially in Iran and Russia), for some it is excelling in warfare (e.g. the knights in the Middle Ages) and for others it is learning (e.g. the Literati in ancient China and for students of the Torah in traditional Judaism).

Although honor has social dimensions, as just indicated, it is affected by moral dialogues and promoted by informal social controls, and it has a strong inner base. Ultimately the person who feels obligated, "honor bound," to live up to whatever his or her concept of honor prescribes, holds that he or she must follow the expected course because it is the right way to conduct themselves, not to please or impress others.

NOTES

I am indebted to Jesse Spafford for his extensive research assistance on this paper.

1. Acts 4:32, *New Revised Standard Bible.*
2. Edmund Burke, *Reflections on the Revolution in France,* ed. J. G. A. Pockock (Indianapolis: Hackett Publishing Co., 1987), 41.
3. See especially in this volume Sharon Krause, "Liberal Honor," and Ryan Rhodes, "Putting One's Best Face Forward: Why Liberalism Needs Honor." Anthony Cunningham's chapter "Good Citizens: Gratitude and Honor" particularly touches on communitarian concerns about the liberal forces that erode habits necessary for social harmony and cooperation in liberal societies.
4. Ronald George Garnett, *Co-Operation and the Owenite Socialist Communities in Britain 1825–45* (Manchester: University of Manchester Press, 1972), 24, 38.
5. Michael Sandel, *Liberalism and the Limits of Justice* (New York: Cambridge University Press, 1982).

6. Milton C. Regan Jr., "Morality, Fault, and Divorce Law," in *Marriage in America: A Communitarian Perspective*, ed. Martin King Whyte (Lanham, MD: Rowan & Littlefield, 2000), 220. See also: William A. Galston, "The Law of Marriage and Divorce: Options for Reform," in *Marriage in America: A Communitarian Perspective*, ed. Martin King Whyte (Lanham MD: Rowman & Littlefield, 2000), and Amitai Etzioni, *The Spirit of Community: The Reinvention of American Society* (New York: Crown Books, 1993), 81–85.

7. Joseph de Maistre, *Considerations on France*, trans. Richard A. Lebrun (Montreal: McGill-Queen's University Press, 1974), 97.

8. Michael Sandel, "The Procedural Republic and the Unencumbered Self," *Political Theory* 12, no. 1 (1984): 81–96.

9. Charles Taylor, "Cross-Purposes: The Liberal-Communitarian Debate," in *Liberalism and the Moral Life*, ed. N. Rosenblum (Cambridge, MA: Harvard University Press, 1989).

10. Michael Walzer, *Spheres of Justice* (Oxford: Basil Blackwell, 1983).

11. Michael Sandel, *Liberalism and the Limits of Justice* (New York: Cambridge University Press, 1982).

12. Dan Avnon and Avner de-Shalit, "Liberalism Between Promise and Practice," in *Liberalism and Its Practice*, eds. Dan Avnon and Avner de-Shalit (London: Routledge, 1999).

13. Shlomo Avineri and Avner de-Shalit, "Introduction," in *Communitarianism and Individualism*, eds. Shlomo Avineri and Avner de-Shalit (Oxford: Oxford University Press, 1992).

14. Seyla Benhabib. "Autonomy, Modernity, and Community: Communitarianism and Critical Social Theory in Dialogue," in *Cultural-Political Interventions in the Unfinished Project of Enlightenment*, eds. Axel Honneth et al., (Cambridge, MA: MIT Press, 1997).

15. Alasdair MacIntyre, *After Virtue* (South Bend, IN: Notre Dame University Press, 1984).

16. John Rawls, *Political Liberalism* (New York: Columbia University Press, 1993).

17. Thomas M. Scanlon, "Rawls' Theory of Justice," *University of Pennsylvania Law Review* 121, no. 5 (1973): 1020–69.

18. Jürgen Habermas, "The New Conservatism: Cultural Criticism and the Historians' Debate," in *Multiculturalism and the Politics of Recognition*, ed. Amy Gutmann (Princeton, NJ: Princeton University Press, 1994).

19. Will Kymlicka, *Liberalism, Community, and Culture* (Oxford: Clarendon Press, 1989). See also: Will Kymlicka, "Appendix I: Some Questions about Justice and Community," in *Communitarianism and Its Critics*, ed. Daniel Bell (Oxford: Clarendon Press, 1993).

20. Ronald Dworkin, *A Matter of Principle* (Cambridge, MA: Harvard University Press, 1985).

21. Ronald Dworkin, "Liberalism," in *Public and Private Morality*, ed. Stuart Hampshire (Cambridge: Cambridge University Press, 1978), 127.

22. John Rawls, *A Theory of Justice* (Cambridge: Belknap Press, 1971), 448.

23. Daniel Bell, "Communitarianism," *The Stanford Encyclopedia of Philosophy*, ed. Edward N. Zalta (2013), http://plato.stanford.edu/entries/communitarianism/.

24. Robert A. Nisbet, *Community Power* (New York: Oxford University Press, 1962).

25. William Kornhauser, *The Politics of Mass Society* (Glencoe, IL: The Free Press, 1959).

26. Philip Selznick, "The Idea of a Communitarian Morality," *California Law Review* 75, no. 1 (1987): 445–63.

27. Robert E. Park and Ernest W. Burgess, *The City* (Chicago: University of Chicago Press, 1967).

28. Georg Simmel, "The Web of Group Affiliations," in *Conflict and the Web of Group Affiliations*, trans. R. Benedix (New York: Free Press, 1955).

29. Stephen Toumlin, "How Medicine Saved the Life of Ethics," in *Bioethics: An Introduction to the History, Methods, and Practice*, 3rd ed., eds. Nancy S. Jecker, Albert R. Johnson, and Robert A. Pearlman (Burlington, MA: Jones & Bartlett Learning, 2012), 26–27.

30. Tom L. Beauchamp and James F. Childress, *Principles of Biomedical Ethics*, 6th edn (New York: Oxford University Press, 2009).

31. For more on such systems, see Amitai Etzioni, *The Active Society: A Theory of Societal and Political Processes* (New York: Collier-MacMillan, 1968).

32. This goal of nationalization was even enshrined in the constitution of the Labour Party whose Clause IV exhorted the party "to secure for the workers by hand or by brain the full fruits of their industry and the most equitable distribution thereof that may be possible on the basis of the common ownership of the means of production, distribution and exchange, and the best obtainable system of popular administration and control of each industry or service." Jim Tomlinson "Labour and the Economy," in *Labour's First Century*, eds. Duncan Tanner, Pat Thane, and Nick Tiratsoo (Cambridge: Cambridge University Press, 2000), 51.

33. Robert Bellah et al., *Habits of the Heart*, 2nd ed. (Oakland, CA: University of California Press, 1996), 333–35.

34. Amitai Etzioni, *The Spirit of Community: Rights, Responsibilities and the Communitarian Agenda* (New York: Crown Books, 1993).

35. The Communitarian Network, "Responsive Communitarian Platform," http://communitariannetwork.org/about-communitarianism/responsive-communitarian-platform/ .

36. Elizabeth Frazer, *The Problem of Communitarian Politics: Unity and Conflict* (Oxford: Oxford University Press, 1999), 41.

37. Sarah Ferguson, "Communitarian Manifesto," *The Village Voice*, August 15, 1992.

38. Paul van Seters, "On Moral Globalization," *The Communitarian Network*, April 2006. http://www.gwu.edu/~ccps/ThirdPlaceWinnerEssayContest.htm

39. Gregory Ferenstein, "Obama's Shift Towards Communitarianism," *The Daily Beast*, June 30, 2013, http://www.thedailybeast.com/articles/2013/06/30/obama-s-shift-toward-communitarianism.html.

40. Paul van Seters, *Communitarianism in Law and Society* (Lanham, MD: Rowman & Littlefield, 2006), 6.

41. Amitai Etzioni, *My Brother's Keeper: A Memoir and a Message* (Lanham, MD: Rowman & Littlefield, 2003), 356–58.

42. Such bills can be found in places as diverse as proposals by the Labour Party in the United Kingdom and the US Advisory Commission on Consumer Protection and Quality in the Health Care Industry, school districts, and the American Catholic Council. Eric Metcalfe, "Rights and Responsibilities," *Justice Journal* 4, no. 2 (2007).

43. Sue L. T. McGregor, "Human Responsibility Movement Initiatives: A Comparative Analysis," *In Factis Pax* 7, no. 1 (2013): 1–26.

44. Elizabeth Frazer, *The Problems of Communitarian Politics: Unity and Conflict* (Oxford: Oxford University Press, 1999). In response to similar objections I sought to clarify the notion, defining "community" as "a web of affect-laden relationships among a group of individuals, relationships that often crisscross and reinforce one another (rather than merely one-on-one or chainlike individual relationships), and a measure of commitment to a set of shared values, norms, and meanings, and a shared history and identity—in short, to a particular culture." Amitai Etzioni, *The New Golden Rule: Community and Morality in a Democratic Society* (New York: Basic Books, 1996), 127.

45. For example: Will Kymlicka, "Appendix I: Some Questions about Justice and Community," in *Communitarianism and Its Critics*, ed. Daniel Bell (Oxford: Clarendon Press, 1993). Amy Gutmann remarked that communitarians "want us to live in Salem." "Communitarian Critics of Liberalism," *Philosophy and Public Affairs* 14, no. 3 (Summer 1985): 319.

46. Though not responding directly to the platform of the political communitarians, authoritarian communitarians defend the position that society must be much less attentive to individual rights than the ideal society envisioned by political communitarians. These include: Russell A. Fox, "Confucian and Communitarian Responses to Liberal Democracy," *The Review of Politics* 59, no. 3 (1997): 561–92.

47. Chang Kyung-Sup, "The Anti-Communitarian Family? Everyday Conditions of Authoritarian Politics in South Korea," in *Communitarian Politics in Asia*, ed. Chua Beng Huat (London, Routledge, 2004), 65–67.

48. Bilahari Kausikan, "Asian versus 'Universal' Human Rights," *The Responsive Community* 7, no. 3 (Summer 1997).

49. Daniel A. Bell, "A Communitarian Critique of Authoritarianism: The Case of Singapore," *Political Theory* 25, no. 1 (Feb. 1997): 6–32.

50. Matahir Bin Mohamad and Ishihara Shintaro, "*'No' to ieru Ajia: tai obei eno hosaku* [The Asia That Can Say 'No': Cards Against the West]," (Tokyo: Kobunsha, 1994).

51. Russell A. Fox, "Confucian and Communitarian Responses to Liberal Democracy," *The Review of Politics* 59, no. 3 (1997): 561–92.

52. Charles Taylor, "The Politics of Recognition" in *Multiculturalism and 'The Politics of Recognition*,' ed. Amy Gutmann (Princeton, NJ: Princeton University Press, 1992).

53. *The Communitarian Network*, "Responsive Communitarian Platform," http://communitariannetwork.org/about-communitarianism/responsive-communitarian-platform/ .

54. Philip Selznick, "Foundations of Communitarian Liberalism," in *The Essential Communitarian Reader*, ed. Amitai Etzioni (Lanham, MD: Rowman & Littlefield, 1998).

55. Robert Nozick, *Anarchy, State, and Utopia* (New York: Basic Books, 1974), 32–33. Nozick's position on this point reportedly evolved over time.

56. Ayn Rand, *Capitalism: The Unknown Ideal* (New York: Penguin, 1986), 20.

57. Margaret Thatcher, as quoted by *The Spectator*, "Margaret Thatcher in Quotes," April 8, 2013, http://blogs.spectator.co.uk/coffeehouse/2013/04/margaret-thatcher-in-quotes/.

58. Charles Taylor, "Cross-Purposes: The Liberal-Communitarian Debate," in *Debates in Contemporary Political Philosophy*, eds. Derek Matravers and Jon Pike (New York: Routledge, 2003), 195.

59. For more on the subject of balance, see: Laurence H. Tribe, "We Can Strike a Balance on Civil Liberties," *The Responsive Community* 12, no. 1 (2002): 28–31.

60. Daniel Solove, *Nothing to Hide: The False Tradeoff Between Privacy and Security* (New Haven, CT: Yale University Press, 2011), 56–60.

61. For example: Gary S. Becker, "Altruism, Egoism, and Genetic Fitness: Economics and Sociobiology," *Journal of Economic Literature* 14, no. 3 (1976): 817–26.

62. For more on "soft communitarianism," see Jonathan Rauch, "Conventional Wisdom: Rediscover the Social Norms That Stand Between Law and Libertinism," *Reason*, February 2000, http://www.jonathanrauch.com/jrauch_articles/hidden_law_2_why_i_am_communitarian/ .

63. Kieran Healy, "Sociology," in *A Companion to Contemporary Political Philosophy*, eds. Robert E. Goodin, Philip Petit, and Thomas Pogge, vol. 2, 2nd edn (Hoboken, NJ: Blackwell Publishing, 2012), 99.

64. James Bohman and William Rehg, "Jürgen Habermas," in *The Stanford Encyclopedia of Philosophy*, ed. Edward N. Zalta, 2011, http://plato.stanford.edu/archives/win2011/entries/habermas/.

65. Jürgen Habermas, *Zwischn Natrualismus und Religion* (Frankfurt am Main: Suhrkamp, 2005) [English translation, 2008], 89.

66. Amitai Etzioni, *Political Unification Revisited: On Building Supranational Communities* (Lanham, MD: Lexington Books, 2001).

67. Amitai Etzioni, *From Empire to Community* (New York: Palgrave MacMillan, 2004).

Part III

Honor: from Citizens to Statesmen

SEVEN

Good Citizens

Gratitude and Honor

Anthony Cunningham

At first glance, notions of honor may seem like a poor bet to keep any close company with the likes of a liberal society. One doesn't have to look long or hard to find glaring examples of honor codes that seem irredeemably incompatible with core liberal ideals. For instance, witness practices like "honor killings" and serious fetters on women predicated on honor, the sorts of everyday examples that are so difficult to square with the notion of a liberal society. Despite these poor prospects, I contend that a robust sense of honor is not only compatible with liberal ideals, but that any liberal society ignores honor at its own peril. Honor can be only as good as the particular forms of life and character deemed honorable by any given society, but a *sense of honor*—the predilection to measure the self by the lights of things deemed noble or shameful—should have a place as an important psychological force in any enlightened conception of a liberal society. Furthermore, substantive elements long associated with traditional honor cultures—"substantive" in the sense of what specifically is deemed honorable—play a key role in ideals at the heart of liberal societies. Honor has wielded a very heavy hand in inhumane practices throughout human history, but as I hope to show by way of some examples of gifts and gratitude, so too has honor been at the center of things that are best and most beautiful about us. So with this in mind, let me turn to gifts and gratitude.

Toward the end of Homer's *Odyssey*, Penelope extends a gracious hand to Odysseus in his disguise as a beggar. The crass and unruly suitors treat Odysseus as a good-for-nothing by mocking and insulting him mercilessly, but Penelope, with no inkling that this man is her husband come back to her after his long journey home, goes out of her way to protect him and to see to his needs. Indeed, she treats the beggar as an honored guest. A woman in her high position certainly doesn't have to lavish such attention on someone like him, but she does. She has nothing obvious to gain, and no external force or threat compels her to treat him so well. This old man is just a beggar, someone who an important person like Penelope could overlook without suffering undesirable consequences. Her gestures on his behalf, both her direct kindness and her pledge to have nothing to do with any suitor who mistreats him again, say something essential about her character and how she sees and moves through the world. Penelope does as she does because she is an honorable woman who would be ashamed to treat the beggar the way her suitors mistreat him. She is above such rudeness and cruelty, and she has contempt for bullies who fail to realize the fact that but for the vagaries of their good fortune, they could easily find themselves in this beggar's rags. In her precarious world, no human being is safe from dramatic reversals in fortune, and this vulnerability should chasten the smug and hard-hearted. As Penelope sees things, a noble person would never stoop so low as to mishandle or have sport with this fellow, so she extends her protection and instructs her servants to take care of him.

> And now, you maids, wash his feet for him, and make him a bed on a couch with rugs and blankets, that he may be warm and quiet till morning. Then, at day break wash him and anoint him again, that he may sit in the cloister and take his meals with Telemachus. It shall be the worse for any one of these hateful people who is uncivil to him; like it or not, he shall have no more to do in this house. For how, sir, shall you be able to learn whether or no I am superior to others of my sex both in goodness of heart and understanding, if I let you dine in my cloisters squalid and ill clad? Men live but for a little season; if they are hard, and deal hardly, people wish them ill so long as they are alive, and speak contemptuously of them when they are dead, but he that is righteous and deals righteously, the people tell of his praise among all lands, and many shall call him blessed.[1]

Penelope's ideal of hospitality plays a significant role not just in Homer's ancient world, but also in many honor stories from disparate times and places. In many cultures, good people take pains and go out of their way as a point of honor to make guests feel welcome and comfortable. Such hospitality is an undeniable gift, and sincere gifts express the conviction that people warrant going to some trouble on their behalf. Gifts not only testify to the importance of the guest; they also say a great deal about the character of the giver, and in particular, about what matters deeply to the giver. Notice that hospitality is not a strict obligation in any way that implies some kind of indefeasible right on the part of a recipient. For instance, if I borrow money from you, then you have a clear right to repayment, and you can duly complain of an injustice if I fail to pay my debt. Likewise, if I make you a solemn promise, I have an obligation to keep it, and devoid of any extenuating circumstances to excuse me, you can hold me to my promise. By contrast, the ideal of hospitality doesn't strictly bind a host as these examples of promises and loans bind people, and yet, neither is hospitality experienced as a matter of purely personal prerogative on the part of an honorable giver. If you are my guest and if I make little effort on your behalf, I insult you in the sense that my modest efforts are an implicit reflection of how much I think you are worth. The thought, "This is my guest," really means something to a hospitable person. Of course, practical considerations can bear on such situations. If I am desperately poor, the best I can do may be quite modest in an absolute sense, but all the same, my efforts may well be an immense effort in a relative one. Well-intentioned hosts can be stretched beyond their means by circumstance, and therefore they can find it impossible to give as they might wish to give. Moreover, gifts can err not only in the direction of being too meager; they can invite troubles by being too grand or by being offered in ways that are not adequately attuned to the circumstances and the recipient. Gifts can be a complicated business that both givers and receivers must manage artfully.

We see interesting examples of the subtleties of gifts in colorful honor stories like the Icelandic sagas, where even benign gifts can create problems. In *Egil's Saga*, a young man meets Egil Skallagrimson, a master poet, and they become good friends. Einar later proves himself a good poet, and after he is rewarded with a magnificent gold shield, he goes to visit Egil. When Einar does not find him at home, he leaves the shield as a gift, and when Egil returns and sees the precious object, he cries out, "'That scoundrel! Does he expect me to stay awake making a poem about his shield? Fetch my horse, I will ride after him and kill him.'"[2] Once Egil learns that Einar is long gone, he turns his attention to composing a poem in return for the younger Einar. No doubt irascible Egil indulges in some curmudgeonly hyperbole in this scene. Nevertheless, even gifts with good intentions can threaten or dishonor someone in the perilous world of the sagas. In this instance, the shield is an extraordinary gift, and since saga recipients incur a debt of honor to gift-givers, a gift can shame them if they can never repay the gift equitably. If they cannot reciprocate, they remain forever in the gift-giver's debt, and they may suffer humiliation for their impotence. And even if they can repay a gift, repayment can be burdensome, an unwelcome onus on the recipient, even if the intentions of the giver are entirely benign. If this saga example seems foreign or irrelevant to modern life, it really shouldn't. For instance, giving to the needy in ways that do not undermine their sense of dignity can be a tricky business in our world. Despite their best intentions, generous people can unwittingly run roughshod over people who genuinely need their help.

When it comes to giving and receiving, both givers and recipients have responsibilities. For their part, recipients should properly appreciate the beneficial things that are done on their behalf, both for the tangible benefits and for the good will in the gifts themselves. A sense of appropriate gratitude manifests the earnest desire to return good for good, both to acknowledge the kindness and to pay it back with something fitting if possible. Grateful people remember what others do on their behalf, and they yearn to return favors if they should get the chance. Such sentiments are on display in Homer's *Iliad* and *Odyssey*, where gratitude is the flipside of something like vengeance, another vital point of honor for Homer's characters. When Agamemnon insults Achilles at the beginning of the *Iliad*, the aggrieved warrior means to make the offending king pay at all costs. Likewise, when Hector kills Patroclus, Achilles will stop at nothing to make the Trojan prince pay the blood price. In much the same way, these Greek warriors usually spare no efforts as a point of honor to return generous deeds done on their behalf. Honor commands that they give people their due, for good or ill, not because they must under pain of external threat or sanction, but because human affairs depend so vitally on it.

In everyday life, grateful people may not always be in a position to return good for good, and in some cases, so doing may even be impossible. For instance, one can be duly grateful for the prodigious efforts and sacrifices of ancestors who are long gone, but in this situation, the best one can do is to be thankful for these people and to be mindful to try to live up to their good example. *Ingrates* take without any thought of returning, whether they fail to reciprocate with the people who benefited them, or whether they enjoy the benefit of those who came before them, only to deny the same benefits to other contemporaries or those who come after them. Thus, as depicted in *Hecuba*, Euripides' version of Odysseus comes off badly because he refuses to return Hecuba's gift of sparing his life after he stole his way within the walls of Troy and was recognized. When the Greeks eventually prove victorious, he not only fails to speak out against sacrificing enslaved Polyxena, but he sways the divided ranks in favor of taking her life as a sacrifice to Achilles. Hecuba reminds him of his precious debt and begs him to sacrifice her and to spare her daughter, but Euripides has Odysseus coldly refuse, putting what must be galling words for Hecuba in Odysseus's mouth: "A man will say anything / anything, to live."[3] Perhaps wily Odysseus is right about what most men would say and do in a life-and-death situation, but Hecuba can hardly be impressed by his hard-hearted ingratitude when he is firmly in her debt. It would be difficult for her to imagine Hector following this Greek warrior's lead in such things.

When honor cultures value hospitality and gratitude as points of honor, they deem them excellences, things that should inspire admiration from observers, pride in those who possess them, shame in those who don't, and contempt for those without them. Thus, the psychological sense of honor connected with these things is a fundamental measure of the self by the person in question *and* by the community. The latter is important to notice because a sense of honor does not get off the ground without some shared social component. If such generosity and gratitude are seen as defining excellences, just what do people who honor these things see so good about them? To appreciate them, consider other sorts of exchanges that we depend upon for the everyday business of living. Thus, I ask you for directions, and I assume that you will answer me honestly. You promise to see me at three o'clock, and I expect you to keep your word. You agree to buy my horse, so I hand over the steed and expect you to pay me. If we could not depend on such basic exchanges, things that have little or nothing to do with gifts and gratitude, the world would be a very different and far more hostile place. Yet, the landscape of hospitality and gratitude is notably different. For instance, suppose that I am a weary traveler, and you bid me to rest on your porch, there to have a cool drink in the shade on a hot day. Say that I am just passing through, so you may never see me again. Hence, any seeds of good will and affection that you sow with your kindness may never bear any discernible fruit for you. As people say, you would have little or nothing to gain. And say that when I am finished, I consider your kind gesture as nothing more than a stroke of good fortune, some much-needed manna from heaven, and I continue on my way without a word of thanks or any desire to return the kindness. However, suppose instead that I am not this kind of person, an ingrate. Say that I understand your gesture for what it was, a small act of kindness freely given without any expectation of recompense, much less any demand for such. In this case, what I am likely to value about the gesture as a grateful person, over and above the tangible benefit I derive from the rest and sustenance, is the fact that you did not *have* to do what you did, and yet you graciously chose to do so. The gesture cost you something in terms of your time and energy and resources, so the gesture expressed an implicit form of intrinsic regard for me. Simply put, I mattered enough to warrant your time and expense in this way. In this case, as a grateful person, I take note of the gesture as a matter of honor, both in the giving and the receiving. I would be loath to take advantage of your kindness without expressing my appreciation. And when I sincerely express my honest thanks, you understand my appreciation as something other than a case of mechanically discharging an obligation. Just as your freely gave, I freely thanked you; our parts in the exchange manifest a kind of mutual regard that is not predicated on any kind of compulsion.

Notice that when it comes to telling the truth, keeping promises, and respecting people and their possessions, people depend on stealth and indirection to get away with not living up to such responsibilities. Others can publicly call us on our misdeeds in this regard, and there is little we can say to defend ourselves, short of disputing the charges and proclaiming our innocence, or else proffering some excuse of extenuating circumstances. The landscape of generous gifts and appropriate gratitude is considerably murkier. Were Penelope to turn a blind eye to how her suitors treat the beggar and simply wash her hands of the affair, or were I to jettison your cool drink from my mind without a word of thanks or any resolve to return the favor, no great hue and cry would likely follow. People can easily get away with such things without being hounded or haunted by their deeds, particularly if an instance is a one-off or if the trail is cold, as it must be when benefactors are long gone or very distant. In this regard, contemporary Americans (along others) surely owe a debt of gratitude to the Allied soldiers who stormed the beaches of Normandy in 1944, but not many of these soldiers are still around to collect on the debt. And even if more of them were with us today, the demands of gifts and gratitude are not always so clear and specific as to demand anything of us *right here and now*. In other words, people can get away with being miserly and unthankful, so when people extend a gracious hand or when they clearly appreciate the generous things done on their behalf, they testify to ways of life and forms of character they prize for their own sake. They effectively say that these things really *matter* to them, that they cannot turn their backs on ideals that *constitute* them at what they see as their best, even if they could easily get away with ignoring such things. Achilles would no sooner fail to repay meaningful gifts than he would fail to repay Agamemnon for insulting him. Doing so would be beneath him, and were he to face up to abandoning such things as a way of life, he would feel shame.

Of course, people can easily go through the motions half-heartedly or mindlessly in these respects. Hospitality and gratitude can assume the form of manners, where behaviors become ingrained habits that are largely perfunctory. Thus, I offer you a scone and a cup of tea, or you offer me the same, and we mouth our appropriate thanks and compliments on the refreshments. For the most part, we pay attention to such things only when they are obviously *missing*. If a person on the street makes a pointed show of refusing me the time of day, or if I hold a door for someone who walks through without a word of thanks or so much as a cursory look, I am taken for granted like someone who warrants no attention. Some victims of such slights learn to brush such things off, while others feel indignant. If the things at stake are relatively small, people are wise to develop the ability to put such slights aside because life is too short to hang on every such insult. In this sense, people can injure themselves on molehills. Nonetheless, most people depend on some backdrop of willful giving and thankful taking in daily life, and as the stakes rise, when the things that are given and taken matter a great deal, or when the giving and taking take on greater import as instances of explicit respect, we tend to care deeply about people extending a kind hand and returning such gestures in kind. In fact, we don't just mildly *prefer* gracious and grateful people, we actually *look down* on stingy ingrates. If we imagine ourselves as such people, we recoil from such ways of life and forms of character as beneath us. Or at least this is how things look and feel to anyone for whom these things are points of honor.

Now suppose that we happen to be people who honor hospitality and gratitude in the sense that I am describing, and suppose we are also citizens of a liberal democracy. No doubt a fair number of people fit this description in everyday life. In this case, can we legitimately extoll generous hospitality and gratitude as requisite virtues for a good citizen in a liberal society? I mean something beyond personally endorsing such traits, the way I might exhort fellow citizens to be fit or to write poetry. Whatever we think about physical fitness or poetry, we do not consider a disinterest in either pursuit as any inherent shortcoming so far as citizenship is concerned. The fundamental ideals of a liberal democracy do not compel such interests, though they allow for citizens to pursue them if they please. Citizens are on their own with respect to these activities, even if it might just so happen that we'd all be indisputably better off as fit poets. Generally, where beliefs about a good life are concerned, interpreters of the notion of a liberal society insist that it must be *neutral* to competing visions of how to live and what sort of person to be. On this interpretation, a liberal democracy should strive not to favor one conception over others. Keep in mind that such neutrality doesn't entail any indifference to citizens leading good lives. Ultimately, a liberal society must have a fundamental interest in its citizens living good lives, but it leaves it up to citizens to figure out and to pursue their own conception of such a life. Neither does a commitment to neutrality call for ignoring the fact that certain conditions must surely be met for citizens to have any realistic chance to pursue their own vision successfully. After all, citizens in all societies undeniably have basic needs that they can ignore only at their own peril. But unlike some societies that embrace a shared conception of the good—a so-called "thick" conception, complete with a shared understanding of and commitment to practices, roles, and forms of character that are faithful to the conception of the good they share—liberal societies usually strive for a "thinner" conception that strives not to privilege one vision over another. Instead, liberal societies look to key ideals that supposedly serve the goal of sustaining the possibility of a pluralistic way of life where the pursuit of conceptions of the good are concerned, as distinct from ordaining favorites.

When it comes to such key ideals, liberty and equality are two pivotal ones for a liberal society. These two ideals obviously speak to vital elements of the human condition. Consider liberty. When constructing any plan for a good life, a person needs to be free in particular ways, free both *from* interference and free *to* pursue choices realistically. If others are dishonest with me, cheat me, break their promises to me, speak falsely about me, usurp my power to choose for myself, lord arbitrary power over me, harass and intimidate me, or harm me physically, my life suffers for these forms of interference. Moreover, even if people leave me alone in these vital respects, my liberty is not apt to flourish unless I happen to be self-sufficient in the myriad ways that matter in human lives. If a liberal society is genuinely committed to people being free to pursue a chosen life plan, it must heed what people need to exercise their liberty effectively. For instance, one can contend that physically handicapped citizens are at liberty to move about the world as they please, but if nobody pays any attention to the design of physical surroundings, such liberty is not apt to be worth much. Stairs, and nothing but steep and foreboding stairs everywhere, might as well be an immense moat or an impregnable wall to a citizen confined to a wheelchair. Lives can be effectively stunted and squashed without intentional interference. Benign neglect can be a killer.

By extolling the value of liberty, a liberal society commits itself to people having a vital say over their own destiny. It does so knowing well that the free exercise of personal choice can sometimes be the downfall of foolish and unfortunate people. In this case, citizens can sensibly rue the actual results of the exercise of such liberty, even while they also acknowledge the inherent value of being the captain of one's own ship, so to speak. Despite this distinct possibility for mistakes, even foolish ones, liberal societies usually take some comfort in the hope and trust that certain liberties tend to grease the wheels of human flourishing. Choosing my company, my loves, my profession, my personal projects—such choices deeply shape a life, and a liberal society's respect for them manifests the conviction that people stand the best chance at flourishing if they can pursue lives that are their own and largely unfettered in significant ways. Sensible people can hardly deny that human vision and imagination can suffer badly when it comes to reckoning the possible elements of a well-lived life, particularly when it comes to judging these things for others, so the experiments in living that one encourages by protecting the liberty to live as one sees fit provide vital opportunities for self-expression and self-development, the sort that can easily be pinched even by the very best of paternalistic intentions.

Keep in mind that when people respect the liberty of their fellow citizens, they usually prize more than just their liberty. On the most basic level, they tend to prize *the people themselves* as the bearers of such liberty. This point warrants explicit mention so that liberty itself isn't misconstrued as the be-all and end-all in a liberal society. As Amitai Etzioni contends, good societies invariably draw upon *multiple* values that can conflict, values that can only be adequately understood in dialogue with each other.[4] The precise shape and boundaries of liberty in a liberal society can only be charted against a larger backdrop of the things that matter, and an essential element of such a backdrop includes a fundamental commitment to the well-being of the bearers of essential liberties.

Of course, liberty and well-being are not conjoined in anything remotely close to some kind of blessed harmony. Life is not so simple. People can make a mess of their lives when left to their own devices, so a concern for their liberty and their well-being can clash, and sometimes clash in tragic and intractable ways. In the case of young children, liberal societies traditionally err on the side of protecting their well-being while trying honestly to cultivate the kind of wise judgment that might eventually allow them to steer a prudent course of their own making. On the other hand, provided that people do no serious harm to others or to the common good, liberal societies usually stay their hand in important ways with respect to the choices of adults out of concern for protecting their say over their own lives. Such respect is not born of indifference to the ultimate results, and neither does it rest on making an unequivocal god of liberty. Instead, this respect embodies the considered judgment that various forms of liberty are necessary for well-being, though they are far from sufficient.

This commitment to the well-being of citizens in a liberal society also finds expression in an ideal of equality: we all count, and we all count the same in some respects. Without a doubt, human beings never have the *same exact* commitment to the well-being of each and all. Most of us care about ourselves, our intimate loved ones, and more distant others, and these distinct forms of concern make considerably different demands on human lives. The things we would do for our intimates ordinarily go well beyond what we would do for strangers or acquaintances; these commitments differ not only in degree, but in kind. Nevertheless, despite these differences, a liberal society must hold fast to the idea that everyone matters. Once again, consider physically handicapped people who may technically be at liberty to go wherever they like so long they have the means to navigate a world designed without them in mind. The failure in such cases is not just a failure of liberty, but also one of equality. Ultimately, handicapped citizens in a liberal democratic community must be able to sustain the plausible conviction that they are not excluded or forgotten if they are to feel like meaningful citizens. Likewise, those who were denied the advantages of white citizens under the guise of "separate but equal" in the Jim Crow South would not have been treated as true equals even if black schools had been equal (and of course, they were not, not even remotely). When Southern whites effectively banished black children to the social periphery, they implicitly proclaimed that black children were worth less (maybe even worthless). True enough, people in any society can be left out inadvertently, rather than by intentional design, but if people care about their fellow citizens, they keep a vigilant eye out for accidental exclusions, and when they spy them, they make a serious effort to redress them. If they refuse, either by way of refusing to look or by refusing to do anything about what they see, the message from those on top can only be clear to those who are ultimately left out or left behind: We, the powerful people, do not care enough to treat you (the powerless or less powerful) as equals, as citizens who matter just as much as us. In this case, the operative rules of association can only feel badly rigged to those left on the outside, and any societal talk of loving liberty and equality must seem like a bold lie. If I cannot plausibly see myself as a free *and* equal citizen in a liberal society, then my supposed "duties" to fellow citizens can hardly seem like any point of high principle.

Notice that these twin ideals of liberty and equality can only be adequately understood in concert, and their practical integration tends to be anything but obvious. Moreover, notice that they are sometimes mentioned in the same breath with a third ideal—fraternity. For instance, the French Republic explicitly embraces the triad of *liberté, egalité, fraternité* as its national motto. Common enough as this famous political triad may be, one can sensibly ask what the relationship between these three elements might possibly be, and depending on the answer, one might argue that fraternity has no appropriate place as an *essential* ideal in a liberal society because even though it may be something laudable, perhaps it is too "thick" for any liberal society committed to remaining neutral to diverse conceptions of the good. A liberal society without a serious commitment to liberty and equality, difficult as that commitment may be to flesh out in both theory and practice, is simply a contradiction in terms, but perhaps the inclusion of fraternity is simply one ideal too many.

One way to imagine fraternity as a member of this triad is to imagine people joined together in a sincere commitment to liberty and equality as *indivisible* ends. If you and I share an interest in money, we share an interest in the same thing, a *divisible* thing in the sense that one of us having it isn't necessarily tied to the other having it (this result may even be unlikely or impossible), and so long as our relationship to money is purely self-interested, we are unlikely to identify with each other psychologically just because of our shared interest. In this case, the sense in which we share this interest is purely accidental and incidental. By contrast, if you and I share an interest in clean air and water, our fates in this respect may well be joined indivisibly (we both enjoy them, or neither does). Nonetheless, our interests may still be purely self-interested. We share the same boat together, but we do so only through sheer circumstance; perhaps we can both get to the other side only by cooperating. This kind of indivisibility needn't encourage any identification with each other. However, suppose we share the end of eradicating a serious disease or saving an endangered species. If so, our end may be indivisible not just in the practical sense that realizing it for one person entails realizing it for everyone, but also in the sense that we prize the sharing of this end because of what it means to us. With this cause, the way in which the end matters makes no fundamental difference to me: I care about eradicating a disease or saving polar bears *for their own sake,* not simply for some personal benefit. When I care about things in this fashion, I am likely to see others who share my ends as brothers and sisters in a common cause, and thus I am likely to identify with them psychologically as a result of our shared ends. When people love what I love in the way I love it, we share a love in a nonincidental sense. Notice that a commitment to liberty and equality can be just like this, and in fact, any attractive conception of a liberal society ultimately depends upon liberty and equality being indivisible ends in this sense. By contrast, in a Hobbesian society, I might campaign vigorously for liberty and equality to protect my vital interests, but in this case, the liberty and equality of my fellow citizens might simply be the invariable price to be paid to advance my own interests. I might not care a whit about my fellow citizens. A more robust commitment to liberty and equality understands these ideals as final ends, not simply as a means to advance one's own interests. And provided we care about liberty and equality in this way, we might naturally come to care about each other as brothers and sisters who prize what we hold dear.

On this description, a sense of fraternity is a possible, but something short of inevitable upshot of sharing an intrinsic interest in liberty and equality. Such a result is hardly improbable, psychologically speaking, but notice that one can conceivably imagine people who are attracted to liberty and equality *in principle* without truly caring deeply about other people. In other words, one can imagine people who love liberty and equality without giving much of a damn about others. I doubt many people actually fit this profile, but the reason for my skepticism is that I believe some sense of fraternity invariably precedes and best explains our concerns for liberty and equality in the first place. In other words, because I care about my fellow citizens, I would ultimately prefer them to be free and be treated as equals. Far from being a superfluous psychological upshot of some *in principle* adoration of liberty and equality, I believe that fraternity is best seen as the psychological bedrock of these two concerns, and as such, at the very least, as first among equals in this famous political triad.

Lest these remarks about fraternity seem too "thick" for any coherent conception of a *liberal* society bent on remaining neutral to the conceptions of the good life—say, well beyond the pale for any standard liberal conception—consider an esteemed liberal source like John Rawls's *A Theory of Justice*. Even those who persevere with this large work may tire before the latter parts of the book where Rawls discusses the idea of a "social union," a notion that fits squarely with his suggestion about how his "difference principle" corresponds

> to a natural meaning of fraternity; namely, to the idea of not wanting to have greater advantages unless this is to the benefit of those less well off. The family, in its ideal conception and often in practice, is one place where the principle of maximizing the sum of advantages is rejected. Members of a family commonly do not wish to gain unless they can do so in ways that further the interests of the rest.[5]

In the years soon after the publication of what is now considered a classic in liberal political thought, interpreters spent a great deal of time on the minutiae of Rawls's "original position," a notion that seemed to embody the concern for avoiding any thick conceptions of the good that might unduly impose upon the lives and choices of free and equal citizens pursuing their own life plan. However, I think that some notion of fraternity was at the heart of Rawls's conception of a liberal democracy as a people sharing a fate in some meaningful sense and mutually committed to liberty and equality because in the end, they genuinely care about each other. The original position and its "veil of ignorance" served the purpose of helping people imagine how to construct a society where people might share a fate together in this meaningful sense, duly guided by ideals of liberty and equality.

Should I be wrong about Rawls, nothing important hangs on the error. I do not advert to *A Theory of Justice* as any "Biblical" authority. Indeed, if I am wrong in my reading of his work, then I say so much the worse for Rawls so far as constructing the most attractive conception of a liberal society is concerned. Ultimately, I think a liberal society is best viewed through an illuminating prism of fraternity. Keep in mind that by claiming that a liberal society should *start* from a foundation of fellow citizens caring meaningfully about each other, I do not intend to engage in any mad flight of fancy about our empirical psychology. If I profess to love my fellow Americans the way I love my family or friends, then I suffer under a fantasy, and potentially a pernicious one at that. Indeed, speaking for myself, if I profess to *like* all my fellow citizens, much less love them, then I am badly exaggerating my actual affections. I don't even like all the people who live on my street. Fortunately, a sense of fraternity as I mean it doesn't hinge on wildly implausible psychological propensities. Return for just a moment to the Allied forces that landed in Normandy in 1944. Or consider the men and women who attempted to make the fifty-four-mile march from Selma to Montgomery slightly more than twenty years after D-Day to defy racial segregation and repression. No single thought can adequately capture all the motivations at work in the participants in these two cases, but hate had to be a key part of the picture. Surely the Allies hated Hitler and would see him defeated, and nonviolent as Martin Luther King and his company may have been, surely they hated Jim Crow without reservation. Thus, hate had its distinct place, but so too did love. Any picture that leaves out the notion of *willing sacrifices* on behalf of the others that these people cared about surely misses a vital element of their courageous efforts. Ultimately, such extreme sacrifices of life and limb—over 200,000 Allied soldiers were killed or wounded during the Normandy invasion, and the long march from Selma was a bloody one—can only be adequately appreciated against a backdrop of caring about those who stood to benefit from the defeat of Nazism and Jim Crow, and this kind of caring doesn't rely on any quixotic view of love. In the end, the operative concern is relatively simple: *Do you care about someone else?* If the answer on the ground is "no," then people are unlikely to make such sacrifices, and the fact that real people regularly make them in everyday and not-so-everyday life provides some compelling psychological evidence that enough people generally care enough about their fellow citizens to make such things possible.

Is this notion of caring too thick to serve as a cornerstone for citizens in a liberal society *in principle*? If it is, I honestly see no way to get any conception of an attractive liberal society off the ground. In that case, where a sense of fraternity is too thick to qualify as a liberal ideal, then suitable ones like liberty and equality by themselves are just too skinny to sustain any robust conception of a real *people* joined together in any true fellowship with any genuine fidelity to each other as fellow citizens. Can something less than this kind of fraternal vision possibly hope to survive as a workable society? Yes, though one should not underestimate the immense hit that widespread indifference to fellow citizens would entail in such a society. By "indifference," I mean something short of outright hostility. In a society where citizens mutually root and vie for each other's downfall or suffering, the prospects are invariably bleak. I mean pervasive disinterest merely in the sense of people having little or no intrinsic interest in reaching out to others or in returning kind-hearted gestures should others be willing to reach out to them. In this regard, we do well to remember that citizens of liberal democracies are human beings before they are citizens, and bringing fundamental human social proclivities to bear on how people might come together as citizens in a liberal society does not run roughshod over the ideals at the heart of such a society. Hospitality, broadly construed in terms of a sense of personal responsibility for reaching out to others generously, and gratitude interpreted as thankfulness for such gifts and the desire to return them when possible, are at the very center of our social lives as human beings. We enter the world entirely dependent on the goodwill and care of others, and if we are fortunate enough to enjoy the great gift of being loved well, we are apt to develop not just the capacity, but also the decided proclivity to care about others in kind. This leap, from the self to others, is the first and most fundamental ethical leap for human beings. Like all psychological leaps, it can be halting and labored, but lives with and without the leap are entirely different.

Of course, one can insist that citizens in a liberal society can't legitimately be compelled to care about others in these ways, and one would be quite right to say so. A liberal society can certainly hold people to various behaviors compelled by reasonable interpretations of the demands of liberty and equality, but it can never *make* people care about each other (no more than it can make people intrinsically care about ideals of liberty or equality either). Yet if there is no such concern—if citizens do not have a fundamental concern for and commitment to each other that goes beyond serving their own interests, a concern that extends over and above holding certain abstract principles dear—then the virtues of such a liberal society might still be noteworthy in key respects, but the vision would be impoverished in a crucial way.

Prone as we are to make the kind of leap I mean here, the habits of the sense of humanity that sustain the bonds that tie us together require abundant and consistent cultivation and sustenance. Perhaps there really are forms of caring that are genuine *no-matter-what* forms of love. Maybe I can deeply love my children no matter who they are, what they do, or how they treat me. To be honest, I have profound doubts about this. At the very least, such love will be seriously tested if children hurt and scorn their parents at every turn. Given our psychology, anything along the lines of unconditional love is bound to suffer enormous stress if burdened in this fashion, and everything in the world eventually breaks under enough weight. Moreover, most of us are undeniably built with a powerful proclivity to answer in kind. When we are the beneficiaries of kindness, we naturally incline toward returning good for good. On the other hand, when we are wronged, most of us wish to get people back, even if some people may do their best to divest themselves of such desires. If one goes back to Homer's world, this view of human nature driven to reciprocate in kind is on full display without any apologies. Achilles cannot turn a blind eye when Agamemnon seeks to humiliate him. Agamemnon must pay, and Achilles thirsts for the day when Agamemnon will tear his heart out and curse himself for what he has done.

Hospitality and gratitude are the bright side to the undeniable darkness of Achilles's profound indignation and desire for vengeance. And just as the capacity for appropriate anger must be duly cultivated, shaped, and moderated (some things really should make good people mad, other things shouldn't make good people *that* mad, and good people must know and feel the difference), so too must our basic proclivities with respect to hospitality and gratitude be cultivated and carefully reinforced. Any society that deeply values these things—and any liberal society *should* prize and herald gracious giving and receiving as pivotal for developing and sustaining the everyday bonds of sentiment that ultimately bind citizens together in the most basic sense—does well to encourage them as vital points of honor. Though the proclivity to return good for good is a well-entrenched part of human psychology, the proclivity requires consistent and plentiful nourishment to keep from withering beyond intimate circles in any given culture. If citizens are inhospitable with their neighbors, or if most citizens are ingrates, the precious soil of gracious giving and gratitude can be rendered barren, and in this case, the bonds of fraternity that are so important as the foundation of a liberal society face a huge uphill battle, and maybe an impossible one at that.

Honor can be a formidable defense against such a calamity. Again, a robust sense of honor has to do with things we deem so important that our very identity hangs in the balance. Shakespeare's "If I lose mine honour, I lose myself" gives voice to the thoughts and feelings at work where honor is concerned.[6] Shame and pride, properly understood as deep measurements of the self, are two psychological reference points for any sense of honor. A shameless person, someone devoid of the *capacity* for shame, is someone without any functional sense of honor. While a sense of honor is rooted in measurements of excellence, not all excellences are points of honor in any given life, and not all the points are equal. If everything is a matter of honor, then in a very real sense, nothing is. Whenever hospitality and gratitude are matters of honor, citizens in a liberal society stand a far better chance to be brothers and sisters in a common cause. When miserliness and ingratitude are occasions for shame, fraternity stands a far better chance.

Notice that the inculcation and sustenance of these proclivities for generous giving and grateful taking are fraught with complexities and possible pitfalls. For instance, consider my comments about an American debt of gratitude to those who invaded Normandy against a backdrop like Paul Robinson's concerns about seeing the Crown's veterans as "super-citizens" entitled to special considerations by virtue of their service.[7] Part of the immense power and beauty of gratitude resides in the fact that it is freely given and not strictly claimed like some straightforward contractual debt. It is one thing for me to express my sincere gratitude to those who served, and quite another for those soldiers to think I do them wrong by not expressing my thanks. Such cases can easily run afoul of a subtle "one thought too many" provision when it comes to an honorable life and character. As Ryan Rhodes details in his story of the poor lady who loses her head, when Lancelot's first thought is that he has suddenly been shamed, we think that he looks in the wrong direction, at himself rather than to the lady's sad fate.[8] In this vein, we admire Penelope's hospitality because she cares about a poor beggar enough to protect him, not because she assiduously checks off some hospitality box so as to preserve a conception of herself as a good host. Though a sense of honor always engages the self deeply, ultimately honor must be about more than just that self and its status, or else it can devolve into nothing more than narcissism and vanity. If Penelope gives with an eye to what her beneficiaries will owe her in the future, she does not give from the heart as a good host gives. And if citizens lionize soldiers and police officers as supercitizens who automatically embody everything that is good and noble, they succumb to a form of cheap sentimentality that does no justice at all to genuine gratitude.

Getting things right in this vein can be a subtle enterprise, one that requires a rich and fine-tuned awareness of the things we might do for each other and what those things cost. In this light, let me conclude with an appropriate literary example drawn from Richard Flanagan's *The Narrow Road to the Deep North*. The protagonist in the tale is an Australian surgeon in World War II, an officer charged with commanding the Allied prisoners working on the impossible task of constructing the Burma railway as prisoners of war. Dorrigo Evans, a flawed man, rises to the occasion to spare as many of the men as possible, day in and day out. He realizes that the men need a strong, inspiring figure—an impossible figure in many respects—to help them survive the brutal conditions, and somehow or other he finds the strength to be more than himself, the man the men know as the *Big Fella*. At one point, an Allied prisoner steals a cow and the men offer Dorrigo a steak as a kind of tribute to his inspiring leadership. In his terrible hunger, he desperately wants to eat the steak before him, but instead, he makes the profound sacrifice of giving it to others who need it more. He understands their need for food, and more importantly, he understands their need for the kind of leader who can set such a magnanimous example. He makes the sacrifice, but not because of vanity or some penchant for virtue; quite simply, he does so for the men. And at another point, a Japanese commander orders him to select one hundred prisoners to march to another work camp. Dorrigo insists that the men are not up to the trek, that they will perish on the way, but the officer insists on the selection. Knowing that the officer will choose the men randomly if he refuses, Dorrigo tries to select the men who stand the best chance of surviving the trek, but he has no illusions about their chances. He knows that many will die, and he bears an enormous burden with the thought that he is sending good men to their deaths. But the anointed surprise him:

> And so Dorrigo continued on, up and down the lines of those he had tried to save and now had to pick, touching, naming, condemning those men he thought might best cope, the men who had the best chance of not dying, who would most likely die nevertheless.
>
> At its end, Dorrigo Evans stepped back and dropped his head in shame. He thought of Jack Rainbow, whom he had made to suffer so, Darky Gardiner, whose prolonged death he could only watch. And now these hundred men.
>
> And when he looked up, there stood around him a circle of the men he had condemned. He expected the men to curse him, to turn away and revile him, for everyone understood it was to be a death march. Jimmy Bigelow stepped forward.
>
> Look after yourself, Colonel, he said, and put out his hand to shake Dorrigo's. Thanks for everything.

> You too, Jimmy, Dorrigo Evans said.
>
> And one by one, the rest of the hundred men shook his hand and thanked him.
>
> When it was done, he walked off into the jungle at the side of the parade ground and wept.[9]

The great beauty of this scene rests in the humane nobility of the participants, nobility marked neither by naïve sentimentality nor crass narcissism. Dorrigo Evans gives his men the incalculable gift of heroically looking out for them at every turn under the savage conditions of the railway line, and in this particular moment, all he can think about is how he cannot protect them from what is to come. The men understand that the march may well be the death of them, but they appreciate Dorrigo Evans, not just for what he has done for them before this fateful day, but for what he suffers on their behalf now by having to choose them. Both the surgeon and the selected testify to the ennobling features of such gifts and gratitude. Together, they all rise to the occasion. Of course, the circumstances and the profound stakes of the situation amplify the poignancy of the scene, but the literary moment makes nothing up about giving and gratitude. The scene simply illuminates the complex innards of gifts and gratitude, delicately weaving together disparate elements of honor and love. The men love Dorrigo Evans, and they are right to do so. Dorrigo Evans loves these men, and he too is right to do so. Without the innumerable instances of looking out for each other in any given day, these soldiers would surely close in upon themselves, concerned only for their own survival, their eyes only on a steak for themselves.

On his thwarted trip to the South Pole in 1908, Ernest Shackleton commanded one of his men, Frank Wild, to accept one of his own biscuits on the uncertain return journey. With rations running low, they were fighting for their lives and they had no way to know whether they would make it. Wild had not begun the expedition as Shackleton's admirer, but this small gesture induced a profound change of heart. Wild's journal gave voice to it with, "I do not suppose that anyone else in the world can thoroughly realize how much generosity and sympathy was shown by this. I DO by GOD I shall never forget it. Thousands of pounds would not have bought that one biscuit."[10] Wild never forgot; thereafter his loyalty to Shackleton was absolutely unwavering. In the end, the gifts we give each other and the appreciation we express for them play crucial roles in forging and sustaining a genuine sense of fraternity in any society, including liberal societies, so we should duly honor them because we are never apt to embody difficult things that we do not hold dear as a point of honor.

NOTES

1. Homer, *The Odyssey*, trans. Samuel Butler, Book XIX, "The Project Gutenberg EBook of the Odyssey, by Homer," http://www.gutenberg.org/files/1727/1727-h/1727-h.htm#link2H_4_0026.

2. *Egil's Saga*, trans. Bernard Scudder, in *The Sagas of the Icelanders* (New York: Viking, 2000), 167.

3. Euripides, *Hecuba*, in *Euripides I*, eds. David Slavitt and Palmer Bovie, trans. Marilyn Nelson, (Philadelphia: University of Pennsylvania Press, 1998), 89.

4. Amitai Etzioni, "Communitarianism Revisited," this volume.

5. John Rawls, *A Theory of Justice* (Cambridge, MA: Belknap Press, 1971), 105. For a discussion of Rawls's work and communitarian critiques, see my "Liberalism, Egalité, Fraternité?" *Journal of Philosophical Research* 16 (1991): 125–44.

6. William Shakespeare, *The Tragedy of Antony & Cleopatra*, 3.4.22–23, in *The Riverside Shakespeare* (Boston: Houghton Mifflin, 1972), 1365.

7. Paul Robinson, "'The Honour of the Crown': The State and Its Soldiers," in this volume.

8. Ryan Rhodes, "Putting One's Best Face Forward," in this volume.

9. Richard Flanagan, *The Narrow Road to the Deep North* (New York: Alfred A. Knopf, 2014), 329.

10. Caroline Alexander, *The Endurance, Shackleton's Legendary Antarctic Expedition* (New York: Alfred A. Knopf, 1998), 13.

EIGHT

Winston Churchill and Honor

The Complexity of Honor and Statesmanship

Mark F. Griffith

Rarely can you find a statesman who exemplified the characteristic of honor better than Winston Churchill. His life was unique, and from a very early age he would lead a life of military valor, political excellence, and writing—all in the public eye. For that reason Churchill earned high honors; moreover, he wrote about honor. A statesman, soldier, writer, rhetorician, hero to many, and the recipient of numerous high honors in several countries, Churchill is uniquely situated for an exploration of honor. Yet in his early life, Churchill was skeptical about the concept of honor and lived in an era of incredible change and uncertainty. Later he would go on to defend honor rhetorically and to symbolize honor to his country, the West, and the world.

The evolution of Churchill's thought is complicated and irregular. One writer claimed that Churchill wrote between eight and ten million words, if you include his speeches, and of course every year more books about Churchill are published.[1] Churchill's writings and speeches make direct and indirect references to honor and dishonor. Everything he wrote was personal: it was deeply affected by Churchill's own life, heritage, and history. He comes to life in his writings, and we can see him making references and judgments throughout. These writings and speeches and his own actions reveal that he identified, considered, and evolved his thoughts on not just one but different aspects of honor. Because of the expansive scope of materials, the challenge is to reveal his understanding of honor.

As a young man Churchill's writings on honor are complex and at times contradictory. He clearly cares about honor, but he has not worked out where it all fits in his way of life. At twenty-three years of age, Churchill published his only novel, *Savrola,* and in that novel he writes that honor is relativistic and of little value,

> [b]ecause it has no true foundation, no ultra-human sanction. Its codes are constantly changing with times and places. At one time it is thought more honourable to kill the man you have wronged than to make amends; at another it is more important to pay a bookmaker than a butcher. Like art it changes with human caprice, and like art it comes from opulence and luxury.[2]

Contrasting what he wrote above was what he wrote to his mother about his desire for great honors like the Victoria Cross and his willingness to do any difficult or heroic thing to get the award:

> I am more ambitious for a reputation for personal courage than [for] anything else in the world. A young man should worship a young man's ideals. The dispatches should be published and I shall know for certain. Meanwhile I live in hope. As to deserving such an honour—I feel that I took every chance and displayed myself with ostentation wherever there was danger—but I had no military command and could not expect to receive credit for what should be after all be merely the behavior of a philosopher—who is also a gentleman.[3]

For Churchill at this stage of life, honor is relative; it comes from civilization, history, and codes of behavior. But all civilizations and codes can be advanced and developed or degenerated and ended. Yet Churchill already had experience with and embraced historic codes, including those of being a "gentleman," British, and a trained military officer. Churchill was a proud man who was always aware of honors but had not yet worked out all of the aspects of honor itself. So, for Churchill, most of these issues will be developed and clarified as his knowledge of history increases. The importance of history to Churchill is far richer and more fundamental than is typical for most people, and his voracious study of history resulted in an all-encompassing worldview. Isaiah Berlin writes,

> Churchill's dominant category, the single, central, organizing principle of his moral and intellectual universe, is his historical imagination so strong, so comprehensive, as to encase the whole of the present and the whole of the future in a framework of a rich and multicoloured past. Such an approach dominated by a desire—and a capacity—to find fixed moral and intellectual bearings, to give shape and character, colour and direction and coherence, to the stream of events.[4]

Throughout his life, history would become the touchstone for all his actions, the source of most of his income, and the way he controlled the debate about events. His view of history would directly affect his vision of honor and would develop over time as his understanding of both deepen and grow.

HONORS AND AWARDS

A necessary digression at this point must be a discussion about the problem of the terms *honor* and *awards*, particularly in relation to Churchill. Clearly, honors and awards bestowed are not the same as the concept of honor; yet for many people, the understanding of these terms and of the concept of honor itself are so interrelated that we need to spend some time clarifying the differences. Churchill was aware of awards and tried during his own career to use the earning of honors as an obvious way to advance his career. He understood that heroic action in battle would gain him prominence and distinction. He received awards and honors throughout his life, but most of these do little to elucidate what the actual concept of honor means. In Great Britain three kinds of honors are given by the government (as opposed to private groups like universities): they are orders, decorations, and medals. Orders are tied to medieval origins in knighthood and to the idea of chivalry, but in modern times they are honors given by kings or queens for commendable service. For example, great diplomatic service might be rewarded. Decorations, which include medals or ribbons that are worn on a uniform, are awarded in recognition of some involvement in a military campaign and heroic effort. Medals are given to all the people who participate in a battle or some other event like a coronation. Orders and decorations give us some insight into the concept of honor, while medals (in Great Britain, unlike the United States) only indicate participation in some event.[5]

Churchill received all kinds of orders, decorations, and medals. Many of them were minor but most were significant. Receiving recognition in terms of high honors does not really define honor, but it provides the contours of the concept. What is most informative are the criteria and the citation that are the basis of the award. The criteria identify whether the award is largely symbolic or whether it is related to substance. The criteria reveal how the awarding group recognizes and defines honor. Honorary or ceremonial honors for political office, longevity, lineage, academic honorary titles, and administrative excellences are largely symbolic.

Military honors for heroism usually result from action. However, *orders* are specific types of honors based on tradition and historical precedent. Churchill coveted the Victoria's Cross (Britain's highest military honor) but was never in a position to earn such an honor.[6] Churchill's highest military honor was the Knight Companion in the Order of the Garter, 1953. The history of the award shows that it is not what it seems to be. It includes the title, the "Order of the Garter," which is the "oldest

British Order of Chivalry and was founded by Edward III in 1348. The Order, consisting of the king and twenty-five knights, honors those who have held public office, who have contributed in a particular way to national life or who have served the Sovereign personally." In other words, although it is a military honor, which is in the category of honors usually reserved for military action, its purpose is actually more about chivalry and government service. It is important to note this distinction because of its link to chivalry, and the code of chivalry is one of the key foundations of honor found in Churchill's writings.[7]

Another example of a significant award that Winston Churchill received was the Nobel Prize for Literature in 1953. Again this high award is less instructive when it comes to defining honor. The citation reads, "The Nobel Prize in Literature 1953 was awarded to Winston Churchill for his mastery of historical and biographical description as well as for brilliant oratory in defending exalted human values."[8] These "human values" would include honor, but otherwise the citation mentions no specific reference to honor as part of the award.

The award ceremony speech provides further enlightenment about the merit and substance of the award. When the award was given to Churchill, the presenter praised the Churchill's oratory and noted the connection between freedom and human dignity in Churchill's oratory. The linking of freedom to human dignity in Churchill's speeches and writings foreshadows the way Churchill would later link freedom to honor: "Churchill's mature oratory is swift, unerring in its aim, and moving in its grandeur. There is the power which forges the links of history. . . . But Churchill's eloquence in the fateful hours of freedom and human dignity was heart-stirring in quite another way. With his great speeches he has, perhaps, himself erected his most enduring monument."[9]

The terms *honors* and *awards* are of course different from the concept of honor. Awards are much more about the common values of a country, the organization, and the giver of the award, rather than about individual honor, collective honor, or a country's honor. Honors and awards are given for some action or excellence, be it honorable or having other characteristics. Nevertheless, they do help point us in the direction of where we can actually look for honor.

INDIVIDUAL AND COLLECTIVE HONOR

The substance of what we call honor requires deeper consideration. For most people, individual heroic actions are required for honor; but for Churchill, individual actions were not honorable until some group established the basis for the honorable action. In other words, a barbarian might have acted honorably, but to Churchill it would not qualify as honorable because no one in the barbarian culture defined it as honorable. For Churchill, honor had to be put in the context of rules that come from civilization, and this was the focus of most of his writings on honor. For him honor came from a long-standing historic alliance like the British Empire. Honor came from values derived from centuries of time-tested tradition. There is no honor without a code. A good example of a code of honor is presented in the discussion of Bushido in the chapter "Honor in Military Culture," by Joe Thomas and Shannon French. They write, "Not surprisingly, are several similar themes in Bushido to those found in other codes, including the importance of maintaining honor and self-discipline, regardless of opposing pressures, and the conviction that voluntarily accepting certain restraints demonstrates strength, not weakness, and separates warriors into an elite group that cannot be confused with mere murderers."[10]

Churchill's own understanding of the complexity of heroism and honor was explored by the philosopher Isaiah Berlin, who worked for Churchill during World War II. Berlin observed that

> [t]he peculiar quality of heroic pride and a sense of the sublimity of the occasion arises [*sic*] in him . . . from a capacity for sustained introspective brooding, great depth and constancy of feeling—in particular, feeling for and fidelity to the great tradition for which he assumes a personal responsibility, a tradition which he bears upon his shoulders and must deliver, not only sound and undamaged but strengthened and embellished, to successors worthy of accepting the sacred burden.[11]

Churchill was aware of the long history of Britain, and that history along with the Empire was the great cause of Churchill's life.

Because Churchill believed that honor is necessarily tied to civilization, much of his discussion of honor was about collective actions rather than individual actions. Churchill wrote both about the honor of Great Britain and about honorable peace.[12] He believed in the distinctive honorable nature of what he called the "English Speaking Peoples." He also thought that France had a long honorable history, and he came to believe that Europe eventually must become one entity. (One of his most famous statements on honor, which is discussed later in this chapter, came from a speech he gave on a united Europe.[13]) All of these great countries and alliances for Churchill formed the foundation of honor. He also wrote about the honor of the British people standing alone against Hitler.

Churchill's evolution on honor took place as he was exposed to and experienced the military and war. Although, for Churchill, individual honors were often associated with military heroism, it is interesting to note how little he wrote about military honor considering how much of his early life was taken up with soldiering.

A political military leader, Churchill was involved with the military for his entire adult life. He attended the Royal Military Academy at Sandhurst. He fought in Cuba, Afghanistan, Sudan, and France. In total, he was present at or fought in a total of fifteen battles. He was a war correspondent and a prisoner of war who escaped during the Boar War in South Africa. He was the first lord of the admiralty twice. He was part of the war cabinet during World War I and was minister of munitions, secretary of state for war, and secretary of state for air. Finally, of course, he was prime minister and minister of defense during World War II. He wrote about all of his war experiences including four volumes about World War I and six volumes about World War II.

As a young man he was taught the classic cavalry tactics that changed dramatically during his lifetime. He wrote, "I wonder often whether any other generation has seen such astounding revolutions of data and values as those through which we have lived. Scarcely anything material or established which I was taught to believe was permanent and vital has lasted. Everything I was sure or thought to be sure was impossible has happened."[14] Churchill believed soldiering to be an honorable profession: "Even after having personally experiencing [*sic*] the horrors of Omdurman and World War I, he never lost his love of all things military and his nostalgia for the battlefield as a place where men proved themselves in the deadly but honorable business of combat."[15] He wrote about honor in regard to never leaving a soldier behind. And he wrote about the honor in making sure that soldiers' votes were counted. He also wrote about bravery, as a form of honor, in regard to the retreat of Dunkirk when the British Expeditionary Force was saved by a force of British boats and ships, both private and military, which moved them from France to Britain.[16] And he wrote about the heroism of the pilots who defended England during the Battle of Britain, famously stating, "Never in the field of human conflict was so much owed by so many to so few."[17] Although he admired individual honor, none of Churchill's writings about individual honor are as well known as his writings about collective honors involving Great Britain.

RHETORIC, WRITING, AND HONOR

Churchill was a great speaker and a Nobel Prize-winning author. A wordsmith who loved language, he wrote all of his speeches by hand, which helps us understand that his speeches were well thought out and edited. Churchill "used words for different purposes: to argue for moral and political causes, to advocate courses of action in the social, national and international spheres, and to tell the story of his own life and that of Britain and its place in the world."[18] Even in his early writings as a young man, he carefully analyzed the craft of writing. In an unpublished essay titled "The Scaffolding of Rhetoric," he explained the method—how to make an argument—emphasizing that rhetoric had to be planned.

For Churchill there were five principal elements of rhetoric that make arguments powerful. The five elements are: (1) correctness of diction, (2) rhythm, (3) accumulation of argument, (4) analogy, and (5) using wildly extravagant language to inspire the crowd. Among the five, the most revealing and informative for a study of honor is the principle of the accumulation of argument. This principle shows how Churchill builds a factual case for his argument or position.[19]

It is instructive to examine some famous examples of Churchill's use of the word *honor* in his rhetoric and what it means for his development of the concept of honor: His rhetorically most sophisticated discussion of honor comes in his first broadcast as prime minister to the British people on May 19, 1940. This broadcast occurred a week after he became prime minister and was among the most famous speeches Churchill ever made. The speech is often referred to as "Be Ye Men of Valour" after the quote at the end of the speech. We will look at the critical paragraph involving honor, where he foreshadows what he will detail in his discussion of Munich. Honor is tied to many of the events of the war and the defense of Britain.

> After this battle in France abates its force, there will come the battle for our Island—for all that Britain is, and all the Britain means. That will be the struggle. In that supreme emergency we shall not hesitate to take every step, even the most drastic, to call forth from our people the last ounce and the last inch of effort of which they are capable. The interests of property, the hours of labour, are nothing compared with the struggle of life and honour, for right and freedom, to which we have vowed ourselves.[20]

Rhetorically, Churchill uses the word *honor* in a familiar and commonly understood way: Honor is linked to the way people act. Here he also introduces two themes about honor that will occur throughout his writings. These themes include the defense of Britain and how that defense connects to right and freedom.

Churchill's most famous quote about honor came in a speech given at Harrow School in November 1941. This was during World War II when everything about Britain's future was still in doubt. Churchill knew his words at this time were critical because it was essential that he keep both the British people and much of the listening world inspired. By this time, his concept of honor had evolved from the concept he had as a young man. In this famous speech he said, "Never give in. Never give in. Never, never, never, never—in nothing, great or small, large or petty—never give in, except to convictions of honour and good sense. Never yield to force. Never yield to the apparently overwhelming might of the enemy."[21] These are the simple clear powerful words that made Winston Churchill legendary as the man who saved Britain and stirred free people everywhere. His speaking about honor this way was clear, without limits, and innate. As a young man, he defined honor in a more limited and relativistic way; whereas in this 1941 speech, his rhetoric and concept of honor more certain and powerful, accessible and conventional, and are less relativistic than what Churchill had written as a younger man. The other difference in this quote is that Churchill ties honor to good sense. "Good sense" will become "judgment" in his later writings; but for most people, the general concept is more likely understood as common sense, practical wisdom, or prudence.

In 1945, Churchill again turns to honor when he describes the importance of achieving the correct results of the war: "On the Continent of Europe we have yet to make sure that the simple and honourable purposes for which we entered the war are not brushed aside or overlooked in the months following our success, and that the words 'freedom,' 'democracy,' and 'liberation' are not distorted from their true meaning as we have understood them."[22] He reminds people that the war was fought for honorable purposes and that those purposes include freedom, democracy, and liberation. In his mature years, Churchill includes an ongoing thread throughout many of his speeches and writings that links honor and freedom. Here he extends the idea of honor and freedom to include not only democracy but also liberation. Churchill's idea of democracy involved a parliamentary system of self-determination, something Churchill defended throughout his life. But his idea of liberation was more complex because, although he advocated self-determination for the countries under Hitler, he certainly wanted to maintain control of the British Empire. This view of liberation was the consistent emphasis of Churchill's time in office and made his relationship with the United States very complicated.

Churchill's final famous quote about honor comes from after the war, in 1947. In a speech in favor of a united Europe, which he strongly believed was necessary for the future common security of everyone, he said, "All greatest things are simple, and many can be expressed in a single word: Freedom; Justice; Honor; Duty; Mercy; Hope."[23] Like his earlier quote, this puts honor in sequence with other innate "things." But what are these things? The ancient Greeks and the Christians would have called them virtues. For Churchill, I think they were simpler parts of his understanding of what it meant to be a gentleman and an Englishman. These are things that everyday people would recognize as good, and it was Churchill's rhetorical brilliance that took complex ideas and made them understandable to all. Yet, for all the brilliance, these speeches never reveal and define his concept of honor as well as his writings do.

CHURCHILL, CHAMBERLAIN, APPEASEMENT, AND HONOR

Churchill spent most of the 1930s in the political wilderness, out of power, and without a party. He wrote extensively, and many people believe he was preparing himself for the challenges he would face in the future. It was during this period that Churchill had to confront the most obvious example of dishonor in his lifetime, and he would use that incident to write the most comprehensive defense of honor in his mature writings.

When Churchill wrote about the betrayal of Czechoslovakia before World War II, he titled the chapter "The Tragedy of Munich."[24] Another Churchill biographer labeled the same incident "The Shame of Munich."[25] What both titles tell us is that the betrayal of Czechoslovakia represented the most important example of what Churchill considered dishonor. A familiar story for many people, Munich sets the backdrop for the most significant events highlighting honor and dishonor in the prewar period. The then Prime Minister of Great Britain, Neville Chamberlain, had to deal with Hitler, and like many in Britain who had seen World War I, he wanted to avoid a second world war at all costs. Hitler, near the beginning of his territorial conquests, had his sights on Czechoslovakia, and after meeting with Chamberlain and the French, he succeeding in obtaining their acquiescence to his takeover of the Sudetenland (a border area of Czechoslovakia) without any military confrontation. Chamberlain had thought Hitler was a "man of honour who would keep his word."[26] Chamberlain's most infamous quote about the deal was, "My good friends, this is the second time there has come back from Germany to Downing Street peace with honour. I believe it is peace in our time."[27] Note that Chamberlain framed his actions in terms of honor; however, the foreign policy lesson that many learned from Chamberlain's actions was that you cannot appease a dictator.

For Churchill the question of Czechoslovakia also turned on honor. In a widely used quote—his immediate reaction to the event—Churchill questions both the policy and the lack of honor in Chamberlain's actions. Colin Coote, who dined with Churchill the night Chamberlain left for Munich, recalled Churchill's reaction: "How, he asked, could honourable men with wide experience and fine records in the Great War condone a policy so cowardly? It was sordid, squalid, sub-human, and suicidal. The sequel to the sacrifice of honour . . . would be the sacrifice of lives, our people's lives."[28] In another quote, Churchill bluntly states, "You were given the choice between war and dishonor. You choose dishonor and you will have war."[29] Although Churchill and Chamberlain were quite different kinds of men, Churchill had always thought highly of Chamberlain and his family; therefore, this remark is particularly serious. Churchill believed that the people who fought in World War I had learned lessons that would make them more honorable, but many of the leaders in World War I had not seen combat like Churchill had. Churchill was a warrior and Chamberlain was not. What Churchill knew in his heart was that there were some things you had to fight for, and sometimes fighting was the best option, and this is what honor was truly about. For Churchill, people who fought in World War I were always given the benefit of the doubt, but appeasement was a betrayal of everything honorable.

Churchill's speech to the House of Commons on Neville Chamberlain's death in 1940 links the issue of Munich to the greater issue of honor and history. This is Churchill's second attempt at making sense of what happened, and it is more measured than his reactions in the immediate aftermath.

> It is not given to human beings, happily for them, for otherwise life would be intolerable, to foresee or to predict to any large extent the unfolding course of events. In one phase men seem to have been right, in another they seem to have been wrong. Then again, a few years later, when the perspective of time has lengthened, all stands in a different setting. There is a new proportion. There is a new scale of values. History with its flickering lamp stumbles along the trail of the past, trying to reconstruct its scenes, to revive its echoes, and kindle with pale gleams of former days. What is the worth of all this? The only guide to a man is his conscience; the only shield to his memory is the rectitude and sincerity of his actions. It is very imprudent to walk through life without this shield, because we are so often mocked by the failure of our hopes and the upsetting of our calculations; but with this shield, however the fates may play, we march always in the rank of honour.[30]

Here, Churchill for the first time gives us the elements of his mature sense of honor: Honor includes conscience, and the rectitude and sincerity of a person's actions. Taken together conscience, rectitude, and sincerity reveal the complexity of honor. All three elements of honor take time to develop, and it helps also to have prudence. Practical wisdom, common sense, and life experience make the need for honor clearer. The development of the elements of honor and prudence comes from age, education, and experience, or as Churchill wrote earlier, they had to be grounded in a code like chivalry. For Churchill, personally, the elements of honor were developed by being a gentleman and warrior, by reading, making, and writing history, and by having a sense of being an Englishman. For soldiers these elements are inculcated by their training. For all of us who value honor, we need to develop our sense of right, conscience, and sincerity through family, education, reading, travel, religion, and exposure to good leaders.

In 1948 in *The Gathering Storm*, Churchill finished his chapter on Munich with the most insightful writing on honor in his maturity. This was the third time he had addressed the issues about Chamberlain's actions and it was his most complete, reasoned approached. It is no surprise that his evaluation of honor at this later stage of his life was different, more complex, and more significant than were his writings as a young man.

He begins by examining the complexity of decision-making rules for leaders using the military. Using Munich as a backdrop, he develops helpful rules that future statesmen could use to guide themselves when they make foreign policy decisions. The rules are clear and would benefit any modern leader, and they could provide a basis, a starting point, for making many of the most important decisions, such as when to go to war. He notes the importance of circumstances, and he delineates the decision involving principles of morals and actions. Problems involving complex interactions of morals, circumstances, and actions make decisions difficult. He suggests a guide for future leaders using doctrines to guide difficult circumstances:

> The facts may be unknown at the time. . . . Those who are prone by temperament and character to seek sharp and clear-cut solutions of difficult and obscure problems, who are ready to fight whenever some challenges comes from a foreign Power, have not always been right. On the other hand, those whose inclination is to bow their heads, to seek patiently and faithfully for peaceful compromise, are not always wrong. On the contrary, in the majority of instances they may be right, not only morally but from a practical standpoint. How many wars have been averted by patience and persisting good will! Religion and virtue alike lend their sanctions to meekness and humility, not only between men but between nations. How many wars have been precipitated by firebrands! How many misunderstandings which led to wars could have been removed by temporizing! How often have countries fought cruel wars and then after a few years peace found themselves not only friends but allies![31]

Judgment is a critical element of Churchill's thought. Circumstances are complicated and often ambiguous. In this quote, he focuses on the peacemakers, something he was not. Yet he understood that in international relations, with all of its uncertainty and changeability, the peacemakers were sometimes correct, and delay might be the right course of action. Under this criterion only, Chamberlain made a good decision, but there is more to the issue.

Churchill next turns to the thorny issue of the conflict between Christian ethics versus political ethics. This matter could be controversial, but Churchill handles the issue adroitly and makes a convincing argument as to why religion cannot be the guide to duty and honor. Churchill understood the temptation to make Christian ethics the basis for leadership ethics but understood it would never work. He references the Sermon on the Mount as the basis for Christian ethics. For Churchill, Christian ethics require one to avoid war and aggression but these tools may be necessary for a political leader. The reason religion cannot be the guide for nation-states is that sometimes both the threat of force and force itself are necessary to keep people safe and free. For Churchill, Christian ethics preclude the use of force, except under very narrow circumstances. Therefore, Christian ethics are not part of what statesmen can use to fulfill their duty to keep a state safe, and this is a problem that continually plagued Christian countries. (There is no evidence that Churchill knew of Just War Theory.) Churchill takes things one step further by insisting that political leadership in wartime must be nimble and take advantage of the situations presented, implying that a leader might have to initiate a war if it will stave off a worse war or one that might be more difficult or deadly. For Churchill, history will judge the actions of those leaders based on a greater knowledge of what happened than any leader will know at the time.[32]

The priority of national defense is where Churchill is most critical of Chamberlain, because Chamberlain neither kept the British people safe nor ensured the freedom of the Czechs and others. He believed that there are times when a statesman must disregard his faith beliefs and do what will keep his people safe. Keeping people safe and free requires judgment and must include the full range of options, including keeping the threat of force as an option. Up to this point Churchill had talked about morals, ethics, and circumstances, but not honor. He is about to show how honor becomes the critical factor in everything he has discussed and points the way for nations to act:

> This guide is called *honour*. It is baffling to reflect that what men call honour does not correspond always to Christian ethics. Honour is often influenced by that element of pride which plays so large a part in its inspiration. An exaggerated code of honour leading to the performance of utterly vain and unreasonable deeds could not be defended, however fine it might look. Here, however, the moment came when Honour pointed the path of Duty . . .[33]

Churchill coalesces in this critical paragraph all he had previously written about honor. Simple justice requires a country to back its allies, keep its word, and live up to its treaty obligations; however, leadership is often more complicated. Pride is the motivation behind honor. But the extremes of honor, including pride, often lead the wrong way, that is, toward personal glory and wrongheaded policies, instead of toward the goal of keeping the citizens of the country safe and free. For Churchill much of what transpired in Munich relates to this. All that Churchill wrote earlier about Christian ethics not applying to honor comes to play in his analysis. Pride is one of the seven deadly sins, and because for Churchill pride is part of honor, then honor cannot correspond to Christian virtue. Instead, pride must be reined in so as not to be used badly. Now we have the final element that the mature Churchill believed involved honor. Honor is tied to pride and can go wrong without having a great deal of experience to moderate and direct it.

If we put together what Churchill wrote in 1940 with what he wrote above, we can finally understand his concept of honor for leaders and the modern world. Uncontrolled pride leads people to act recklessly. Pride controlled by duty, judgment, and the circumstances usually yields an honorable end. Duty is tied to countries, civilizations, and codes of behavior like chivalry. Duty helps moderate pride because it makes individuals part of something larger: For Churchill it was his sense of being an Englishman that gave him a sense of duty and moderated his outsized pride. Judgment involves conscience, rectitude, and sincerity. Conscience moderates pride by giving the person a sense of right and wrong and a preference for doing right. Rectitude moderates pride by emphasizing the goodness in moral choices and includes kindness and respect. Sincerity moderates pride by illuminating genuine actions free of deception or treachery. Taken all together, conscience, rectitude, and sincerity make it more difficult to succumb to false pride. Duty and judgment help leaders make good decisions.

Returning to Munich, Churchill blames the French for their dishonorable betrayal of Czechoslovakia. He wrote, "Not only wise and fair policy, but chivalry, honour, and sympathy for a small threatened people made an overwhelming concentration [of evidence against the Munich Agreement]." And he goes on to blame Great Britain for the same reasons. For Churchill, Chamberlain's actions fail all the important tests. Munich was not a wise course of action. Keeping the Sudetenland in Czech hands was the wise and prudent thing to do, because it would have slowed Hitler's advance. Britain had no business abrogating the treaty with the Czechs, and no authority to act for them.[34]

CONCLUSION

Winston Churchill was an excellent example of a statesman who wrote about honor, but what he wrote and believed were unconventional. Anyone who spent as much time in and around the military would be expected to focus on individual heroic action as the focus of honor in the modern world; however, although Churchill acknowledged heroism and knew it led to great recognition, it was not the focus of his beliefs, especially as he matured.

Instead, Churchill went through an evolution in his thinking about honor. As a young writer Churchill believed that honor was relative, subject to variation in societies and within any society over time, without any guiding principle. He modified this belief over time, but in much of his writing, he still remained convinced that honor was not innate but pertained to civilized codes of behavior. Churchill also desired awards and honors as a young man, while understanding the great challenges and danger of military life that went with the awards. Yet most of the awards yielded very little in the way of understanding the concept of honor.

For Churchill the most important theory that generally dominated his life and writing was his expansive vision of history. Churchill's historicism is familial, personal, distinguished, largely British, and unique. Churchill's view of honor is always linked with his writing of history. The more sophisticated Churchill's histories became, the more deep his understanding of honor became. Churchill's cultivated intellectual worldliness in the 1930s finally led to his mature understanding of honor.

Churchill was not a religious man, but he had an understanding of religion and referred to it many times in his writings. He concluded that religion could not be the guide for statesmen because they must focus on what would make their country safe and free. To make people safe, politicians must do things that went against the tenets of most religions, like attacking other countries and executing traitors. Therefore, honor becomes more important for Churchill because honor becomes the guide to action when religion cannot.

For Churchill honor is associated with Great Britain, other Western countries, civilization, and codes of honor like chivalry. Honor was a product of those institutions, which means it can change over time, but because it was tied to great, historic, generally good places like Great Britain, it was good. Implied, but not stated, is that any claim to honor by a country like Nazi Germany would be corrupt because the underlying régime is corrupt.

Churchill understood that the nuances of honor could not be refined rhetorically. He knew that honor could be understood simply as a natural, good thing. He never defines honor in speeches, but instead it stands as something that the beholder can define. Implied is that honor is good: keeping one's word; fulfilling treaty obligations; fighting for your family, friends, and country. Honor was an inspirational point for Churchill in speeches that helped his people and insured his place in history.

Pride is the motivating emotion that drives people to act honorably. Yet pride can go wrong and become too dominant, and then people can err in their judgment. Churchill was a proud man who understood how pride drove him. Yet he stayed within the bounds of honor by having an unambiguous understanding about his own place in history. Churchill limited his pride by having a sense of duty to Great Britain and a commitment to continue that greatness for the next generation.

Honor must involve judgment and common sense. Churchill had a clear belief that because of pride and error, all honor must be limited necessarily by common sense. The quest for honor is an intense motivation, and practical wisdom about how to live is important to keep it from going wrong. Even more important is mature, considered, judgment, because it is integral for ensuring that individuals use honor correctly. Honor is also rightly constrained by conscience, rectitude, and sincerity. All of these elements are as instructive for leadership and for statecraft in Churchill's day as they are for statecraft today. Churchill never formally defines honor, but it is clear from what he wrote that honor is keeping your word, abiding by your treaties, backing your allies, and keeping people free and safe. These qualities guide us toward honor and fortify leaders for making difficult decisions with honor.

NOTES

1. Paul Johnson, *Churchill* (New York: Penguin, 2009), 11.
2. Winston S. Churchill, *Savrola* (London: Octopus Publishing Group, 1990), 77.
3. Randolph S. Churchill, *Winston S. Churchill, Vol. 1, Youth, 1874–1900* (Boston: Houghton Mifflin, 1966), 349.
4. Isaiah Berlin, *Personal Impressions* (New York: Penguin, 1980), 4.
5. Douglas S. Russell, excerpt from "The Orders, Decorations and Medals of Sir Winston Churchill," *Winston Churchill Centre*, accessed 5/31/14, http://www.winstonchurchill.org/learn/biography/the-soldier/orders-decorations-and-medals.
6. Carlo D'Este, *Warlord, A Life of Winston Churchill at War, 1874–1945* (New York: Harper, 2008), 114.
7. "National Churchill Museum," accessed 5/25/2014, http://www.nationalchurchillmuseum.org/winston-churchill-knight-of-the-garter.html.
8. "Winston Churchill's Nobel Prize in Literature 1953," *Nobel Prize*, accessed 5/25/2014, http://www.nobelprize.org/nobel_prizes/literature/laureates/1953/.
9. "Presentation Speech by S. Siwertz, Member of the Swedish Academy, The Nobel Prize in Literature 1953 Winston Churchill," *Nobel Prize*, accessed 5/25/2014, http://www.nobelprize.org/nobel_prizes/literature/laureates/1953/press.html.
10. Joe Thomas and Shannon French, "Honor in Military Culture: A Standard of Integrity and Framework for Moral Restraint," in this volume.
11. Berlin, *Personal Impressions*, 15.
12. Martin Gilbert, *Churchill: The Power of Words* (Boston: Da Capo Press, 2012), 336, 358.
13. Winston S. Churchill, *Never Give In! The Best of Winston Churchill's Speeches* (New York: Hyperion, 2003), 436.
14. Winston Churchill, *My Early Life, 1874–1904* (New York: Touchstone, 1996), 67.
15. D'Este, *Warlord*, 33.
16. Max Hastings, *Winston's War: Churchill 1940–1945* (New York: Alfred A. Knopf, 2011), 59–63.
17. Winston S. Churchill, *Their Finest Hour: The Second World War, Vol. 2* (Boston: Houghton Mifflin, 1949), 340.
18. Gilbert, *Words*, vii.
19. Winston S. Churchill, "The Scaffolding of Rhetoric," *Winston Churchill Centre*, accessed 5/26/2014, http://www.winstonchurchill.org/images/pdfs/for_educators/THE_SCAFFOLDING_OF_RHETORIC.pdf.
20. Winston S. Churchill, *Never Give In!* 209.
21. Winston S. Churchill, *Never Give In!* 307.
22. Winston S. Churchill, *Never Give In!* 394.
23. Winston S. Churchill, *Never Give In!* 406.
24. Winston S. Churchill, *The Gathering Storm: The Second World War, Vol. 1* (Boston: Houghton Mifflin, 1948), 298.
25. D'este, *Warlord*, 249.
26. Graham Stewart, *Burying Caesar: The Churchill-Chamberlain Rivalry* (New York: Overlook, 1999), 310.
27. Stewart, *Burying Caesar*, 310.

28. Martin Gilbert, *Prophet of Truth: Winston S. Churchill, 1922–1939* (London: Minerva, 1976), 989.
29. D'este, *Warlord,* 253.
30. David Cannadine, ed., *Blood, Toil, Tears and Sweat: The Speeches of Winston Churchill* (Boston: Houghton Mifflin, 1989), 194.
31. Churchill, *Gathering Storm,* 319.
32. Churchill, *Gathering Storm,* 320.
33. Churchill, *Gathering Storm,* 320–21.
34. Churchill, *Gathering Storm,* 321.

NINE

Life in Death

Democracy and Civic Honor

Ajume Wingo

Why do young Africans cling so desperately to life and peace at any cost to their freedom, justice and happiness? Why for so long haven't they fought back with the full measure of their own lives? Our sage ancestors taught us that life and death should not be judged by mere superficial physical qualities alone. While death is a total loss of physical functioning, *life* in its fullest form is more than just the absence of physical death, but is ultimately an active purpose writ large in the life of the state. Life in that fullest form is intimately tied to freedom or civic activity. Just as the usual understanding of immortality refers to an unending physical life, there is an analogous sense of civic immortality based on the continuing effect of one's civic life on others. As such civic immortality conjures up political life as life over and beyond biological life.

Consider a scene from Chinua Achebe's novel, *Things Fall Apart* :

> Ezeudu was a great man, and so all the clan was at his funeral. [. . .] Ezeudu had taken three titles in his life. It was a rare achievement. There were only four titles in the clan, and only one or two men in any generation ever achieved the fourth and highest. When they did, they became the lords of the land. Because he has taken titles, Ezeudu was to be buried after dark with only a glowing brand to light the sacred ceremony. [. . .] But before this quiet and final rite, the tumult increased tenfold. Drums beat violently and men leaped up and down in frenzy. Guns were fired on all sides and sparks flew out as machetes clanged together in warriors' salutes. The air was full of dust and the smell of gunpowder. It was then that the one-handed spirit came, carrying a

> basket full of water. People made way for him on all sides and the noise subsided. [. . .] He danced a few steps to the funeral drums and then went to see the corpse. "Ezeudu" he called in his guttural voice. "If you had been poor in your last life I would have asked you to be rich when you come again. But you were rich. If you had been a coward, I would have asked you to bring courage. But you were a fearless warrior. If you had died young, I would have asked you to get life. But you lived long. So I shall ask you to come again the way you came before. If your death was the death of nature go in peace. But if a man caused it, do not allow him a moment's rest." He danced a few more steps and went away.[1]

Here Achebe describes the death celebration of a hero. Traditional African societies recognized multiple human lives and deaths. There is the biological life of an individual common to all living organisms, which ends in biological death, and then there is political life, which is more than or less than but not equal to biological life. In the African parlance, this is life beyond *biological* life, or "bio-life" as we may put it. Ezeudu, though biologically dead, has a continuing *social and political* life. The clan has gathered not merely to celebrate the life lived but to immortalize him by weaving his life, as it were, into the intricate fabric of societal life. He is being asked to come back—not in a biological or physical sense, but in a political sense. It is the continuation of life by other means.

Among the people of Nso in Cameroon, the honor of immortalization is more explicit. Once every year for the eight days of the Nso calendar week in December the progenies of Ngonnso, the thirteenth-century matriarch who founded the state of Nso (named after her) in the northwest region of Cameroon, gather in Kumbo, the political capital of the Nso Fondom. The eight days are celebrated with communal music, dance, gunfire, bonfire, Nso cuisine, open-air-theater and art of all genres, along with the enactment of the Nso communal ways of life: war is enacted through war songs, bloodletting animal sacrifices are made to the heroes and heroines of Nso, now ancestors. In the spirit of the dignitarian society that Nso is, occupants of all ranks participate. Everyone from the Fon (King), a Yaa (female leaders), a Mforme ver a baa (the two Nso Generals, "a" stands for plural); Vibay (cabinet members of the Fon), a Taa Ntoh and a Taa Nwerong (Supreme Court Justices and retainers of Nso laws), a Shu-Fai and Fai (elected representatives of large families), down to the rank of Shey (a recently invented nonhereditary title open to anyone by merit) gather together with dignitaries from neighboring communities. Through this annual celebration, Ngonnso's life is woven into the lives of Nso people.

Achebe's fictional event and the Nso annual celebration are parts of complex institutions that support a particular conception of political freedom within those societies. This chapter examines that conception of political freedom and an associated conception of citizenship. I argue that, at their core, those conceptions of political freedom and citizenship for an individual citizen involve the transformation of the self by deeds and words into the intricate artificial sovereign entity, the state, which is ultimately responsible for political life and death.

CITIZENSHIP IN CONTEMPORARY AFRICAN DEMOCRACIES

While African traditions conceive of individuals and citizens in a variety of ways, modern African elites and intellectuals have largely abandoned that perspective. For instance, when a Nigerian boasts of 170 million Nigerian citizens, she is referring to a body count. This physical body-based conception of citizenship is nowadays the norm of modern democratic states the world over. The body conception of citizen has a *recorded* history in modern Western world extending back to the writ of the habeas corpus, which literally means "produce the body" or "you may have the body."[2] The opening of the writs in the fourteenth-century Anglo-French document requiring a person to be brought before a court or judge to determine if that person is legally detained reads as follows:

> We command you, that the body of A.B. in Our prison under your custody detained, as it is said, together with the day and cause of his taking and detention, by whatever name the said A.B. may be known therein, you have at our Court . . . to undergo and to receive that which our Court shall then and there consider and order in that behalf. Hereof in no way fail, at your peril. And have you then there this writ.[3]

One can further see how the conceptions of the body and the citizen have been joined in the Universal Declaration of Human Rights (UDHR). Enacted shortly after World War II, the Universal Declaration of Human Rights provides that "Everyone has the right to life, liberty and security of person." Mimicking the writ, Article 5.4 of the European Convention on Human Rights reads "Everyone who is deprived of his liberty by arrest or detention shall be entitled to take proceedings by which the lawfulness of his detention shall be decided speedily by a court and his releases ordered if the detention is not lawful." While the UDHR was clearly intended to protect individual rights, it did so in a way that that "leveled down" the requirements for citizenship. Bio-life became the new norm for enjoying the political life.

In some ways, this conception of citizenship was a momentous achievement of modern politics, for it universalized citizenship (at least among humans).[4] At the same time, however, it highlighted the problem of how to reconcile the two lives—the political life and the bio-life: *What are the implications for our understanding and practice of politics when citizenship is divorced from active political participation?*

The answer to that question may be troubling, for in many ways the good provided by politics depends on the participation of the members of the political community. Politics, as Aristotle taught, is of value to the extent that it allows citizens to realize the good life—a life in which those citizens have a say in determining their destiny.

THE KNOT OF POLITICAL LIFE: THE RELATIONSHIPS AMONG THE STATE, CITIZENS, AND HUMAN BEINGS

In his political treatise, *De Cive*, Thomas Hobbes observed that:

> If we look at adult men and consider the fragility of the unity of human body (whose ruin marks the end of every strength, vigor, and force) and the ease with which the weakest man can kill the strongest man, there is no reason for someone to trust in his strength and think himself superior to others by nature. Those who can do the same things to each other are equals. And those who can do the supreme thing—that is, kill—are by nature equal among themselves.[5]

According to Hobbes, the main cause of conflict is human equality: we are by nature approximately equal in our capacity to bring about the violence end of life of each other. The ultimate aim of political life is to upset that natural equality by endowing one actor—the state—with the power to do to others what others *cannot* do. Politics, that is, marks the transition from the equality of vulnerability to the inequality in the service of human security.

This transition is also the difference between a bio-life—a life dictated by the necessities of survival and self-preservation—and the life of a person—one directed by intention and design. Herein is the difference between "Life," writ large, and life as animal existence, the distinction the people of Nso make. They say "not life but Life in life is what we celebrate" for political life is "our life" and the bio-life is anything but "ours." Life as existence is given to us by nature; political life is given to nature by us. The former is imposed on us; the latter is an aesthetic achievement of the individual.

A central problem in political thought concerns the creation of an entity—the state—with the capability and authority to order the lives of its constituent members so as to allow those members to live the good life. Few efforts have come close to solving that problem, and throughout history, most have bought the capacity to order by diminishing the liberty of the population. A traditional method of addressing the problem of equality is *tribalism*, whereby individuals with a natural affinity to one another (e.g., family members) come together as groups. Within the group, individuals generally remain equal in power. The dangers posed by equipollent individuals to each other are, however, counteracted by bonds of common blood or descent. Those bonds of common blood or descent also create a cadre of natural allies in fending off threats from nonmembers.

Tribalism is best thought of as a means of managing the problem of equality, rather than as a solution. That is, it operates by sorting individuals by blood or other innate traits to minimize conflict within the group. It does not, in itself, create a superior force—to do unto others what they cannot do unto it—that orders the individuals composing the group. Instead, it relies on the ability of groups to cast out those individuals who are not compatible with the groups' identifying characteristic (e.g., descent or familial relationship).

The "sorting" nature of tribes is a means of reducing intratribal conflict among individuals. A form of the problem of equality remains, however, in that those equally powerful individuals may have very different ideas about which policies the tribe should adopt as a group. This problem is most evident in circumstances of conflict *between* tribes, where the survival of the tribe is at stake. In those situations, there is an advantage to having a single individual with the authority to decide for the group. Often the man (or, as is the case of some African communities like the Nso, the woman) who performs extraordinary deeds defending their community at war is singled out for that role. The practice of the ancient Greeks (according to Aristotle) was to banish such a being from the community of equals. In the case of many African communities, rather than expel him, he was deliberately recognized, honored and made King. Therein lies the origin of the "big-man" phenomenon, which haunts Africa today.

Tribalism *manages* the problem of equality by latching onto largely immutable circumstances of individuals' birth. A political state, in contrast, attempts to *solve* the problem by shaping individuals' dispositions and character in some way or another—sometimes through persuasion and education, and sometimes through brute force. Whatever the means used, a key distinction between tribalism and the political state is that whereas the former seeks harmony among its constituents by sifting out the disharmonious, the latter seeks to harmonize the actions of its constituents by *making* them act in harmony.

This view of the political state as having a hand in reshaping or even creating the actions and characters of the individuals in them suggests a complementary relationship between the state and the subject: a political state is itself an artificial entity constituted by individuals who themselves are also a kind of artificial being—what the Romans and the Athenians referred to as the *citizen*, and what the Nso of Cameroon and the Akan of Ghana refer to as *wir* and *onipa* (or "person"), respectively.[6]

Our understanding of the life (and death) of political individuals thus is bound up with our understanding of the state. A natural place to start, then, is with Hobbes's analysis of the origins and nature of the state as presented in *Leviathan*, his seminal political treatise. Significantly, Hobbes presents the state not as embodied in a human figure (as tribal societies would have it in the name of a King), but as a nonhuman—indeed, as the sea monster described in the Book of Job.

Abraham Bosse's famous frontispiece of *Leviathan* captured the image of the state even better. In it, a giant figure of a "big-man" wearing a churchly crown emerges from a landscape holding a sword and a crosier. Beneath is a quote from the Book of Job: "*Non est potestas Super Terram quae Comparetur*" ("There is no power on earth to be compared to him"), linking the figure to the monster of that book. More interestingly, his torso and arms are composed of the images of many small persons all facing inward, with only the giant face showing visible features. (In some other manuscripts, the faces are looking outward from the body with a range of expressions.) The sword and the crosier symbolize the union of the secular and the spiritual in the state, the sovereign. According to Hobbes, the state of nature is characterized by the "war of all against all," and life there is "solitary, poor, nasty, brutish and short." The only hope for a secured and good life becomes the state as symbolized by the leviathan.

But the frontispiece itself, though evocative of the relationship between the state and individuals, does not exactly capture the interactive nature of that relationship, for the state itself is not merely an association or collection of individual humans. There is, instead, a more complex relationship, one in which the individuals that compose the state take on additional qualities by virtue of their relationship to the state: they are transformed from mere humans into *citizens*. This is just to say, again, that there is more to being a citizen than one's physical status as a human being. The honor of being called "citizen" is not due merely to being a living organism—even one as highly developed as a human being. Citizenship is earned through one's activity—particularly one's political activity and involvement in public matters.[7]

What, then, follows from this distinction between citizens and humans? At the very least, this view suggests there is something quite wrongheaded about the outlook that made the concrete body of the human being the benchmark for citizenship and the law, as in the writ of the habeas corpus act and the UNDHR.

A second consequence concerns how states and citizens should interact. The distinction between humans as mere biological organisms and citizens lies in the latter's capacity for purposeful activity in the political life of the state. Citizens participate in the creation and maintenance of their political institutions; they do not merely react to their political circumstances according to their instincts and habits, like a mouse in a lab. Indeed, citizens influence in purposeful ways the state through politics.

That citizens and the state interact through politics imposes an important constraint on how citizens should interact amongst themselves and how the state should interact with them. Politics is, as Aristotle taught, concerned with how we should live a secured and good life *together*, and because life together comes with constant contacts with others who disagree over aims and conceptions of the good, politics invariably involves conflict. What distinguishes politics as a means of handling conflict is that it is dedicated to the use of negotiation, conciliation, compromise, and persuasion in the service of pursuing those shared purposes that require the state. The use of physical force or coercion is diametrically opposed to politics. *Pace* Clausewitz, while war and politics are necessarily involved with conflict, they are utterly different responses to ("means" of addressing) that conflict. War—and coercion in general—results from the belief that there is no point to arguing with the other side. Politics, no matter how abased or undignified it may be in practice, rests on the entirely honorable belief that others can be persuaded, and that reasons and an understanding of others' motives and priorities can make a difference.[8]

A third consequence of the distinction between citizens and humans concerns the effect of that distinction on the lives of those humans who do not meet the standards of citizenship. What I've argued to this point concerns the status of *citizens* and their relationship to each other and to the state. But that leaves out all those human *noncitizens*. The effects of the citizen-human distinction on those noncitizens will in some cases be quite positive. If, that is, citizens are concerned with protecting individual liberty and autonomy, then they are likely to demand broad limits on state power. By demanding what is essentially a kind of public good, citizens secure benefits for themselves and for noncitizens. Historically this has often been the case with highly active citizens—e.g., America's founding generation, civil rights activists, labor leaders—who make demands of the state that affect the entire population. Often, those citizens may be seen by those who have little or no interest in politics as members of the "lunatic fringe" or "agitators," yet their efforts may have long-term benefits for all.

Citizens do not, of course have only the capacity to steer states in a *positive* direction. The nature of a citizen is to engage with the state in an intelligent and purposeful way through politics. None of that requires the citizen to act altruistically or morally, and so it is quite possible—indeed, predictable—that some citizens will attempt to harness the state's power in order to benefit themselves at the cost of others or even to persecute others.

The tremendous potential negative consequences for noncitizens is evident in Africa. For instance, not all who *think* of themselves as Nigerian citizens (and who are *counted* as Nigerian citizens on the body-based conception) are actually treated that way by the so-called Nigerian state. That is, the majority of Nigerian *subjects* are not *citizens*—not engaged with the state, making demands of it, and voicing their expectations of it. For instance, on the night of April 14, 2014, 276 girls were kidnapped from a government secondary school in the town of Chibok in Borno state, Nigeria. Boko Haram, an Islamic extremist and terrorist group based in northern Nigeria, claimed responsibility for the abduction. And there most of the victims remain. What would have happened if those girls were *citizens*—if those girls *mattered* to the Nigerian state? In Edmund Burke's words, ten thousand swords would have leaped from their scabbards to avenge them. Instead, the girls are still being held. Indeed, Boko Haram has spread since then, preventing thousands of young people from attending school in Borno state. How else can the Nigerian state's failure to heed the cries of these girls and their parents be explained other than by the fact that, as far as the state is concerned, *Boko Haram isn't harming anyone who really matters*.

The difference between citizens and noncitizens makes a difference when the protections afforded to citizens do not "spill over" to noncitizens. This is evident in Nigeria, where even Boko Haram is careful to leave full-fledged citizens alone. Let Boko Haram abduct or kill a real citizen of Nigeria—say the minister of oil and energy, or some other official, or any of their children—and you will see the full force of the Nigerian state unleashed on them and the organization destroyed overnight. Let it abduct or kill a United States citizen and see the United States' drones unleashed upon them overnight. As I write, the girls are still in the custody of Boko Haram. Should the Nigerian government act, it will be thanks to the pressure put on the government, either by its citizens or by outside forces (e.g., the international community). But it will not be because of some spontaneous urge to protect the welfare of the girls and their parents, for they do not (as a matter of fact) show up on the radar of citizenship of the state of Nigeria.

HONOR AND CIVIC IMMORTALITY AS THE UPLOADING OF THE SELF BY DEEDS AND WORDS INTO THE COMMON PURPOSE (THE STATE)

The activities of Boko Haram and the reluctance of the Nigerian state to react illustrates the negative effects of the distinction between citizens and noncitizens not just in Nigeria but in African states in general. Those negative effects are, I believe, likely only to get worse over time if we continue to ignore the distinction between citizens and mere humans, and focus instead on the body-based conception of citizenship that has become so dominant the world over, promulgated by the Western world in the name of democracy.

The leveling down of persons or citizens into bare human beings has not served democracies well, and certainly hasn't served Africans in their quest for democratic political life. When we come to a point where everyone is entitled to a trophy whether they participate in the competition or not, then we've lost not only the meaning of a trophy but the essence of competition. That has been the case in politics, wherever the Kantian conception of dignity has been improperly appropriated into democratic politics. This is not lost on Catholics and Muslims. Autonomy that is attached to the kind of human dignity advocated by Jeremy Waldron, and which is taken for granted in liberal democratic states, is not always taken for granted. Here is Michael Rosen musing on the aporia of freedom without autonomy:

> Not surprisingly, the voluntarism associated with the autonomy conception of human dignity is forcefully rejected by the Catholic Church (as well as many other religious groups), for example by Pope John Paul II in his encyclicals *Veritatis Splendor* (1993) and *Evangelium Vitae* (1995). In *Veritatis Splendor* the pope recognizes that "[the] heightened sense of the dignity of the human person . . . certainly represents one of the positive achievements of modern culture." On the other hand, it is characteristic of atheism and "doctrines which have lost the sense of the transcendent" that they should "exalt freedom to such an extent that it becomes an absolute, which would then be the source of values." . . . [T]he problem, in the pope's view, is a voluntarist conception of human dignity, "the mentality which carries the concept of subjectivity to an extreme and even distorts it, and recognizes as a subject of rights only the person who enjoys full or at least incipient autonomy."[9]

These concerns about autonomy are not confined to Catholics. The *Cairo Declaration of Human Rights in Islam* (1990) is telling. Its Article 6, in contrast to the *Universal Declaration*, asserts that women have "equal dignity" but, conspicuously, not equal rights.[10]

Wittingly or not, African political outlooks are bad copies of the Western systems. They were appropriated from, and handed over to elite Africans by, their colonial masters, and they've done nothing to change their states for the better. The new African elites, with neither prior local social standing nor political experience (none was from the royal or ruling houses in African indigenous societies), for the first time in their lives had a taste of political life. The result? They went wild in their craving for more at any cost to those they were supposed to be serving in the first place. They were recruited from the margin of African indigenous communities, trained and schooled by missionaries and colonial masters. Their craving for political power hastened the demise of colonization and their ascent into the cockpit of new African states at independence. The African elites were recruited by the colonialists to serve them, not the people, a legacy that is still alive and well.

The postcolonial states that Crawford Young described so well (in *The African Colonial State in Comparative Perspective*[11]) were synonymous with the African ruling elites, who sought to maintain the veneer of democracy. If seeing is learning, then no one should be surprised, since what African elites had seen were the colonial masters beating Africans like dumb animals, commanding them around like nutty children refusing to leave the playground, and in many cases killing them with impunity as if they were cattle in slaughter houses.[12] When these elites imagined how to govern, they had nothing of their own to hold onto and so adopted the methods of their colonial masters. What the new elites never could figure out even up to today is that the behavior of the colonial masters towards Africans was markedly the opposite of their behavior to their citizens in their home countries.

It is as if African elites (especially those who traveled to the West) were exposed to Western citizens exuding not only a secure state, but more centrally the good life, but without any witness of the sacrifices of citizens. The likes of Frederick Douglass, John Brown, Patrick Henry, Rosa Parks, and Martin Luther King, Jr. made political life in the United States possible and achievable for many through their sacrifice of, or their readiness to sacrifice, their bio-lives for higher purposes of the state. The African elites were exposed to laws but not to what it takes to make the laws functional and agreeable to the citizens. They were exposed to the executive offices of presidents but not to other offices, which together make political life legitimate. When they imagined how to govern legitimately, they immediately focused their attention on the Office of the President or Prime Minister at the helm making decisions all alone, without the equal contributing power of the judiciary, legislators, and, most importantly, the nonoffice-bearing citizens and their elective associations and organizations that Tocqueville talks about in his *Democracy in America*. They saw Western elites taking office but not leaving those offices. The "President for Life" tradition continues unabated in African states today.[13] If and when African elites do leave office, it is generally either by what Africans has dubbed a "coup from heaven" (death in office) or by an outright coup d'état. It is as if African elites are exposed to the invention, but not the inventor's labor and imagination: they have seen the light bulb, but not Thomas Edison.

What is missing from the legitimate political life in African states cannot be compensated for by yet more political trappings. Africans have a superabundance of the trappings of modern states—competitive multiparty democratic elections, parliaments, judicial systems, memberships in the United Nations, and the like. But behind these trappings very often lies a state that is corrupt, repressive, and unbound by the rule of law. For the African citizens living in these states, the arbitrary force of their leaders does not become law simply by being clad in the trappings of law, and a systematic oppression of people can quite easily coexist with modern—even liberal—trappings.

The trappings of modern states are most important to the leaders with the least claim to legitimacy, providing them with a kind of sublime power, serving as "palm wine with which the private wills of tyrants are drank." In even a legitimately constituted state, the trappings are important in supporting the effectiveness of the state and its use of power by making the state and its authority concrete. Much as the Catholic Church has incorporated a range of sensory experience to make itself concrete—the visual sensations of stained glass and tapestries, aural experience of hymns and choirs, the tangible, tactile qualities of the Eucharist, and the olfactory dimension of burning incense—states can use these trappings to make themselves present to citizens by enabling the state to be seen, heard, touched, felt, contemplated, and appreciated in real time and place.

But the trappings are not sufficient for a government's legitimacy. If they were, then any band of gun-toting hoodlums who violently seized power and adorned themselves appropriately in various trappings—as happened in Africa following the string of coup d'états that characterized the early days of independence, and recently in Mali, Guinea Bissau, and Central African Republic—could make themselves legitimate. But the legitimacy of a government depends not just on its own qualities (such as the substantial features of its organization or its more superficial trappings), but more importantly on its *relationship* to citizens and the state. Leaders' mere ability to impose their will from behind the trappings is not sufficient to ensure actual legitimacy. Might does not make right.[14]

What is still missing from African political life is something that only Africans can supply themselves. African youth are well positioned to transform themselves into the general purposes of states that not only make life meaningful for them but also for generations to follow. African youth as citizens are responsible for bringing about responsive states. Just as new African elites got the colonialists who were maltreating them and stopped them from exercising the full blast of power, African youth will need to get rid of the new African elites. To do so, they will need a type of motivation which transcends the material world of things and even bio-life. Clinging to bio-life in the manner of a mere animal does not foster the conditions needed for the establishment of a responsive state to provide security and, more importantly, political life.

The exclusive focus on bio-life is responsible for the brain drain caused by African youth flying to Europe. It is as if Western technological development in aerial transportation, cell phones and internet have paved the way for an exodus of the most promising young Africans from their homeland. African youth from troubled African spots in the continent (which is virtually everywhere and anywhere in Africa) are in flight—for the most part sharing the desire to go anywhere other than where they have been. *Staying alive*, at bottom, has been the prime mover of emigration. Faced with a tyrannical regime or political, economic, and social setbacks, the choice for young Africans is either flight or fight the regime responsible with their bio-lives. It is as if Africans would prefer to die on their dangerous voyage out of Africa than to die in Africa fighting the setbacks in their various states. This could be said, for example, of the more than eight hundred who recently risked their souls on the Mediterranean Sea during their flight out of Africa rather than risk their bio-lives for the common good and live on politically in the lives of later generations of Africans. Those able-minded and able-bodied youths who stay behind do so because there is nowhere else to go. They may embark on a different sort of flight, a virtual flight into the cyber world of the West with their bodies in Africa but their spirits in the West and now China and Dubai.

What is missing from African states is as simple as it is important to a well-ordered political life: it is the lack of a citizenry with the readiness to sacrifice "life for Life." African youth need to convert their physical flight into political activity, as did the likes of Steve Biko, Mohamed Bouazizi, and Nelson Mandela of South Africa, who risked and sometimes sacrificed their physical lives for the communal purposes that make political life possible and rich. What those three had in common was that they gave up their biological *mortal* life for civic *immortal* Life so that young Africans will not have to leave their homes in flight to Europe or elsewhere.

Contemporary political philosophers are fond of talking about institutions and leaders without citizens. My intention here is to draw a focus back to the nature of citizens and their key role in creating responsive states. To that end, I outline some general types of individuals that populate states, ranging from merely human noncitizens to different categories of citizens:

Human Beings: Death in Death

A human being is a biological entity. Unlike citizenship, the status of being human is not subject to degrees or gradations: one is either a human being or one is not. The factors ruling the actions and conduct of human beings are not freedom, justice, and equality but necessities of life and concern for its preservation. The actions of human beings are necessitated by internal laws of self-preservation. The life of self-preservation is shared by all members of the species. As remarkably complex organisms, humans interact with their physical environment in amazingly complicated ways, but they do not create or manipulate their political environment.

Citizen Simpliciter: Dignity and Life in Life

This is the run-of-the-mill member of a state. A citizen simpliciter enjoys the status of self-representation, self-legislation, self-application of the law, self-improvement, and consequently self-piloting of her life in the state. She is a full participant in the life of the state. It is appropriate to speak of the *dignity* of such citizens, in the sense of dignity being the desire not to be dominated, repressed, or oppressed. In short, it is to be free from the arbitrary commands of others and capricious laws.[15] The dignity of the citizen simpliciter is displayed in the communal sphere where they can see and be seen, listen and be heard, feel and be felt. Exemplars of such displays are in public assemblies, Jane Mansbridge's "town hall meetings," and deliberate voting for representatives, laws, and all other things that ensure their freedom, justice, and equality.

Liminal Citizens: Straddling between Life and Death

A *liminal citizen* straddles the gap between the mere human and the citizen simpliciter. She is more or less caught in between a citizen and a human being; but because she is entitled to the benefits and obligations of political life (especially in a democracy), she is considered a citizen rather than merely a human being. The factors controlling her actions and conduct are still partly internally necessitated. Her political enterprise is an unending struggle to climb out of a noncitizen status of a human being into the rank of a citizen and to avoid falling back into a nonstatus entity. As a human being, her life is governed by the fear of death.[16]

The forces of law and order are put into place in the service of these kinds of liminal citizens. Thanks to the coercive forces of the police, penal devices, jails and prisons, which enable this category of citizens to assume responsibilities of citizenship such as the toleration of other citizens, respect for traffic, payment of taxes, performance of jury duty, and so on. To recruit this category of citizens into the military, emphasis is given to material and immediate benefits such as attractive salaries and professional training. Such citizens are more attracted to the military when warfare is conducted at a safe distance from the enemy, firing from far in the sky or from the shores of the great oceans unreachable by the enemy. When they leave for war they tell their loved ones they will be back. Contrast this to those serving the state in the indigenous Nso polity who upon leaving for war bid their loved ones goodbye.

Taxation is another place where liminal citizens are treated as equals. In the United States, the IRS must make it clear that they are poised to audit anyone at random with heavy penalties for not complying with tax codes. Liminal citizens are expected to pay taxes to keep the state up and running. The state also coerces these kinds of semicitizens as fathers into the performance of their parental responsibilities otherwise they may conduct themselves in a kind of Rousseauian reproductive state of nature, as men who are just interested in spreading their seeds wherever they can and with zero responsibility.

Liminal citizens do just enough to enjoy the benefits of political life. They see the state as an impediment to their freedom because the state in their minds is *external* to their lives and a kind of threat to their bio-lives. As a result, they see freedom as beginning where the state ends. These are the classic Benjamin Constant-type citizens, who want to be left alone to enjoy their private lives.[17] If and when they face a challenge from the government, as when a tyrant takes power, they are often the first to run for their lives. In Africa, they are those who respond to conflict and strife by flight. Human beings are hardly an issue for tyrants. In contrast, liminal citizens are because they are unpredictably partly citizens and partly human beings, with at the least the potential of evolving or devolving further. More often they are the kind of citizens who clear the spaces for nonresponsive "big man" politics and, even worse, tyranny in Africa. Tocqueville (in a different context) was perhaps referring to liminal citizens when he said, "I tremble, I confess that [democratic citizens] may permit themselves to be fully possessed by a cowardly love of present pleasure that . . . they may prefer to follow feebly the course of their destiny rather than make a sudden energetic effort needed to set things right."[18] This category of citizens is what Mahmood Mamdani, in his book *Citizen and Subject*, refers to as "subjects."[19]

Most of Africa is made up of these kind of liminal citizens, who cling to life by all means and as such never have the benefit of spiritual civic life, the kind of life in which the body has no significance to the citizen. When the body is insignificant, one can begin to enjoy a life that under other circumstances is not available. That is the sweetest of aesthetic lives, and it does not end with bio-death for one has already renounced that life in order to enjoy a full-fledged civic life of the highest order.

Citizen-Statespersons: Dignity, Honor and Civic Immortality

The highest degree of citizenship is that of the *citizen-statesperson*. Those are the few whose participation in civic life and politics—often at the expense of their own physical lives—confer upon them civic immortality. While the human being aims at bio-life, statespersons aim at the highest political life, that of the state (as the stem of the word *statesperson* suggests), and only incidentally do they enjoy any other life.

Of these few we can speak not just of dignity but of *honor*. Honorable actions are extraordinary. Sharon Krause in this volume compares honorable action to Hannah Arendt's concept of action. "Action, on Arendt's account, means asserting one's capacity for what she calls 'natality,' or new beginnings, against the 'automatic' process, in whose context they constitute a wholly unexpected." They represent a person's capacity to begin something new. "Honor," Krause goes on, "is difficult to categorize. It cannot be reduced to self-interest, even self-interest well-understood, partly because honor may motivate the sacrifice of one's most fundamental interest (life itself) and partly because honor as quality of character is always tied to principled codes of conduct."[20] Fear of physical death is a powerful instinct, and those who have the audacity to override it bring honor to life. As such an honorable person so conceived is far above the Hobbesian citizens who are moved around by the fear of bio-death. The object of the citizen-statesman's being is not material life or bio-life. Such a person is neither open to obsequious rank climbing nor to the venality of vain citizens. The state is to politics what God is to religious practices, and the statesperson's deeds and words are for the highest, God-like purposes, which ultimately translate into the meme-like spiritual life of the state and inheres in the purposes and lives of the citizenry at large.

CONCLUSION

This talk of dignity, honor, and civic immortality will undoubtedly strike most as peculiar. It is particularly out of step with the way political theorists in the West talk. But that is because, I believe, those in the West have lived with the products of dignified and honorable citizens for a very long time. Unlike most Africans, they have been blessed with the traditions created by the Founding Fathers of the United States and other citizen-statesmen—and -stateswomen. As a result, political theorists in the West tend to overlook the extraordinary agency that citizens must harbor in order to create and recreate their states so that it is as responsive to them as they want it to be. Except for the purpose of repudiation, the concept of honor in relation to democracy is not something that comes closer to their democratic vocabulary. Western contemporary political philosophers and their African acolytes have not seen the resolve of a whole citizenry—as in many African countries—as it dissolves into the perfect unity of the unopposed will of a tyrant. They tend to mistake an instance of honor killings in backward states of the Middle East for the whole of that people's conception of honor.

Putting law over men is a problem in politics that Rousseau likes to compare to that of "squaring the circle" in geometry: "Solve that problem correctly, and the government based upon your solution will be a good government, proof against corruption. But until you solve it, rest assured of this: you may think you have made the laws govern; but men will do the governing."[21] Historically those who have engaged in extraordinary acts of legislations—such as founding a free state, freeing a people from the yoke of slavery and obsequiousness, enforcing the law and creating peace where anarchy and despotism reign—have been the few extraordinary citizens for whom honor and life in death were the inspirations. These honor-driven citizens may occupy the same sphere with the citizen simpliciter and liminal citizen, but they are miles apart from them in terms of what it is that makes them tick in political life. The citizen simpliciter and liminal citizen enjoy the political life in life while clinging to their bio-lives. That is not so for honor citizens, whose civic object is life in death or immortal life.

Africa has its own citizen-statesmen and -stateswomen, and Africans can find hope in their example. The leading exemplar is arguably Nelson Mandela, a citizen equal in greatness and honor to a George Washington.[22] Using nothing but his imagination, creativity, audacity, and, more centrally, his readiness to sacrifice his bio-life, he turned to his people torn apart by vicious conflict brought about by the inhuman apartheid system, a conflict that went on for far too long, to the point where no one could anymore discern its purpose for purposeful citizens. He planted in them seeds of civility, which, if cultivated with care, could turn the people of South Africa into the best democrats not only in Africa but in the world. His object was to found a responsive state, not simply to reform this or that aspect of the government. That is why in our contemporary time he should be considered the first statesman to have come out of the African soil.

In his "I am Prepared to Die" speech, Mandela expressed indifference to his bio-life. His aim was to end domination (whatever the source) and to found a democratic free society. That he was prepared to die in order to found a democratic South Africa could be seen from the words that concluded his speech: "It is an ideal for which I hope to live for and to see realized. But, my Lord, if it needs be, it is an ideal for which I am prepared to die."[23] The death is bio-death. Mandela's lawyers urged him to leave out this conclusion, lest it provoke the judge into sentencing him to death, but Mandela refused. He felt that he was likely to be sentenced to death regardless of the statement. He metaphorically died on April 20, 1964, the day of "I am Prepared to Die." Mandela was convicted and sentenced to life imprisonment. He served twenty-seven years of the sentence before being released and elected the first president of a democratic South Africa. Upon his release he quoted the last sentence of the "I am Prepared to Die." As an honorable person who did not fear death, and for whom the material life and bodily suffering was nothing but a curiosity, daring the judge to sentence him to death as he did could only have frustrated the aim of Judge de Wet, who, like a Hobbesian Leviathan, realized that there is nothing one can do to a person who is not afraid of death but to separate him from society. Bishop Desmond Tutu, a fellow South African Nobel Peace Prize Laureate said Mandela's legacy will live on in South Africa forever in these words: "Like a most precious diamond honed deep beneath that surface of the earth, the Mandela who emerged from prison in January 1990 was virtually flawless." The last lines from the "I am Prepared to Die" speech are thoughtfully etched on the wall of South Africa's Constitutional Court building in Johannesburg, one of the many ways in which Mandela has been and continues to be honored.

But there are others worthy of honor, whose examples should also be celebrated as civic immortals. Ngonnso, the founder of the political life of the Nso people in Cameroon, is often referred to as a god or the lord of the Nso people. Ngonnso was an extraordinary woman who unified and led dispossessed people who were scattered all over the North-West Region of Cameroon. She brought them together and transformed their physical lives into political lives, and gave them a collective identity through rituals, symbols, ceremonies, and a constitution. The legacy of those rituals and institutions formed a comprehensive *paideia* for the Nso, which strengthened them and gave them the ability to defend themselves against threats to enslave them.[24] This extraordinary woman expended her imagination and creativity in founding the laws that even at this time of modernity still fend off tyranny because the laws are so stubbornly enshrined in the whole being of her citizens. Among the citizens of Nso, Ngonnso is alive, well, and flourishing. She's been immortalized and is basking in the purposes of the people of Nso, enjoying her civic immortality.

NOTES

1. Achebe, Chinua. *Things Fall Apart*. Classics in Context series. Halley Court, Jordan Hill, Oxford: Heinemann Educational Publishers, 2000, 87.
2. The complete phrase is "habeas corpus ad *subjiciendum*" meaning "you may have the body for the purpose of subjecting him/her to examination."
3. Rollin Carlos Hurd, *Treatise on the Right of Personal Liberty, and on the Writ of Habeas Corpus and the Practice Connected with It: With a View of the Law of Extradition of Fugitives* Vol. 3, (Albany, NY: W. C. Little and Company, 1858), 232.
4. In fact, there is a new debate about giving or bestowing onto chimpanzees living in the Western world in recreational zoos the status of citizens.
5. Thomas Hobbes, *De Cive: The Latin Version*, ed. Howard Warrender (Oxford: Clarendon Press, 1983), 93.
6. For details on the etymology of the word "person" see Ajume Wingo, "The Aesthetics of Freedom," in *New Waves in Political Philosophy*, eds. Boudewijn de Bruin and Christopher Zurn (New York: Palgrave Macmillan 2009).
7. This is, of course, not to discount the importance of the body as the physical manifestation of citizens. But just as Kant distinguished between the appearances of things (*phenomena*) and the things-in-themselves (*noumena*), we can draw a significant difference between the underlying "material basis" of citizens and the qualities that distinguish citizens from *mere* humans. At the same time, we should acknowledge that, as Wittgenstein said, "The human body is the best picture of the human soul," the physical body is perhaps the best "picture" of the citizen. It's no accident that we commemorate civic heroes with statutes. For instance, visit the Union Building in Pretoria and you will be taken aback by a gigantic statue of Mandela so majestic and striking that it is meant to capture the proportion of his contribution to the life of the state that is now synonymous with him. Many who visit the Union Building even say metaphorically that they are going to visit Mandela, and they pose for pictures by the statue to send home to their loved ones.
8. Violence and coercion, then, are *alternatives* to politics. Indeed, it is the implicit contrast between politics and war that gives Clausewitz's aphorism its ironic power. That the commitment to politics is a commitment to nonviolent means (at least in dealing with political peers) was evident for the ancient Greeks, who relegated violence to the sphere of international relations and noncitizens. A similar view of politics as a disavowal of violence was echoed by John Stuart Mill, who insisted that "Liberty, as a principle, has no application to any state of things anterior to the time when

mankind have become capable of being improved by free and equal discussion. Until then, there is nothing for them but implicit obedience to an Akbar or a Charlemagne if they are so fortunate as to find one." See John Stuart Mill, *Utilitarianism, On Liberty, Considerations on Representative Government, Remarks on Bentham's Philosophy*, ed. Geraint Williams (London: J. M. Dent, 1993), 79.

9. Michael Rosen, "Dignity Past and Present" in *Dignity, Rank, and Rights*, ed. Jeremy Waldron, (New York: Oxford University Press, 2012), 92–3

10. Rosen, "Dignity Past and Present," 89.

11. Crawford Young, *The African Colonial State in Comparative Perspective* (New Haven, CT: Yale University Press, 1994).

12. See Adam Hochschild, *King Leopold's Ghost: A Story of Greed, Terror, and Heroism in Colonial Africa* (New York: Houghton Mifflin, 1998).

13. As I write, Pierre Nkurunziza's term as president of Burundi is up and he has refused to leave office, announcing on April 25 that he will seek a third term, in violation of the constitutional mandate limit of two terms, sparking a riot in Bujumbura, the capital. So far at least six people have been killed and 25,000 are said to have fled across the borders. A handful of presidents represent exceptions to the general rule: Zambia's Frederick Chiluba in 2002, Malawi's Bakili Muluzi in 2004 and Nigeria's Olusegun Obasanjo in 2007 stepped down only after trying abortively to maneuver the people into allowing them to stay. In 2013, Blaise Compore of Burkina Faso was driven from office by mass protests. Many have found ways to hoodwink their people to allow them to stay in power by the ballot. Uganda's Yoweri Museveni, who was given ten years in office by the Constitution of 1995, has now served twenty-nine years. Paul Biya has been the President of Cameroon since 1982. In April 2015 Togo's Faure Gnassingbe was reelected to a third term, extending his family's unbroken tenure to forty-eight years. Others who will follow suit include, Joseph Kabila of the Democratic Republic of Congo, who should retire next year, and Denis Sassou-Nguesso of Congo Brazzaville, who has ruled for most of the past thirty-one years. The Ethiopian constitution established a limit of six two-year terms but Mules Zenawi has been Prime Minister for seventeen years, with no end in sight. Zimbabwe's Robert Mugabe has been Prime Minister since 1980, with a new constitution in 2013 limiting the head of state to two terms—but only from that date. So he hopes to retire at the age of ninety-nine years ("Apres Moi, Moi," *The Economist*, May 2, 2015, www.economist.com/news/middle-east-and-africa/21650190-more-africans-are-resisting-presidential-efforts-flout-constitutional-term).

14. On the Thrasymachean view, the only question is whether the group of people called the government is strong enough to enforce their will upon a territorially constituted people. This should take the sting out of the word "right" from someone who protests that *right* implies morally right or something like that. What I am implying here is similar to the idea of legal positivism or the idea that the law is what the judges say it is and nothing else.

15. According to Waldron "[W]hen we hear the claim that someone has dignity what comes to mind are ideas such as: having a certain sort of presence; uprightness of bearing; self-possession and self-control; self-presentation as someone to be reckoned with; not being the abject, pitiable, distressed, or overly submissive in circumstances of adversity." Jeremy Waldron, *Dignity, Rank, and Rights* (New York: Oxford University Press, 2012), 22.

16. Hannah Arendt placed such lives among the "automatic processes" of nature. According to her: "Human life placed on earth, is surrounded by automatic processes—by the natural processes of the earth, which, in turn, are surrounded by cosmic processes, and we ourselves are driven by similar forces insofar as we too are part of organic nature. Our political life, moreover, . . . also takes place in the midst of processes which we call historical and which tend to become as automatic as natural or cosmic processes, although they were started by men." Hannah Arendt, *The Human Condition* (Chicago: University of Chicago Press, 1958), 168f.

17. Benjamin Constant, "Liberty of the Ancients compared with that of the Moderns," http://www.uark.edu/depts/comminfo/cambridge/ancients.html.

18. Cited in Sharon Krause, *Liberalism with Honor* (Cambridge, MA: Harvard University Press, 2002), 88.

19. Mahmood Mamdani, *Citizen and Subject* (Princeton, NJ: Princeton University Press, 1996).

20. Sharon Krause, in this volume.

21. Jean-Jacques Rousseau, *The Government of Poland*, trans. Willmoore Kendall, (Indianapolis: Hackett Publishing Company, 1985), 3.

22. For detail, see Ajume Wingo, "Nelson Mandela's Greatness? He Stepped Aside," *Denver Post*, December 8, 2013, www.denverpost.com/opinion/ci_24672937/wingo-nelson-mandelas-greatness-he-stepped-aside.

23. Nelson Mandela, 1964, "An Ideal for Which I am Prepared to Die," *Guardian*: http://www.theguardian.com/world/2007/apr/23/nelsonmandela.

24. Part of the *paideia* has to do with the conduct of a Nso person in the public. She taught Nso, and her lessons are enshrined in artworks and also in performance art which teaches the youth by demonstration on how to conduct themselves in political life. In everyday life, an honorable person stands upright and looks at people in the eye without shifting the body or wincing; he walks in an upright position without slouching or hunching and is always humble to those citizens who occupy lower ranks in the society. The Nso people are taught not to "catch a sleeping rabbit" and to take the bullet on the chest and not to fight one's enemies at night or in foggy weather.

Part IV

Women and Honor

TEN

The Female Point of Honor in Postrevolutionary France

Andrea Mansker

In 1869, the feminist travel writer, journalist, and public speaker, Olympe Audouard, judged herself insulted by a few lines published in the conservative newspaper *Le Figaro*. A brief report on one of her recent lectures on women's emancipation, the piece accused her of being such an ineffective and inarticulate speaker that the small audience present for her talk "laughed in her face," while others "whistled at her."[1] Taking her complaint directly to the paper's audacious director, Hippolyte de Villemessant, himself no stranger to the dueling field, Audouard alerted him that due to the anonymous personal insult made against her in the columns of *Le Figaro*, "I judged that my honor as a woman and as a writer [*écrivain*] required a reparation. I asked you for your day and hour."[2]

This was one of a number of high-profile dueling challenges made by French feminists from the period of the late Second Empire to the First World War. Audouard, like other individuals who issued provocations to male journalists and editors, opted for this violent solution due to muckrakers' unchecked libel of any woman who attempted to forge a public persona. Framing *Le Figaro*'s insult as one that not only affected her personally, but that outraged all women writers, Audouard expressed her belief that as long as women were excluded from the masculine point of honor, they would not be taken seriously as political actors. By issuing her cartel, Audouard enacted a popular script increasingly used by French men in this period, one which followed a discernible pattern of language, gestures, behavior, and values of the extralegal honor system. This system thrived in France during a prolonged era that witnessed the rise of republicanism as the dominant focus of the nation's political loyalties as well as the growth of the mass press from the 1860s. Historians of modern France have demonstrated that the exclusive, aristocratic honor culture was retained and democratized by bourgeois men after the French Revolution of 1789. The revolutionaries proclaimed an end to privilege and initiated liberal economic and political policies that favored individualism. But scholars argue that the public code of honor remained the exclusive prerogative of men and became a key way of defining masculinity prior to the Great War.[3]

Feminists Olympe Audouard and Marie-Rose Astié de Valsayre both faced the problem of inserting themselves into the increasingly contentious and competitive world of journalism in the late nineteenth century. But they also exploited the contradictions of different "republican moments" to expand the boundaries of the public honor code and to redefine liberalism in practice to include women. Liberal democracy in France paradoxically championed universal suffrage and individual rights, but continued to look to the seemingly anachronistic ritual of the duel to settle conflicts over personal reputation. While the Third Republic failed to grant women full civil and civic rights, the honor code treated them as weak physical beings whose reputation was defended by the men in their families. By issuing their dueling challenges, Audouard and Astié de Valsayre engaged in "occasional, extraordinary instances of resistance" that Sharon Krause links to honor in modern democratic political systems.[4] They appropriated the supposedly masculine qualities of courage and will to object to women's exclusion from public honor and from republican citizenship. In this chapter, I suggest that approaching French honor from the perspective of individuals considered marginal to the code demonstrates a more flexible and nuanced understanding of its gendered boundaries among contemporaries than historians have recognized.

OLYMPE AUDOUARD

Audouard outlined her grievances against Villemessant in a letter published by *Le Figaro* shortly after the issue containing the insulting review. She indicated that after friends had drawn her attention to the offending passage, she presented herself at the paper's office in Paris. She asked a staff member to convey the message to Villemessant, who was reportedly away from the capital, that the article in question was "completely inaccurate" and that she wanted a retraction. In response to the journal's characterization of her as a bad speaker, Audouard admitted that though she might have been a poor "*conférencière*," "what is certain is that my audience listened to me with the most courteous attention for one and a half hours, and that it had the benevolence to applaud me much more than my weak talent merited." In reply to the paper's accusation that Audouard failed to attract a large audience to her talk, she made it clear that "my room was full." Upon hearing her complaint, Villemessant replied, "This is possible, but I will not rectify it."[5] The refusal of *Le Figaro*'s editor in chief to publicly correct his journalist's false statements prompted Audouard to escalate the conflict and to invoke the language of honor more directly. She explained to Villemessant that not only was the review "inaccurate," but it was "rude [*grossier*] and impertinent."[6] Such a base attack on her character demanded a reparation by arms.

In her insistence that Villemessant settle the conflict violently on the dueling terrain, Audouard appealed to both legal and extralegal codes. She reminded her adversary of his legal responsibilities as *Le Figaro*'s director. The press laws of the Second Empire required a paper's editor in chief to not only personally sign every number of the newspaper but to "insert the responses of any person named or designated" therein in the following edition, and typically within three days of receiving the individual's letter. If directors refused to print the letter in a timely fashion, they could face a fine of anywhere from fifty to five hundred francs. They could also be sued for other penalties and damages to which the original, incriminating article gave rise.[7] *Le Figaro*'s disparaging remarks about Audouard might have constituted defamation of character were she to pursue him in court. She thereby reminded Villemessant of his obligations as the paper's director, which made him responsible for all content in his publication. Villemessant believed he had fulfilled his legal duty by printing Audouard's letter of riposte within the required time frame. What he refused to do was to publish a rectification to an article that she considered not only false, but damaging to her public reputation as a speaker.

Though Audouard reminded Villemessant of the law, she immediately clarified in her published letter that she had no intention of taking her adversary to court. This was suggested by her demand that he specify his "day and hour." By indicating that she would settle for nothing less than a duel in the absence of a retraction, Audouard implied that *Le Figaro*'s insult to her honor was so damaging that it could only be settled by violence. Hence, the Audouard-Villemessant affair explains how and why a personal conflict in the increasingly liberal world of journalism during the last years of the Second Empire could require an extralegal solution. The press was undergoing a dramatic shift in the late 1860s. During most of the imperial period, the government imposed heavy censorship on newspapers through a series of decrees that required directors to apply for prior government authorization and to deposit substantial caution money to found political papers. In 1868, as part of his attempt to liberalize the regime, Napoleon III agreed to a new press law that allowed any man enjoying his civil and political rights to establish a paper without prior government approval. Within one year, one hundred and forty new papers were created in Paris as a result of the law.[8]

Even in the earlier 1860s, however, there had been a proliferation of periodicals that used their "nonpolitical" status to avoid paying caution money.[9] In 1863, the entrepreneur and journalist Polydore Millaud began a penny press revolution when he launched *Le Petit Journal*, a daily paper in reduced format that sold for five centimes, bringing it within the reach of the masses.[10] *Le Figaro* is a good example of this nonpolitical press under the Second Empire, characterized by its rumormongering and its general "desire to distract." Villemessant, the founder and animating spirit of the publication, was known as a businessman already responsible for establishing a number of failed newspapers when he revived *Le Figaro* in 1854. He was widely criticized by contemporaries for his methods of selling papers, accused of trading in insults and even of blackmailing his enemies.[11] The paper often mercilessly targeted specific victims and Villemessant himself was frequently brought to court or onto the terrain as a result.[12] Due to these democratic developments, the journalistic world was increasingly regulated by the point of honor. In moving beyond the threat of legal action to a call to arms based on a journalistic slur, Audouard was on solid ground according to the nineteenth-century dueling manuals. Historian Robert Nye has shown that, in spite of the principle that honor constituted an implicit, unwritten code, detailed instruction booklets on dueling abounded in France from the seminal publication of the Comte de Chateauvillard's *Essai sur le duel* in 1836. French men viewed Chateauvillard's book as an authoritative guide to the rules governing the practice, and it attained a quasi-legal status in both civil and criminal courts.[13] The press was not the principal concern in Chateauvillard's day that it would become later in the century. Correspondingly, one can see in the proliferation of dueling guides from the 1870s a prominent consideration of journalists' and editors' personal obligations when faced with readers' charges of libel. These unofficial rules were often more rigorous than the law during the Third Republic, suggesting a higher value placed on public reputation by participants. As the 1900 *Conseils pour les duels* by Prince Georges Bibesco and Duke Féry d'Esclands made clear, "Any person insulted in a periodical publication will be able to demand reparation either from the article's author or from the editor in chief of the paper, at his choice."[14] A proper mode of "satisfaction" when outraged in this fashion was, as the manuals made clear, "either a retraction of his affronts or a reparation by arms."[15]

In adhering to the rules and regulations of the point of honor, Audouard did what any man might do who found himself libeled in a similar fashion. The problem with her challenge and the main reason Villemessant did not take her seriously as an adversary was her sex. Many of the responses that Audouard received from *Le Figaro* and from other male journalists demonstrate the masculine boundaries of public honor and the hostility and ridicule that a woman experienced when she attempted to access such an exclusive domain. Though Villemessant published Audouard's response to his perceived slight to her honor, he refused to grant her satisfaction through extralegal means. His reply to her request for reparation was that he "would not fight a woman." Villemessant nonetheless appointed *Le Figaro*'s journalist Jules Richard to serve as his proxy to handle the affair in his absence. According to Audouard, Richard listened to her grievance with the "courtesy of a gallant man," but echoed Villemessant in asserting that he would not cross swords with a woman. Richard then gave her the option of having a man fight in her place, invoking the idea of a substitute.[16] Dueling manuals throughout the nineteenth century had specified that minors along with old or incapacitated men required that their able-bodied male relatives stand in for them on the terrain.[17] Significantly, authors of these guides did not feel compelled to specifically mention the need to "protect the honor of a woman without defenders" or to provide a male substitute for a woman who delivered a public insult herself until the 1870s.[18] The novel inclusion of specific instructions for such situations suggests both an augmentation in the number of offended single women who lacked men in their families to defend them as well as an increase in the number of women who sought to participate autonomously in the point of honor. When the manuals did begin to mention these possibilities, they sought to preclude women by equating them with minors, old men and the physically disabled.[19]

Though Villemessant and Richard treated Audouard in a strictly legal manner, *Le Figaro* inserted an insulting poem about her written by Albert Millaud directly after Audouard's letter of riposte. Derisively presenting his poem as the official "response to Madame Olympe Audouard," Millaud openly mocked her pretensions to speak the language of male honor and to fashion herself as a female duelist: "I am the one who will respond, Madame / To your virulent style / It is in verse that one speaks to the woman / You see how gallant we are." Millaud scoffed not only at her attempt to demonstrate masculine courage, but at what he saw as her desire to revive bygone traditions of medieval chivalry. Gallantry, he implied, had been destroyed in current times by "virulent" women like Audouard, who tried to establish public identities as writers and who adopted the combative style and idiom of the duel. Sexualizing her and making it clear which qualities excluded her from active combat, Millaud continued: "In this duel, I must say to you / One of the fighters would be duped / Madame, for the target / Is more developed in you."[20] In this allusion to Audouard's breasts, Millaud made it clear that her physiology as a woman was the primary hindrance to her viability as an adversary. In medical and popular thought, women were held to be weaker than men and their bodies subject to irregular fluctuations based on their biological cycles. This was reflected in the dueling manuals' provision of a male substitute, and Audouard commented on this assumption numerous times in her writings. As she stated sarcastically in her 1866 book *War on Men*, which highlighted men's repeated "slander" and "calumniation" of women writers, "Messieurs, it is well and truly war that I declare on you. I attack what is stronger than me. I attack the strong sex, whereas I belong to the weak sex. I must therefore have for me *gens de coeur* [men of courage] always ready to rescue the weak against the strong."[21] A woman's need for protection was a principal justification for the honor code, and her reputation, primarily sexual, was supposed to be safeguarded by the men in her family.

Millaud's assessment was echoed by other papers that commented on the affair. *La Presse* treated her cartel as farcical, characterizing Audouard as a French "*bas-bleu*" who, like her bluestocking counterparts in England and America, violated their sex by speaking in public and demanding the vote for women. Referring to an upcoming republican congress where women would be allowed to vote on an equal footing to men, the journalist wrote, "I already imagine . . . the blond Olympe Audouard mounting the rostrum to excite [the crowd], and preaching her traditional War on Men!" He then joked that Audouard might even send a cartel to Victor Hugo if he dared to disagree with her.[22] Jules Valette in *La Bibliographie contemporaine* echoed this assessment when he joked that, "Mme. O. Audouard is first class at wielding the épée [sword], and she ruthlessly provokes to single combat the unfortunate critics of whom she complains. It is written: 'He who has struck by the pen will perish by the sword.'"[23]

Much of the language Millaud and others used to describe Audouard's public persona invoked the *bas-bleu* stereotype, which was linked to women's reemerging identities as feminists and public figures during a period of liberal reform. As Millaud admonished her in a rather unimaginative stanza, "Since one says that your intellect shines / Remove your dreadful bluestockings / Be a mother of the family / And look after the *pot-au-feu* [stew]."[24] Writers and caricaturists deployed the bluestocking label from the first half of the nineteenth century to address the literary prominence of female writers such as George Sand and Marie d'Agoult. Honoré Daumier's caricatures of bluestockings in the 1840s depicted them as ugly, unsexed, domineering, neglectful of their domestic responsibilities, and ridiculous in their intellectual pretensions. Daumier and others played on and inverted the axiom that "genius has no sex" by suggesting that any woman who pursued literary or intellectual activities in the public sphere proved, in fact, that genius was sexed, belonging exclusively to men. As Whitney Walton points out, this stereotype thrived in a context of anxiety and important changes in publishing and journalism under the July Monarchy. Technological and commercial innovations in printing allowed larger numbers of women writers to publish their works but also created increased competition among all authors for jobs. As a result, many male writers attributed a supposed decline in literary quality and commercialization to the increased presence of female authors.[25]

A similar dynamic appeared to be at work in the last years of the Second Empire when the government relaxed not only the press laws but began to reintroduce freedom of association. Prior to this, women were banned from giving public speeches in addition to the prohibition against addressing political topics in periodicals. As freedom of assembly was slowly extended, public lectures, or *conférences*, became important features of the French political landscape. The reappearance of the female journalist and *conférencière* in this period appeared to be a novel and unusual phenomenon to contemporaries.[26] Along with feminists such as Maria Deraismes, Louise Michel, and André Léo, Audouard became one of the first women in this period to speak publicly on women's rights. By the late 1860s, she had established her reputation as an activist writer and world traveler, publishing a number of books about her extensive journeys in Egypt, Turkey, and the United States. As Rachel Nuñez demonstrates, Audouard used the liberal concept of cosmopolitanism in these travelogues to expose and criticize the legal, political and social condition of French women.[27] Often delivering speeches on women's rights to accompany her books, Audouard's public identity in the literary world as well as her self-publicity and willingness to travel independently linked her to the bluestocking stereotype in the public mind. Audouard's dueling provocation simply confirmed for many writers the bluestocking's challenge to male privilege and public prerogatives.

Many of the journalistic responses to Audouard's affront, in fact, emphasized it as a desperate, frivolous publicity stunt that she orchestrated to gain exposure for her subpar books and lectures. The satirical paper *Le Tintamarre* attributed this self-realization to her:

> I could publish eighty volumes a year and I would never succeed in attracting public attention. I will knock over my inkwell and seek a noisier advertisement than that of talent and work. And taking her strong head into her hands, Mme. Audouard found an idea that will probably furnish Crémieux and Hervé buffoonery for next winter. *She seeks to fight a duel.* At present, Mme. Audouard wanders through the editorial offices, a box of pistols under her arm, and asks for a journalist who wants to line up with her. The person is not important to her. Above all, she wants blood and victims.[28]

Le Tintamarre suggested that Audouard's cartel was yet another feminist ploy to attract the attention of journalists, always on the hunt for the next sensationalist story. She tried to mimic the behavior of men by appropriating the language and gestures of the honor system but her willingness to fight the first man regardless of whether or not he had insulted her demonstrated her complete misunderstanding of the code. Her provocation, the author implied, was not based on a deep feeling of personal injury but was all for show. Central to her preoccupation was the celebrity status she hoped to obtain from her theatrical display and thus, she was driven by a shameful desire for material gain. Finally, rather than meriting literary acclaim through hard work and talent as a man would, she sought to make a spectacular and superficial gesture befitting of her sex.

Yet accusing Audouard of shallowness and a quest for self-publicity was ironic considering the meaning and function of the honor code for French men in this era. Central to practically all honor grievances was the accusation of lying. To "give the lie" to an individual meant to challenge his word and his self-constructed persona as an *honnête homme* [honest man]. As historians have demonstrated, the point of the duel or threat of the duel was not in fact, to determine the "truth" of any insult or to dig beneath the surface of appearances to some underlying reality. Rather, it was to suggest that you would not allow another person to call into question the public identity that you projected of yourself.[29] While individuals outraged in the French press may have wanted some version of the truth to be reflected in the editor's rectification, the duel itself certainly did not establish or discredit the veracity of any claim. Rather, the duel verified that the individual had the ability and will to defend her public reputation from defamation and proved the duelist's equality with her opponent.[30] When a man showed that he was willing to risk his life on the field of honor, this was expected to silence his opponents and protect his good name.

In Audouard's case, the perceived insult had been over her abilities as a feminist speaker. Audouard may have wanted Villemessant to rectify the offending article to reflect the reality of her audience's appreciative reception. But at stake was her self-constructed persona as a talented "*conférencière*" and writer in the combative and masculine world of journalism. She had spent her career carefully crafting this self-image and was attracting large, paying crowds to her lectures. Her speeches were also frequently reviewed and praised in the press.[31] In seeking publicity through the duel and defending her reputation as a public figure, she acted in the same manner as did French men of honor. The duel was, as Kenneth Greenberg makes clear in his study of the Old South, "a theatrical display for public consumption, and the parties expected descriptions of the events to be widely circulated."[32] This observation is equally accurate for France in these decades, when dueling manuals specified the all-important role of public opinion in determining the point of honor and when both parties in an affair outlined their grievances in full in the press. In enacting this script of the dueling affair and demonstrating that a woman could adhere to its rules, Audouard exposed both the superficiality of the French interpretation of honor and its changing and constructed nature.

Audouard also laid heavy emphasis in this affair and others on "unmasking" her male opponents, thereby calling them out as "cowards" in public.[33] For her, male journalists' dishonorable behavior toward women demonstrated their modern distortion of France's chivalric history and customs. She mocked the way that writers of her day claimed to be "gallant men" who protected and defended female honor but repeatedly violated the code when they outraged women publicly their newspapers. As she stated in her book *War on Men*, "You attack [women], even insult them in your writings and newspapers, forgetting completely that to insult she who cannot respond to you with a good blow of the épée is characterized by a very nasty word in the French language!"[34] Similarly, in the 1869 affair, she turned Villemessant's refusal to fight a woman against him, retorting,

> I am a woman, you say, and prejudices hold that it is ridiculous to fight a woman. Monsieur, the laws of chivalry required that, not only did one never insult a woman, but that one always placed his sword at her service! Certain men of the nineteenth century have trampled on these laws. It seems to me that it is much less severe to stamp out prejudices.[35]

She pointed out that her adversary's "gallant" desire not to harm her was not honorable at all since he used women's exclusion from the public code and their inability to respond violently as an excuse to shamefully defame them in print. Audouard implied that if republican men had misconstrued and disfigured the point of honor so drastically, then what was the purpose of clinging to such rituals?

Furthermore, she noted, many women in the modern era did not have men to duel in their stead. Alluding to the reality of increasing numbers of single, professional women who threatened the honor code's gendered exclusivity, she explained, "I am a widow, and no longer have either a father nor a brother. This means that it falls to me alone to ensure that my dignity and honor are respected." This idea of a male substitute, she made clear, was a "prejudice":

> I will not tolerate a gratuitous impertinence, and I persist in demanding a reparation from you, either in writing or by the pistol. As for the rest, to place your sensitive nature at ease, I will tell you that I know how to handle a firearm, and that a bullet, whether fired by a female or male hand, kills just the same. I hope, monsieur, that if you believe you have the right to publish an impertinence against me, you will understand that you do not have the right to persist in refusing me a reparation.[36]

Audouard made it clear that she was willing to risk her life to have her reputation respected, and that she was no shrinking violet who had never handled weapons. In fact, Audouard had been taught to use guns by her father as a child and continued to hunt as an adult, despite the difficulties women often faced in obtaining permits.[37]

Audouard's gendered challenge to the code and her reference to journalists' lack of chivalry may not have convinced her adversaries that they should take up their pistols against women. But she did expose some of the new democratic social conditions and realities to which the honor system struggled to adapt. Her critique revealed the contradictions of maintaining the noble practice of the duel in a republican society that challenged the imperial rule of Napoleon III and professed its firm belief in liberal democracy. This conflict was also given voice by the major critic Audouard faced in the wake of her provocation to Villemessant, the royalist writer and literary critic, Jules-Amédée Barbey d'Aurevilly. In his published response to Audouard's actions in the conservative paper *Le Gaulois*, Barbey d'Aurevilly continued along the lines of Millaud in his mockery of his feminist rival. Yet rather than simply highlight Audouard's perversion of the point of honor, Barbey d'Aurevilly used her provocation to make a larger point about the anachronism of the duel in an increasingly republican society. If, he wrote, "the coachman is your equal, if the domestic servant is your equal as the noblemen were among themselves, if women are our equals, there is nothing to say or to laugh at; one must fight the coachman, the servant, . . . and even Mme Audouard."[38] Audouard, he argued, was simply, "the most advanced, best-armed expression of the woman's right to civil, political, and social equality."[39] Though Barbey d'Aurevilly deplored bluestockings such as Audouard as "monsters of creation, errors of nature,"[40] he nonetheless joined her in suggesting that republican men's interpretation of the code was a pale and distorted imitation of its chivalric predecessor, and that by clinging to it, they created numerous contradictions in relation to their political ideology.

The extensive debate that unfolded in the press regarding the Audouard-Villemessant affair demonstrated that the nineteenth-century honor system and even the ritual of the duel itself did not function as an unequivocal, natural marker of masculine identity and prowess. Rather, Audouard's challenge revealed that men and women constantly questioned the meaning and relevance of the honor system in the democratizing context of the late Empire and openly flouted its gendered prescriptions. By doing so, Audouard and her critics exposed the honor culture for what it was: a shifting and malleable construct whose contradictions could be exploited by women to realize in practice republicanism's promise of equality.

MARIE-ROSE ASTIÉ DE VALSAYRE

In a rather bizarre 1886 cartel, an eccentric feminist writer and activist named Marie-Rose Astié de Valsayre challenged the female cofounder and director of the English Salvation Army, the "*maréchale*" Catherine

Booth, to cross swords with her if Booth would not cease to proselytize in France. Following the sensationalized French trial of Euphrasie Mercier in which Mercier used religious mysticism as an excuse for her criminal behavior, Astié de Valsayre felt that the Salvation Army's militaristic evangelicalism and its flashy, unconventional methods for converting the popular classes carried a grave danger for the newly-stabilized, secular Third Republic.[41] Though established in 1870, the Republic had experienced a humiliating war against Prussia, the Paris Commune, and nearly six years of rule by Patrice de MacMahon's Catholic "Government of Moral Order." Finally winning both houses of the legislature by 1879, republicans embarked on a decades-long campaign to wean citizens' loyalty away from the Church. Explaining her motives in an open letter to Booth dated April 24th and published in a number of prominent newspapers, Astié de Valsayre suggested that the duty to reprimand Booth's "soldiers" would normally fall to the French government. However, "since it does not suffice to suppress all that 'wounds' the glory of France in the name of patriots worried about this glory," she would personally take responsibility for redressing this injury to her country. Because Booth's doctrines were "pernicious for weak or depraved minds, especially in our provinces," and threatened to create a "schism" in France, Astié de Valsayre demanded that Booth leave the country. Delivering her ultimatum in the case of Booth's refusal, she wrote, "Judging myself as wronged in the person of my country, I will be constrained to ask you for a reparation by arms, to my great regret. [I] hope that you will not fall short of your compatriot Miss Shelby, my loyal adversary."[42]

Astié de Valsayre's provocation of Booth did not stem from a direct personal insult. Indeed, she had never met Booth, much less had a direct exchange with her. Whereas Audouard's challenge addressed women's emerging public and political identities at a moment of liberal reform, Astié de Valsayre calibrated her feminist cartel to a period of nationalistic revival. Her strategy was to raise the possibility of active female citizenship through women's participation in the project of national regeneration. Emphasizing that she defended the nation's interests by attacking one of the Republic's supposed enemies, she suggested that women also had a stake in civic life and in the government's anticlerical initiatives. In fact, she highlighted the correlation between nationalism and the honor code by stating that she was "wronged in the person of my country," insisting on the deeply personal nature of Booth's affront despite its abstract political character. Historians have shown that a growing number French duels were fought over political and ideological conflicts in the 1880s. Nye notes that political duels, together with those he characterizes as "journalistic" made up the majority of all public duels in the early Third Republic. At stake in these conflicts was the "authenticity of the bond between a man and his ideals at any moment in time."[43] A growing sense of parliamentary crisis in these years helped create countless affairs of honor between men. The divisive party politics of the Republic and a growing desire to avenge France's defeat by the Prussians helped fuel the Boulanger Affair. Minister of war between January 1886 and June 1887, General Georges Boulanger gained popularity among nationalists thanks to his reforms within the army, his persecution of royalist army officers in favor of "republicanizing" the military, and his aggressive stance toward Germany.[44] Though Astié de Valsayre was not a Boulangist, her provocation should be understood partly in this context. She used the duel for political purposes, issuing her challenge to Booth against a background of rising nationalist sentiment in France.

By emphasizing women's embodiment of national identity and by showing that a woman could substantiate her words with violence, Astié de Valsayre sought to demonstrate her fitness for full membership in both the public honor code and the Republic. Strategically referring to a duel she had fought one month prior with an American feminist, Miss Shelby, on the site of the famous battle of Waterloo, Astié de Valsayre made it clear to Booth that her cartel was no empty threat. Attended by four American seconds, this former duel by épée ended after Astié de Valsayre slightly wounded Shelby's arm. The national and international press had commented widely on this *"duel des femmes."*[45] Astié de Valsayre had also been the instigator of this challenge, citing both nationalistic and feminist motives. In an interview, she explained her conflict with Shelby in these terms:

> My adversary Miss Shelby maintained that American female doctors were superior to those in our country. I refuted her, she called me an "idiot." We went onto the terrain fifteen days later. I gave her a delay so that she could practice a little, her inferiority being great next to mine. I wounded her slightly on the arm and immediately after she made her excuses to me.[46]

On the one hand, Astié de Valsayre emphasized that this duel was not the result of some petty spat between women, but revolved around her patriotic defense of female doctors in her country. French women had only begun to receive medical degrees in 1870 and the number of practicing female doctors in France was still small in 1886.[47] Astié de Valsayre herself had studied medicine seriously in Paris for a number of years and obtained the rank of *"officier de santé et de pharmacie."*[48] She also reportedly entered the ambulance service during the Franco-Prussian War of 1870 and was wounded on plateau d'Avron.[49] Thus, Astié de Valsayre provoked Shelby in defense of French women's professional abilities and achievements and fought in the name of these female doctors rather than simply on her own behalf. On the other hand, by alluding to her previous dueling affair in her letter to Booth, Astié de Valsayre established her credentials as a *"fine lame,"* or a skilled swordsperson, on the field of honor. As in her cartel to Booth, she adopted the language and gestures of the French honor code to assert women's equal physical and political capabilities to men. She made her successful reenactment of the masculine ritual clear in the triumphant letter she sent to the press following her duel. Lest the public think that this affair constituted playacting among women or that the two adversaries lacked courage, she insisted that Shelby's conduct had been "noble":

> She called me an "idiot"—in response, I threw my glove in her face. Even though knowing herself to be inferior in advance, she did not withdraw. But afterwards, she extended her hand to me with these loyal words: *Now, I can offer you my apologies.* How small I found myself next to her! Such are women dispossessed of what one is used to calling *their charm* [*leur grâce*], meaning their frivolity![50]

Astié de Valsayre sought to demonstrate that the two combatants adhered faultlessly to the point of honor from Shelby's insult and Astié de Valsayre's throwing of her glove to Shelby's gallant proffering of her apologies once Astié de Valsayre had wounded her on the field. Newspapers even reported that the four seconds declared that "all had passed loyally."[51] By ensuring that proper form had been followed, she demonstrated that women were perfectly capable of practicing the elaborate rituals of the point of honor, including the physical exertion of swordplay. Astié de Valsayre's duel not only gave lie to men's insistence on the strict gendered boundaries of the honor code, but to the central justification for women's exclusion from full citizenship: their purported physical weakness that led republicans to categorize them as minors.

Despite Astié de Valsayre's attempt to force Booth onto the terrain as she did to Shelby, her English adversary seemed completely baffled by Astié de Valsayre's aggressive behavior. Booth's identity as a woman, but also as a leader of a pacifist evangelical organization and a citizen of a country that had abandoned the duel in the eighteenth century, led her to reject the violent honor code of her continental neighbors. When asked by a French reporter for her comment, she replied, "What does this woman want? That I leave France? What gives her the right to speak to me this way? Am I sticking my nose into her business?" Describing the Salvation Army's doctrine as antithetical to the mores of the duel, she explained, "Our goal is to bring back lost souls to good, to give back to God the sheep he lost, etc.; our mission is thus a mission of peace and comfort. So, would I go fight? Let Mme de Valsayre, who has probably not seen us at work, come to our lectures. . . . This is the only reparation that I can give her."[52] Astié de Valsayre responded with an even more belligerent letter in which she referred to Booth as an "exploiter of human credulity," and an "assassin of intelligence."[53] Because Booth had suggested that she would respond to her adversary at the upcoming Salvation Army lecture, French journalists crowded into the hall on the Blvd. des Capucines in hopes of seeing a confrontation between the two women. The press was disappointed to report that Booth used her "soldiers" to ban Astié de Valsayre from the proceedings when she arrived despite her loud protest at the door of the meeting hall. Along with many English devotees of the Salvation Army, French journalists were subjected to a "long" sermon by Booth that "lacked much interest" and "provided very little amusement for the public who expected a tournament and not a lecture."[54]

Despite Astié de Valsayre's failure to drag Booth onto the dueling terrain, she cleverly used the affair as a springboard to launch her career as a feminist speaker and to attract attention to her principal cause: fencing for women. She elaborated this purpose fully in a lecture she delivered in the same meeting hall where Booth had addressed the Parisian public one month earlier. Her talk, entitled "L'Escrime et la femme," outlined her ideas on the utility of fencing for women's physical rehabilitation as well as its centrality to their national mission as mothers. Léon Richer's feminist newspaper *Le Droit des femmes* claimed that Astié de Valsayre sought "nothing less than a hygienic and moral revolution." Drawing from "the most rigorously scientific data" to explain fencing's multiple benefits for women's reproductive organs and general mental health, she promised that the sport would correct a number of female maladies. Currently, she explained, the urban woman suffered from infirmities due to "the sedentary regime where she atrophies" and, especially from hysteria, "which causes so much malaise and enigma." Fencing's cultivation of "an energetic and well-regulated muscular activity," along with the development of the chest, the seat of lactation, could help correct the nation's precipitous fall into physical and mental decline.[55]

The Terrible Year of 1870–1871 spurred bleak ruminations on the "degeneration" of the nation, and these assumptions were reaffirmed for many by publicized statistics of declining birth rates, a sex ratio imbalance, and rising rates of disease and crime. In her lecture, Astié de Valsayre took up the theme of degeneration as it related to French women's widespread use of wet nurses in lieu of breastfeeding their children. She blamed this phenomenon for a host of France's ills, including the poor health and insufficient military height of the country's soldiers.[56] Summarizing her class-based condemnation of wet nurses, *Le Droit des femmes* noted with approval that Astié de Valsayre attacked the "plague of mercenary breastfeeding [that] expands with all its consequences: mortality of newborns, degeneration of the race by an unnatural diet consumed at the feeding bottle, without taking into account the disorganization of the wetnurse's family."[57] By creating fit mothers who delivered easily and could physically provide the nutrition their children required, fencing would not only revitalize women, but the nation.

At a time when women were beginning to participate in sports such as gymnastics, bicycling, swimming, and even shooting, Astié de Valsayre suggested that fencing was perfectly compatible with women's maternal duties.[58] For her, it was not a sport that "virilized" women, but that accentuated and improved their feminine functions. A decade later, Astié de Valsayre similarly made waves by submitting a petition to the Chamber of Deputies in favor of the "liberty of female dress." Her petition referred to women whose "skirts and petticoats cut off retreat and multiplied the number of female victims" at the Bazar de la Charité fire of that year.[59] A suffragist favorable to equality of salaries and the opening of all studies and professions to women, Astié de Valsayre advocated sport and dress reform as a means to gain autonomy of action for women. In 1886, her ultimate goal was to allow other women to experience the vitality, confidence, and strength that fencing could instill in them. To this end, she hoped to establish an organization for young women of fencing, gymnastics, and shooting.[60] These sports, she predicted, would soon be practiced by girls at an early age in boarding schools across France.[61]

Though Astié de Valsayre received little support in the press or from her feminist colleagues for her duel, her advocacy of female fencing drew strong acclaim from many quarters. Journalists' reactions to her behavior clearly represented growing public interest in women's sport as well as an increased respect for feminist attempts to exercise a public form of honor. Whereas Audouard's challenge attracted some media attention, Astié de Valsayre's provocation of Booth unleashed a veritable wave of articles and commentary devoted to "*femmes d'épée*" and famous "*escrimeuses*" in French history. Writers would continue to publicize Astié de Valsayre's exploits well into the early 1900s. The conservative paper *Le Gaulois*, for example, featured a number of extensive articles devoted to her in 1886 under titles such as "Femmes d'épée."[62] Georges Lefèvre of the republican *Le Radical* included a long commentary on her in one of his pieces. Though Lefèvre mocked Astié de Valsayre for trying to form a "future battalion of swordswomen," he acknowledged that her advocacy of female fencing had become mainstream:

> For a long time now, gymnastics has won its rightful place in the female boarding schools and even in the most timid convents. Fencing also takes its place there. In the manipulation of the sword and in the daily practice of fencing, there is a bringing into play of the chest muscles, a heightening of movements of the lungs, which could only be completely salutary for young women.[63]

In 1888, Jean Frollo of *Le Petit Parisien* published a piece entitled "Women's Duels," which placed Astié de Valsayre's challenge and ideas within a history of female duelists and fencers reaching back to the seventeenth century.[64] As Henri Nicolle confirmed in an article for an 1894 issue of *Revue illustré*, "Our Astié de Valsayre—if I dare express myself thus—is, as everyone knows, what we call a *fine lame*. She wields language and the foil with equal agility. She lectures and she fights."[65] Though ridiculing Astié de Valsayre for her masculine behavior, Nicolle nonetheless concluded that "fencing with a foil is an excellent exercise for women. It demands neither strength nor a powerful muscle structure. A good eye, presence of mind, and flexibility are all that is needed, and you know that [women] hardly lack these."[66] A number of books were published in the 1890s that supported Nicolle's assessment, including Alexandre Bergès's *L'Escrime et la femme* and Carl Albert Thimm's *A Complete Bibliograpy of Fencing and Dueling*.[67]

Though Astié de Valsayre linked her defense of dueling to a rising culture of sport and physical fitness as well as to the feminist movement that entered a more militant phase in the 1880s, her use of the point of honor, like Audouard's, ultimately stemmed from a conflict in the journalistic milieu. Explaining her motives for championing the duel rather than some other form of conflict resolution, she argued that, "it is necessary to close the mouth of slanderers as long as they will be restrained so little by the law." Acknowledging that the duel could be abused, she nonetheless suggested that "one does not give up eating and drinking because there are drunks or indigestion."[68] Fencing, as she described it in her 1886 lecture, was not just a sport, but "a school of courage and sang-froid as well as a badge of respect [*porte-respect*] in a democratic society where each person often only has himself to rely on."[69] She thereby described the duel as a regrettable necessity for women as it was for men due to the lack of effective libel laws or other checks on the press under the democratized Third Republic. The liberal press law of 1881 superseded all previous legislation and removed the remaining censorship that had lingered from the Second Empire. Though the new law allowed individuals to sue for libel, it limited penalties for defaming private persons to eighteen francs or six days in jail. Also forbidding investigation into the truth of allegations in a libel suit, the law's laxity tended to encourage attacks on personal reputation in the press. Journalists' use of insinuations and half-truths to protect themselves made it hard to obtain a positive judgment against them in court.[70]

In the early 1880s, Astié de Valsayre took advantage of the liberal press laws to establish a reputation as a female journalist. In a press interview regarding her challenge to Booth, she recounted the event that led her to rely on the duel as the only method to "close the mouth of slanderers": "The taste for weapons came to me only recently. A young man, who signed [his name] Polignac in a morning newspaper, insulted me and refused to give me reparation. I had to whip him in public, but I nearly fought [a duel]."[71] The 1884 incident Astié de Valsayre describes helped launch her career as a "*femme d'épée*" in the exclusive world of the press and was most likely instrumental in attracting her to feminism. The editor of the newspaper *Le Cri du peuple*, a man named M. de la Bretèche, wrote an insulting piece about Astié de Valsayre and her journalistic collaborator, Albin Rousselet.[72] La Bretèche was, at the time, writing under the pseudonym M. de Polignac, and according to *La Presse*, he made "acerbic and even violent critiques of Mme. Astié de Valsayre's personality" in *Le Cri du peuple*.[73] Following their failure to receive an adequate retraction from La Bretèche or to engage him in a duel, Astié de Valsayre and Rousselet ambushed him at the café rue Montmartre accompanied by their "second," Léon Roux, director of *Le Capitan*.[74] *La Presse* described La Bretèche's account of this loud and colorful confrontation in the following terms:

> "You are M. de Polignac?" "Yes, Monsieur." "Are you the one who wrote the article of September 19 about Mme Astié de Valsayre and M. Albin Rousselet?" "Certainly." No sooner had these two fallen on me with doubled blows when unknown individuals seized me from behind thus placing me in the absolute impossibility of defending myself. I have learned since then that these were police agents.[75]

Claiming he had been jumped by Rousselet, Roux, and their band of policemen, La Bretèche sought to restore his honor that had been called into question by his inability to defend himself before a crowd of onlookers. Most likely at issue was the fact that Rousselet was able to advance toward him and strike him on the face, a symbolic gesture in the honor code that led to an inevitable duel.[76] According to the *Journal des débats*, after several persons were able to separate Rousselet and La Bretèche, "one believed the affair had ended when Mme. Astié de Valsayre asked M. Roux to deliver her card to M. de La Bretèche and to inform him that she asked him for a reparation by arms."[77]

Astié de Valsayre wrote to the mass-circulation newspaper *Le Matin* after the affair to emphasize her prominent role in the scuffle, which many papers had overlooked or misinterpreted. Making it clear that she asked Roux to be her second and that she acted autonomously, she wrote:

> As for me, reckoning that from the moment one insults a woman, one must find her adequate to cross swords, I asked M. Roux, second of M. Rousselet, to ask M. Polignac for a reparation by arms *on my behalf alone*. This request has nothing in common with that of M. Rousselet. I had decided to whip M. Polignac if he refused, and I would have done so had twenty of his friends not rushed forward to protect a man from a woman and had not broken my whip.[78]

Ridiculing Polignac in print for needing protection from a woman armed only with a whip, Astié de Valsayre demonstrated her ability to speak the language of honor and to present herself as a worthy adversary of a man. Polignac, she implied, had dared to denigrate a woman in his newspaper because he knew she could not force him onto the field of honor. She offered an alternative account of the affair that portrayed Rousselet not as her substitute whom she had charged with demanding reparation from La Bretèche, but as an individual who wanted his own satisfaction from the editor. She thereby subverted the code of honor to stress her ability to enact vengeance independently on her opponent.

CONCLUSION

In her insistence on female autonomy within the point of honor, Astié de Valsayre echoed Audouard's response to Villemessant's proposal of a male substitute. Both feminists manipulated the gendered assumptions of the code of honor to women's benefit and unmasked its supposed natural basis in the male sex as an artificial construct. Taking advantage of two different "republican moments" in France to expose the contradictions of a liberal democracy that excluded women both politically and culturally, Audouard and Astié de Valsayre suggested that practice should align with principle. Just as there were no physical or mental disabilities that prevented women from exercising their equality on the dueling field, there was no logical rationale for excluding them from citizenship. Reacting initially to liberal changes in the press, these women's feminist appropriations of the public code fundamentally altered the gendered meanings of both liberalism and honor in France.

NOTES

1. *Le Figaro*, August 23, 1869.
2. Audouard's account in *Le Figaro*, August 29, 1869.
3. Robert A. Nye, *Masculinity and Male Codes of Honor in Modern France* (Berkeley: University of California Press, 1993), vii; 127–47; William M. Reddy, *The Invisible Code: Honor and Sentiment in Postrevolutionary France, 1814–1848* (Berkeley: University of California Press, 1997), 5–13; Edward Berenson, *The Trial of Madame Caillaux* (Berkeley: University of California Press, 1992), 169–207; Christopher E. Forth, *The Dreyfus Affair and the Crisis of French Manhood* (Baltimore: Johns Hopkins University Press, 2004), 103–22.
4. See Sharon Krause's chapter "Liberal Honor" in this volume.
5. Audouard's account in *Le Figaro*, August 29, 1869.
6. Audouard's account in *Le Figaro*, August 29, 1869.
7. A. F. Teulet, *Les Codes de l'Empire Français*, 9th edition (Paris: Librairie Videcoq, 1860), 176–75; Claude Bellanger, Jacques Godechot, Pierre Guiral, and Fernand Terrou, *Histoire générale de la presse française*, vol. 2 (Paris: Presses Universitaires de France, 1972), 408–409.
8. Bellanger et al., *Histoire générale*, vol. 2, 346–47.
9. Bellanger et al., *Histoire générale*, vol. 2, 346–47.
10. Michael B. Palmer, *Des petits journaux aux grandes agences: naissance du journalisme moderne* (Paris: Aubier, 1983), 23–40.
11. Bellanger et al., *Histoire générale*, vol. 2, 298–300.
12. Henry Vizetelly, *Glances Back Through Seventy Years*, vol. 2 (London: Kegan Paul, Trench, Turner & Co., 1893), 322–25.
13. Nye, *Masculinity*, 137–43.
14. Georges Bibesco and Camille Féry d'Esclands, *Conseils pour les duels à l'épée, au fleuret, au sabre et au pistolet*, 2nd edition (Paris: A. Lemerre, 1900), 11–12.
15. Charles du Verger de St. Thomas, *Nouveau code du duel: histoire, législation, droit contemporain* (Paris: Dentu, 1879), 319.
16. Audouard's letter in *Le Figaro*, Aug. 29, 1869.
17. See, e.g., Comte de Chateauvillard, *Essai sur le duel* (Paris: Chez Bohaire, 1836), 11.

18. Emile Bruneau de Laborie, *Les Lois du duel* (Paris: Manzi, Joyant, et Cie, 1906), 101–04; Verger de St. Thomas, *Nouveau code*, 164–65; 200.
19. Bruneau de Laborie, *Les Lois du duel*, 101–104; Bibesco and Féry d'Esclands, *Conseils*, 179–80.
20. Albert Millaud, "Réponse à Madame Olympe Audouard," *Le Figaro*, Aug. 29, 1869.
21. Olympe Audouard, *Guerre aux hommes*, 2nd ed. (Paris: Dentu, 1866), 3.
22. Georges Maillard, "Causerie," *La Presse*, Sept. 10, 1869.
23. Jules Valette, review of Audouard's *L'Amie intime* in *La Bibliographie contemporaine* (Paris), March 15, 1873.
24. Millaud, "Réponse," *Le Figaro*, Aug. 29, 1869.
25. Whitney Walton, *Eve's Proud Descendants: Four Women Writers and Republican Politics in Nineteenth-Century France* (Stanford, CA: Stanford University Press, 2000), 84–5.
26. Claire Goldberg Moses, *French Feminism in the 19th Century* (Albany, NY: SUNY Press, 1984), 151–52; 173.
27. Rachel Nuñez, "Between France and the World: The Gender Politics of Cosmopolitanism, 1835–1914," Ph.D. Dissertation, Stanford University, 2006, 115–16.
28. "Lettres de Faust à Marguerite," *Le Tintamarre*, Sept. 5, 1869.
29. Kenneth S. Greenberg, *Honor & Slavery* (Princeton, NJ: Princeton University Press, 1996), 7–8; Nye, *Masculinity*, 177.
30. For development of this argument, see Mansker, *Sex, Honor, and Citizenship in Early Third Republic France* (Houndsmills, Basingstoke, Hampshire: Palgrave, 2011), 19–41; Berenson, *Trial*, 204–207.
31. For a journalistic account that mocks Audouard as a speaker, but nonetheless admits that the large number of journalists present at her lectures "inflates ticket sales," see Charles Yriarti, "Courrier de Paris," *Le Monde illustré*, April 16, 1870, 243.
32. Greenberg, *Honor & Slavery*, 8.
33. For an earlier example of her efforts to expose her opponents as "liars," see Audouard's account of the successful defamation suit she brought against Ernest Dréole: Audouard, *Voyage à travers mes souvenirs* (Paris: Dentu, 1884), 62–67.
34. Audouard, *Guerre aux hommes*, (Paris: E. Dentu), 4.
35. Audouard's letter in *Le Figaro*, Aug. 29, 1869.
36. Audouard's letter in *Le Figaro*, Aug. 29, 1869.
37. Nuñez, "Between France and the World," 125–26; Audouard, "La Femme, estelle individu?" *Revue cosmopolite* 16 (May 2, 1867): 97–103.
38. Jules Barbey d'Aurevilly, "Le duel tombé en quenouille," *Le Gaulois*, Sept. 2, 1869.
39. Jules Barbey d'Aurevilly, "Le duel tombé en quenouille," *Le Gaulois*, Sept. 2, 1869.
40. Barbey quoted by Audouard, "A Monsieur Barbey d'Aurevilly en réponse à son article 'Le Duel tombé en quenouille,'" *Le Gaulois*, Sept. 15, 1869.
41. *Gazette anecdotique, littéraire, artistique, et bibliographique* (Paris) 1, no. 9 (May 15, 1886): 197–200. For Mercier, see Henry Brodribb Irving, *Studies of French Criminals of the Nineteenth Century* (London: William Heinemann, 1901), 283–301.
42. *Gazette anecdotique*, 197–98; Astié de Valsayre's letter was also published in *Le Temps*, April 28, 1886; *Le XIXe siècle* (Paris), April 29, 1886; *La Justice*, April 28, 1886; *Le Rappel* (Paris), April 29, 1886.
43. Nye, *Masculinity*, 185–86; 191–93.
44. Robert Lynn Fuller, *The Origins of the French Nationalist Movement, 1886–1914* (London: McFarland & Co., 2012), 23–36.
45. "Un Duel des femmes," *Le Petit Parisien*, March 27, 1886; *La Justice*, March 27, 1886; *Le XIXe siècle*, March 30, 1886; *Le Gaulois*, March 26, 1886; *Sacramento Daily Union* 55, no. 29 (March 26, 1886): 221.
46. "Une femme d'épée," *Le Gaulois*, April 5, 1886.

47. Karen Offen, *European Feminisms, 1700–1950* (Stanford, CA: Stanford University Press, 2000), 134–35.
48. Camille Delaville, "Chronique mondaine" column, October 6, 1884.
49. Entry "Valsayre (Marie-Rose Astié de)," in Pierre Larousse, *Grand dictionnaire universel du XIXe siècle*, vol. 17, 2nd supplement (Paris: Administration du Grand Dictionnaire Universel, 1866–77), 1969.
50. *Le XIXe siècle*, March 30, 1886.
51. "Un Duel des femmes," *Le Petit Parisien*, March 27, 1886.
52. *La Justice*, April 29, 1886.
53. "Duel des femmes," *Le Petit Parisien*, May 11, 1886.
54. Paul Roche, "La Maréchale Booth à la Salle des Capucines," *Le Gaulois*, May 10, 1886; "Duel des femmes," *Le Petit Parisien*, May 11, 1886; L'armée du Salut," *Journal des débats politiques et littéraires*, May 10, 1886.
55. Léon Giraud, "L'Escrime et la femme," *Le Droit des femmes*, June 20, 1886, 143–4.
56. *Journal d'hygiène* (Paris), no. 512 (July 15, 1886): 344; "L'Escrime et la femme," *Journal des débats politiques et littéraires*, June 5, 1886.
57. Giraud, "L'Escrime et la femme," 144.
58. For this culture of sport, see Hélène Salomon, "Le corset: entre la beauté et la santé, 1880–1920," and Gilbert Andrieu, "A propos d'un livre: 'Pour devenir belle . . . et le rester' ou La culture physique au féminin avant 1914." Both in *Histoire du sport féminin*. Edited by Pierre Arnaud and Thierry Terret, vol. 2 (Paris: L'Harmattan, 1996), 11–26.
59. *Cincinnati Lancet-Clinic* 39 (July 3, 1897): 13; "Costume," in *Grand dictionnaire*, 925.
60. Giraud, "L'Escrime et la femme," 145.
61. *Journal d'hygiène*, 344.
62. "Une femme d'épée," April 5, 1886 and June 5, 1886, "Femmes d'Épée," August 20, 1886 in *Le Gaulois*.
63. Georges Lefèvre, "Les Femmes d'épée," *Le Radical* (Paris), May 10, 1886.
64. Jean Frollo, "Duels des femmes," *Le Petit Parisien*, August 22, 1888.
65. Henri Nicolle, "Escrime pour dames," *Revue illustré* 19 (December 15, 1894): 80.
66. Henri Nicolle, "Escrime pour dames," *Revue illustré* 19 (December 15, 1894): 82.
67. Alexandre Bergès, *L'Escrime et la femme* (Paris: D. Benoist, 1896); Carl Albert Thimm, *A Complete Bibliography of Fencing and Dueling* (Gretna, LA: Pelican Publishing Co., 1896), 528 on Astié de Valsayre.
68. Giraud, "L'Escrime et la femme," 143.
69. Giraud, "L'Escrime et la femme," 143.
70. Nye, *Masculinity*, 175–76.
71. "Une femme d'épée," *Le Gaulois*, April 5, 1886.
72. Camille Delaville, "Chronique mondaine," *La Presse*, October 6, 1884.
73. Delaville, "Un Nouveau scandale," *La Presse*, October 4, 1884.
74. *Journal des débats politiques et littéraires*, October 4, 1884.
75. Delaville, "Un Nouveau scandale," *La Presse*, October 4, 1884.
76. *Journal des débats*, October 4, 1884.
77. *Journal des débats*, October 4, 1884.
78. "Provocation en duel par une femme," *Le Matin*, October 7, 1884.

ELEVEN

A Woman's Honor

Purity Norms and Male Violence

Joseph A. Vandello and Vanessa Hettinger

What does it mean to have "honor"? The answer differs for men and women. Although the specific behaviors may take different forms across cultures and times, being an honorable man usually means protecting and providing for one's family, and standing up for one's reputation.[1] For women, honor and virtue center much more on moral purity. We venerate women who protect their purity by being chaste and modest, and not overindulging in vices that pollute the body and mind. In the West, societal focus on female moral purity has waxed and waned, but it has always been considered more important than male purity. Female purity emphasis may have reached its zenith in America in the nineteenth and early twentieth centuries, when femininity centered around the "cult of true womanhood," which emphasized women's virtuous behavior, sexual purity, and religious piety.[2] For example, the New York Female Moral Reform Society was established in 1834 to promote sexual abstinence and prevent women from entering prostitution.[3] "Good" women would avoid moral vices like drinking and smoking at all costs. Women played a prominent role in leading temperance movements in the United States in the early twentieth century (e.g., the Women's Christian Temperance Union).[4] Smoking was considered a dirty habit and a moral taboo for women through much of the history of the United States and was almost exclusively a male behavior until after World War I.[5] As changes in women's roles in society were accompanied by relaxed purity norms, some suggested that women's advancements came with a moral price tag. The *Buffalo Evening Post* noted the transition to women's new independence and freedoms during the 1920s with moral disapproval: "It may be true that women have the same right as men to drink and smoke and indulge habits peculiar to masculinity, but that means the lowering of the standards of womanhood to the level of men."[6]

Although Americans may be less obsessed with women's purity today than in past generations, female purity is still relevant in contemporary Western cultures, a point upon which we will expand later in the chapter. Outside of U.S. culture, concerns about female purity, and behavioral rituals to enforce it are often much more overt. In many cultures, particularly those organized around cultural codes of honor, the purity of girls and women continues to be a defining theme and is treated with an urgency that men's purity is not accorded. Consider the practice of female genital mutilation in parts of Africa and the Middle East, used to control women's supposedly dangerous sexual urges and to protect their purity—a custom that Grand Sheikh Gad al-Haq Ali Gad al-Haq, an Egyptian religious leader, called "a noble practice which does honor to women."[7] Clothing traditions in such cultures often reflect an emphasis on female purity. Consider the skin-covering *hijabs, abayas, chadors,* or *burkas* women wear in many Muslim countries to protect their 'modesty' and demonstrate their obedience to the tenets of Islam. Within Western societies, several subcultures also reflect this emphasis—for example, the long, modest dresses worn by ultra-orthodox Jewish women and some Mormons.

Female purity or impurity is even sometimes endowed with great powers or assumed to play a causal or magical role in external events. For instance, an Iranian cleric blamed earthquakes in the region on women's supposed impurity.[8] Even American evangelical preacher Pat Robertson implied that the moral sins of New Orleans (such as legalized abortion) caused Hurricane Katrina in 2005.[9] Among the Kamano of Papua New Guinea, men believe that women's polluting sexuality can weaken a man so that he is vulnerable to sorcery from his enemies.[10] Just as moral impurity can contaminate, female purity is also believed to have the power to heal. It is still commonly believed in some rural parts of sub-Saharan Africa that having sex with a female virgin can cure a man with AIDS.[11]

Purity violations are also typically met with more severe punishment for females than males. For example, among the Guajiro of northern Venezuela, mothers enforce the purity of their daughters by placing hot branding irons on their daughters' vaginas as punishment for suspected premarital sexual activities.[12] Honor killings, in which male family members kill female family members for violations of family honor that range from premarital sex, suspected infidelity, or being a victim of rape, are still common in parts of the Middle East, South Asia, and beyond.[13] Such punishments serve to not only discipline individuals but to enforce expectations for female purity more broadly among communities.

In this chapter, we review gender-related expectations for men and women in honor cultures and explore specifically why female sexuality is seen as a powerful, sometimes dangerous, force that must be tightly controlled. We also ponder the broader socio-psychological functions of these norms beyond honor cultures. We will speculate on the economic and cultural forces that give rise to and fertilize female purity concerns. Then, we will discuss the relevance of female purity among modern, liberal democracies. Finally, we will say a few words on the future of female purity as a moral code and whether it has a beneficial place in cultures low and high in honor orientation.

PURITY, GENDER, AND HONOR

Broadly speaking, purity can be defined as avoiding pollutants of the body or mind, or "preserving the sanctity of the body and mind."[14] Humans' concerns with purity are adaptive, evolved strategies that originated in avoiding the ingestion of dangerous toxins or the exposure to harmful pathogens. Over time, purity concerns expanded to incorporate more abstract concerns with spiritual purity and hedonistic vices.[15] Sexual and religious purity concerns, and accompanying emotions like moral disgust, thus reflect the abstraction and moralization of concerns with contamination of the body.[16]

This helps to explain why people universally care about purity, but not why female moral purity is almost always of greater concern than male purity, and why this is especially the case in honor cultures. While certain cultural and religious customs do prescribe purity rituals for men (for example, various cleansing rituals), obsessions with male purity are rare and of lesser magnitude than female purity concerns. To understand the disproportionate importance given to female over male purity, it is necessary to consider the economic and social functions of heterosexual pairings and marriage and their relation to the meanings of cultural prescriptions and proscriptions for men and women in honor cultures. Men demonstrate their honor through active, public demonstrations—thus, a man's honor must be earned. As anthropologist David Gilmore[17] noted, "real manhood is different from simple anatomical maleness . . . it is not a natural condition that comes about spontaneously through biological maturation but rather is a precarious or artificial state that boys must win against powerful odds." In contrast, for women, the demonstration of honor rests largely on the avoidance of "impure" acts—a woman's honor must be "preserved." This chapter focuses specifically on this latter operationalization of honor as the preservation of female purity. Male honor is fundamentally tied to female purity. Female purity (most notably, sexual purity) is the currency by which male honor and family honor is measured.[18] Thus, not only women's but men's honorable reputations are built on female moral purity, and this is the case in a remarkably wide range of societies.[19] Writing on the importance of honor in Latin America, for instance, Youssef notes that "Family 'honor' or male 'honor' is symbolized in the idea of two sex-linked characteristics that distinguish the ideal character of a man and woman: the manliness of the man (*machismo*) and the sexual purity of the woman (*verguenza*)."[20] In the Middle East "status and acceptance in the context of traditional society rest on the clan or family honor, an honor that largely depends on the behavior of its female members."[21] This can have consequences not only for the social reputation of families, but for their economic outcomes as well. In most honor cultures (and indeed, in most traditional cultures), marriage was and is a means of creating economic and political alliances between families.[22] Families can protect or increase their economic and social position in a community by marrying upward in the social hierarchy (hypergamy). Women, more often than men, marry "up,"[23] meaning that in many honor cultures both the social and economic standing of a family depends upon successfully protecting, controlling, and managing the public perception of its women. Men, it is often said, "own" the honor of women in their families. James Bowman noted in his *History of Honor*," in honor cultures, a woman's honor normally belongs to her husband or father and the dishonor of any sexual contact outside marriage, whether consensual or otherwise, falls upon him exactly alike, since it shows him up before the world as a man incapable of either controlling or protecting her."[24]

Reproduction versus Economic Production

Women's moral purity thus represent their "value" as a measure of their (and by association, their families') reputation. As Jane Schneider noted in her ethnographic review of honor cultures in the Mediterranean: "The repository of family and lineage honor, the focus of common interest among the men of the family or lineage, is its women. A woman's status defines the status of all the men who are related to her in determinate ways. These men share the consequences of what happens to her, and share therefore the commitment to protect her virtue."[25] Thus, a reputation for moral purity became the primary signal of a woman's value in the marriage market, and their families' economic and social livelihood depended on it.[26]

In short, economic and cultural features help explain how purity norms come to be stronger in some places and weaker in others, depending on whether a woman's marriage value is her primary means of contributing to her family and to the community at large. While no doubt an oversimplification of the diversity of gender roles around the world, across cultures women are valued relatively more for either their domestic, reproductive capacity or their economic, productive capacity. Given the relationships discussed above, we can expect that female purity should be most highly valued and enforced in cultures in which women's familial role stresses reproduction over economic production. Many (but not all) traditional cultures subscribe to some version of the doctrine of separate spheres: a woman's role is primarily defined as producing and raising children in the home, and men are tasked with economic production. In contrast, in modern liberal societies in which women are economic contributors, they should be valued relatively less for their purity, chastity, and fertility and use these attributes less in attracting mates.[27]

We recently sought empirical evidence for the prediction that female purity is associated with the cultural valuing of women's reproduction over their economic production.[28] We began by creating a quantitative measure of the degree to which cultures emphasize the moral purity of their women. Taking a broad view of purity as avoidance of bodily or spiritual pollutants, we sought behavioral and attitudinal measures that reflected concerns with sexual chastity (e.g., average age of brides—a reflection of prizing virginity), avoidance of chemical vices (e.g. smoking and drinking rates), and religious piety (e.g., percentage of women praying daily). Averaging these various measures together, we were able to create a six-item "Female Purity Index" and score nations on this index. As expected, the highest scoring nations tended to be Islamic or African cultures organized around honor norms, whereas the lowest scoring nations were predominantly situated in northern Europe. We then used this measure to explore the correlates of cultural concerns with purity.

We predicted that female purity would be emphasized most strongly in cultures in which women are valued the most for reproduction and childrearing (rather than as potential economic producers). To measure nations' relative emphasis on women's reproductive value versus economic productive value, we used two measures that reflected a cultural emphasis on reproduction (fertility rates and polygamy) and two indicators of women's economic output (labor force participation and relative income).

Fertility rates, measured as the average number of children born per woman[29] were strongly correlated with a cultural emphasis on female purity. As a second measure of prioritizing reproductive value, we collected data on the legal status of polygamy across cultures.[30] In these sorts of cultures, women are considered reproductive vehicles, tightly controlled by their families and usually married off young.[31] (Indeed, the vast majority of polygamous societies are polygynous, in which men may marry multiple wives).[32] As predicted, the cultural tradition of polygamy was also associated with female purity emphasis.

Just as the cultural prioritizing of women's reproductive value should be associated with an emphasis on female purity, we predicted that cultures that prioritize women's economic value (in terms of becoming producers outside the home) should *de-emphasize* the importance of female purity. Stated differently, as women gain economic independence, the less they need to safeguard and advertise their purity in hopes of finding a mate. Indeed, both female labor force participation and women's income relative to men's are significantly negatively associated with female purity emphasis.

Purity and Family Ties

Because potential partners carry the possible reward of strengthening family alliances and standing within a community (or damaging family standing), purity should be especially important in collectivist cultures in which the ties among family members are strongest—where women have the greatest potential to bring honor or shame to their families. Ethnographers and cultural anthropologists have noted women's key role in building marital alliances that can lead to the acquisition of resources such as land, rights to water, inheritance of herds, and grazing rights.[33] More generally, families in collectivist cultures should be more likely and better able to enforce purity norms in their women, because everyone in the family has a bigger stake in preserving the family reputation and because collectivist socialization means that family units have greater power to bring about conformity in their members.

In our cross-cultural research,[34] we examined the connection between collectivism and female purity. Indeed, our Female Purity Index correlated quite strongly with national scores on cultural collectivism versus individualism. Further demonstrating the interconnectedness of these concepts, one collectivist social custom that reflects a prioritization of family alliances as a conduit to prosperity and social standing is the practice of arranged marriages. As mentioned above, when family status is tied to economic welfare through marriage alliances (which provides an orderly passing of land and material resources), reputational concerns should be especially strong. Using data from Georgas and colleagues' cross-cultural examination of family practices across thirty nations,[35] we coded for whether arranged marriages were common in a sample of nations. The presence of arranged marriages also correlated strongly with our Female Purity Index.

Finally, reputational concerns should also be heightened in cultures where residential mobility is low, because people's indiscretions are most likely to stay with them when they lack the ability or motivation to move to new communities.[36] Furthermore, when people live close to their families, reputational stains are more likely to extend to affect one's entire family. Using measures of the percentage of households moving in the past two years and the percentage of parents living more than twenty-five kilometers from their children as proxies of residential mobility, we found that both measures correlated negatively with the Female Purity Index.

Taken together, these data indicate that in collectivist cultures where family units are tighter (less likely to move or live apart, and more likely to play an active role in marriage arrangements), and where women typically have a larger reproductive and smaller economic role, the family and the culture as a whole tend to exhibit greater concern with the preservation and maintenance of women's honor.

THE BROADER PSYCHOLOGICAL AND SOCIAL FUNCTIONS OF FEMALE PURITY EMPHASIS

Beyond the specific context of honor cultures, social psychologists have theorized that heterosexual romantic relationships are similar in many ways to economic transactions.[37] Because of women's role in reproduction, female sexuality (much more than male sexuality) is often commoditized and accorded value, which (following basic economic principles) increases to the extent that it is scarce. Thus, a woman's purity (e.g., chastity, fidelity, piety) increases the perceived value of her sexuality, and perhaps by extension of herself. A wealth of research has provided evidence that diverse cultures value, regulate, and often suppress female sexuality. Women may be complicit in this suppression themselves, particularly when they have little societal power, as sexuality can be one of the few resources women have available to negotiate other material and social resources.[38]

Social psychological theories of sexism also take into account the fact that relationships between men and women are characterized by both inequality and interdependence.[39] Ambivalent sexism theory proposes that inequality leads to sexism, but men's and women's mutual interdependence means that prejudice is not uniformly hostile. Rather, sexism is marked by deep ambivalence. Hostile sexism results from men's greater strength and status, but subjectively benevolent forms of sexism result from men's dependence on women for children and for psychological intimacy.[40] Benevolently sexist attitudes help to justify gender inequality by romanticizing the purity of women, and placing the responsibility on men (as the dominant group) to "protect" the honor of women. This idealizing of purity by placing women on a pedestal also helps to pacify women's resistance to inequality, as women will often trade independence and equality for protection, particularly in cultures high in hostile sexism—a theme to which we return later in the chapter.

This is consistent with codes of chivalry as well.[41] Chivalrous men will protect "virtuous" women, but if women argue for equality, they risk losing the protection that this paternalism provides. Chivalrous norms rely upon two stereotypes about women: First, that (some) women are more virtuous than men, which explains why women are thought to deserve chivalry. Second, that women are less agentic than men, which explains why women are thought to require chivalry. Chivalry acts as a contract between men and women: Men withdraw their willingness to protect women who fail to conform to these twin gender roles of moral purity and submission.

IMPLICATIONS OF A CULTURAL EMPHASIS ON FEMALE PURITY

The above theorizing suggests that the cultural preoccupation with female purity, and the behaviors taken to enforce it, require a steep tradeoff. Male honor is especially tenuous because it not only depends on a man's behavior but on the behavior of women in the family (wives, sisters, daughters, etc.) as well. An Arab expression captures this interdependence bluntly: "a man's honor lies between the legs of a woman."[42] Maintenance of male honor thus requires control over the behavior of women, suggesting two related implications. First, to the extent that male honor requires female purity and fidelity, women in high purity cultures should have less autonomy, lower status, and fewer rights. Second, as their behavior is highly scrutinized, women may also be more vulnerable to men's violence as well.

In our cross-cultural analysis of correlates of female purity emphasis, we examined outcomes for women's autonomy and well-being.[43] Specifically, we looked for indicators suggesting women had: political influence and political freedoms, and vulnerability to violent victimization in the home.

Political Influence and Freedoms

To measure the extent to which women hold positions of influence, we compiled data from the World Economic Forum's Global Gender Gap Index[44] on the percent of minister-level positions held by women and percent of parliamentary positions held by women. As expected, as countries emphasize female purity more, women are less represented in government positions of power. As a second measure, we also gathered data on women's political rights across nations, using data from the Cingranelli-Richards (CIRI) Human Rights Dataset.[45] This database includes an index of women's political rights (e.g. right to vote, right to run for political office, right to petition government officials). As expected, political rights for women correlated negatively with the Female Purity Index.

Partner Violence

Prescriptions for "protecting" the honor of women can mean using violence or the threat of violence in an attempt to deter possible infidelity, desertion, or shame-producing actions. Prescriptions for female purity are part of this equation as well. Because violations of purity can threaten not only women's honor but also the honor of related men, violence in the service of honor restoration can be culturally sanctioned. Sometimes this violence is explicitly sanctioned but other times people simply look the other way or minimize it.

In our cross-cultural survey of female purity correlates, we gathered two types of data on intimate partner violence. First, we compiled prevalence rates of men's physical violence against women, from a variety of nationally representative surveys of women. Second, to measure women's acceptance and endorsement of the legitimacy of men's partner violence, we used survey data compiled by UNICEF,[46] asking whether a husband or partner is justified in hitting or beating his wife under certain circumstances (i.e., if his wife neglects the children, goes out without telling him, argues with him, refuses sexual relations, or burns the food).

Male intimate partner violence was significantly more prevalent in nations that emphasized female purity. In addition, and perhaps more disturbingly, women also endorse men's violence in purity cultures: women were more likely to respond that a partner is justified in hitting his wife in cultures that emphasize female purity. This underscores the challenge in changing deeply entrenched cultural norms, as women often assume the role of moral educators of children and enforcers of their daughters' moral purity.

In other experimental research, one of the authors has examined people's responses to hypothetical conflict scenarios, comparing people from Latin American cultures of honor to people from the northern United States, a culture without a strong honor tradition.[47] In these studies, we find evidence that a woman's infidelity or suspected infidelity diminishes her partner's reputation, and the man's reputation can be partially redeemed through his use of violence against the woman.

For instance, in one study,[48] we compared college students from Brazil (a culture with strong honor roots)[49] and the U.S. respondents were told either about a man whose wife was faithful to him or one whose wife was unfaithful to him. They then had to rate the man on honorable traits (e.g., trustworthiness and good character), strength, and masculinity. For U.S. respondents, the woman's infidelity had little effect on ratings of the man: his trustworthiness and good character were unaffected and his masculinity and strength were slightly diminished. In contrast, for Brazilian respondents, the man whose wife was unfaithful was rated much less favorably on these dimensions than the man whose wife remained loyal. These findings were extended in a study comparing Canadian respondents to those from Chile (an honor culture), with an important caveat.[50] Participants listened to an audiotape of a man who told of a violent encounter with his wife. Both Canadians and Chileans were equally condemning of the man's violence when it was unrelated to honor (i.e., when she overspent a credit card), but Chileans rated the husband and his actions more positively when her actions called into question her purity and his honor (i.e., when he suspected his wife of flirting with another man). This study echoes results from Spain,[51] in which Spanish participants saw a victim of domestic violence as more guilty, and British participants saw the abuser as more guilty, when the victim's suspected infidelity was a motive for the violence. Sometimes the sanctioning of violence can affect law enforcement and public policy as well. For example, in a recent study of an Afghan police force, officers were asked about their attitudes and intentions to intervene in hypothetical cases of domestic violence. When the female victim admitted to infidelity, the officers expressed reluctance to intervene and arrest the perpetrator or aid the victim.[52]

Not only do men's honor norms work to (at least partially) excuse violence, but feminine honor norms in some cultures may demand women's acceptance of such violence. One such feminine honor norm is referred to as *marianismo* (the female counterpart to *machismo*) in Latin cultures, an ideology in which purity, loyalty, sacrifice, and relational altruism are venerated.[53] In a dramatic laboratory experiment, we staged a conflict between an engaged couple in a hallway that ended with the man violently shoving his partner against a wall, all in view of unsuspecting participants who were waiting for a psychology experiment some distance down a hallway. When the woman later interacted with participants, those from American cultural groups with relatively strong traditions of honor (southern Anglos and Latinos) were more approving of the woman, compared with a group of northern Anglos, when she expressed contrition and loyalty after the altercation. In contrast, participants from the northern United States liked her and approved of her more when she was assertive and threatened to leave the relationship. In addition, participants from the honor groups sent more messages condoning the aggression and encouraging her to tolerate it and remain loyal to her partner, compared with the northern Anglo group.

IS FEMALE PURITY RELEVANT IN CONTEMPORARY LIBERAL SOCIETIES?

The research cited in this chapter has focused mainly on traditional honor cultures, in which gender relations, customs about marriage and relationships, and women's economic and social status are often quite different from the majority of the United States and similar economically advanced, democratic societies. Turning to a major question of this book, one might ask whether the question of female moral purity is relevant to contemporary Western liberal democracies.

On the one hand, women's roles in many cultures have changed greatly over the past two centuries. Women are no longer valued primarily for their reproductive capacities and marriage is no longer primarily about building familial and economic alliances. It is tempting to conclude that honor norms that prize and enforce female purity are antiquated and have no place in modern, liberal American society. On the other hand, recent news stories as well as evidence from psychologists studying morality make clear that concerns with purity, and women's purity in particular, continue to resonate beyond traditional honor cultures.

Within the United States well-publicized examples of the gender policing of morality and the sexual double standard are still easy to find. To name of few recent examples: In Virginia, a teenage girl was kicked out of prom for an "inappropriate dress" that some parents complained was arousing "impure thoughts" among the male chaperones.[54] In Utah, a high school digitally edited the yearbook photos of several female students whose tops were deemed too revealing.[55] In 2012, Georgetown law student Sandra Fluke spoke at a Congressional hearing to advocate for including contraception drugs in healthcare coverage. Radio talk show host Rush Limbaugh called Ms. Fluke a "slut" and a "prostitute" based on her speech to Congress.[56] In fact, many of the supposed "culture wars" that differentiate American social conservatives and liberals revolve around matters of moral purity. Conservatives endorse attitudes and prescriptive norms that are aligned with traditional honor codes—chivalry, female modesty, aversion to sex education, and the like. Social psychologist Jonathan Haidt[57] has noted that conservatives in general are more apt to consider purity or divinity a moral domain than are liberals, who see purity issues as personal preferences.

A spate of recent experimental work also confirms continued concerns with female (more than male) purity among American college students. Women who dress provocatively (e.g., low-cut blouse, high-heeled shoes) are judged more harshly (by both men and women) and disparaged by their female peers, compared with women who wear more conservative clothing (e.g., buttoned-up blouse, flat shoes).[58]

In a series of recent studies with American undergraduates, we have also found evidence that purity concerns are more central to how women (compared with men) evaluate themselves and in how people judge women (compared to men).[59] In one study, we asked female and male students to rate a number of purity and nonpurity-related traits on a continuum from "much more important for women to possess" to "much more important for men to possess." Purity-related traits were considered more important for women than men to possess, and these perceptions did not differ depending on whether a male or female participant was making the ratings. In a separate study directing participants to consider these same traits in relation to themselves, women rated the purity related traits as more personally important than men did, and women's self-ratings of their own purity-related traits significantly predicted their self-esteem—especially among women who were strongly gender identified. Follow-up studies showed that purity was a more salient theme in evaluations of a woman's character than of a man's, and that women were judged more harshly than men for purity violations, as contrasted with other kinds of moral violations.

DO PURITY NORMS HAVE ANYTHING TO OFFER WOMEN?

Clearly, female purity norms still hold sway in much of the world. Even in cultures with fairly liberal views of sexuality and in which women enjoy relatively high status, purity informs third-party judgments of women, as well as women's self-perceptions. At least among some groups of Americans, the moral purity of girls and women remains a central concern.

Who benefits from these norms? Purity and chivalry certainly have their defenders. Cultural tensions exist between champions of chivalry who wish to save it from extinction and those who see it as a barrier to true gender equality. It's easy to see how the enforcement of purity can benefit men. However, honor codes that paint women as pure creatures who ought to be cherished and protected can be seductive for women as well, due to the implicit promise of adoration and protection. Norms of honor, purity, and chivalry may indeed offer (some) women protection from things like sexual harassment from strangers and violence outside of the home. Thus, in cultures where the dangers women face are greater, one might expect the implicit promise inherent in chivalry to be especially valued. Indeed, in Peter Glick and colleagues' cross-cultural investigation of hostile and benevolent sexism,[60] they found that in cultures in which men's hostile sexist attitudes were highest, women were also most endorsing of benevolent sexism (sometimes more endorsing than men in these cultures). So, while women reject hostile sexism, they may in fact accept benevolent, patronizing forms of sexism precisely to the extent buying into that system could be perceived as protecting them from greater risk of hostile sexism.

Benevolent sexism is disarming;[61] but ultimately, though individual women might benefit from the protection that the honor system provides, women as a whole pay a high cost for this bargain. As Gloria Steinem once remarked, "A pedestal is as much a prison as any small, confined space." Belief in women's virtue goes hand in hand with a prescriptive belief in lack of agency,[62] which serves to maintain status differences between men and women. Women who play by the rules must accept their subordinate position in order to be rewarded. Indeed, women who seek equality are often perceived as ungrateful and unfeminine and are therefore acceptable targets for punishment and harassment.[63] As gender equality increases and hostile sexism decreases (in mostly non-honor cultures) women are less likely to need to accept this tradeoff. That is, these women are less likely to require the more material benefits that benevolent sexist ideology provides, and are also less likely to be targets of hostile sexism.[64]

The gendered nature of honor codes exposes a contradiction, elaborated in more detail by both Andrea Mansker and Dan Demetriou in this volume. Honor is a commodity that is traded among parties of equal status, yet it flourishes in societies in which men have much greater status and power than women. Demetriou notes how honor systems create intermural coordination between competing parties of *similar rank*, and as such lead to courtesies even among enemies. Of course, this system is relevant to men only. In Demetriou's terminology, membership in horizontal honor groups must be earned rather than inherited. Once admitted to such groups, members may compete for vertical honor, or ranked prestige. Given that men already jockey for status amongst themselves, they will be reluctant to dilute the value of their horizontal honor by broadening it to include women as well.

Mansker writes eloquently about how nineteenth-century French feminists used the traditional honor code to undermine their society's sexism and gender inequality. When the feminist journalist and speaker Olympe Audouard was libeled in a newspaper, she challenged the writer to a duel. The writer was then forced to choose between refusing the duel, thereby formally exposing the unequal position of women by denying Audouard the right of challenge, or to dueling against a woman—a losing proposition no matter the outcome. As Mansker notes, Audouard was thus able to show how the honor code failed as a system by excluding women and not treating them as equals ("her adversary's 'gallant' desire not to harm her was not honorable at all since he used women's exclusion from the public code and their inability to respond violently as an excuse to shamefully defame them in print."). The irony, then, is that, as contemporary democracies move to greater gender equality, men and women could come closer to being seen as equals due mutual respect and honor. However, as equality begins to be formally recognized, but before it really penetrates social customs, women may no longer be "protected" in the patronizing way they once were, but neither are they fully admitted into the realm of men who have access to the tools of a "horizontal" honor code for defending against challenges to their own honor. In addition, as women gain equality with men, they have less *need* for the paternalistic protections of that the traditional honor system afforded them.

Does honor have a future? Defenders of honor will argue that as modern liberal societies have favored ever-increasing individualism at the expense of traditional collective institutions (family, religion, etc.), we lose our moral consensus. One might argue that the gendered honor system we have discussed here is necessary to reign in some of society's moral ills. However, the empirical record does not back this up. In addition to the troubling link between purity emphasis and intimate partner violence, other moral problems appear greater, not lesser, in places where honor is still taken seriously, at least in the United States. In the South, for instance, where honor still has its strongest foothold,[65] rates of teen pregnancy and divorce are highest.[66] In modern, pluralistic democracies, "honor as purity" is outmoded and harmful. Elements of the honor code may yet have a future in liberal democracies, as others in this volume have advocated, but to do so, they must be extricated from their historical gender trappings to a gender-neutral and more narrowly defined construct. Any system that denies the equality of women, even when couched in benevolence, will and should ultimately be rejected.

NOTES

1. David D. Gilmore, *Manhood in the Making* (New Haven, CT: Yale University Press, 1990).
2. Barbara Welter, "The Cult of True Womanhood: 1820–1860," *American Quarterly* 18 (1966) : 151–74.
3. Steven Mintz, *Moralists and Modernizers: America's Pre-Civil War Reformers* (Baltimore: Johns Hopkins University Press, 1995).
4. See Ruth Bordin, *Woman and Temperance: The Quest for Power and Liberty, 1873–1900* (Philadelphia: Temple University Press, 1981). Women also led reformist movements in England in the sixteenth and seventeenth centuries. See Jessica Warner, "The Naturalization of Beer and Gin in Early Modern England," *Contemporary Drug Problems* 24 (1997): 373–402.
5. Allan Brandt, *The Cigarette Century: The Rise, Fall, and Deadly Persistence of the Product that Defined America* (New York: Basic Books, 2009); Joseph R. Gusfield, "The Social Symbolism of Smoking and Health," in Robert L. Rabin and Stephen D. Sugarman (eds.), *Smoking Policy: Law, Politics, and Culture* (New York: Oxford University Press, 1993), 49–68.
6. Cited in Brandt (2009), 57.
7. Alan Sipress, "Egyptian Rights Group Sues Sheik on Support of Female Circumcision," *Philadelphia Inquirer*, April 5, 1995, http://articles.philly.com/1995–04–13/news/25684816_1_female-circumcision-islamic-law-traditional-practice.
8. BBC, "Iranian Cleric Blames Quakes on Promiscuous Women," *British Broadcasting Corporation*, April 10, 2010, http://news.bbc.co.uk/2/hi/8631775.stm.
9. Pat Robertson linked Katrina to America's abortion policy; see Media Matters, "Religious Conservatives Claim Katrina was God's Omen, Punishment of the United States," September 13, 2005, http://mediamatters.org/research/2005/09/13/religious-conserv
atives-claim-katrina-was-gods/133804. Gerhard Maria Wagner, a Catholic bishop in Austria, suggested that Katrina was caused by New Orleans's lax sexual attitudes, noting that it had "the best brothels and the prettiest prostitutes." See Veronika Oleksyn, "Pope's Bishop Pick Criticized over Katrina Comments," *Huffington Post*, March 4, 2009, http://www.huffingtonpost.com/2009/02/02/rev-gerhard-maria-wagner-_n_162920.html.
10. Elizabeth Mandeville, "Sexual Pollution in the New Guinea Highlands," *Sociology of Health and Illness* 1 (1979): 226–41.
11. Steve Vickers, *Staging Sex Myths to Save Zimbabwe's Girls*, BBC News, October, 26, 2006, television.
12. Lawrence C. Watson, "Sexual Socialization in Guajiro Society," *Ethnology* 11 (1972): 150–56.

13. Nancy V. Baker, Peter R. Gregware, and Margery A. Cassidy, "Family Killing Fields: Honor Rationales in the Murder of Women, *Violence Against Women* 5 (1999): 164–84; Mark Cooney, "Death by Family: Honor Violence as Punishment," *Punishment & Society* 16 (2014): 406–27.

14. E. J. Horberg, Christopher Oveis, Dacher Keltner and Adam B. Cohen, "Disgust and the Moralization of Purity," *Journal of Personality and Social Psychology* 97 (2009): 963.

15. Jonathan Haidt, Paul Rozin, Clark Mccauley, and Sumio Imada, "Body, Psyche, and Culture: The Relationship of Disgust to Morality," *Psychology and Developing Societies* 9 (1997): 107–31; Paul Rozin and April Fallon, "A Perspective on Disgust," *Psychological Review* 94 (1987): 23–41; Joshua M. Tybur, Debra Lieberman, and Vladas Griskevicius, "Microbes, Mating and Morality: Individual Differences in Three Functional Domains of Disgust," *Journal of Personality and Social Psychology* 97 (2009): 103–22.

16. Horberg, Oveis, Keltner and Cohen, "Disgust."

17. Gilmore, *Manhood*, 11.

18. S. Cihangir, "Gender Specific Honor Codes and Cultural Change," *Group Processes & Intergroup Relations* 16 (2012): 319–33.

19. Richard E. Nisbett and Dov Cohen, *Culture of Honor: The Psychology of Violence in the South* (Boulder, CO: Westview Press, 1996); Sherry B. Ortner, "The Virgin and the State," *Feminist Studies* 4 (1978): 19–35; Joseph A. Vandello and Dov Cohen, "Male Honor and Female Fidelity: Implicit Cultural Scripts that Perpetuate Domestic Violence," *Journal of Personality and Social Psychology* 84 (2003): 997–1010; Jospeh A. Vandello and Dov Cohen, "Gender, Culture, and Men's Intimate Partner Violence," *Social and Personality Psychology Compass* 2 (2008): 652–67; Joseph A. Vandello, Dov Cohen, Ruth Grandon and Renae Franiuk, "Stand By Your Man: Indirect Prescriptions for Honorable Violence and Feminine Loyalty in Canada, Chile, and the United States, *Journal of Cross-Cultural Psychology* 40 (2009): 81–104.

20. Nadia Youssef, "Cultural Ideals, Feminine Behavior, and Family Control," *Comparative Studies in Society and History* 13 (1973): 326–47, 329.

21. Baker, Gregware and Cassidy, "Family Killing Fields," 165

22. Stephanie Coontz, *Marriage: A History* (New York: Penguin, 2006).

23. Kingsley Davis, "Intermarriage in Caste Societies," *American Anthropologist* 43 (1941): 376–95; Lena Edlund, "Son Preference, Sex Ratios, and Marriage Patterns," *Journal of Political Economy* 107 (1999): 1275–1304; Norval D. Glenn, Adreain Ross and Judy C. Tully, "Patterns of Inter-generational Mobility of Females Through Marriage," *American Sociological Review* 39 (1974): 683–99; Robert Merton, "Intermarriage and the Social Structure: Fact and Theory," *Psychiatry* 4 (1941): 361–74.

24. James Bowman, *Honor: A History* (New York: Encounter Books, 2006), 18.

25. Jane Schneider, "Of Vigilance and Virgins," *Ethnology* 9 (1971): 1–24, 18.

26. Joseph A. Vandello, Vanessa Hettinger and Dov Cohen, *Female Moral Purity and the Market for Women: A Global Study*, 2015.

27. Richard Posner, *Sex and Reason* (Cambridge, MA: Harvard University Press, 1991).

28. Vandello, Hettinger, and Cohen, *Female Moral Purity*.

29. Central Intelligence Agency, *The World Factbook* (2012).

30. OECD Development Centre, *Social Institutions and Gender Index Database*, 2012.

31. See Joseph Heinrich, Robert Boyd, and Peter Richerson, "The Puzzle of Monogamous Marriage," *Philosophical Transactions of the Royal Society* 367 (2012): 657–69.

32. George P. Murdock, *Ethnographic Atlas* (Pittsburgh, PA: University of Pittsburgh Press, 1967).

33. Sherry B. Ortner, "The Virgin and the State," *Feminist Studies* 4 (1978): 19–35; Julian Pitt-Rivers, "Honour and Social Status," in Jean G. Peristiany (ed.), *Honour and Shame: The Values of Mediterranean Society* (London: Weidenfield & Nicolson, 1965); Jane Schneider, "Of Vigilence and Virgins, *Ethnology* 9 (1971): 1–24.

34. Vandello, Hettinger and Cohen, *Female Moral Purity*.

35. James Georgas, John W. Berry, Fons J. R. van de Vijver, Cigdem Kagitsibasi, and Ype H. Poortinga, eds., *Families Across Cultures: A 30-nation Psychological Study* (Cambridge: Cambridge University Press, 2006).

36. Shigehiro Oishi, "The Psychology of Residential Mobility: Implications for the Self, Social Relationships, and Well-Being," *Perspectives on Psychological Science* 5 (2010): 5–21; Masaki Yuki and Joanna Schug, "Relational Mobility: A Socio-Ecological Approach to Personal Relationships," in Omri Gillath, Glenn E. Adams, and Adrianne D. Kunkel, eds., *Relationship Science: Integrating Evolutionary, Neuroscience, and Sociocultural Approaches* (Washington, DC: American Psychological Association, 2012): 137–52.

37. Roy Baumeister and Kathleen Vohs, "Sexual Economics: Sex as Female Resource for Social Exchange in Heterosexual Interactions," *Personality and Social Psychology Review* 8 (2004): 339–63; Harold H. Kelley and John Thibaut, *Interpersonal Relations: A Theory of Interdependence* (New York: Wiley, 1978); Richard Posner, *Sex and Reason* (Cambridge, MA: Harvard University Press, 1991).

38. Roy F. Baumeister and Jean M. Twenge, "Cultural Suppression of Female Sexuality," *Review of General Psychology* 6 (2002): 166–203; Baumeister and Vohs, *Interpersonal Relations*.

39. Peter Glick and Susan T. Fiske, "An Ambivalent Alliance: Hostile and Benevolent Sexism as Justifications for Gender Inequality," *American Psychologist* 56 (2001): 109–118.

40. Peter Glick and Susan T. Fiske, "The Ambivalent Sexism Inventory: Differentiating Hostile and Benevolent Sexism," *Journal of Personality and Social Psychology* 70 (1996): 491–512.

41. Maurice Keen, *Chivalry* (New Haven, CT: Yale University Press, 1984).

42. Lisa Beyer, "The Price of Honor," *Time*, January 18, 1999, 55.

43. Vandello, Hettinger and Cohen, *Female Moral Purity*.

44. Ricardo Hausmann, Laura D. Tyson, and Saadia Zahidi, *The Global Gender Gap Report 2011*. (Geneva, Switzerland: World Economic Forum, 2011).

45. David L. Cingranelli and David L. Richards, "The Cingranelli-Richards (CIRI) Human Rights Dataset," 2010, accessed May 23, 2012, http://www.humanrightsdata.org.

46. UNICEF, *The state of the world's children 2008* (New York: UNICEF, 2008), Table 9, 146–47, http://www.unicef.org/publications/files/The_State_of_the_Worlds_Children_2008.pdf.

47. Vandello and Cohen, "Male Honor"; Vandello, Cohen, Grandon, and Franiuk, "Stand By Your Man."

48. Vandello and Cohen, "Male Honor," Study 1.

49. Sueann Caulfield, Sarah Chambers and Lara Putnam, eds., *Honor, Status, and Law in Modern Latin America* (Durham, NC: Duke University Press, 2005); Lyman Johnson and Sonya Lipsett-Rivera, eds., *The Faces of Honor: Sex, Shame, and Violence in Colonial Latin America* (Albuquerque: University of New Mexico Press, 1998).

50. Vandello, Cohen, Grandon and Franiuk, "Stand by Your Man."

51. Ana Delgado, Gerardo Prieto and Roderick Bond, "The Cultural Factor in Lay Perceptions of Jealousy as a Motive for Wife Battery," *Journal of Applied Social Psychology* 107 (1997): 1824–41.

52. Anna C. Baldry, Stefano Pagliaro, and Cesare Procaro, "The Rule of Law at Time of Masculine Honor: Afghan Police Attitudes and Intimate Partner Violence," *Group Processes & Intergroup Relations* 16 (2013): 363–74.

53. Maria A. Lara-Cantu, "A Sex-Role Inventory with Scales for 'Machismo' and 'Self-Sacrificing Woman,'" *Journal of Cross-Cultural Psychology* 20 (1989): 386–98; Evelyn Stevens, "Machismo and Marianismo," *Transaction Society* 10 (1973): 57–63.

54. "Homeschooled teen says she was kicked out of the prom because of dress." CBS, May 13, 2014, television. http://www.cbs5az.com/story/25509214/homeschool-prom

55. CNN, "Utah High School's Yearbook Photo Editing Angers Female Students," May 29, 2014, http://www.cnn.com/2014/05/29/us/utah-high-school-yearbook-photos-editing/.

56. Jenna Johnson, "Sandra Fluke Says She Expected Criticism, Not Personal Attacks, Over Contraception Issue," *Washington Post* (Washington, DC), March 3, 2012.

57. Jonathan Haidt, Silvia Helena Koller, and Maria Dias, "Affect, Cultures, and Morality, or is it Wrong to Eat Your Dog?" *Journal of Personality and Social Psychology* 65 (1993): 613–28.

58. Antonia Abbey, Catherine Cozzarelli, Kimberly McLaughlin and Richard Harnish, "The Effects of Clothing and Dyad Sex Composition on Perceptions of Sexual Intent: Do Women and Men Evaluate These Cues Differently?" *Journal of Applied Social Psychology* 17 (1987): 108–26; Delwin D. Cahoon and Ed M. Edmonds, "Male-Female Estimates of Opposite-Sex First Impressions Concerning Females' Clothing Styles," *Bulletin of the Psychonomic Society* 27 (1989): 280–81.; Martina Infanger, Laurie Rudman, and Sabine Sczesny, "Sex as a Source of Power? Backlash Against Self-Sexualizing Women," *Group Processes and Intergroup Relations* (2014); Tracy Vaillancourt and Aanchal Sharma, "Intolerance of Sexy Peers: Intrasexual Competition Among Women," *Aggressive Behavior* 37 (2011): 569–77.

59. Vanessa Hettinger and Joseph A. Vandello, *It's Different for Girls: Purity as a Gendered Moral Code*, 2014.

60. Peter Glick, Susan T. Fiske, Antonio Mladinic, José Saiz, Dominic Abrams, Barbara Masser, Bolanle Adetoun, et. al., "Beyond Prejudice as Simple Antipathy: Hostile and Benevolent Sexism Across Cultures," *Journal of Personality and Social Psychology* 79 (2000): 763–75.

61. Peter Glick and Susan T. Fiske, "An Ambivalent Alliance: Hostile and Benevolent Sexism as Justifications for Gender Inequality," *American Psychologist* 56 (2001): 109–118.

62. T. William Altermatt, Nathan DeWall and Emily Leskinen, "Agency and Virtue: Dimensions Underlying Subgroups of Women," *Sex Roles* 49 (2003): 631–41.

63. Jennifer Berdahl, "The Sexual Harassment of Uppity Women," *Journal of Applied Psychology* 92 (2007): 425–37; Anne Maass, Mara Cadinu, and Annalisa Grasselli, "Sexual Harassment Under Social Identity Threat: The Computer Harassment Paradigm," *Journal of Personality and Social Psychology* 85 (2003): 853–70; Laurie A. Rudman and Peter Glick, "Prescriptive Gender Stereotypes and Backlash Toward Agentic Women," *Journal of Social Issues* 57 (2001): 743–62.

64. Glick et. al., "Beyond Prejudice."

65. See Richard E. Nisbett and Dov Cohen, *Culture of Honor: The Psychology of Violence in the South* (Boulder, CO: Westview Press, 1996).

66. CDC, "Divorce rates by state, 1999–2012," *Centers for Disease Control*, http://www.cdc.gov/nchs/data/dvs/state_divorce_rates_90_95_and_99–12.pdf; Kathryn Kost and Stanley Henshaw, "U.S. teenage pregnancies, births, and abortions, 2010: National and state trends by age, race, and ethnicity," *Guttmacher Institute*, https://www.guttmacher.org/pubs/USTPtrends10.pdf

Part V

Honor and National Defense

TWELVE

Restoring Order

The Ancient Greeks on Taming Honor and Appetite

Richard Ned Lebow

Since the end of the Cold War, the problem of order at the domestic, regional, and international levels, has been high on the agenda of policy makers and scholars. How do these orders arise? What sustains them? Why and how do they decay or collapse? What can be done to shore up existing orders, supplant them with more successful arrangements, and bring some degree of stability to the more chaotic countries and regions of the world? I do not propose any answers to these questions, but offer a novel way of looking at them based on ancient Greek thought about the nature of individual and political order and their relationship to justice. Such a framework, I believe, has the potential to offer important and useful insights about the nature of political order.

For Greeks writing in the late fourth and fifth centuries, order was as grave a problem as it is for us today. The Peloponnesian War (431–404 B.C.E.) devastated Hellas and led to a short-lived but bloody tyranny in Athens. A shaky democracy—that would ultimately prove robust—was restored on the basis of the first known amnesty for criminal offenders of the previous regime. As in today's world, interstate war and domestic turmoil alike were to a great extent reflections of socioeconomic changes that brought about new practices and ways of thinking that threatened the power and identities of traditional elites and political units. Thucydides, Plato, and Aristotle grappled with these problems, and developed valuable insights and perspectives that are substantially different from those of most modern scholars. They are not directly applicable to problems of the twenty-first century. Instead, they reflect the wisdom of a pre-industrial Greek world where people lived in city states in which slavery was the norm, women were disenfranchised and citizenship and access to power severely restricted. These thinkers provide a vantage point to interrogate our understandings of order and expose their limitations.

With these ends in mind, I elaborate key aspects of the thought of Thucydides, Plato, and Aristotle about the nature of order. I refer to order in the generic sense, because all three thinkers thought individual and political orders were sustained by the same kind of balance, and deteriorated as a result of imbalances. All three described important connections between order and disorder at different levels of social aggregation. One of the principal goals of this section of the chapter is to show how key foundational assumptions and arguments of Plato and Aristotle are implicitly embedded in Thucydides. There are, of course, many important differences among the three thinkers, but they are closer together than is usually acknowledged in their understanding of how order is created, maintained, and restored. Individually and collectively, their understanding of order represents one of humanity's greatest and most useful intellectual achievements.

RESTORING ORDER

The Peloponnesian War transformed the social and political climate of Athens. Nearly three decades of a costly and ultimately unsuccessful struggle had destroyed a fragile political consensus and pitted the well-born against the *dēmos* and the rich against the poor in increasingly bitter factional struggles. This strife occurred against a background of growing cynicism in which laws, conventions, and practices (*nomoi*) had increasingly come to be regarded as artifice. The courts and assembly were exploited by individuals and factions for parochial ends, and especially revenge against enemies.

Thucydides and Plato recognized that the "ancient simplicity" they both admired so much could no longer be reproduced through everyday practice. The old ways had not only been discredited, they were no longer "natural" as other alternatives had emerged. Thucydides believed that the way out of this impasse was to create a synthetic order that would combine good features of the old and the new, while avoiding, as far as possible, their respective pitfalls. The best of the new was its spirit of equality (*isonomia*), and the opportunity it offered to all citizens to serve their *polis*. The best of the old was its emphasis on civic excellence (*aretē*), which encouraged members of the elite to suppress their appetite for wealth and power, and even their instinct for survival, in pursuit of valor, good judgment, and public service. Thucydides offered an idealized view of Periclean Athens as the kind of synthesis he envisaged. As noted earlier, he described it as a mixed constitution (*xunkrasis*) that allowed the capable to rule and the *dēmos* to participate in government in meaningful ways. It muted tensions between the rich and the poor and the wellborn and men of talent, in sharp contrast to the acute class tensions and near stasis of *fin de siècle* Athens.

Thucydides may have believed that intercity relations could be reconstituted on similar foundations. The same kinds of inequalities prevailed between *poleis* as within them. If the power of tyrants could give way to aristocracy and mixed democracy, and the drive for power and wealth constrained by the restoration of community, this achievement could be duplicated at the regional level. Powerful states might once again see it in their interest to wield influence on the basis of *hēgemonia*: recognition by others of one's right to lead in return for having provided extraordinary services to the community. Power imbalances could be "equalized" through the principle of proportionality (*to analogon*), more powerful states would receive honor (*timē*) to the degree they provided benefits for less powerful *poleis*.

The extension of Thucydides's domestic project to foreign policy would have been in keeping with Greek practice. Relations between *poleis*, and before that, between households, were traditionally regarded as extensions of domestic relations. There was a strong sense of "pan-Hellenic" community going back at least as far as the seventh-century poetry of Archilocus. A century later, Herodotus tells us, the Athenians resisted the Persians in the name of "our common brotherhood with the Greeks: our common language, the altars and sacrifices of which we all partake, the common character which we bear."[1] In the aftermath of the Peloponnesian War, this sentiment was very strong and something akin to the hopes of many Europeans after World War II that a peaceful Europe could be constructed on the basis of a common identity that transcended national differences and antagonisms. Plato described the "natural relationship" between Greeks as a form of kinship.[2]

Thucydides was a stern skeptic and rationalist who gives evidence of having believed that radical sophists had done a great disservice to Athens by convincing people that *nomos* (laws, conventions, rules, customs) was arbitrary and a self-serving justification for various forms of inequality. He could not have had much hope for the restoration, at least in the short-term, of stable orders at home or abroad, let alone for the kind of restructuring he considered essential to civil and international harmony. Thucydides wrote for an intellectual elite, who, like himself, was unlikely to accept *nomos* as gods-given. He appealed to them with a more sophisticated defense of *nomos* that did not require rooting it in nature (*phusis*). By describing the destructive consequences of the breakdown of *nomos*, he made the case for its utility and the wisdom of those in authority to act *as if* they believed *nomos* derived from nature. For Thucydides, unlike Plato, language and conventions were arbitrary but essential.[3]

Plato was, if anything, less optimistic than Thucydides. He had no illusions about Pericles, the political order he had cobbled together, or the less than straightforward means he used to hold it together. In the *Republic*, Socrates criticizes Pericles for failing to display or teach excellence (*aretē*). Plato's fundamental disagreement with Thucydides was over the nature of *aretē*, which Plato associated with suffering injustice, not committing it, as he thought Pericles had. Athens could only become just when each citizen overcame his own tyrannical impulses. Plato's solution to *stasis* entailed a more thoroughgoing revolution whose starting point was the moral reeducation of citizens.

Plato agreed with Thucydides that civil order, when not enforced by a tyrant, had to rest on a foundation of *nomos* that was adhered to by citizens in a nonreflexive way, and law that was followed as the result of a deliberate and reasoned commitment. He did not believe that leaders of a corrupt city could bring such an order about through reforms, and would have considered Thucydides's project unrealistic. His *Republic* and *Laws* establish new cities at some remove from Athens. The *Republic* offers a radical solution to the seemingly intractable problem of institutionalizing justice. Philosophers derive the constitution of the *Kallipolis* from first principles that reflect their holistic understanding of the good. They know how to order the life of the *polis* to the benefit of all citizens regardless of their particular skills and intellectual potential. A class of carefully educated Guardians, who understand the principle of justice, will impose correct opinion (*orthodoxa*) on the *polis* and enforce the constitution, including its provision of denying its citizens, as far as reasonably possible, contact with outsiders.[4]

Plato does not trust in education alone to restrain his Guardians. He wants to deprive them of wealth and family, widely considered the principal sources of corruption in ancient Greece.[5] In the *Laws*, he acknowledges that unconstrained authority—which the Guardians possess—is likely to corrupt even the best educated of human beings.[6] He also expresses doubts that citizens would willingly follow the lead of the Guardians if they were not godlike in their appearance and qualities. Otherwise, the natural envy of people for the wealth or power of others they regard as otherwise similar to themselves will dispose them to rebellion. As the Guardians are merely human beings, the *Republic* is unrealistic by Plato's own admission and is best regarded as a "thought experiment" to help him and his readers come to a better understanding of the nature of justice and the difficulty of achieving it in practice.

The *Laws* acknowledge what for Plato must have been a more unpleasant political truth: good laws are the product of reason, but reason has little to do with their success or failure. People obey laws because they are conditioned to do so through socialization and practice. Belief can reinforce compliance, but it is not the kind of belief that is reached through ratiocination. It is quasi-religious belief in the laws as "sacred" and "immutable," and a corresponding understanding of citizens as their servants. To foster this myth, Plato wanted to locate his city in far-off Magnesia and brainwash its citizens into forgetting that their constitution was a man-made artifice to which they or their ancestors had initially given their assent.[7]

It is interesting to read Plato against Thucydides, whose prescription for order relied on both reason and custom. Thucydides appealed to the elite on grounds of enlightened self-interest to establish and abide by reasonably just *nomos*. Their exemplary behavior would facilitate compliance by the *dēmos,* and might ultimately transform laws into deeply ingrained habits that became part of everyday life. Plato's preferred solution to the problem of order was to use dialogue and its associated *elenchos* to help people develop a conception of self-interest based on an intellectually sophisticated but emotionally empathetic understanding of the human condition. In a society populated by enlightened people, law and justice would be unproblematic. His fallback position, articulated in the *Laws,* is to institutionalize good laws by any possible means, including subterfuge. The latter is necessary to keep society intact and create the minimum conditions in which reason and dialogue might ultimately lead to a more enlightened citizenry. The strategy of the mature Plato is almost indistinguishable from that of Thucydides.

Aristotle was closer to Thucydides than Plato in his down-to-earth interest in empirical reality and ordinary politics. Like Plato, he constructed a constitution for an ideal *polis,* but only to have a template to evaluate existing political systems. In his ideal community, ordinary citizens, not by philosophers, make laws. What distinguishes his citizens from their real-life counterparts is agreement about the ends of life and a corresponding commitment to the law to help the community realize those ends.[8] Aristotle recognized that no such consensus existed in Greek cities. He nevertheless valued differences within and across *poleis* because of the range of lessons they offered. Good government relied on others' experiences as well as one's own. Diversity within cities made it likely that a wider range of policy options would be considered and evaluated from different perspectives. Aristotle sought a compromise that would preserve diversity while still making the city "common and one" in the sense of citizens accepting its *nomos* as legitimate. This was the minimum condition for civil order.[9]

Aristotle favored kingship, aristocracy, and polity because they were more likely to put the good of the community before that of individuals. Tyrannies, oligarchies, and democracies were defective because their rulers—individuals, groups and the *dēmos*—used power to advance their interests at the expense of the community. In oligarchy and democracy, such shortsightedness exacerbated conflict between the rich and the poor. Conflict was particularly acute in oligarchy because leaders were jealous of one another and fought among themselves as well as with the people.

In a democracy, the middle class could sometimes moderate the passions of the *dēmos*.[10]

Richard Kraut rightly considers Aristotle's typology of constitutions somewhat deceptive because Aristotle acknowledged that most political systems to some degree incorporated the principle of majority rule. Even when only a few ruled, as in aristocracies and oligarchies, they turned to larger groups of citizens to break deadlocks. Minority factions within ruling groups also brought issues to a wider forum when they thought they could garner support for their demands. Most systems were mixed in one form or another; the real distinction was between those where the interests of the community came first and all others where it did not.[11]

Aristotle was no democrat. He was adamantly opposed to giving much power to the people, especially laborers and mechanics, and made crude arguments against women, slaves, and non-Greeks. He had an even stronger dislike of the wealthy, wellborn, and refined, and, like a latter-day Leninist, proclaimed that a city that eliminated its elites was better than one that merely controlled them.[12] Extraordinary kings aside, Aristotle maintained that all men needed to be constrained by laws. The principle of majority rule benefited the degenerate city by limiting the power of its rulers. Aristotle accordingly wanted ordinary citizens to participate in the assembly and the courts when they chose officials or tried them for misconduct. Citizens would learn to think for themselves, ask pertinent questions, and perhaps come to understand how politics could serve the community. Aristotle nevertheless wanted to curb the power of assemblies and give rulers broad discretionary powers of enforcement. He opposed the use of decrees in lieu of legislation because they were responses to single cases and usually served selfish interests or destructive passions. Through the rule of law and a balanced constitution, he hoped to foster the kind of cooperative political culture (*koinōnia*) that would allow a *polis* to make at least some progress toward stability, justice and the good life.[13]

Such a society would still be second best in two important ways. A *koinōnia* was an association designed to advance the interests of its members. Cooperation was interest-based, but could become sufficiently routinized that members followed its rules and customs in an unreflective way. A *koinōnia* could be a source of conflict when its members distrusted one another and feared that some sought wealth or honor at their expense. Aristotle envisaged his ideal community as a *homonoia*, whose members agreed about the nature of the good life and how it could be achieved. Disagreements would still exist, but would not threaten the peace because they would take place within an environment based on mutual respect and trust. Plato would have insisted that people who followed *nomos* without understanding and accepting it on philosophical grounds did not qualify as virtuous. Aristotle considered perfect virtue beside the point. It was probably the best that most human beings could achieve. And when it became a habit, conformity could lead people closer to virtue.[14]

ARCHEO INSIGHTS

Plato and Aristotle base their metaphysics on a combination of deductive reasoning and extensive empirical observation. Thucydides's account of the Peloponnesian War is framed as an historical narrative, but he relies on many of the same conceptual categories used more explicitly by his successors. Their collective analysis of politics is based almost entirely on the experience of Greek city states, which even for its time was a highly idiosyncratic form of political community. And the *polis*, like all other political units of its era, existed before media, education, and industrialization made mass politics possible. Some of their insights are nevertheless applicable to the modern era, in particular, their thoughts about how orders decay and might be restored. They represent the outlines of a holistic prototheory of order that bridges materialist and ideational explanations and levels of analysis. Their common starting point—which Nietzsche would later made central to his philosophy—is recognition that human societies can be divided into those in which practice is nonreflective, and those in which actors recognize that their norms and practices are part of an overall social system. Both kinds of societies are fragile, but vulnerable to different kinds of threats. The former is most at risk when people become aware of their *nomos* (laws, rules, conventions, norms) as a system, and of the possibility that it is not gods-given, but man-made. The latter is most vulnerable when *nomos* itself is questioned, usually on the grounds that it is unjust.

Improvements in shipbuilding and navigation had stimulated trade and given rise to encounters with civilized peoples who had different customs and gods. These encounters triggered an active debate in the fifth century about the relative merits of *nomos* and *phusis* (nature), with some sophists, like Plato's Callicles, asserting that law merely reflected the interests of the rich and powerful. Lack of consensus about the source of law and convention, and by extension, of the meaning of justice was an increasingly acute problem in fifth-century Greece. It divided democrats from aristocrats, and was the principal cause of *stasis* (acute domestic conflict and civil war). In his account of the Corcyraean revolution, Thucydides provides us with chilling descriptions of how violent such conflict could become.

Some way had to be found to justify *nomos*, and here there are important shades of difference among our three thinkers. We have observed that Thucydides hoped to convince the elite of the utility of treating *nomos* as if it were *phusis* and the will of the gods. Plato appears to reject such a duplicitous strategy in favor of providing a rational foundation for *nomos*, but his willingness to base *ē* on a foundational lie, in which at least the first generation of Guardians must be complicit, suggests that he is not that distant from Thucydides in his approach. Following Plato, Aristotle emphasizes the role of socialization through imitation and education, but, unlike Plato, he gives an important role to reflection and independent learning. All three are deeply pessimistic about the ability of human beings to construct and maintain viable political orders that endure. In the *Symposium*, Plato recognizes that lawgivers and philosophers alike aspire to create something enduring, and laments that only philosophers have any hope of success.[15] In the *Republic*, he acknowledges that this is true even of his *Kallipolis*.[16] Thucydides and Aristotle understood the rise and decline of political orders as a cyclical process. For Aristotle, the life cycle of a constitution was no different in principle from that of all living things.

Order and Justice

Homer's epics are built around such conceptions of justice and the conflicts to which violations of them give rise. Thucydides, Plato, and Aristotle were close readers of Homer as well as careful observers of their own societies. They are adamant that all successful social orders—including preconscious ones—embody some principle of justice. Stable societies were those in which practices were to some degree concomitant with underlying principles of justice. Societies that had become reflective about the social order also required some kind of consensus about the nature of justice.

The materialist explanation, most often associated with Karl Marx, interprets competing conceptions of justice as ideologies of competing class interests. It is generally true that demands for democracy were most pronounced in *poleis* that were actively engaged in foreign trade and had sizeable commercial "classes"—a term that can be applied to ancient Greece only with the utmost caution. An alternative, ideational explanation, associated with constructivism, contends that class conflict requires prior development of relevant language in terms of which class can be conceptualized and claims formulated. The debate over the relative importance of *nomos* and *phusis* in the second half of the fifth century facilitated the emergence of the concept of self-interest, which is central to such a discourse. Plato was convinced that philosophers played a critical role in problematizing social orders that were previously reproduced as natural practice. By doing so, they undermined the values that encouraged public service, sacrifice and self-restraint on the part of the elite.

Of our three thinkers, Aristotle is the closest to Marx. As we have seen, he describes the wealthy and highborn as exploiters of the *dēmos*, and the poor as envious of the goods of the wealthy. Thucydides resorts more to ideational explanations; he is attentive to ways in which language shapes thinking and how the misuse and transformation of words can undermine *nomos* and the civic association it sustains. It is no coincidence that his description of how language was degraded by a negative reinforcement cycle of word and deed, follows immediately on his description of a particularly nasty civil war. He also appears to recognize—following Homer—that alternative discourses must emerge and become available before people can step outside of their own practices, problematize and reflect on them, and act, or organize, to bring about social-political change.[17]

Thucydides, Plato, and Aristotle recognize that even when there is a consensus about the meaning of justice, those ideals will never be fully realized in practice. Thucydides and Aristotle were less concerned about this discrepancy than Plato who was more of a perfectionist. Greek constitutional history indicated to them that citizens would tolerate inconsistencies between ideals and practice as long as their appetites and spirits were to some degree assuaged. For Thucydides this required some form of popular political participation and with it, a public discourse that accepted the ultimate sovereignty and wisdom of the *dēmos*. The democratic ideology, with which Pericles publicly associated, reconciled the *dēmos* to the economic and political advantages of the elite in a Gramscian manner.[18] When the gap between ideology and practice was blatantly exposed by the post-Periclean demagogues, class conflict became more acute and politics more vicious, leading to the violent overthrow of democracy by the regime of the Thirty in 404 and its restoration a year later. Thucydides's depiction of the Periclean constitution closely resembles what Aristotle would later call a polity, and describe with favor.

Balance and Imbalance

Thucydides's portrayal of Cleon and Alcibiades offer a sharp contrast to his portrait of Pericles, who had acted with restraint and maintained his authority by convincing the *dēmos* that he had their best interests at stake. His successors sought power as an end in itself and achieved it by pandering to the appetites of the masses. Alcibiades's speech in support of the Sicilian expedition offers a striking example. For leaders and led alike, reason lost control over both spirit and appetite. Plato and Aristotle, as we have seen, gave this insight the status of a general principle. For all three thinkers, the operative cause of breakdown is failure of rulers to govern in accordance with the principles on which their legitimacy is based. Succeeding generations of rulers—whether kings, aristocrats or democratic politicians—fail to sustain the commitment to justice, prudence, and self-restraint (*sophrosunē*) of their predecessors. In our time, Mao Zedong made a parallel argument about revolutionary bureaucracies.

The gradual abandonment of self-restraint by rulers encourages imitation by the *dēmos*. By the time of the Sicilian debate, a majority of the assembly appears as self-indulgent as Alcibiades, and are persuaded to support him by the prospect of pecuniary gain. A relatively united Athens accordingly embarked upon the riskiest and most disastrous campaign of the war. Their defeat led to other defeats, internal bickering about who was responsible for them, intensification of class and political differences, and an oligarchic coup. Politicians skilled in the art of rhetoric were catalysts of political corruption. According to Thucydides, they used "fair phrases to arrive at guilty ends."[19] They twisted and deconstructed the language, giving words meanings that were often the opposite of their traditional ones, and using them to justify behavior at odds with conventional practices and values. By the late fifth century, the code of "ancient simplicity" (*euēthēs*), so admired by Thucydides and Plato, had not merely declined, it had been "laughed down and disappeared."[20]

Phase Transition

On the eve of the Peloponnesian War, Athenians justified their city's behavior to the Spartan assembly by invoking the three traditional Greek motives: interest, honor, and fear. The first two represent appetite and spirit respectively, while fear comes into play when individuals (or states) come to believe that other actors have the power and desire to gain so much wealth or honor for themselves, and that this can only be accomplished at their expense. When this happens, there is a sudden and dramatic reorientation in the priority in peoples' motives—what physical scientists call a phase transition. In Corcyra and Athens, and in Greece more generally, there was a shift from what we might call a constructivist world to a realist one.

For Thucydides and Aristotle, the shift to fear and realism occurs when an individual or faction has captured the institutions of state and exploits them for partisan ends. These institutions no longer regulate and constrain competition for wealth and honor, but intensify it by enabling one faction to enrich itself or advance its standing, at the expense of others. In extreme cases, factions may use the institutions of state to punish or kill their opponents. Aristotle notes that the very expectation of such a process can encourage one faction to grab power preemptively in the belief that they must strike out before their adversaries do. Once such a cycle of violence and retribution begins, it becomes difficult to contain. Thucydides provides a chilling description of how runaway civic tensions escalated into an utterly destructive civil war (*stasis*) in Corcyra.[21] Aristotle offers Rhodes, Thebes, Megara, and Syracuse as examples.[22] Realist worlds are readily made self-fulfilling, and once in them it is hard to escape.

The process of civic breakdown illuminates a key tension of Greek society. Honor, and its social manifestation as standing, was a central value for Greeks, so much so that Plato and Aristotle made the spirit an independent part of the psyche. Honor is, by definition, a relational concept. It is a scarce commodity because if it is available to everyone it is attainable by no one. Worlds in which honor is an important value are highly competitive. For Aristotle, as Steven Skultety observes in chapter 4 of this volume, honor is an important source of stability and legitimacy for societies, but also a source of instability and disorder when it is pursued for the wrong reason.[23] Paradoxically, the competition for honor requires a high degree of consensus and cooperation. External honor is only meaningful when recognized and praised by others. *Kleos* (fame) is derived from the verb *kluein* (to hear). It indicates recognition, as Homer knew so well, that fame requires heroic deeds, bards to sing about those deeds, and folks willing to listen and be impressed by them. In the absence of a society with important shared values, functioning institutions, or at least, procedures for recognizing accomplishments and establishing standing, external honor cannot exist. Self-advancement found expression in Greece primarily in a quest for honor, but enlightened self-interest imposed restraints on that quest, just as it did on the striving for wealth and power. Greek myth and tragedy were replete with tales of figures like Croesus and Agamemnon whose downfall was brought about by their exaggerated ambitions or self-importance.

In industrial and postindustrial societies, appetite, especially wealth, is thought to be the driving motive—although, as Veblen realized, wealth, and the conspicuous consumption it allows, are often just another means of achieving standing.[24] In either case, the dynamic is the same: competition within a structured environment. Plunder aside, the acquisition of wealth depends upon such things as enforceable contracts, negotiable instruments and flow of people, money, and ideas. They all depend on the existence of norms, rules, laws, and voluntary compliance to them by large numbers of actors. When competition for wealth gets out of hand it threatens the very institutions and practices that make it possible.

Class Analysis in Perspective

Since Marx, many analysts of civil unrest and revolution had emphasized the role of class conflict. Plato, Aristotle, and Thucydides are not insensitive to class conflict, but consider it only one cause of civil disorder, and one moreover, that is mediated by other factors. Wealth was unevenly distributed within all *poleis*. Thucydides and Aristotle do not consider this inequality in itself sufficient to provoke serious internal conflict. This occurred when discourses that reconcile diverse classes through a widely shared and overarching commitment to the community as a whole lose their authority.[25] When this happens, the wealthy and the aspiring become more rapacious and the *dēmos* less accepting of their subordinate economic and political status. Class division becomes more evident and consequential. Thucydides's account of post-Periclean Athens indicates that he considered the collapse of civic discourse and its restraining effects as both a cause and effect of psychological imbalance. The plague and war helped to undermine that discourse, giving freer rein to the individual pursuit of wealth and power. They in turn further undermined traditional discourses and civic values. The causes of class conflict were as much psychological, social, and political as they were economic. The importance of the plague indicates that there was also an element of chance.

A second, equally important source of civil disorder is *intraclass* conflict. Class conflict was primarily, although not entirely, attributable to appetite. The unequal distribution of wealth created envy and encouraged those who had less to band together to exploit the strength of numbers to improve their situation. The unequal distribution of wealth meant that some men had to sell their labor to others and become subordinate in ways that diminished their self-esteem. So the spirit also comes into the picture. Intraclass conflict is primarily about the spirit, and concerns social standing within classes. As noted, conflict over standing was endemic to fourth- and fifth-century Greek elites, and was often more acute because honor, unlike wealth, is a zero-sum quality. The two forms of conflict were, of course, related, as they were both due to psychological imbalances caused by reason's loss of control of either the appetite or spirit. They could also be synergistic when intraelite conflict becomes sufficient to destroy the respect of the *dēmos* for the elite, thus making inequalities in wealth and status less tolerable or threatening the well-being, and perhaps the survival, of the *polis*. Such a dynamic was at play in Corcyra, where leaders of competing factions set in motion a process of escalating conflict that led to a destructive civil war.

Thucydides, Plato, and Aristotle understood that neither wealth nor poverty produce *stasis*; civil disorder is due to failures of self-restraint and empathy. Plato nevertheless considers too much of either to be destabilizing because wealth makes for luxury and idleness, and poverty for mean-mindedness and bad work.[26]

Domestic and International Parallels

Plato and Aristotle described politics at the individual and state levels, as did Thucydides, who extended his analysis to what we call the regional level. None of them thought in terms of levels of analysis, and efforts to map their analyses on to this formulation do not do justice to their understandings of the social world. Their explanations bridge levels of analysis in ways that indicate they did not conceptualize political behavior in horizontal, if permeable, layers, each with its own appropriate mode of explanation. They conceived of social interactions of all kinds as taking place in a discrete number of nested domains, each characterized by similar dynamics and amenable to the same kind of analysis. Plato and Aristotle begin with a description of the individual psyche, whose categories and pathologies they extend to the *polis*. People and *poleis* alike are motivated by appetite, spirit, and reason. Order and disorder in both domains is attributable to balance or imbalance among these components. Plato's *Republic* describes a city, but portrays it as a collective representation of a human psyche, with its philosophers embodying reason. The constitution he lays out for this city is similar in all important respects to what he believes is best for the individual. The principal difference—the physical isolation of his city—is due to the absence of other virtuous cities with which it might associate. Aristotle's analysis of constitutions also parallels his understanding the individual; lack of discipline in individuals and cities leads to instability. The institutional arrangements he thinks most likely to maintain discipline in *poleis* are an extrapolation from his preferred regimen for the individual. It is self-evident to him that "the same life is best for each individual, and for states and for mankind collectively."[27] If we need a modern analogy, fractals come closest to capturing the Greek understanding of human behavior. They replicate the same pattern at different orders of magnification.

Thucydides not only extends this kind of analysis to foreign policy, he demonstrates how imbalance in one social domain can help bring about imbalance in another. His account of the Peloponnesian War can be read as a discourse on how psychological imbalance in individuals replicates itself in the city and then in Hellas more generally. Pericles appears to be the model of the wise statesman because of his ability to get citizens to rise above their parochial concerns to support policies that are in the best interest of their *polis*. Thucydides attributes his success to self-mastery; Pericles suppressed his appetites in pursuit of honor for himself and his city. He was successful as long as his appetite and *thumos* were constrained and guided by reason. In 431 B.C.E., Pericles succumbed to hubris when he convinced himself, and an initially reluctant Athenian assembly, that a defensive alliance with Corcyra was a low-cost means of increasing Athenian power and humbling its Corinthian rival. He was irrationally confident about his ability to manage events to prevent the outbreak of war, or failing that, to limit its scope and duration.[28] Pericles's hubris was emblematic of his city's; Thucydides has Corinthian and other speakers describe Athenians as restless, ambitious, risk-prone, and never content with what they have.[29] These characteristics became increasingly more pronounced as the war progressed, and found their most extreme and destructive expression in the assembly's enthusiasm for the Sicilian expedition. Events in Greece as a whole recapitulate the horrors of *stasis* in Corcyra, and for much the same reasons.

If Athenians were increasingly dominated by appetite, Spartans were in thrall to *thumos*, which led them to act in equally irrational ways. Eager for war to preserve their standing and gain new honors, they brushed aside the warning of their astute king Archidamus that Athens was rich and powerful and impervious to assault by land. The precipitating cause of war between the two hegemons was third party conflicts, and once the war was under way, it greatly exacerbated these conflicts and factional divisions within cities. At every level of conflict, conventions broke down, enlightened self-interest disappeared and unrestrained barbarism became the order of the day. Writing in the aftermath of the Peloponnesian War, Plato reflected the pessimism of his generation when he described peace as a fiction because cities, by their very nature (*kata phusin*), lived in a state of undeclared war with every other city.[30]

Thucydides was writing about relations among Greeks, and not about international relations more generally. Social relations for Greeks were embedded in a dense web of interlocking relationships, governed by an elaborate set of conventions that encouraged expectations of support while imposing constraints and obligations. Relations with fellow citizens were conceptualized as an extension of domestic relations, as were, to a significant extent, relations with other Greeks. The fifth-century lexicon did not have a word for international relations. Like Herodotus, Greeks most often used *xenia*—a Homeric concept that meant "guest friendship"—to describe relations between *poleis*.[31]

Greeks distinguished themselves from "barbarians," and had higher expectations for intra-Greek relations. Fifth-century Greeks had extensive dealings with local tribes and the Persian, Egyptian, and Carthaginian empires. Many of these encounters were violent; Greece had suffered two Persian invasions, and Athens fought Carthage for control of Sicily and had briefly achieved control over Egypt. Until the Peloponnesian War, conflicts among Greeks had mostly been about disputed territory or relative standing. Battles were bloody, but wars were limited and governed by extensive rules. Warfare never threatened the existence of combatant cities. By contrast, conflicts with barbarians—whether tribesmen or empires—were about security, often about survival, and frequently fought with no holds barred.

JUSTICE AND PHILOSOPHY

Greek philosophy is rich in organic analogies. The life cycle of birth, growth, decline, and death is routinely applied not only to people but also to social entities such as the regime and city. It provides the basis for their *telos*. For Aristotle, this is the kind of growth and maturation that enables living things to express their respective natures. *Phuein*, the verb "to grow," may have given rise to the noun *phusis*, meaning "nature," indicating that, for Greeks, the two concepts were inseparable almost from the beginning.

Proportion (*to analogon*) comes into play because growth is an expression of one's nature, and healthy growth is by definition proportional. Growth in turn is made possible by power. In speaking of power, Greeks distinguished between *kratos* and *dunamis*. *Kratos* is the capability that makes the exercise of power possible. *Dunamis* is the expression of power through process—from which our words dynamism and dynamic derive. For Greeks, power could not be easily understood apart from its purpose, and this was usually considered to be expansion and growth. These understandings couple power to proportionality, and indirectly, to fairness and justice, because proportionality is a measure and expression of fairness and justice. The several parts of the individual psyche must be in balance, as must the constituent parts of the city. Each needs to perform its particular function and cooperate with the others in a harmonious manner. Fairness, justice, and balance are so closely related that it is not too much of a stretch to understand them as different expressions of the same thing.[32]

The organic understanding of human life and social organizations has important implications for how Greeks thought about structure and process. For modern social science, they are separate categories, and structure is given ontological priority. It is the "reality" we want to understand because it has substance, while process is thought to be fleeting. Philosophers routinely trace this ontological preference back to Plato and Aristotle, both of whom are routinely read as defenders of invariance against Parmenides's conception of nature as flux.

In many of his dialogues, Plato follows Heraclitus in describing the observable world as one of fleeting "appearances." He insists that as reason demands stability, there must be imperceptible, enduring, ideational forms, whose understanding would confer wisdom. Appearances are an expression of the forms, and can only be understood by reference to these universals.[33] Aristotle rejects Plato's forms in an effort to put his ontology on a firmer footing. He tries to prove that descriptions based on appearances inevitably lead to inconsistencies and paradoxes. In Book Gamma of *Metaphysics*, he argues for the necessity of first principles that are fixed in their own right and not a reflection of ourselves or our understanding of the world. They inhere in things and constitute their fixed essences. In *De Anima*, he expresses his belief that we are endowed with the cognitive capability (*nous*) to intuit these essences. This is possible because our rational thought processes match the structures of reality. In such a philosophical system, change can be understood by reference to that which is changeless.

Neither Plato nor Aristotle are as one-sided as they are sometimes depicted. Plato never claims any knowledge of universals, and conducts his inquiries in the *Statesmen* and the *Republic* without any assurance that they are in conformity with underlying verities. His understanding of politics, like that of Aristotle's, is one of process. The master metaphor of growth and decay provides the framework for inferring the ends of peoples and cities and the various pathologies to which they are subject. Constitutions are abstract representations of an evolutionary process. Plato's descriptions of these constitutions are a frozen frame, or snapshot, of underlying flux. For Plato, the forms are a goal that philosophers seek but may never reach. What counts is the voyage of discovery, just as it did for Odysseus—and for all he disparaged poets, Plato was a close reader of Homer, and there are striking parallels in their works. The voyage of discovery directs our attention away from narrow and selfish concerns and toward broader social truths. It leads us into dialogue with our peers, which, we have observed, Plato considers essential to create the empathy and friendship that sustains justice and the civic culture.

Something similar can be said for Aristotle. He makes first principles the centerpiece of *Metaphysics*, but his analysis of social affairs is framed in terms of the life cycle. It focuses on transitions and relies heavily on procedural concepts such as *dunamis* (potency), *energeia* (activity), kinesis (motion), and *metabolē* (change). He discusses first principles at length, but nowhere claims substantive knowledge of them. His principal social inferences concern the social nature of man and the hierarchy of his activities. At the top is the contemplative life, which Aristotle pursued. If he had been able to grasp the most important first principles, his extraordinary accomplishment would have undercut the value of the contemplative life for others. The only task remaining would have been deductions from those principles to account for the variety of their natural and social manifestations. The goal of subsequent philosophers would have been something akin to that of our less imaginative graduate students who defend their dissertations as efforts "to fill in gaps in the literature."

In *De Anima*, Aristotle asserts that first principles are independent of context, but in the *Politics* and *Nicomachean Ethics*, he acknowledges that their applications must be tailored to circumstances. Natural justice (*phusikos*) has the same force everywhere, and is quite independent of how people conceive of it. Legal justice, by contrast, exists only by virtue of being recognized and practiced. It displays considerable variation, and in the same *polis*, within limits, different systems of justice might function just as effectively.[34]

Before the development of the *polis* it would have been difficult, if not impossible, for any philosopher to intuit that individuals could only fulfill their natures through participation in the life of the *polis*. Aristotle must have understood that the *polis*, like all forms of human organization, could not endure. With his pupil Alexander's conquest of so much of the known world, he watched new military practices and political forms emerge that signaled the decline of the *polis*. Even if first principles were universal, their implications for human life needed periodic revision and updating in light of evolving circumstances. Aristotelian disciples must gaze in two directions: outwards, toward abstract principles and universal truths; and over their shoulders, at their own societies, their principles of justice, constitution, laws, and educational practices. Deliberation about natural, customary, and rationally constituted orders, provides perspectives necessary to critique and improve current practices and encourage human excellence. Contemplation is the highest form of activity because it benefits not just the individual, but the entire community.

The tension between invariance in flux in the works of Plato and Aristotle cannot easily be resolved, but it does become explicable when we consider the multiple and somewhat contradictory goals of both philosophers. In *Metaphysics*, Aristotle considers nature perfect in its organization, in what we might call the proliferation of genotypes, but acknowledges that it makes mistakes in the expression of individual phenotypes. We encounter all kinds of living things that are deformed in one way or another; this is true of individual psyches and city constitutions. Greeks left deformed and unwanted infants to die—one of the many ironic reversals of Oedipus is that it was the process of abandonment that made him lame. Plato approves of this practice, and of the execution of incurable psychopaths.[35] But like Thucydides and Aristotle, he believes that people and cities can overcome their psychological "deformities." To do this, they require a careful diagnosis, based on an understanding of the true ends of people and cities. In theory, the appeal to first principles can anchor such analyses, and can make arguments based on them appear more persuasive. At the level of philosophy, the appeal to forms or first principles allowed Plato and Aristotle to fold *nomos* (convention) back into *phusis* (nature) and attempt to overcome the politically dangerous dualism that had opened up in the course of the fifth century.

NOTES

1. Herodotus, *The Histories*, trans. George Rawlinson (New York: Knopf, 1997), 8.144.
2. Plato, *Republic*, in *The Collected Dialogues*, trans, Edith Hamilton and Huntington Cairns (Princeton, NJ: Princeton University Press, 1989), 469b–471c.
3. Richard Ned Lebow, *The Tragic Vision of Politics* (Cambridge: Cambridge University Press, 2003), elaborates this argument.
4. Plato, *Republic*, 506c; *Statesman*, in *The Collected Dialogues*, trans. Edith Hamilton and Huntington Cairns (Princeton, NJ: Princeton University Press, 1989), 309c6–10
5. *Republic*, 464c5–e1.
6. Plato, *Laws* in *The Collected Dialogues*, trans. Edith Hamilton and Huntington Cairns (Princeton: Princeton University Press, 1989), 875a–d.
7. *Laws*, 875a–d, 860e, 919d, 946b, 969a.
8. Aristotle, *Politics* in *The Complete Works of Aristotle*, ed. Jonathan Barnes (Princeton, NJ: Princeton University Press, 1984), 2 vols, Books 7 & 8.
9. *Politics*, Books 7 & 8, 1261a18, 1263b36–37.

10. *Politics*, Books 7 & 8 1279b8–9, 1289b4–51, 307a15–20.

11. Richard Kraut, *Aristotle: Political Philosophy* (Oxford: Oxford University Press, 2002), 312.

12. *Politics*, 1248113–14.

13. *Politics*, 1252a1–7, 1328b7–9, 1335b38–1336a2, 1336b8–12.

14. *Politics*, 1155a22–613, 162b5–21, 1328b7–9, 1335b38–1336a2, 1336b8–12.

15. Plato, *Symposium* in *The Collected Dialogues*, trans. Edith Hamilton and Huntington Cairns (Princeton, NJ: Princeton University Press, 1989), 206c–207c.

16. *Republic*, 546d5–547a5.

17. Homer, *Iliad*, trans. Robert Fagles (New York: Viking, 1990), Book IX.

18. Thucydides, *The Landmark Thucydides: A Comprehensive Guide to the Peloponnesian War*, ed. Robert B. Strassler (New York: Free Press, 1996), 2.37.1 and 2.65.9–10.

19. Thucydides, 3.82.

20. Thucydides, 3.83.

21. Thucydides, 3.83.

22. *Politics*, 1302b22–34.

23. Skultety, "A Neo-Aristotelian Theory of Political Honor," in this volume.

24. Thorstein Veblen, *The Theory of the Leisure Class: An Economic Study in the Evolution of Institutions* (New York: Modern Library, 1934 [1898]).

25. *Politics*, 1302b34–1303a21.

26. *Republic*, 421e4–422a3.

27. *Politics*, 1325b30–32.

28. Lebow, *Tragic Vision of Politics*, ch. 7.

29. Thucydides, 1.70.6, 2.37.1, 40.4, 2.63.3 and 64.4.

30. *Laws*, 62a2–5.

31. *The Histories*, 1.69.

32. *Politics*, 11.6–9.

33. Especially *Theaetetus*, *Timaeus*, *Symposium*, *Phaedrus*, and *Republic*.

34. Aristotle, *Nicomachean Ethics* in *The Complete Works of Aristotle*, ed. Jonathan Barnes (Princeton, NJ: Princeton University Press, 1984), 2 vols., 1134b18–20.

35. *Republic*, 460c3–461c7 and 410a3–4.

THIRTEEN

"The Honour of the Crown"

The State and Its Soldiers

Paul Robinson

In summer 2013 a group of military veterans filed a suit against the Canadian government, complaining that the benefits provided to injured soldiers by the New Veterans Charter (NVC) passed by Parliament in 2006 were insufficient. The NVC replaced the disability pensions previously awarded with lump sum payments, which the veterans claimed were "arbitrary, substandard and inadequate for supporting themselves and their families." The case was said to be "about promises the Canadian Government made to men and women injured while in service to their country and whether it is obliged to fulfill those promises," and the veterans based their suit in part on the claims that a) "a social covenant" exists between the state and its soldiers, and b) the "honour of the Crown" makes the Canadian government obliged to implement its promises to veterans.[1]

Against this, lawyers for the Crown have argued that the Canadian government owes veterans only what is promised in the NVC. They claim that, "There are no similarities between the origin, foundation, and history of the Honour of the Crown doctrine as it is known in Canadian law and the way in which the plaintiffs seek to apply it in this action." Furthermore, "Even if the Honour of the Crown doctrine could be said to extend to the relationship between Canada and members of the Canadian Armed Forces (which is denied) the doctrine cannot be used to invalidate legislation. . . . Any attempt to use the Honour of the Crown to invalidate legislation would violate the principle of parliamentary sovereignty."[2]

The aim of this chapter is not to examine the validity of the legal claim concerning the "honour of the Crown," nor to determine whether the veterans' complaints about the provisions of the NVC are correct. Rather the chapter uses the idea of the "honour of the Crown" as a starting point to undertake a broader examination of the appropriate status of military personnel and of Western liberal democracies' relationship with their soldiers. It will argue that the veterans' appeal to the principle of the "honour of the Crown" appears to reflect a common contemporary view of civil-military relations, according to which the military and the state have a quasi-feudal relationship in which each is bound to fulfill certain obligations towards the other not by contract but by vaguer ties of honor. The chapter will look briefly at one attempt to codify such ties, namely the "Armed Forces Covenant" enacted by the Parliament of the United Kingdom.

The chapter will conclude that nowadays a quasi-feudal relationship between the state and its soldiers may work to neither side's benefit. In modern liberal democracies, soldiers should neither be disadvantaged compared with other citizens nor enjoy special privileges. There may be some advantages in converting military service into something more comparable to other professions. This would fit with a process of what Anthony Forster calls the "juridification of the armed forces," which is already underway in Europe, and by which European armed forces are losing their special legal status.[3] Furthermore, in strictly practical terms this may be of more benefit to soldiers than existing arrangements.

In the context of Commonwealth countries such as Canada, which share the British monarchy, the term "Crown" refers not to the person of the monarch herself but rather to the "State," although the fact there is a monarch whose honor is connected to that of her state is perhaps not entirely irrelevant. "The honour of the Crown" refers to "the principle that servants of the Crown must conduct themselves with honour when acting on behalf of the sovereign."[4] According to David Arnot,

> Canadians have inherited the British tradition of acting honourably for the sake of the Sovereign. This convention has roots in pre-Norman England, a time when every yeoman swore personal allegiance to the king and anyone who was charged with speaking or acting on behalf of him bore an absolute personal responsibility to lend credit to the king's good name. Should he fail in this responsibility or cause embarrassment, he was required to answer personally to the king with his life and fortune. The Crown was not an abstract or an imaginary essence in those days, but a real person whose powers and prestige were directly dependent on the conduct of his advisers, captains and messengers.[5]

The modern version of the "honour of the Crown" was enshrined in Canadian law in the Supreme Court's 1984 decision in the case *Guerin v The Queen*, which established that there is a "fiduciary relationship between the Crown and the Indians"[6] (a fiduciary relationship being one in which "one party is required to look after the best interests of the other in an exemplary manner," for instance, the relationship between lawyers and their clients or physicians and their patients).[7] Arnot notes that, "the court restored the concept of holding ministers to a standard of fairness that demands forethought as to what conduct lends credibility and honour to the Crown, instead of what conduct can be technically justified under the current law."[8] The concept has since been further developed in other cases involving First Nations. For instance, in *R. v Marshall* in 1999, the Supreme Court declared at paragraph forty-nine that, "the honour of the Crown is always at stake in its dealings with Indian people. . . . It is always assumed that the Crown intends to fulfill its promises. No appearance of 'sharp dealings' will be sanctioned."[9]

Arnot comments that "The concept of honour was the basis of the First Nations leaders' understanding of what they were doing when they entered into treaties with the British Crown. They were entering into a personal relationship . . . with the British sovereign."[10] As yet, Canadian courts have not applied the concept of the "honour of the Crown" to any cases not involving First Nations. The legal relationship between the Crown and the First Nations is *sui generis*. Were the veterans to win their case, it would constitute a dramatic extension of the principle.

The veterans' decision to appeal to the principle also reflects their own understanding of their relationship with the state; that like that of the First Nations, it is a "personal relationship" with the Crown based on honor. The fact that Canadian soldiers, unlike American ones, do not swear allegiance to the Constitution but rather to the Queen may serve to reinforce this impression. For even if it is symbolic in practice, in form the oath, as Patrick Mileham says, is "an inter-personal promise, not one made to an abstract concept."[11]

Furthermore, the language which veterans suing the Canadian government have used to describe their relationship with the Canadian government is similar to that used by the First Nations. Arnot comments that the First Nations regard the treaties which they signed with the British Crown as "sacred," taking the form of a "covenant."[12] "Elders speak about treaties and the Crown in consistent terms: treaties as establishing a lasting relationship with the Crown and her subjects, with the creator as witness."[13] In the same vein, the veterans' lawsuit talks of a "social covenant" between the Crown and its soldiers, language which, as we shall see, has been duplicated by the armed forces in the United Kingdom. Michael Blais, leader of the lobby group Canadian Veterans Advocacy, has repeatedly argued that the Canadian government has a "sacred obligation" to its soldiers.[14] He has had some success in getting others to adopt this phraseology. Justin Trudeau, leader of the Liberal Party of Canada, for instance, used the "sacred" description in a radio advertisement in December 2014, saying that, "We have a sacred duty to Canadians who risk their lives for us."[15]

The foundation of the veterans' claim against the Canadian government, then, is that they have a "unique relationship with the Crown. . . . In return for undertaking . . . onerous and often dangerous obligations, armed forces members were promised that they and their dependents would be fairly and adequately compensated."[16] This relationship is not a contractual one, however. At no stage do soldiers sign a contract which specifically stipulates that in return for their service they will receive a certain level of support. The veterans pursuing the court case seem to view their relationship with the Crown in quasi-feudal terms. Although the reality was far more complex (thus the use of the term "quasi-feudal"), feudalism is often portrayed as being a system of reciprocal obligations between vassals and their lords. As Susan Reynolds puts it, free men "entered into vassalage by a ritual known as commendation and by taking an oath of fidelity. Commendation and oath bound them to the service of their lords. . . . In return for the vassal's service the lord offered protection and some form or degree of maintenance."[17]

In the modern manifestation of this quasi-feudal relationship, soldiers swear allegiance to the person of the Queen, and in return for their service to her receive an implied promise of support which the Queen's representatives are honor bound to fulfill. The swearing of an oath adds to the allegedly sacred quality of this relationship, which binds together God, the Crown, and the soldier through ties of honor.

One problem with this model is that it is largely a figment of soldiers' imaginations. Many of them may view their relationship with the Crown in this way, but the historical evidence would suggest that the Crown never has. For the Crown, soldiers are simply its servants, whom it pays to do its bidding, from whom it expects more or less unquestioning obedience, and to whom it has no contractual obligations. In Canada, the legal case of *Gallant v The Queen*, which follows British precedent, has established that, "Both English and Canadian Courts have always considered . . . that the Crown is in no way contractually bound to the members of the Armed Forces, that a person who joins the Forces enters into a unilateral commitment in return for which the Queen assumes no obligations."[18] This has been confirmed in subsequent cases. According to *McClennan v Canada*, for instance, "members of the Forces serve at pleasure. They do not have contractual rights enforceable against the Crown. . . . there is no contract of employment between Her Majesty and members of the Forces."[19] Not only is there no contract, but in the case *Manuge v Canada*, the Crown argued that it did not have a fiduciary duty to members of the armed forces either, saying: "The relationship of the Crown to its employees, including CF [Canadian Forces] members . . . does not create the basis for a fiduciary duty."[20]

In fact, Sarah Ingram argues that the idea that a covenant exists between the state and its soldiers is an "invented tradition," based in part on "erroneous assumptions concerning its antiquity."[21] The historical reality of the British Crown's relationship with its soldiers has been that "successive governments since the sixteenth century tried to evade their responsibilities or were begrudging in their attitude towards veterans."[22] The concept of a covenant represents an "idealized past that does not withstand scrutiny,"[23] and "claims concerning the nation's unbreakable bonds of responsibility, identity, and loyalty to soldiers cannot be substantiated."[24]

Given that there is no convincing evidence that the Crown ever did agree to a sacred covenant with its soldiers, it is curious that this archaic concept has suddenly gained acceptance in many circles. Anthony Forster suggests that it is a "conservative" reaction to social changes deemed hostile to traditional military values, and represents an attempt to assert the right of military institutions to be "different" from civilian society.[25] In effect it is a new claim to a distinct status.

Here, we confront some confusion, as it would appear that different soldiers and veterans make different claims about what that distinct status should be. Andrew Murrison, a member of the British Parliament, remarks that there are two models of what soldiers' status should be: "no disadvantage" and "citizen-plus." The first implies that service men and women should not be disadvantaged because of being in the military. In the case of medical care, for instance, that would mean that wounded veterans should receive the same benefits as civilians who suffer similar injuries. The second, however, implies that because of the unique nature of their service, military personnel should enjoy special privileges which civilians do not.

In their case against their government, the Canadian veterans fail to make a distinction. On the one hand, "they say that they are being treated unequally because the benefits and compensation available under the NVC are substantially less favourable than those that are available to injured persons claiming under tort law or workers compensation,"[26] a claim which fits with the "no disadvantage" model. On the other hand, they appeal to the armed forces' "unique relationship with the Crown."[27] Lobbyist Michael Blais has made it clear that he views the military's status in terms of "status plus," saying:

> Nor do we agree with or support the Royal Canadian Legion or the many prominent veterans organizations they have united under the banner of the consultation group on this issue. They would propose solutions that compare the sacrifice of Major Mark Campbell—whose legs were explosively amputated, who suffered serious internal injuries, including the loss of a testicle, who has a brain stem injury and complex PTSD—with the plight of a civilian awarded legal damages due to negligence at the workplace in Ontario. This is unconscionable.

> There is no comparison. The sacred obligation is not accorded to a litigant in a lawsuit. The sacred obligation is reserved for Canadians who have sworn allegiance to this great nation, who have borne arms in our name and bled in battle, who have suffered in peace with unwavering loyalty and offered great sacrifice while treading in harm's way in Canada's name. Clearly the compensation quotient of the lump sum award must reflect and respect the sacrifice borne.[28]

There is a similar failure to distinguish between the two models in other countries. For instance, the Confederation of British Service and Ex-Service Organizations said in a 2009 statement that, "The Armed Forces do not demand privileged status, but expect to be treated as a special group within the public sector to reflect the Unique Nature of Military Service." As Andrew Murrison says, "It is difficult to know what to make of this."[29]

The confusion finds further expression in the Military Covenant which the British Army introduced in 2000, and which subsequently led to the adoption of an Armed Forces Covenant by the British government in 2010.

The UK's Covenants attempt to define the Crown-soldier relationship in the twenty-first century. The very use of the word "covenant" is revealing. The three authors of the 2000 covenant consisted of a general educated at a Catholic private school, another who was the son of a Church of England clergyman, and a military chaplain. The first of these people drafted the Covenant with "Thomas Jefferson's Declaration of Independence and the Rule of St Benedict . . . at [his] elbow."[30] The Military Covenant of 2000 had decidedly religious overtones.

The later Armed Forces Covenant, which gave flesh to the earlier version and expanded it to include the Royal Navy and the Royal Air Force as well as the British Army, declares that, "Those who serve in the Armed Forces . . . should face no disadvantage compared to other citizens in the provision of public and commercial services. Special consideration is appropriate in some cases, especially for those who have given most such as the injured and the bereaved."[31] The document thus combines the language of "no disadvantage" with elements of "citizen-plus." Examples of the latter are provisions specifying that veterans should receive "priority treatment" in the National Health Service if their injuries were service-related, and that service personnel should have "priority status in applying for Government-sponsored affordable housing schemes." The Covenant also established a "Community Covenant Scheme," which it said "could take the form of, for example, additional support in accessing local service delivery such as social housing or free access to leisure facilities, discounts in shops and restaurants."[32] In this way, the Covenant clearly seeks to extend perks to military personnel that other citizens do not have. Sarah Ingram thus concludes that, "inherent in the Armed Forces Covenant are implied notions of military moral superiority. Service personnel are, by implication, deemed to be 'citizens-plus' . . . all automatically deserving of civilian society's respect."[33]

This too reflects a relatively new phenomenon in civil-military relations in the English speaking world. Once, the prevailing view was that soldiers were, as the Duke of Wellington so colorfully put it, "the mere scum of the earth."[34] Nowadays, however, there is a growing belief among the public that members of the armed forces are rather super-citizens, or as Andrew Bacevich writes in his book *The New American Militarism*, "a repository of traditional values and old-fashioned virtue." In the United States, there is, says Bacevich, "a tendency to elevate the soldier to the status of national icon, the apotheosis of all that is great and good about contemporary America."[35] Soldiers, Bacevich also writes, "have tended to concur with this evaluation of their own moral superiority."[36]

This phenomenon is perhaps most pronounced in the United States, but it has spread elsewhere. In the United Kingdom, Helen McCartney notes, there is "a general feeling, at all levels of the British military, that where public support is concerned, the Americans have got it right. Senior officers have highlighted the military discounts for serving soldiers and the free tickets offered to attractions and sports games. . . . There is corresponding disappointment as soldiers make the comparison with the reception they are afforded by the British public."[37]

It is clear that the "disappointment" McCartney observes does not spring from soldiers being unable to afford to pay for attractions and sports games or to pay full price in the shops. If that were the problem, they would not seek military discounts but better pay. It would appear that it is not the money which is important, it is the special status. According to McCartney, "Serving soldiers want to feel that they are making a difference on their deployments and they want the public to be proud of what they do and the roles they play as well as respect who they are. . . . If service personnel are risking death and injury, they want to know that this sacrifice is valued and appreciated."[38] The former head of the British Army, Sir Richard Dannatt says that, "soldiers do not ask why but they do ask for respect and honour for what they have been sent to do."[39]

The language of covenants in the United Kingdom and Canada thus covers a desire for citizen-plus status for military personnel, which in turn reflects a belief that such personnel are uniquely deserving of honor. Yet as Murrison points out, citizen-plus has never been government policy. "With the notable exception of America, it tends to be more prevalent in repressive states where the military has to be bought off by the regimes it protects with special favours."[40] In liberal democratic states, and in particular in Commonwealth countries such as the UK and Canada, where the head of state is the Queen, there is a clear disconnect between this expectation by the soldiers and the Crown's view on the matter.

There are good reasons for this. In this volume, Steven Skultety comments that, "Liberalism would never claim that for any given citizen to exercise liberty, she must serve in office. . . . If an honor-friendly liberalism attempted to accommodate Aristotelian honor by making it an enabling condition for the meaningful exercise of freedom, it would end up claiming that freedom belongs only to the subset of inhabitants who have the good fortune of occupying political office." Similarly, Skultety remarks that it is difficult to see how liberalism could consider that serving in government office makes somebody "ethically superior." "Giving freedom priority value certainly gives us no reason to value government service over any other kind of job," writes Skultety, "nor does it suggest that some citizens are ethically superior to one another." If this is true of political office and government service more generally, then it is true of military service more specifically. While "no disadvantage" is evidently fair, citizen-plus is hard to reconcile with a liberal democratic order.

General Sebastien Roberts, one of the authors of the Military Covenant, remarks that in drafting it, "I wanted . . . it to be widely understood that soldiers potentially give everything. In return, the nation, private or public, must be prepared to give everything back."[41] Some Canadian veterans have used similar language, claiming that as soldiers have an "unlimited liability" (in other words may be killed in line of duty), in response the state has an equally unlimited liability towards them. This is an untenable position for governments. No state can issue a blank check. Resources in any society are limited. Those which go to one group must come from another. When veterans make a claim for additional resources from the state, they are in fact making a claim for the money of fellow citizens, which the state will have to collect for them through taxes.

As noted above, the trend is possibly strongest in the United States and may have spread from there. However, the historical situation of the United States is different from that of Commonwealth countries. Theda Skocpol observes that in the aftermath of the Civil War the United States constructed a welfare state for veterans and their families, but not for others: "the nation's help was lavished on a selected subset of the working- and middle-class people . . . who by their own choices and efforts as young men had *earned aid* . . . the morally undeserving or less deserving were not the nation's responsibility."[42] In Europe, by contrast, in the late nineteenth century governments developed nascent welfare states designed to provide "modest amounts for whole categories of workers and the less economically privileged. State help was being more or less uniformly offered to those who economically needed it."[43] This was the experience of Canada also.

Liberal welfare states today are for the most part morally neutral. The European rather than the American model prevails, in that states do not generally differentiate between the "deserving" and "undeserving"—for instance, Canada's taxation-funded, state-run health service, like the National Health Service in Britain, treats the patient whose lung cancer is self-inflicted through smoking equally to the lung cancer patient who never smoked. Their need is the same. In short, most states consider everybody to have equal rights and status, and distribute public resources upon the basis of what people need rather than who they are.

In line with this, Israeli military ethicist Michael Gross argues that injured soldiers who cannot return to duty should not receive privileged access to civilian health care but only the same treatment that equally needy civilians receive. Soldiers, he says, "*should* be satisfied with military medical care when it a) is sufficient to maintain their health and fitness, b) can return many of the wounded to battle, c) does not abandon the seriously wounded, and d) provides the seriously wounded with short and long term health care on par with what their compatriots receive."[44] Gross notes that past behavior is not considered a reason for assigning priorities in health care—the bike rider whose serious head injuries are due to his failure to wear a helmet is still rushed to the head of the line in the emergency room, for the "distribution principle that governs the distribution of health care . . . [is] medical need."[45] If poor behavior is not a reason for giving people less access to care, then behavior which society considers good (e.g. military service) is not a reason for giving more: "the right to health care is an unconditional, universal human right, guaranteed solely by virtue of one's status as a human being and unaffected by merit or past contribution. . . . Military service should not add to or detract from an individual's right to health care."[46]

The same principle applies equally to other forms of state assistance. "The principle of not harming should trump that of not rewarding," says Gross, "that is, it is better, morally, that the faultless should not be harmed rather than the meritorious not rewarded."[47] The citizen-plus model is incompatible with this principle.

A danger also exists that citizen-plus can create a sense of entitlement among service personnel. In his chapter in this volume, Anthony Cunningham comments that, "contemporary Americans (along with those liberated from Nazi occupation) surely owe a huge debt of gratitude to the Allied soldiers who stormed the beaches of Normandy in 1944." Problems can arise, however, when veterans feel that they are entitled to such gratitude and become disgruntled when they do not receive what they believe is their due. In contemporary Britain, for instance, Helen McCartney says, "Historical and international comparisons, together with the steady rise in the number of casualties in current operations, have begun to create greater expectations of public support than ever before."[48] Furthermore, "The concept of the military covenant itself has greatly increased the military's expectations of the public."[49]

As one U.S. Marine writes:

> I think that there's a culture of entitlement being bred in new veterans. I suspect that this is product of the AVF [All Volunteer Force] and the Vietnam era; no one wants to be accused of being anti-military so folks bend over backwards to extend various privileges and perks to vets. This is compounded by veterans organizations . . . which encourage service members . . . to fight for disability benefits which may or may not be legitimate (at least that was my experience). New veterans are leaving the military thinking that society owes them something besides a little appreciation.[50]

Another veteran similarly notes that:

> In our attempt to heal, to be generous, and to be thankful to those who volunteered to serve, Americans inadvertently created a cadre of veterans for whom nothing would ever be good enough. . . . Our generation is easily the best supported generation of veterans since those of World War II. . . . However, we have been nervous to say out loud that service alone should not guarantee free admission and the front of the line every time for every service member.[51]

Bacevich explains the danger of going down this path: "Retired admiral Stanley Arthur has expressed concern that 'more and more, enlisted as well as officers are beginning to feel that they are special, better than the society they serve.' Such tendencies, concluded Arthur, are 'not healthy in an armed force serving a democracy.'" Bacevich continues that, "In public life today, paying homage to those in uniform has become obligatory and the one unforgivable sin is to be found guilty of failing to 'support the troops.'"[52]

In his book *Killing in War*, Jeff McMahan comments that, "Our own societies are, however, perpetually in danger of fighting unjust wars. And I believe that part of the explanation for this lies in an idea that we share with the Nazis, and indeed with most people in most cultures at all times in history. This is the idea that no one does wrong, or acts impermissibly, merely by fighting in a war that turns out to be unjust."[53] McMahan's remarks illustrate the hazards inherent in the idea that one should "support the troops" even if one considers the missions they undertake to be unjust. In the Western world, criticism of recent wars, many of which have been morally questionable and also decidedly unsuccessful, has been muted. One reason is that the elevation of the soldier into a figure worthy of special respect has made it easy for war supporters to silence critics by claiming that in criticizing the war they are criticizing the soldiers also. Bacevich points out that before the 2003 invasion of Iraq, there was considerable public disquiet about the planned war, but:

> No politician of national stature offered himself or herself as the movement's champion. No would-be statesman nursing even the slightest prospects of winning high national office was willing to risk being

> tagged with not supporting those whom President Bush was ordering into harm's way. . . . Opposition to war had become something of a third rail: only the very brave or the very foolhardy dared to venture anywhere near it.[54]

Furthermore, making it impossible to criticize the soldiers also makes it more difficult to render the military as a whole accountable when errors are made. Accountability is the bedrock of liberal democracy. When an institution's failures (such as the U.S. military's in Iraq or the UK military's in Afghanistan) are not believed to be a reason for holding that institution to account but rather to blame elected officials for allegedly failing to "support the troops," and those failures are even used as a reason to lobby for even more resources for the institution in question, then there is no accountability. The raising of military personnel into "citizens-plus" places them beyond the realm of democratic control. This is not a desirable development.

Finally, even in cold practical terms, a covenant as the model of soldier-state relations does not necessarily best serve military personnel. Ingram notes that:

> Covenants are "outside the world of contracts and exchange" and the parties to them are bound by moral reciprocity. While this sort of exchange arrangement might have suited tribal societies in the Bronze age, they may not be the most practical arrangement today. . . . Unlike soldiers, few other professions would rely upon a covenant to ensure that they were properly cared for in case of a workplace accident.[55]

This is true. The state does not have "sacred obligations" and does not keep "covenants" with any of its other servants other than soldiers. Rather it signs contracts with those servants. If it breaks those contracts, then it can be sued, but there is no need to resort to the idea of the "honour of the crown" to explain the suit. Furthermore, it is clear from the start precisely what people are entitled to.

By contrast, the quasi-feudal vision of civil-military relations creates expectations among soldiers which are never likely to be met because the state has never specifically promised what soldiers believe has been promised. The feudal relationship is lopsided. While theoretically there are reciprocal obligations, in practice those obligations flow largely one way. Soldiers may view their relationship with the state as a sacred covenant, but, as we have seen, the state does not.

As noted above, veterans' welfare systems are a historical anomaly in most states. They came into being at times when fully developed welfare states did not exist. Special provision thus had to be made for soldiers, as in the United States after the Civil War. Now, however, such welfare states are well established. It is questionable whether a parallel welfare state for veterans is really necessary or even desirable.

In Europe the trend in recent years has been to bring the legal status of the armed forces and their members more and more in line with that of civilian institutions and of ordinary citizens. Both European and national courts have ruled that armed forces are, for instance, bound by European human rights legislation. Among other things, this means that soldiers have a right to join a trade union. In Britain, the courts have determined that the Ministry of Defense is subject to health and safety legislation, and that soldiers can sue the Ministry for negligence. This process of "juridification" of the armed forces means that they are increasingly unable to operate outside of the framework of civilian law. The honor-based idea of a sacred covenant between the state and its soldiers runs counter to this trend, and may not in the long term be sustainable.

In the case of *Manuge v Canada*, former service personnel succeeded in overturning the military's policy of reducing the long-term disability benefits payable to disabled Canadian Forces members under the Service Income Security Insurance Plan (SISIP) by the amounts payable to them under the *Pension Act*. The Forces' policy was found to be in breach of the terms of the contract with the insurer, Manulife.[56] In this case it seems clear that the plaintiffs benefited from the fact that they had, in the form of SISIP, a clearly defined documented basis for the entitlement they claimed. It thus reveals the advantages which may accrue from contractual arrangements.

Many soldiers would probably resist the idea that they are public servants like any other, and that their relationship with their employer should be on the same type of contractual basis. There is a feeling that this would change their identity from selfless defenders of the Crown to mercenaries. Yet there is no inherent reason why having contracts should render soldiering any less an honorable profession than, say, being a police officer or a judge. Furthermore, such a system would give soldiers clearly defined and legally enforceable rights.

In conclusion, therefore, it would seem that the model of honor-based civil-military relations which many soldiers adhere to does not serve their interests well any more. Nor does it serve the interests of the state or of society as a whole. Service based on legal contract may well be more desirable than service founded on feudal concepts of honor.

NOTES

1. *Scott v Canada*, 2013 BCSC 1651.
2. *Scott v Canada*, (2 January 2014), Vancouver, CA041232 (BCCA) (Factum of the Appellant), http://equitassociety.ca/11035228_1_Appellant's%20Factum%20.pdf.
3. Anthony Forster, "British Judicial Engagement and the Juridification of the Armed Forces," *International Affairs* 88, no. 2 (2012): 283–300.
4. *Scott v Canada*, 2013 BCSC 1651.
5. David Arnot, "The Honour of the First Nations—The Honour of the Crown: The Unique Relationship of First Nations with the Crown," in *The Evolving Canadian*

Crown, eds. Jennifer Smith and D. Michael Jones (Montreal: McGill-Queen's University Press, 2012), 161.

6. *Guerin v The Queen*, [1984] 2 SCR 335, 1984 CanLII 25 (SCC). The term "Indian" is used in the sense of the *Indian Act*, RSC 1985, c I-5.

7. M. M. Litman, "The Law of Fiduciary Obligation," *The Canadian Encyclopedia*, Feb. 7, 2006, http://www.thecanadianencyclopedia.ca/en/article/law-of-fiduciary-obligation/.

8. Arnot, "The Honour of the First Nations," 161.

9. Arnot, "The Honour of the First Nations," 162.

10. Arnot, "The Honour of the First Nations," 160, 163.

11. Patrick Mileham, "Unlimited Liability and the Military Covenant," *Journal of Military Ethics* 9, no. 1 (2010): 26. The exact words of the oath are: "I, [name], do swear that I will be faithful and bear true allegiance to Her Majesty Queen Elizabeth the Second, Queen of Canada, Her Heirs and Successors. So help me God." Contrary to Mileham's assertion, the Ontario Court of Appeal ruled in 2014 that the oath of allegiance is not in fact an expression of loyalty to the specific person of the Queen, but rather "an oath to our form of government, as symbolized by the Queen as the apex of our Canadian parliamentary system of constitutional monarchy," *McAteer v Canada (Attorney General)*, 2014 ONCA 578 (CanLII). This author once suggested this to a group of British army officers, only for one of them to immediately object, "No, it isn't, it's the Queen."

12. Arnot, "The Honour of the First Nations," 156.

13. Arnot, "The Honour of the First Nations," 160.

14. Murray Brewster and Dene Moore, "Vets Outraged as Federal Lawyers Argue that Ottawa has No Social Obligation to Soldiers," *The Globe and Mail* (Toronto, ON) July 30, 2013, http://www.theglobeandmail.com/news/politics/vets-outraged-as-federal-lawyers-argue-ottawa-has-no-social-obligation-to-soldiers/article13498389/.

15. "Our New Radio Ad on Veterans Affairs," *Liberal Party*, December 17, 2014, https://www.liberal.ca/listen-our-new-radio-ad-on-veterans-affairs/.

16. *Scott v Canada*, 2013 BCSC 1651.

17. Susan Reynolds, *Fiefs and Vassals: The Medieval Evidence Reinterpreted* (Oxford: Oxford University Press, 1994), 19.

18. *Gallant v The Queen* (1978), 91 DLR (3d) 695, 1978 CarswellNat 560 (WL) (FCTD) at para 4.

19. *McClennan v Canada (Minister of National Defence)*, 2002 FCT 244 at para 11.

20. *Manuge v Canada*, 2008 FC 624 at para 40.

21. Sarah Ingram, *The Military Covenant: Its Impact on Civil-Military Relations in Britain* (Farnham, UK: Ashgate, 2014), 17 & 18.

22. Ingram, *The Military Covenant*, 36.

23. Ingram, *The Military Covenant*, 31.

24. Ingram, *The Military Covenant*, 39.

25. Anthony Forster, "The Military Covenant and British Civil-Military Relations: Letting the Genie out of the Bottle," *Armed Forces & Society* 38, no. 2 (2012): 276.

26. *Scott v Canada*, 2013 BCSC 1651.

27. *Scott v Canada*, 2013 BCSC 1651.

28. "Michael Blais at the Veterans Affairs Committee," *Openparliament.ca*, March 27, 2014, https://openparliament.ca/committees/veterans-affairs/41–2/18/michael-blais-1/on
ly/.

29. Andrew Murrison, *Tommy This An' Tommy That: The Military Covenant* (London: Biteback, 2011), 113.

30. Murrison, *Tommy*, 61.

31. *The Armed Forces Covenant: Today and Tomorrow* (London: Ministry of Defence, 2010).

32. *The Armed Forces Covenant*, 71.

33. Ingram, *The Military Covenant*, 171.

34. *The Oxford Dictionary of Quotations*, 2nd edition with revisions (Oxford: Oxford University Press, 1978), 564.
35. Andrew J. Bacevich, *The New American Militarism: How Americans Are Seduced By War* (Oxford: Oxford University Press, 2005), 23.
36. Bacevich, *The New American Militarism*, 24.
37. Helen McCartney, "The Military Covenant and the Civil-Military Contract in Britain," *International Affairs* 86, no. 2 (2010): 426
38. McCartney, "The Military Covenant," 423–24.
39. Murrison, *Tommy*, 70.
40. Murrison, *Tommy*, 117.
41. Ingram, *The Military Covenant*, 60.
42. Theda Skocpol, *Protecting Soldiers and Mothers: The Political Origins of Social Policy in the United States* (Cambridge, MA: Belknap Press, 1992), 151.
43. Skocpol, *Protecting Soldiers*, 151.
44. Michael Gross, "Why Treat the Wounded? Warrior Care, Military Salvage, and National Health," *The American Journal of Bioethics* 8, no. 2 (2008): 6.
45. Gross, "Why Treat the Wounded?" 7.
46. Gross, "Why Treat the Wounded?" 7–8.
47. Gross, "Why Treat the Wounded?" 8.
48. McCartney, "The Military Covenant," 419.
49. McCartney, "The Military Covenant," 420.
50. Thomas E. Ricks, "Sure, You're a Vet, But That Doesn't Mean You Have License to Act Like a Jerk," *Foreign Policy*, June 17, 2011, http://foreignpolicy.com/2011/06/17/sure-youre-a-vet-but-that-doesnt-mean-you-have-license-to-act-like-a-jerk.
51. Stacy Bare, "On Veterans' Sense of Entitlement: Hey, If Your Country Is Good Enough to Fight for, Then It Is Good Enough to Come Home to," *Foreign Policy*, June 7, 2012, http://foreignpolicy.com/2012/06/07/on-veterans-sense-of-entitlement-hey-if-your-country-is-good-enough-to-fight-for-then-it-is-good-enough-to-come-home-to.
52. Bacevich, *The New American Militarism*, 24.
53. Jeff McMahan, *Killing in War* (Oxford: Clarendon Press, 2009), 3.
54. Bacevich, *The New American Militarism*, 26.
55. Ingram, *The Military Covenant*, 77–78.
56. *Manuge v Canada*, 2012 FC 499.

FOURTEEN

Honor in Military Culture

A Standard of Integrity and Framework for Moral Restraint

Joe Thomas and Shannon E. French

Subcultures within American society have their own distinct practices, norms, and languages. This chapter will explore the varied meanings of honor in the unique subculture of the U.S. military, describe the teaching methods used to encourage and enhance honorable conduct, and demonstrate how the military's operationalization of honor serves modern liberal society. Unlike in other subcultures, the concept of honor rarely takes on a pejorative connotation or produces pernicious outcomes within the military. Understanding how to embody honor and, more specifically, display consistent honorable conduct, is an explicit learning outcome set for professional military education. Yet we may be at a turning point in military usage of the terms "honor" and "honorable conduct." What will these terms mean within the U.S. military as we head deeper into the twenty-first century?

Ultimately, the concept of honor entails a very complex and elusive framework of ethical behavior. Two of the most common uses of the concept are as a standard of integrity (e.g., a cadet does not lie, cheat, or steal, nor tolerate those who do) and as an implicit code of moral restraint (e.g., honorable treatment of noncombatants on the battlefield). It is the second conception that will be explored in this chapter. How does the concept of honor serve to guide the moral life of service members and the profession as a whole? Is there a danger of honor actually becoming a glorified relic, as some like Roger Spiller would have us believe about the term "military ethos . . . a pseudo philosophy, a pastiche of militarism and romanticism that appealed to the immature mind?"[1]

As a point of comparison, consider "glory" as an example of a richly meaningful word that has changed dramatically over time. In pre-twentieth century military vocabulary, glory represented a positive goal, an ideal, and a significant part of the objective of fighting. Soldiers sought fame and glory for their acts of courage and physical accomplishment on the battlefield and were encouraged to do so. Without a sense of irony or embarrassment, officers would often compel their subordinates to action by invoking their opportunity for glory. Certainly defense of home and family has always been a motivation to fight, but glory implied there was something more to be gained, as well. In many ways, it was a far more attractive motivator to young men. It implied immortality, and thus helped conquer the fear of death.

One is reminded of the speech of the Trojan hero Sarpedon, mortal son of Zeus in Homer's *Iliad*, who explains the primary reason for risking death and facing the rigors of combat in terms of the opportunity for glory:

> O my friend! Could we,
> Shunning this war, forever be exempt
> From feeble age and death, I would not then
> Among the foremost of the field advance,
> Nor to the glorious combat thee exhort.
> But since the fates press on us ne'ertheless,
> And death, from causes numberless, impends,
> Which man by care or flight can ne'er evade,
> Now let us march, to give some foe renown,
> If fall we must, or glory to win ourselves.[2]

Today, of course, the usage of the term glory is more than passé. The concept is almost never invoked as motivation for fighting, and for good reason. The horrors of war (including lasting physical and psychological costs for troops) are too well understood and honestly faced by contemporary military service members to allow for appeals to such an abstract, external, and ephemeral notion such as glory. Nor is there any realistic expectation among service members that their individual deeds will afford them the lasting adoration of their society the way the term "glory" implies.

Does the future hold the same for honor as for glory within the military subculture of the United States? Or is the concept of honor more resilient, more timeless? Evidence in the attitudes of those currently serving in uniform suggests it may be more timeless. The overwhelmingly positive conception of honor is, perhaps temporarily, being kept alive because it has evolved to address the underlying attractiveness of military life for those who serve. But the reasons for its resilience may run much deeper, into the core of military ethics and defense of the lines that separate warriors from murderers. While honor may not always be part of the daily conversation within the profession, it is sufficiently enshrined in doctrine and curriculum to survive additive negative connotations implied by the larger society. And as long as the term serves the dual purpose of being a standard of integrity and a system of moral restraint, perhaps it must not be allowed to pass into disuse.

HONOR AS UNIVERSAL MILITARY STANDARD

There is much about the military profession, for better or worse, which has persisted virtually unchanged for centuries, even millennia. Admiral John Paul Jones professed in 1777 that "I would lay down my life for America, but I cannot trifle with my honor."[3] Clausewitz declared that "[t]he soldier trade, if it is to mean anything at all, has to be anchored to an unshakable code of honor[:] otherwise, those of us who follow the drums become nothing more than a bunch of hired assassins walking around in gaudy clothes . . . a disgrace to God and mankind."[4] Brigadier General S. L. A. Marshall taught that "[a] man has honor if he holds himself to a course of conduct because of a conviction that it is in the general interest, even though he is well aware that it may lead to inconvenience, personal loss, humiliation, or grave personal risk."[5]

Military service is often regarded as more of a calling than a profession, and it is noteworthy for its exclusivity. Soldiers tend to bond instantly with veterans of earlier wars with whom they share little in common other than the experience of battle. These same soldiers will often separate themselves from the larger society and even withdraw from family relationships. Exclusive claims to understanding the real meaning of sacrifice and an isolating anguish born from combat trauma often drive these views. To the combat veteran, certain key abstract notions such as honor take on a more concrete meaning. Whether conceptually defined through near-synonyms such as integrity or via antonyms such as shame, honor has taken up an exalted place in military culture. It plays a necessary role in helping make sense of war. What human undertaking is more chaotic and destructive than war? The sheer chaos that is war creates in the human mind a need for clarity and consistency. The concept of honor has stepped into that void to provide comfort and reassurance.

The ancient Greeks were obsessed with *timē*, a view of honor often associated with fame or glory. This is a conception of honor that is externally focused. Perhaps the most well-known example is again found in Homer's *Iliad*. When Hector, Prince of Troy, contemplates having to face the extremely intimidating wrath of the "god-like" Achilles, he wishes that he could simply refuse to battle his foe. But this option is unavailable to him because it would leave him without honor in the eyes of his fellow Trojans. This sense of honor is tied to public perception. The otherwise courageous prince quakes in terror at the thought of being judged a coward by the matrons of Troy:

> [F]rom the Trojans much I dread reproach,
> and Trojan dames whose garments sweep the ground,
> if, like a coward, I should shun the war.
> Nor does my soul to such disgrace incline,
> since to be always bravest I have learned,
> and with the first of Troy to lead the fight;
> asserting so my father's lofty claim to glory,
> and my own renown in arms.[6]

The Greeks believed strongly in fate, and so Hector does not really think he can determine the outcome of the war by his own actions. If Troy is fated to fall, it will, no matter what he does. He can, however, control his own legacy. There are standards of honor set by his people, and he must abide by them. What matters most to him is being judged to be an honorable warrior by his public. If he succeeds at that, he achieves immortality; he will live on in hearts and legends. If he fails, he will be reviled and potentially even forgotten (which he would regard as the worst fate of all). His death will then be without meaning.

As an interesting point of contrast, Hector's opponent, the Greek champion Achilles, seems in some ways to have a much more personal, private conception of honor. Earlier in the story of the *Iliad*, Achilles does not care that his fellow Greeks pass negative judgment on him for withdrawing from the fighting in response to King Agamemnon's insulting action of stripping Achilles of his prize woman, Briseis. What is more important to him is that his personal sense of honor has been outraged. He explains that he cannot endure the injustice of Agamemnon taking what is rightfully his:

> Not for wrongs to me came I so far from home,
> this war to wage against the Trojans.
> They had never driven my steeds or cattle, nor laid waste
> the fields of fertile Phthia, my well-peopled realm; [. . .]
> But thee, . . . we have followed, for thy pleasure, here,
> to win revenge for Menelaus, and for thee, . . . a favor now
> repaid with base ingratitude and reckless scorn!
> For thou hast threatened to usurp my prize,
> the precious meed of many bloody toils; [. . .]
> Compared with thine, my share is always small, [. . .]
> [T]he greater part of war's laborious task
> these hands perform; but, when the spoil is shared,
> thine are the richest prizes![7]

Achilles knows that the Greeks need him to win against the Trojans. This fact becomes more obvious the longer he sulks in his tent. The other Greeks beg him to return to the fight and suggest that his honor depends on it, but he is unmoved. Finally, his best friend, Patroclus, tries his hand at convincing Achilles to return to war.

Patroclus's arguments all depend on appeals to honor. He lists off all the Greek warriors who will likely die if Achilles does not return to fight beside them. The clear message is that honor demands Achilles stand by his friends. Achilles is unmoved by this. Defending his personal honor is more important to him than defending his fellow Greeks, and Achilles is angry with them all for allowing Agamemnon's insult to stand.

Patroclus then shifts to the very point that was so persuasive to Prince Hector: "What will future generations have to thank you for, if you will not help the [Greeks] in their direst need?"[8] Achilles dismisses this, asking in return why he should care if lesser men misjudge him? Unlike Hector, Achilles places himself in a category apart from other men. A near immortal with extraordinary martial prowess, he is closer to the gods.

Achilles's attitude shifts dramatically when Hector and other Trojan fighters kill Patroclus, while Patroclus is masquerading as Achilles, in an attempt to rally the Greeks. He is literally haunted by the ghost of his fallen comrade and tortured by the pain and guilt of not having been on hand to defend him. He vows to return to battle and kill Hector. Achilles's mother, the sea goddess Thetis, tries to persuade him against this course of action, warning him that his death will follow soon after Hector's (according to prophesy). He is unmoved by her words:

> [Mother], let me die; since t'was my doom
> not to defend my comrade slain in fight!
> Unaided in his dying hour, he fell,
> far distant from his country; [. . .]
> my prowess needed to repel the blow.
> [I] . . . was no light in darkness to Patroclus,
> and the rest of my unhappy countrymen, [. . .]
> Now to war I go to meet the murderer of my friend.
> And death I will embrace whenever decreed by Zeus [. . .][9]

This exchange with his mother seems to indicate that Achilles is now concerned again with the standards of honor set by his people. Yet after he kills Hector, avenging Patroclus, Achilles again transgresses against the public ideal of honorable conduct by desecrating Hector's corpse. For this, he earns condemnation even from the gods. Homer has the god Apollo call out Achilles' shameful behavior:

> The terrible Achilles, ruthless chief [. . .]
> Like a fell lion, confident in strength,
> Who, by ungovernable rage impell'd,

> And thirsting still for blood, invades at night
> The trembling fold, Achilles has renounc'd
> All pity, and indeed all sense of shame [. . .]
> But, savage-like, he fastens to his car,
> And rudely drags illustrious Hector's corpse
> Around his comrade's tomb; no honor this,
> Or benefit to him![10]

Achilles's attitude is certainly not celebrated by Homer. Instead, he shows that this rejection of the rules of honorable combat only causes Achilles continued despair. He finds no peace through his dishonorable actions. He only experiences some measure of redemption in the closing book of the epic when he finally sets aside his rage long enough to agree to allow the Trojans to give their prince a decent burial. The *Iliad* closes with the funeral of Hector, as he is eulogized with great praise. The ignominious death of Achilles, struck by an arrow shot from the bow of the slimy Prince Paris, is outside the scope of the poem.

Homer's work can be seen as a warning to warriors of any age that failing to respect the lines that separate honorable acts from dishonorable acts (as Achilles does when he desecrates Hector's corpse) isolates the warrior from his or her comrades and community to a harmful degree. The bond that sustains the exclusivity of military cultures depends on it being possible to distinguish those who belong from those who do not. Dishonorable actions disrupt that bond. By virtue of being given a mandate to kill on behalf of their community, those who fight (soldiers) are already isolated from ordinary citizens (civilians). If soldiers' actions violate the norms of the military subculture, too, then they have nowhere left to turn for comfort, just like Achilles. This suggests that it would be a grave disservice to combat troops to let the concept of honor fade out of use in the modern U.S. military.

There are other such insights to be found in past conceptions of warrior honor. As Richard Ned Lebow points out in this volume, the Greek conception of honor shifted somewhat around the time of the Peloponnesian War. After the Greeks, arguably no culture was more obsessed with honor than the Romans. *Honoris causa* or "for the sake of honor" was the reasoning behind much of Rome's accomplishment and crimes. The Roman philosophy that had the most to say about honor that is relevant to modern troops, however, was Stoicism.

Marcus Aurelius was a Roman emperor and general who lived by deeply held Stoic beliefs, which he explicated in his *Meditations*. Since he understood and had lived the Roman way of war, he was able to tie many of his teachings in the *Meditations* directly to the challenges faced by his legionnaires and to use examples relating to combat and other military experiences. There are some strong parallels that can be drawn between the subculture in the Roman legions in Marcus's day and that of the modern U.S. military.

Classical scholar Maxwell Staniforth captures the attraction of the code of honor found in stoicism for the average Roman soldier: "A code which was manly, rational, and temperate, a code which insisted on just and virtuous dealing, self-discipline, unflinching fortitude, and complete freedom from the storms of passion was admirably suited to the Roman character."[11] Emperor Aurelius wanted his soldiers to make their sense of honor central to their identity. They should not act dishonorably in response to any provocation, he argued; because all provocations are external and can be resisted by those of strong will with a clear sense of duty.

Roman troops fought in close formation, relying on one another to perform exactly as they had drilled, ignoring any distractions. Honor was defined as maintaining that perfect discipline and thus not letting down your comrades. Stoic philosophy asserts that nothing should be able to shake a person away from the pursuit of duty. Just as the Greeks believed that each individual had an unchangeable fate, the Stoics taught that every person has a specific role to play in life, and playing that role as well as possible is the only thing capable of giving life any meaning. A stoic person should not fear death or any other harm to self or loved ones, except the grievous harm of failing to life a good life (where a good life is defined as one spent fulfilling one's duties to the best of one's ability).

Emperor Aurelius took this ideal so far as to demand that his legionnaires should not only embody the ethic of "death before dishonor," but should care more about their honor than anything else they could possibly conceive. The average Roman soldier had less than a fifty percent chance of surviving until retirement.[12] Like Epictetus before him, Marcus wrote pitilessly about the need not to allow the death of a close comrade or other loved one to distract one from doing one's duty. Seeing your best friend skewered by a Gaulish spear would be no excuse for falling out of step in an advance or failing to keep an adequate watch the following day. His troops should even resist the agonies of torture, he insisted, if the alternative was to commit an unworthy act (especially one such as betraying Rome). Pain, after all, is just external stimuli (everything material, including the body, was external in the view of the Stoics), whereas honor is a precious internal good: "33. Of Pain. If it is past bearing, it makes an end of us; if it lasts, it can be borne. The mind, holding itself aloof from the body, retains its calm, and the master-reason remains unaffected. As for the parts injured by the pain, let them, if they can, declare their own grief."[13]

Interestingly, the emperor made the same move as the modern U.S. military away from ideas of pursing glory and fame, while retaining the emphasis on honor. Glory is just another external item beyond anyone's control. Reputations are at the mercy of other people's opinions and interpretations of events. So Marcus writes: "34. Of Fame. Take a look at the minds of her suitors, their ambitions and their aversions. Furthermore, reflect how speedily in this life the things of today are buried under those of tomorrow, even as one layer of drifting sand is quickly covered by the next."[14]

The reward for honorable behavior was not to be lauded by others, but to know inside oneself that one had done one's duty and accomplished the tasks one was born to accomplish. The goal of maintaining honor gave life purpose. In theory, the stoic Roman soldier could die enjoying the inner peace that came with the conviction that he had played his part well and not let down his emperor, his state, his legion, or himself.

The motivational power of the ideal of living (and dying) with honor is undeniable. As the Stoics emphasized, privileging honor above other values gives the individual a sense of control. Integrity is defined as having one's values and actions perfectly aligned. The reward of personal integrity, analogous to the structural integrity of an aqueduct, is strength and endurance. Accepting restraint—refusing to take certain actions in war because they are dishonorable—may initially seem an irrational, weakening move, like tying one's hand behind one's back. In reality, adopting a code that allows you to have absolute faith in what your fellow warriors will and will not do while at the same time investing your life with greater purpose and meaning is a choice that is both rational and compelling.

Even historical military cultures that do not call to mind contemporary views of honor or honorable conduct, such as the Mongol hordes of Genghis Khan, recognized the power of having the maintenance of honor as an explicit goal. The Yasa Code and associated *biligs* or maxims defining honor that have come down to us through Petis de la Croix's 1710 *History of Genghis Khan the Great* are an excellent example of non-Western conceptions of the requirements for preserving a warrior's honor. The thirty or more elements of the Yasa Code were designed to regulate the affairs of an expeditionary force. The Mongols in the time of the Great Khans were nothing if not expeditionary. In a period of just over four decades the light cavalry of Genghis and his successors conquered an area of over 40,000 square miles. They occupied all of Central Asia, much of East Asia, and had penetrated into the heart of Europe. Part of this success can be attributed to the strict discipline enforced on its soldiers. Yasa provided a framework for that discipline.

While much of Yasa describes administrative requirements of warriors such as rituals for eating, assignment of leaders, and respect for authority, other aspects concisely define conceptions of honor. Perhaps the best and most widely cited, is from the chronicler Vartang, "The Yasa of Genghis Khan forbids lies, theft, and adultery and prescribes love of one's neighbors as one's self; it orders men not to hurt each other and to forget offences completely, to spare countries and cities which submit voluntarily, to free from taxes temples consecrated to God, and to respect the temples of God and their servants."[15] Cleary such a code was aspirational at best. The rate at which Mongol warriors subscribed to such lofty demands of honorable conduct is left to the imagination of the reader. Nevertheless, even Genghis Khan's biographers sought to define the best aspects of the spirit that animated the force, at least in principle if not in practice. The constraint of behavior on the battlefield was key. That the Mongols even possessed such a formal code comes as a surprise to most Westerners. It is important to remember, however, that the reputation of the Mongols comes down to us primarily through the written records of the vanquished. The Mongols themselves scarcely kept any record of their exploits. What little exists includes the Yasa and its attempt at the definition of a warrior's honor.

It is worth reflecting on one more non-Western warrior subculture, which is much better known. Undoubtedly the most famous historical code of honor from Asia is that of Japan's samurai, generally referred to as Bushido. Not surprisingly, there are several similar themes in Bushido to those found in other codes, including the importance of maintaining honor and self-discipline, regardless of opposing pressures, and the conviction that voluntarily accepting certain restraints demonstrates strength, not weakness, and separates warriors into an elite group that cannot be confused with mere murderers.

In common with the Roman Stoics, the samurai found meaning and purpose in doing their duty. However, like the Homeric Greeks, the samurai also cared a great deal about appearances. "Saving face" was essential. Loyalty to one's superiors was also of paramount importance, and that loyalty was often defined in terms of ensuring that one's superiors—even more than oneself—maintained the appearance of honor.

The *Budoshoshinshu*, a later work that attempted to revive samurai values after the subculture had gone into decline, presents the central lessons of Bushido training. The fifth lesson of the *Budoshoshinshu*, "A Sense of Shame Will Uphold Justice," tells a story laying out the role that shame should play in motivating the actions of a samurai. A samurai is asked to carry money for a stranger who then suddenly dies, leaving the samurai holding the bag of coins. No one but the samurai now knows that the money was given to him. What should the samurai do? The lesson spells out three possible paths the samurai could take: (1) immediately begin hunting down the dead man's heirs in order to give the money to them, (2) decide to keep the money for himself, but then feel ashamed of that decision and begin to search for the dead man's family, or (3) decide to keep the money for himself and not feel shame about that choice, but then begin to fear that someone may somehow find out about his action and publicly shame him for it—so deciding, once again, that he must start looking for the deceased's next of kin.[16]

All three paths lead to the same conclusion: the samurai cannot keep the money. The richness of the lesson is that while it emphasizes that the preferred choice is the first one, in which the samurai does the right thing for the right reasons right off the bat, it offers two other motivations, one internal and one external, both shame-based, that could compel the man to do the right thing. In this way, this code of honor is both prescriptive and aspirational. It sets the ultimate goal for the warrior to be motivated purely by an internal standard of integrity, but for those samurai who have not yet developed their good character to that degree, it provides other persuasive reasons to act with honor.

Lesson 44, "Accept Difficult Orders Positively," implies that honor requires not only right actions, but also the right attitude. The argument embedded in the lesson is that if a samurai is given a particularly tough challenge, he faces the choice of taking it on in a grumbling, discontented way, or with a positive, can-do attitude. If he displays a negative attitude but nevertheless succeeds, people will assume the task was not really that much of a challenge (since it could be completed even by one with such a bad attitude). If he has a negative attitude and fails, people will think that he failed because of the bad attitude, not because the task was hard. If he has a good attitude but fails to complete the task, he will at least be seen as someone who tried his best and was fully committed to the job. And if he has a positive attitude and succeeds, he will get full credit for his great performance. Furthermore, he will gain the trust of his superiors. The lesson goes on to say that a positive attitude adopted for these reasons of expediency will eventually become habit or second nature to the samurai (a notion that the Greek philosopher Aristotle would have applauded). In this way, external motivations breed internal ones.

Samurai honor required constant efforts at self-improvement. Samurai were expected to think of their lives holistically, and strive for perfection just as much in their behavior away from the battlefield as when in combat. Practicing restraint in the form of observing precise social etiquette, for example, was thought to be a way to strengthen the same virtue needed to show restraint in the face of one's enemies.

The *Budoshoshinshu* concludes by celebrating the guardian role of the samurai warriors:

> If there were only one such deeply resolved warrior at the side of every feudal lord, thoughtful only of putting his life on the line for his master and being his safeguard, . . . evil and treacherous men with the minds of devils and vicious spirits would hesitate to act, and, perverse and unrighteous deeds would cease to be done.[17]

This, too, is an aspect of the warrior archetype that still appeals to members of the modern U.S. military. A recent recruiting ad for the U.S. Navy and Marine Corps showed happy and flourishing civilians surrounded by circles of "deeply resolved" service members ready to lay down their lives to protect those citizens from harm. The tag line was, "To get to you, they'd have to get past us."[18] This illustrates the lasting allure of adopting the honorable role of guardian. And in order to be trusted, guardians must accept restraint. A guardian cannot be simply an indiscriminate killer. This is the covenant between the state and its warriors which is discussed and critiqued by Paul Robinson in his chapter in this volume.

Relinquishing the fear of death so that one is willing to die, if necessary, to achieve noble ends (such as guarding one's community) is central to Bushido. The *Budoshoshinshu* speaks of "practicing death," or coming to be at peace with the idea that one cannot count on having more time to fulfill one's responsibilities: "Lesson 33: *Complete One's Duties Within the Day: One Second Ahead is Uncertain*. [. . .] [I]f one thinks that the world will go on without change and that he will have unlimited time in which to perform his duties, as time passes he will become bored with things, his mind will slacken, and his spirit will become negligent."[19] However, Bushido's perspective on death involves more than just being aware that one's life could be cut short by circumstance or the actions of others. Famously, Bushido also advocated the use of ritual suicide, or *seppuku*, to maintain honor in certain situations. This takes the idea of "death before dishonor" in a direction less appealing to Westerners, for whom suicide often carries a heavy taboo.

Seppuku stands out for both its elaborate procedure and for its uses. It was usually done as a final, desperate act of redemption. A samurai who had acted dishonorably in any way could be asked by his superior or could request for himself the right to commit this act that would, in the eyes of the members of his subculture and the broader Japanese culture of the time, thoroughly and permanently erase the stain upon his honor.[20] Suicide was also the only honorable way for a samurai to protest an action by his master. Before being made illegal, another form of seppuku called *junshi* was practiced to follow a beloved superior to his death.[21] All of these practices were tied to the same philosophy: that death was far preferable to losing that which gave a samurai's life meaning and purpose—honor.

Members of the modern U.S. military may not (and should not) be expected to commit ritual suicide any time they fail to be paragons. Nevertheless, embracing a less extreme version of the "death before dishonor" mentality, holding them to the high standard of being willing to risk or even face certain death rather than abandon their sworn principles, remains essential to their moral survival. Experiencing war and combat has the power to strip away much of what makes men and women feel human. Retaining a sense of honor through it all restores their sense of humanity. It gives them one thing that remains within their control, even in the chaos of the so-called "fog of war." It allows them to feel bonded to their peers, who also strive to hold the same standards despite the many tangible and psychological pressures not to, as well as to retain the respect of the broader human communities to which they belong. This, in turn, makes it possible for them to accomplish the difficult transition out of the world of war to their own post-combat lives with their families and friends back home. Honor is the unseen force that holds together both individuals and social units that might otherwise be shattered by war. As such, it is not an antiquated concept that should be abandoned. It is a timeless one that must be nurtured.

NOTES

1. Roger Spiller, *An Instinct for War* (Cambridge, MA: Harvard University Press, 2005), 386.
2. Homer, *Iliad*, trans. William Munford (Boston: Little & Brown, 1846), 12.437–46.
3. 3 Qtd. in *Dictionary of Military and Naval Quotation*, ed. Robert Debs Heinl, Jr. (Annapolis, MD: U.S. Naval Institute Press, 1978).
4. 4 Qtd. in *The Book of Military Quotations*, ed. Peter G. Tsouras (St. Paul, MN: Zenith, 2015), 216.
5. 5 *The Armed Forces Officer*, ed. S. L. A Marshall (Washington, DC: United States Government Printing Office, 1950).
6. Homer, *Iliad*, trans. Munford (Boston: Little & Brown, 1846), 6.441–46.
7. Homer, *Iliad*, trans. Munford, 1.203–222.
8. Homer, *Iliad*, trans. E. V. Rieu (Harmondsworth, UK: Penguin Books, 1950), 16.31–32.
9. Homer, *Iliad*, trans. Munford, 18.138–1.
10. 10 Homer, Iliad, trans. Munford, 24.56-74.
11. Marcus Aurelius. *Meditations*, trans. Maxwell Staniforth (New York: Penguin Books, 1964), 10.
12. Those who did make it to retirement, however, were given a fairly generous pension, their own parcel of land on which to live and farm, and of course all the benefits of Roman citizenship. Please see Colin Wells, *The Roman Empire* (Stanford, CA: Stanford University Press, 1984), 136–40.
13. Marcus Aurelius, *Meditations*, trans. Staniforth, Book Seven, 110–11.
14. Aurelius, *Meditations*, Book Seven, 111.
15. D. O. Morgan, "The Great Yasa of Chingiz Khan and Mongol Law in the Ilkhanate," in *Bulletin of the School of Oriental and African Studies*, University of London 49, no. 1 (London: Cambridge University Press, 1986), 173.
16. William Scott Wilson, trans., *Budoshoshinshu: The Warrior's Primer of Daidoji Yuzan* (Santa Clara, CA: O'Hara Publications, 1984), 28.
17. *Budoshoshinshu*, 127.
18. https://www.youtube.com/watch?v=ThImmlN-I8s
19. *Budoshoshinshu*, 81.
20. H. Paul Varley, *Samurai* (New York: Delacourte Press, 1970), 36.
21. *Budoshoshinshu*, 125.

Conclusion

Laurie M. Johnson

As Richard Ned Lebow points out, concerns about the destructive nature of honor predate the development of liberalism. Thucydides identified three motivations that supposedly compelled Athens to aggressively pursue empire to the point of goading Sparta into a regional war: fear, honor, and interest. Of these three, honor proved the most problematic in Thucydides's chronicle of the Peloponnesian War because, long after the war could be said to have harmed Athens and Sparta more than it benefited either side, the drive for honor, especially (and oddly) on the part of the democratic side, drove the Greeks to continue to fight rather than to reach a lasting peace. The price of Athens's hunger for honor was that it transformed into *hubris*, which eventually led to Athens's total defeat.

Thucydides was far from the only ancient thinker to argue that honor could be dangerous, that it needed to be channeled appropriately so that it would not become destructive. Achilles and Agamemnon embodied the tension between personal honor and the common good. Plato found value in timocratic honor but found it ultimately lacking in philosophic wisdom and dangerously prone to creating unnecessary conflict. Aristotle identified the end of political life as honor but went on to point out that its need for external confirmation made it a lesser motivation than virtue or wisdom. In other words, when Hobbes argued that honor was a problematic beast to be tamed by a leviathan, he had learned that lesson especially from Thucydides, but also from the ancient Greeks more generally. He then initiated the liberal rejection of at least the kind of honor associated with characters like Achilles and Alcibiades.

For liberal theorists like Hobbes and Locke, the drive for honor was generally not good. It was about the sin of vanity or pride. Honor was at best an unattractive aspect of human nature, and at its worst it was the reason for unnecessary civil and international wars. Hobbes's solution was for an absolute sovereign to establish the definition and rules of honor and to enforce them in such a way that loyalty and obedience to the sovereign were primary characteristics of the honorable man. Locke's concern for the destructiveness of honor was similar to Hobbes's, but his solution was to redirect our attention to something much more rational than honor—namely self-interest, especially as it played out in the healthy competition of the marketplace. As a result, today the liberal societies philosophers like Hobbes and Locke helped to shape, with the partial exception of their military establishments, do not speak in terms of honor for the most part. They speak instead in terms of self-interest, but also in the language of liberty and equality.

For many of the authors in this volume the diminishment of honor's importance in both our private and public lives has created a void that has not been completely filled by rational self-interest, and is also not quite captured by the love of liberty or equality, though these may play a role in developing a liberal democratic version of honor. They ask, despite the skepticism with which liberal political theorists have dealt with honor, is there a way that honor can be compatible with liberalism? The authors in this volume have explored various aspects of honor, and arguments for and against its inclusion in the values of liberal society. Some of our authors definitely reject honor in this older sense.

Paul Robinson questions military honor at least insofar as it is used to claim any special economic benefits for those who have served in the armed forces. In doing so, he reveals very well the seeming incompatibility between thinking in terms of honor and thinking in terms of equality and fairness. Steven Skultety asks a similar question, whether democracy can be compatible with the idea that the leaders we choose should be in some way superior and deserving of special honor. Vandello and Hettinger criticize the old gender-based honor that extols feminine purity on the grounds that it unfairly discriminates against women. Others, like Joe Thomas and Shannon French, champion old-fashioned honor, at least in the military, where people must be motivated to risk their lives, if necessary, to defend the liberty of their fellow citizens.

The founder of communitarianism Amitai Etzioni reviewed in his chapter the development of the communitarian critique of liberalism, and in the process he drew out those signal aspects of liberal democracy that tend not only to erode a strong sense of community but, through some of the same mechanisms, challenge the aristocratic view of honor and call into question whether or not honor can be re-visioned within a liberal context. Skultety, as mentioned above, likewise highlighted the seeming incompatibility of honor with liberalism but found a point of reconciliation in political honor. The demand for full equality and universal rights and liberties within liberal democracy creates a situation in which citizens are loath to recognize any leadership as morally authoritative, as deserving more honor and thus obedience. This leads to the situation, so well described by Alexis de Tocqueville, in which democratically elected officials behave no better, and sometimes noticeably worse, than the average citizen. Liberalism's focus on the individual, and liberalism's insistence on the efficacy of rational self-interest in guiding individuals' actions for the overall good, pose significant problems for honor. And yet, for most of the authors in this volume, the value of honor for the regulation of behavior and the cohesion of community and/or community's subgroupings, is too great to simply let go.

So, within this volume we see a wide range of responses to the problem of honor and liberalism—from an assumption that the two can continue to coexist either generally or at least within certain subgroups, to a conclusion that the two are basically incompatible and that honor may simply be outmoded as a source of order, restraint and obligation in the West. Clearly, we remain uncomfortable in a democratic society with any way of thinking that accepts some form of inequality as part of its framework.

Demetriou's chapter on agonistic honor demonstrates that in order to develop an honor code for democratic politics and social interactions generally, we have to acknowledge differences in power and position as relevant for how we treat people. When Demetriou insists that people in public life do not "punch down" and only "pick on someone their own size," he acknowledges (and urges us to acknowledge) that some people are somehow above others, that not everyone is, in fact, the same size. While absolutely true, and hard to deny, people are still very uncomfortable with so openly acknowledging *de facto* inequality, and tend to attribute motives such as condescension and paternalism to those who suggest that we ought to acknowledge or obey honorable codes of conduct. As Demetriou and many other authors in this volume point out, the greatest benefit of doing so is to create not less, but more order, by establishing "rules of the game" that are inherently compelling to human beings with a healthy sense of self-regard, given the inevitability of competition and conflict among such human beings.

Vandello and Hettinger express the liberal discomfort with honor very well in their chapter on gendered honor, which particularly deals with the value of sexual purity for women. They argue that women derive no benefit from the old view of female honor and the subsequent chivalrous code for men. In the U.S. South where, they argue, the old-fashioned view of female honor is most likely to be found, teen pregnancy and divorce rates are at their highest. Yet, even today, and not just in the South, sexual purity is considered more important for women than for men, and many men and women still value it, creating sexist double standards when viewed against our egalitarian expectations. For instance, recently Senator Mitch Holmes, chairman of the Kansas House Pensions and Benefits Committee, attempted to impose a dress code exclusively on women who came before his committee to provide testimony. The code did not allow skirts that were considered too short, or tops considered too low-cut, though these were not clearly defined by the chairman, whose code said nothing about male attire. According to published reports, "Holmes said he considered requiring men to wear suits and ties during testimony but decided males didn't need any guidance."[1] Within a few days, Holmes had retracted the rule and apologized, but not before taking a great deal of heat from his fellow lawmakers, male and female alike, being referred to as a caveman and a sexist, and being reminded that this was 2016.

Vandello and Hettinger argue that any notion of honorable behavior is more likely to survive if it applies equally to men and women. Andrea Mansker's chapter on women who tried to insert themselves into the nineteenth century dueling culture shows one way this can happen—for women, in this case, to try to adopt a masculine code of honor and, by doing so, make it gender neutral. This was certainly the strategy of many feminists even into the 1970s in America who adopted masculine dress, mannerisms and strategies. This mode of feminism has faded in recent decades in favor of recognizing some differences between men and women. However, new feminist ideas do not necessitate that men take on any special obligation of concern for women as such, instead simply acknowledging that women may communicate differently, think differently, love differently, and more or less relate to the world differently, with, for instance, less aggressiveness and more nurturance, or with a stronger intuitive sense. Feminists who recognize gender differences as legitimate and even good do not normally commit to the idea that these differences are inherent, and this makes it harder to conceive of an honor code that might recognize gender without committing sexism. But it does not make it impossible. Differences can be recognized inasmuch as they exist, whether they are permanent or temporary in nature. And, inasmuch as they translate into differential power and influence, these differences may still be useful for developing a code of honor in even a strongly egalitarian environment.

It would seem to be more "natural" for an "alpha male" or an elite to emerge within any human group, and therefore to think of democracy as an artificial social contract, an unnatural but desirable imposition because it brings order and peace by enforcing an albeit unnatural equal respect. However, several of our authors in one way or another reject the idea that inequality and elite formation are natural, or at least the *only* natural choice. Because of this, they more easily re-vision honor as quite compatible with democratic equality. Steven Forde, for instance, explores the views of Francis Fukuyama, corroborated by recent primate and anthropological research, that a social configuration that acknowledges equal dignity is quite natural and instinctual. Sharon Krause argues that the historic liberation movements within democracies show us this animating spirit of equal dignity which demands what is, in effect, unnaturally withheld—equal honor. In her view, democracy takes the same sense of pride or honor which supported the stratified system of aristocracy and bestows it on citizens equally.

If a hard-won agreement to equal human dignity is enduring and natural attribute of the human experience, democratic honor is viable, and can be called upon to raise liberalism above the crass materialism and selfishness that authors like Etzioni are concerned to moderate, bringing forth the potential for true citizenship. If that is the case, then at least one item on the honor agenda should be to bring more citizens into the life of the *polis* so that they can experience not just the legal acknowledgment of their equal human dignity but aspire to a greater sense of honor that comes from full participation in spirited debate, deliberation and voting.

Too many citizens of democracies are citizens in name only. If voter turnout is a decent measure of active citizenship, we find that there are more citizens in some democracies than in others. U.S. turnout in the 2012 presidential election was 53.6 percent of registered voters. The democracy with the highest turnout in recent elections (excluding Belgium and Turkey where voting is compulsory) was Sweden with 82.6 percent of voters. Switzerland, on the other hand, routinely has the lowest voter turnout, with 40 percent of the eligible voters participating in the 2011 election there.[2] It is of course impossible to fully explain this difference, but certainly much of it must lie within the cultures of these countries, that is, in their understanding of what it means to be a citizen, and how much the activities of a citizen are considered honorable and are honored. In the United States, the old language of duty and honor when it comes to political participation has largely been abandoned in public discourse, indicating that perhaps the countervailing liberal values of individualism and rational self-interest have at least temporarily gotten the upper hand against the more uplifting drive of *isothymia*.

In this regard, not only Krause's implicit call for us to model our citizenship after a hero of civil rights such as Martin Luther King Jr., or Mark Griffith's appeal to contemplate the democratic leadership of the defender of Western liberty, Winston Churchill, but Ajume Wingo's appeal for young Africans to admire those African liberationists like Nelson Mandela, all point up the value of those who lead the way and provide the inspiration and models for honorable citizenship. Such role models have a way not only of defining what is honorable but also of shaming us into honorable actions, long after they have achieved worldly immortality. In fact, Wingo himself employs the rhetorical weapon of honor and shame (maybe particularly shame) at the very beginning of his chapter by directly addressing young Africans who "cling so desperately to life and peace at any cost to their freedom, justice and happiness," and he soon suggests that they be more like Mandela.

Wingo's appeal resonates, and not unintentionally, with Martin Luther King Jr.'s calls for justice, and Churchill's criticism of Neville Chamberlain's "peace for our time" as shameful appeasement. The chapters by Wingo, Krause, and Griffith remind us of the ultimate connection between the vision of the honorable democratic life and the possibility of hardship and/or death as the price of maintaining that freedom. The African experience gives us a model of civic immortality which addresses this frightening prospect—an image that shows us how we can envision our lives as extending beyond our individual existences to the life of the larger community. This heroic image of the liberationist hero, in its most radical expression, makes understandable and honorable the sacrifice of one's life for the well-being of current and future generations. In its less extreme expression it speaks to those daily sacrifices of our selfish ends to free up time and space for true citizenship practices like becoming informed and voting.

But appealing to heroes of liberty and equality and expecting ordinary citizens to emulate them in motivation, and perhaps in action, is asking for a fairly big leap all at once. If so, Anthony Cunningham's approach of growing honor from the ground up is particularly helpful. Cunningham's chapter validates the experience of our everyday lives that honor is alive and well even if we do not speak explicitly in those terms, in this case in the largely unspoken rules governing hospitality and gratitude. There, even in a context in which citizenship might not be fully understood or lived, we have an abundance of examples of the type of thinking that could be a foundation for the development of citizen honor. When we are treated with rudeness, disrespect, or ingratitude we feel that the other person has not recognized our equal dignity, that our honor has been wounded, and we may reevaluate our respect and our willingness to cooperate with that other person.

If there is more disrespect than respect coming from the people around us (which arguably is the case at times), how can we envision ourselves as citizens? Indeed, the bedrock of citizen honor lies in this universal experience of supposedly private honor, and Cunningham's treatment of it highlights that there is, after all, no bright liberal dividing line between public and private when it comes to honor. Private honorable behavior forms the model for honorable public and civic behavior. And, as Ryan Rhodes points out, the law of reputation that Cunningham develops in the realm of our everyday interactions, can also be seen in the fact that, despite our discomfort with its undemocratic implications, the coinage of democratic political power is still reputation, which is indeed publicly instituted honor and shame based upon anything from a politician's private indiscretions made public, to his or her public behavior violating commonsense notions of honor that we experience first in our private life.

While the subject matter in this volume has spanned from ancient to modern thought, from the international level to that of the local community and family, from the male to the female experience, and from Western to non-Western conceptions of honor, what unites it is a concern for the future of honor in liberal societies. To the extent that liberal democracy is either the fact or at least an aspiration for a significant part of the world, its weaknesses and its strengths regarding honor are of global significance. To the extent that different conceptions of honor hold sway in nonliberal regimes, scholars and citizens alike should be well motivated to learn not only about how well the concept works within liberalism (or does not) but how theirs may differ with other cultural conceptions of honor.

We hope that this inaugural volume in the Lexington Books series *Honor and Obligation in Liberal Societies* is just the beginning of a conversation about honor in all contexts and in all its dimensions. Perhaps some of these authors will contribute a longer work to the series. Hopefully, too, many scholars, students, and members of the public and the armed forces will be able to use this volume as a source of information and inspiration for their own analysis of honor. Anyone wishing to know more about the series of which this book is a part, or potentially contribute to this series, can find more information at *lexingtonliberalism.com.*

NOTES

1. Associated Press, "A dress code imposed by a Kansas Senate committee chairman that prohibits women testifying on bills from wearing low-cut necklines and miniskirts is drawing bipartisan ridicule from female legislators," U.S. News and World Report, http://www.usnews.com/news/offbeat/articles/2016–01–22/kansas-lawmaker-imposes-dress-code-on-female-witnesses, accessed 3:15 p.m., Feb. 4, 2016.

2. Drew Desilver, "U.S. Voter Turnout Trails Most Developed Countries," Pew Research Center, http://www.pewresearch.org/fact-tank/2015/05/06/u-s-voter-turnout-trails-most-developed-countries/, accessed Feb. 9, 2016.

Bibliography

INTRODUCTION (DEMETRIOU AND JOHNSON)

Adair, Douglass. *Fame and the Founding Fathers: Essays by Douglass Adair*. New York: Norton, 1974.

Anderson, Elijah. *Code of the Street*. New York: Norton, 1999.

Aristotle. *Nicomachean Ethics*. Translated by Terence Irwin. Indianapolis, IN: Hackett, 1999.

Bell, David. *The First Total War: Napoleon's Europe and the Birth of Warfare as We Know It*. Boston: Houghton Mifflin, 2007.

Berger, Peter. "On the Obsolescence of the Concept of Honor" in *Revisions: Changing Perspectives in Moral Philosophy*. Notre Dame, IN: University Notre Dame Press, 1983.

Bloom, Mia. "In Defense of Honor: Women and Terrorist Recruitment on the Internet." *Journal of Postcolonial Cultures and Societies* 4, no. 1 (2013): 150–95.

Bourdieu, Pierre. "The Sentiment of Honor in Kabyle Society," in *Honour and Shame: The Values of Mediterranean Society*. Edited by J. G. Peristiany. Chicago: University of Chicago Press, 1966: 191–241.

Brennan, Geoffrey and Philip Pettit. *The Economy of Esteem*. New York: Oxford University Press, 2004.

Campbell, John K. *Honour, Family, and Patronage: A Study of Institutions and Moral Values in a Greek Mountain Community*. Oxford: Clarendon, 2004.

Cunningham, Anthony. *Modern Honor*. New York: Routledge, 2013.

Demetriou, Dan. "Honor War Theory: Romance or Reality?" *Philosophical Papers* 42, no. 3 (2013): 285–313.

Freeman, Joanne. *Affairs of Honor: National Politics in the New Republic*. New Haven, CT: Yale University Press, 2002.

French, Shannon. *Code of the Warrior*. Lanham, MD: Rowman & Littlefield, 2003.

Johnson, Laurie. *Thomas Hobbes: Turning Point for Honor*. Lanham, MD: Lexington Books, 2009.

———. *Locke and Rousseau: Two Enlightenment Responses to Honor*. Lanham, MD: Lexington Books, 2012.

Jones, George Fenwick. *Honor Bright: Honor in Western Literature*. Savannah, GA: Frederic C. Bell, 2000.

Krause, Sharon. *Liberalism with Honor*. Cambridge, MA: Harvard University Press, 2002.

Lebow, Ned. *Why Nations Fight*. New York: Cambridge University Press, 2010.

Livy. *History of Rome*. Translated by C. Roberts. New York: E. P. Dutton and Co., 1912.

Mandeville, Bernard. *An Enquiry into the Origin of Honour, and the Usefulness of Christianity in War*. London: Brotherton, 1732.

McPherson, Jeffrey. *Honor System Marketing*. Austin, TX: Acres USA, 2011.

Miller, William Ian. *Bloodtaking and Peacemaking: Feud, Law, and Society in Saga Iceland*. Chicago: University of Chicago Press, 1990.

Montaigne, Michel de. *The Complete Essays*. Translated by M. A. Screech. London: Penguin, 1987.

Montesquieu, Charles-Louis. *The Spirit of the Laws*. Edited by Anne Cohler, Basia Carolyn Miller, and Harold Stone. Cambridge: Cambridge University Press, 1989.

Nisbett, Richard and Dov Cohen. *Culture of Honor: The Psychology of Violence in the South*. Boulder, CO: Westview Press, 1996.
Olsthoorn, Peter. *Honor in Political and Moral Philosophy*. Albany, NY: SUNY Press, 2014.
Oprisko, Robert. *Honor: A Phenomenology*. New York: Routledge, 2012.
Peristiany, J. G. *Honor and Shame: the Values of Mediterranean Society*. Chicago: University of Chicago Press, 1966.
Pinker, Steven. *The Better Angels of Our Nature*. New York: Penguin, 2011.
Pitt-Rivers, Julian. "Honour and Social Status," in *Honor and Shame: The Values of Mediterranean Society*. Edited by J. G. Peristiany. Chicago: University of Chicago Press, 1966, 19–77.
Regan Tom. *Defending Animal Rights*. Urbana-Champaign: University of Illinois Press, 2001.
Robinson, Paul. *Military Honour and the Conduct of War*. Oxford: Oxford University Press, 2006.
Schneider, Jane. "Of Vigilance and Virgins: Honor, Shame, and Access to Resources." *Mediterranean Societies Ethnology* 10, no. 1 (1971): 1–24.
Sessions, Lad. *Honor for Us*. New York: Continuum, 2010.
Singer, Peter. *Animal Liberation*. New York: Random House, 1975.
Sommers, Tamler. *Relative Justice*. Princeton, NJ: Princeton University Press, 2012.
Stewart, James Henderson. *Honor*. Chicago: University of Chicago Press, 1994.
Waldron, Jeremy. *Dignity, Rand, and Rights*. New York: 2009.
Welsh, Alexander. *What is Honor?* New Haven, CT: Yale University Press, 2008.
Willis, Garry. *Cincinnatus: George Washington and the Enlightenment*. Garden City, NY: Doubleday, 1984.
Wood, Gordon. *Revolutionary Characters: What Made the Founders Different*. New York: Penguin, 2006.
Wyatt-Brown, Bertram. *Southern Honor: Ethics and Behavior in the Old South*. New York: Oxford University Press, 2007.
———. *Honor and Violence in the Old South*. New York: Oxford University Press, 1986.

CHAPTER 1: FIGHTING TOGETHER: CIVIL DISCOURSE AND AGONISTIC HONOR (DEMETRIOU)

Arendt, Hannah. *The Human Condition*. Chicago: Chicago University Press, 1958.
Chagnon, Napoleon. *Noble Savages: My Life Among Two Dangerous Tribes—The Yanomamo and the Anthropologists*. New York: Simon & Schuster, 2013.
Connolly, William. *Identity/Difference: Democratic Negotiations of Political Paradox*. Ithaca, NY: Cornell University Press, 1991.
Demetriou, Dan. "Honor War Theory: Romance or Reality?" *Philosophical Papers* 42, no. 3 (2013): 285–313.
———. "What Should Realists Say About Honor Cultures?" *Ethical Theory and Moral Practice* 17, no. 5 (2014): 893–911.
———. "The Ecology of Honor in Humans and Animals," in *Beastly Morality*. Edited by Jonathan Crane. New York: Columbia University Press, 2015.
Gladwell, Malcolm. *David and Goliath: Underdogs, Misfits, and the Art of Battling Giants*. New York: Little, Brown and Company, 2013.
Habermas, Jürgen. *Between Facts and Norms: Contributions to a Discourse Theory of Law and Democracy*. Cambridge, MA: MIT Press, 1996.
Hall, Leslie, trans., *Beowulf*. Boston: D. C. Heath & Co., 1892. http://www.gut enberg.org/files/16328/16328-h/16328-h.htm
Herodotus. *History, Volume III*. Translated by George Rawlinson. London: John Murray, 1862.

Hillenbrand, Carole. "The Evolution of the Saladin Legend in the West," in *Mélanges*. Edited by Louis Pouzet. Beirut: Dar El-Marchreq, 2006, 1–13.
Hobbes, Thomas. *Leviathan*. Edited by Richard Tuck. Cambridge: Cambridge University Press, 1996.
Hoffer, Eric. *The True Believer: Thoughts on the Nature of Mass Movements*. New York: HarperCollins, 2010.
Honig, Bonnie. *Political Theory and the Displacement of Politics*. Ithaca, NY: Cornell University Press, 1993.
Johnson, Laurie. *Thomas Hobbes: Turning Point for Honor*. Lanham, MD: Lexington Books, 2009.
Krause, Sharon. *Liberalism with Honor*. Cambridge: Harvard University Press, 2002.
Kuhn, Thomas. *The Structure of Scientific Revolutions: 50th Anniversary Edition*. Chicago: University of Chicago Press, 2012.
Montesquieu, Charles-Louis. *The Spirit of the Laws*. Edited by Anne Cohler, Basia Carolyn Miller, and Harold Stone. Cambridge: Cambridge University Press, 1989.
Mouffe, Chantal. *Agonistics*. New York: Verso, 2013.
Pinker, Steven. *The Better Angels of Our Nature* New York: Viking, 2011.
Rawls, John. *Political Liberalism*. New York: Columbia University Press, 1993.
Regan, Geoffrey. *Lionhearts: Richard I, Saladin, and the Era of the Third Crusade*. New York: Bloomsbury, 1999.
Robinson, Paul. "The Moral Equality of Combatants." *Irrussianality*. Blog entry. December 17, 2014. https://irrussianality.wordpress.com/2014/12/17/the-moral-equality-of-combatants/
———. "The Moral Equality of Combatants," *Honorethics.org*. Comment. December 19, 2014. http://honorethics.org/2014/12/18/the-moral-equality-of-combatants/#commen ts.
Ruskin, John. *Crown of Wild Olive* . Boston: Colonial Press, 2008. http://www .gutenberg.org/files/26716/26716-h/26716-h.htm#Page_66
Singh, Sarva Daman. *Ancient Indian Warfare: With Special Reference to the Vedic Period*. Delhi: Motilal Bararsidass Publishers, 1965.
Stewart, James Henderson. *Honor*. Chicago: University of Chicago Press, 1994.
Toll, Ian. *Six Frigates: The Epic History of the Founding of the U.S. Navy*. New York: Norton, 2006.
Wingenbach, Ed. *Institutionalizing Agonistic Democracy*. Burlington: Ashgate, 2011.

CHAPTER 2: LIBERALISM AND HONOR THROUGH THE LENS OF DARWIN (FORDE)

Arnhart, Larry. *Darwinian Natural Right: The Biological Ethics of Human Nature*. Albany, NY: SUNY Press, 1998.
———. *Darwinian Conservatism*. Charlottesville, VA: Imprint Academic, 2005.
Bekoff, Marc. "Wild Justice and Fair Play: Cooperation, Forgiveness, and Morality in Animals." *Biology and Philosophy* 19 (2004): 489–520.
Boehm, Christopher. *Hierarchy in the Forest: the Evolution of Egalitarian Behavior*. Cambridge, MA: Harvard University Press, 1999.
Bowles, Samuel and Herbert Gintis. *A Cooperative Species: Human Reciprocity and its Evolution*. Princeton, NJ: Princeton University Press, 2011.
Darwin, Charles. "The Descent of Man and Selection in Relation to Sex," in Darwin, *The Origin of Species by Means of Natural Selection* and *The Descent of Man and Selection in Relation to Sex*. Chicago: Encyclopedia Britannica/Great Books of the Western World, 1952, 253–600.
Dawkins, Richard. *The Selfish Gene*. Oxford: Oxford University Press, 1989.
Forde, Steven. *Locke, Science, and Politics*. New York: Cambridge University Press, 2013.

Fukuyama, Francis. *The End of History and the Last Man*. New York: The Free Press, 1992.

———. *Our Posthuman Future*, New York: Farrar, Straus and Giroux, 2002.

Galston, William. *Liberal Purposes: Goods, Virtues, and Diversity in the Liberal State*. Cambridge: Cambridge University Press, 1991.

Gould, S. J. and R. C. Lewontin. "The Spandrels of San Marco and the Panglossian Paradigm: A Critique of the Adaptationist Programme," in *Proceedings of the Royal Society of London* B 205 (1979): 581–98.

Haidt, Jonathan. "'Dialogue between My Head and My Heart:' Affective Influences on Moral Judgment." *Psychological Inquiry* 13, no. 1 (2002): 54–56.

Hegel, Georg Wilhelm Friedrich. *Philosophy of Right and Law*, in *The Philosophy of Hegel*. Edited by Carl L. Friedrich. New York: Modern Library, 1954, 21–329.

Hobbes, Thomas. *Leviathan*. Edited by Edwin Curley. Indianapolis, IN: Hackett, 1994.

Johnson, Laurie M. *Locke & Rousseau: Two Enlightenment Responses to Honor*, Lanham, MD: Lexington Books, 2012.

———. *Thomas Hobbes: Turning Point for Honor*. Lanham, MD: Lexington Books, 2009.

Jonas, Hans. *The Phenomenon of Life: Toward a Philosophical Biology*. Evanston, IL: Northwestern University Press, 2001.

Kitcher, Philip. "Ethics and Evolution: How to Get Here from There," in *Primates and Philosophers: How Morality Evolved*. Edited by Stephen Macedo and Josiah Ober. Princeton, NJ: Princeton University Press, 2006, 120–39.

Knauft, Bruce M. "Violence and Sociality in Human Evolution." *Current Anthropology* 32, no. 4 (1991): 391–428.

Kojève, Alexandre. *Introduction to the Reading of Hegel*. Translated by James H. Nichols, Jr. Edited by Allan Bloom. New York: Basic Books, 1969.

Krause, Sharon. *Liberalism with Honor*. Cambridge, MA: Harvard University Press, 2002.

Locke, John. *Some Thoughts Concerning Education*, in *Some Thoughts Concerning Education and of the Conduct of the Understanding*. Edited by Ruth Weissbourd Grant and Nathan Tarcov. Indianapolis, IN: Hackett, 1996. 1–162.

Masters, Roger D. *The Nature of Politics*. New Haven, CT: Yale University Press, 1989.

Mayr, Ernst. *The Growth of Biological Thought: Diversity, Evolution, and Inheritance*. Cambridge, MA: Harvard University Press, 1982.

Nisbett, Richard E. and Dov Cohen. *Culture of Honor: The Psychology of Violence in the South*. Boulder, CO: Westview Press, 1996.

Ober, Josiah. "Democracy's Dignity." *American Political Science Review* 106, no. 4 (2012): 827–46.

Peterson, Dale and Richard Wrangham. *Demonic Males: Apes and the Origins of Human Violence*. New York: Houghton Mifflin, 1996.

Philosophy of Right and Law, in *The Philosophy of Hegel*. Edited by Carl L. Friedrich. New York: Modern Library, 1954, 221–329, 404ff.

Pinker, Steven. *The Better Angels of Our Nature: Why Violence Has Declined*. New York: Penguin, 2012.

Sommers, Tamler. "The Two Faces of Revenge: Moral Responsibility and the Culture of Honor." *Biology and Philosophy* 24 (2009): 35–50.

Taylor, Charles. *Multiculturalism and the "Politics of Recognition."* Princeton, NJ: Princeton University Press, 1992.

———. "The Politics of Recognition," in *Multiculturalism*. Edited by Amy Gutmann. Princeton, NJ: Princeton University Press, 1994. 25–74.

Thayer, Bradley A. *Darwin and International Relations: On the Evolutionary Origins of War and Ethnic Conflict*. Lexington, KY: University Press of Kentucky, 2009.

Tocqueville, Alexis de. *Democracy in America*. Translated by Harvey C. Mansfield and Delba Winthrop. Chicago: University of Chicago Press, 2000.

Tomasello, Michael. *Why We Cooperate*. Cambridge, MA: MIT Press, 2009.

Waldron, Jeremy. "Dignity, Rank, and Rights: The 2009 Tanner Lectures at UC Berkeley." *Public Law and Legal Theory Research Paper No. 09–50*. New York: New York University School of Law, 2009.

Wright, Robert. *The Moral Animal: Evolutionary Psychology and Everyday Life*. New York: Vintage Books, 1994.

CHAPTER 3: LIBERAL HONOR (KRAUSE)

Althusser, Louis. *Politics and History: Montesquieu, Rousseau, Marx*. Translated by Ben Brewster. London: Verso, 1982.

Appiah, Kwame Anthony. *The Honor Code: How Moral Revolutions Happen*. New York: W. W. Norton, 2010.

Arendt, Hannah. *The Human Condition*. Chicago: University of Chicago Press, 1958.

Aristotle. *The Politics*. Translated by Carnes Lord. Chicago: University of Chicago Press, 1984.

Baker, Keith Michael. *The Old Regime and the French Revolution*. Chicago: University of Chicago Press, 1987.

Bayefsky, Rachel. "Dignity, Honour, and Human Rights: Kant's Perspective," *Political Theory* 41, no. 6 (2013): 809–37.

Berger, Peter. "On the Obsolescence of the Concept of Honor," in *Liberalism and Its Critics*. Edited by Michael J. Sandel. New York: New York University Press, 1984.

Bien, David. "Old Regime Origins of Democratic Liberty," in *The French Idea of Freedom: The Old Regime and the Declaration of the Rights of 1789*. Edited by Dale VanKley. Stanford, CA: Stanford University Press, 1994.

Blight, David W. *Frederick Douglass' Civil War: Keeping Faith in Jubilee*. Baton Rouge, LA: Louisiana State University Press, 1989.

Blits, Jan H. "Redeeming Lost Honor: Shakespeare's *Rape of Lucrece*." *The Review of Politics* 71, no. 3 (2009): 411–27.

Bowman, James. *Honor: A History*. New York: Encounter Books, 2006.

Brotz, Howard, ed., *African-American Social & Political Thought*. New Brunswick, NJ: Transaction Publishers, 1995.

Bush, M. L. *Noble Privilege*. Manchester: Manchester University Press, 1983.

Carrithers, David. "Montesquieu's Philosophy of History." *Journal of the History of Ideas* 47, no. 1 (1986): 61–80.

Chaussinand-Nogaret, Guy. *La noblesse au XVIIIe siècle: De la féodalité aux lumières*. Paris: Librairie Hachette, 1976.

Cox, Iris. *Montesquieu and the History of French Laws*. Oxford: Voltaire Foundation, 1983.

Demetriou, Daniel George. *Honor Among Theories*. Ann Arbor, MI: Proquest UMI Dissertation Pubishing, 2011.

Destutt de Tracy, Antoine Louis Claude. *A Commentary and Review of Montesquieu's* Spirit of the Laws. Translated by Thomas Jefferson. New York: Burt Franklin, 1969.

Dewald, Jonathan. *The European Nobility, 1400–1800*. Cambridge: Cambridge University Press, 1996.

Douglass, Frederick. *Frederick Douglass: Selected Speeches and Writings*. Edited by Philip S. Foner. Chicago: Lawrence Hill, 1999.

———. *My Bondage and My Freedom*. New York: Dover, 1969.

DuBois, W. E. B. "Resolutions of the Niagara Movement," in *African-American Social & Political Thought*. Edited by Howard Brotz. New Brunswick, NJ: Transaction Publishers, 1995, 539.

Ford, Franklin. *Robe and Sword: The Regrouping of the French Aristocracy after Louis XIV*. Cambridge, MA: Harvard University Press, 1953.

Garrow, David J. *Bearing the Cross*. New York: Quill, 1986.

Genicot, Léopold. *La noblesse dans l'occident medieval*. London: Variorum Reprints, 1982.

Hegel, G. W. F. *Philosophy of Right*. Translated by T. M. Knox. Oxford: Oxford University Press, 1967.

Hulliung, Mark. *Montesquieu and the Old Regime*. Berkeley: University of California Press, 1976.

Johnson, Laurie M. *Thomas Hobbes: Turning Point for Honor*. Lanham, MD: Lexington Books, 2009.

———. *Locke and Rousseau: Two Enlightenment Responses to Honor*. Lanham, MD: Lexington Books, 2012.

Johnson, Lyman L. and Lipsett-Rivera, Sonya. *The Faces of Honor: Sex, Shame, and Violence in Colonial Latin America*. Albuquerque, NM: University of New Mexico Press, 1998.

King, Martin Luther, Jr. *Testament of Hope: The Essential Writings and Speeches of Martin Luther King, Jr*. Edited by James M. Washington. New York: HarperCollins, 1986.

King, Richard H. *Civil Rights and the Idea of Freedom*. New York: Oxford University Press, 1992.

Kinneging, Andreas A. M. *Aristocracy, Antiquity and History*. New Brunswick, NJ: Transaction Publishers, 1997.

Krause, Sharon R. "Review of *The Honor Code*." *Ethics and International Affairs* 25, no. 4 (2011): 475–78.

———. *Liberalism with Honor*. Cambridge, MA.: Harvard University Press, 2002.

Labatut, Jean-Pierre. *Les noblesses européennes de la fin du XVe siècle à la fin du XVIIIe siècle*. Paris: Presses Universitaires de France, 1978.

LaVaque-Manty, Mika. "Dueling for Equality: Masculine Honor and the Modern Politics of Dignity." *Political Theory* 34, no. 6 (2006): 715–40.

Lewis, David L. *King: A Critical Biography*. New York: Praeger, 1970.

Martin, Kingsley. *French Liberal Thought in the Eighteenth Century*. London: Turnstile Press, 1954.

Martin, Waldo E., Jr. *The Mind of Frederick Douglass*. Chapel Hill, NC: University of North Carolina Press, 1984.

McClure, Christopher Scott. "War, Madness, and Death: The Paradox of Honor in Hobbes's *Leviathan*." *The Journal of Politics* 76, no. (2014): 114–25.

Meyer, Jean. *La noblesse française à l'époque moderne (XVIe-XVIIIe siècle)*. Paris: Presses Universitaires de France, 1991.

Miller, Kelly. "Radicals and Conservatives," in *Critical Essays on Frederick Douglass*. Edited by William L. Andrews. Boston: G. K. Hall, 1991.

Mills, Charles W. "Whose Fourth of July? Frederick Douglass and 'Original Intent,'" in *Frederick Douglass: A Critical Reader*. Edited by Bill E. Lawson and Frank M. Kirkland. Malden, MA: Blackwell Publishers, 1999.

Miroff, Bruce. *Icons of Democracy*. Lawrence, KS: University of Kansas Press, 2000.

Montesquieu, Charles-Louis de Secondat baron de la Brède et de. *De l'esprit des lois*, in *Oeuvres complètes*, 2 vols. Edited by Roger Caillois. Paris: Gallimard, "Bibliothèque de la Pléiade," 1949–1951, vol. II.

———. *The Spirit of the Laws*. Translated by Anne M. Cohler, Basia Carolyn Miller and Harold Samuel Stone. Cambridge: Cambridge University Press, 1989.

———. *Mes pensées, Oeuvres complètes*, vol. I.

Mosher, Michael A. "The Particulars of a Universal Politics: Hegel's Adaptation of Montesquieu's Typology." *American Political Science Review*, 78, no. 1 (1984): 179–88.

Oates, Stephen B. *Let the Trumpet Sound: A Life of Martin Luther King, Jr.*. New York: Harper Perennial, 1982.

Olsthoorn, Peter. "Honour, Face and Reputation in Political Theory." *European Journal of Political Theory* 7, no. 4 (2008): 472–91.

Peristiany, J. G. *Honor and Shame*. Chicago: University of Chicago Press, 1966.

Rawls, John. A *Theory of Justice*. Cambridge, MA.: Harvard University Press, 1971.

Rosso, Corrado. *Montesquieu moraliste*. Bordeaux, FR: Ducros, 1971.

Schaub, Diana. "Frederick Douglass's Constitution," in *The American Experiment: Essays on the Theory and Practice of Liberty*. Edited by Peter Augustine Lawler and Robert Martin Schaefer. Lanham, MD: Rowman & Littlefield, 1994.

Schrader, David E. "Natural Law in the Constitutional Thought of Frederick Douglass," in *Frederick Douglass: A Critical Reader*. Edited by Bill E. Lawson and Frank M. Kirkland. Malden, MA: Blackwell Publishers, 1999.
Shklar, Judith. *Ordinary Vices*. Cambridge, MA: Harvard University Press, 1984.
Stewart, Frank Henderson. *Honor*. Chicago: University of Chicago Press, 1994.
Storing, Herbert. "Frederick Douglass," in *American Political Thought*. Edited by Morton Frisch and Richard Stevens. Itasca, IL.: F. E. Peacock, 1983.
Taylor, Charles. "The Politics of Recognition," in *Multiculturalism*. Edited by Amy Gutmann. Princeton, NJ: Princeton University Press, 1994.
Tocqueville, Alexis de. *La démocratie en Amérique* (2 vols.) in *Oeuvres complètes d'Alexis de Tocqueville*. Edited by J. P. Mayer, 13 vols. Paris: Gallimard, 1951, vol. I.
———. *L'ancien régime et la révolution*, 3 vols., in *Oeuvres complètes*, vol. II.
Walzer, Michael. *Spheres of Justice*. New York: Basic Books, 1983.
Washington, Booker T. "Early Problems of Freedom," in *African-American Social & Political Thought*, 388f.

CHAPTER 4: A NEO-ARISTOTELIAN THEORY OF POLITICAL HONOR (SKULTETY)

Aristotle. *Ethica Nicomachea*. Edited by I. Bywater. Oxford: Oxford University Press, 1894.
———. *Nicomachean Ethics*. Translated by Terence Irwin, 2nd edn. Indianapolis, IN: Hackett, 2000.
———. *Politica*. Edited by W. D. Ross. Oxford: Oxford University Press, 1957.
———. *Politics*. Translated by C. D. C. Reeve. Indianapolis, IN: Hackett, 1998.
Berger, Peter. "The Obsolescence of the Concept of Honour." *European Journal of Sociology* 11, no. 2 (1970): 338–47.
Hobbes, Thomas. *Leviathan*. Edited by A. P. Martinich and Brian Battiste. Toronto: Broadview, 2011.
Lennox, James. "Teleology," in *Keywords in Evolutionary Biology*. Edited by E. F. Keller and E. A. Lloyd. Cambridge, MA: Harvard University Press, 1992.
Locke, John. *The Second Treatise of Civil Government*. Edited by J. W. Gough. Oxford: Basil Blackwell, 1946.
Sandel, Michael. *Justice*. New York: Farrar, Straus and Giroux, 2009.

CHAPTER 5: PUTTING ONE'S BEST FACE FORWARD: WHY LIBERALISM NEEDS HONOR (RHODES)

Ackerman, Felicia. "'Never to Do Outrageously or Murder': The World of Malory's *Morte D'arthur*," in Shannon French, *The Code of the Warrior*. Lanham, MD: Rowman & Littlefield, 2004, 119.
Aristotle. *Nicomachean Ethics*. Translated by Terence Irwin. Indianapolis, IN: Hackett, 1985.
Baker, Alan. *The Knight: An Introduction to the Most Admired Warriors in History*. New York: Barnes & Noble Books, 2005.
Bowman, James. *Honor: A History*. New York: Encounter Books, 2006.
Bouchard, Constance Brittain. *"Strong of Body, Brave and Noble": Chivalry and Society in Medieval France*. Ithaca, NY: Cornell University Press, 1998.
Geuss, Raymond. "Liberalism and its Discontents." *Political Theory* 30, no. 3 (2002): 320–38.
Homer. *The Iliad*. Translated by Robert Fagles. New York: Penguin Books, 1991.

Homer. *The Iliad*. Translated by William Cowper. Edited by Robert Southey. Notes by M. A. Dwight. New York: D. Appleton & Co., 1849. Accessed through Project Gutenberg, www.gutenberg.org. Bk. II, 298–305.
Knowles, Sir James. *King Arthur and His Knights*. New York: Children's Classics, 1986.
Lear, Jonathan. *Radical Hope: Ethics in the Face of Cultural Devastation*. Cambridge, MA: Harvard University Press, 2006.
Leland, R. J. and Han van Wietmarschen. "Reasonableness, Intellectual Modesty, and Reciprocity in Political Justification." *Ethics* 122, no. 4 (2012): 721–47.
MacIntyre, Alasdair. *After Virtue*, 2nd edn. Notre Dame, IN: University of Notre Dame, 2003.
Mallory, Sir Thomas. *Le Morte DArthur*. Edited by Tom Griffith. Hertfordshire: Wordsworth Classics of World Literature, 1996.
McKinnon, Christine. "Hypocrisy, with a Note on Integrity." *American Philosophical Quarterly* 28, no. 4 (1991): 321–30.
Moore, Matthew J. "Pluralism, Relativism, and Liberalism." *Political Research Quarterly* 62, no. 2 (2009): 244–56.
Tsunetomo, Yamamoto. *Bushido: The Way of the Samurai*. Translated by Minoru Tanaka. Edited by Justin F. Stone. New York: Square One Publishers, 2002.
Williams, Bernard. *Shame and Necessity*. Oakland, CA: University of California Press, 1993.

CHAPTER 6: COMMUNITARIANISM AND HONOR (ETZIONI)

Avineri, Shlomo and Avner de-Shalit. "Introduction," in *Communitarianism and Individualism*. Edited by Shlomo Avineri and Avner de-Shalit. Oxford: Oxford University Press, 1992.
Avnon, Dan and Avner de-Shalit. "Liberalism Between Promise and Practice," in *Liberalism and Its Practice*. Edited by Dan Avnon and Avner de-Shalit. London: Routledge, 1999.
Beauchamp, Tom L. and James F. Childress. *Principles of Biomedical Ethics*. 6th edn. New York: Oxford University Press, 2009.
Bellah, Robert et al. *Habits of the Heart*, 2nd edn. University of California Press, 1996.
Bell, Daniel A. "A Communitarian Critique of Authoritarianism: The Case of Singapore." *Political Theory* 25, no. 1 (1997): 6–32.
Benhabib, Seyla. "Autonomy, Modernity, and Community: Communitarianism and Critical Social Theory in Dialogue," in *Cultural-Political Interventions in the Unfinished Project of Enlightenment*. Edited by Axel Honneth et al. Cambridge, MA: MIT Press, 1997.
Burke, Edmund. *Reflections on the Revolution in France*. Edited by J. G. A. Pockock. Indianapolis, IN: Hackett, 1987.
Dworkin, Ronald. "Liberalism," in *Public and Private Morality*. Edited by Stuart Hampshire. Cambridge: Cambridge University Press, 1978, 127.
Dworkin, Ronald. *A Matter of Principle*. Cambridge, MA: Harvard University Press, 1985.
Etzioni, Amitai. *From Empire to Community*. New York: Palgrave MacMillan, 2004.
———. *My Brother's Keeper: A Memoir and a Message*. Lanham, MD: Rowman & Littlefield, 2003.
———. *The New Golden Rule: Community and Morality in a Democratic Society*. New York: Basic Books, 1996.
———. *Political Unification Revisited: On Building Supranational Communities*. Lanham, MD: Lexington Books, 2001.
———. *The Spirit of Community: Rights, Responsibilities and the Communitarian Agenda*. New York: Crown Books, 1993.
Fox, Russell A. "Confucian and Communitarian Responses to Liberal Democracy." *The Review of Politics* 59, no. 3 (1997): 561–92.

Frazer, Elizabeth. *The Problem of Communitarian Politics: Unity and Conflict*. Oxford: Oxford University Press, 1999.

Galston, William A. "The Law of Marriage and Divorce: Options for Reform," in *Marriage in America: A Communitarian Perspective*. Edited by Martin King White. Lanham, MD: Rowman & Littlefield, 2000.

Garnett, Rondald George. *Co-Operation and the Owenite Socialist Communities in Britain 1825–45*. Manchester: University of Manchester Press, 1972.

Habermas, Jürgen. "The New Conservatism: Cultural Criticism and the Historians' Debate," in *Multiculturalism and the Politics of Recognition*. Edited by Amy Gutmann. Princeton, NJ: Princeton University Press, 1994.

———. *Zwischn Natrualismus und Religion*. Frankfurt am Main: Suhrkamp, 2005.

Healy, Kieran. "Sociology," in *A Companion to Contemporary Political Philosopy*. Edited by Robert E. Goodin, Philip Petit, and Thomas Pogge. Vol. 2, 2nd edn. Hoboken, NJ: Blackwell Publishing, 2012.

Kausikan, Bilahari. "Asian versus 'Universal' Human Rights." *The Responsive Community* 7, no. 3 (Summer 1997): 9–21.

Kornhauser, William. *The Politics of Mass Society*. Glencoe, IL: The Free Press, 1959.

Kymlicka, Will. "Appendix I: Some Questions about Justice and Community," in *Communitarianism and Its Critics*. Edited by Daniel Bell. Oxford: Clarendon, 1993.

Kymlicka, Will. *Liberalism, Community, and Culture*. Oxford: Clarendon, 1989.

Kyung-Sup, Chang. "The Anti-Communitarian Family? Everyday Conditions of Authoritarian Politics in South Korea," in *Communitarian Politics in Asia*. Edited by Chua Beng Huat. London: Routledge, 2004.

MacIntyre, Alasdair. *After Virtue*. South Bend, IN: Notre Dame University Press, 1984.

de Maistre, Joseph. *Considerations on France*. Translated by Richard A. Lebrun. Montreal: McGill-Queen's University Press, 1974.

McGregor, Sue L. T. "Human Responsibility Movement Initiatives: A Comparative Analysis." *Factis Pax* 7, no. 1 (2013): 1–26.

bin Mohamad, Matahir and Ishihara Shintaro, "'*No' to ieru Ajia: tai obei eno hosaku* [The Asia That Can Say 'No': Cards Against the West]." Tokyo: Kobunsha, 1994.

New Revised Standard Bible. Christian Education of the National Council of the Churches of Christ (1989).

Nisbet, Robert A. *Community Power*. New York: Oxford University Press, 1962.

Nozick, Robert. *Anarchy, State, and Utopia*. New York: Basic Books, 1974.

Park, Robert E. and Ernest W. Burgess. *The City*. Chicago: University of Chicago Press, 1967.

Rand, Ayn. *Capitalism: The Unknown Ideal*. New York: Penguin, 1986, 20.

Rawls, John. *A Theory of Justice*. Cambridge, MA: Belknap Press, 1971.

———. *Political Liberalism*. New York: Columbia University Press, 1993.

Regan, Milton C. "Morality, Fault, and Divorce Law," in *Marriage in America: A Communitarian Perspective*. Edited by Martin King Whyte. Lanham, MD: Rowman & Littlefield, 2000.

Sandel, Michael. *Liberalism and the Limits of Justice*. New York: Cambridge University Press, 1982.

———. "The Procedural Republic and the Unencumbered Self." *Political Theory* 12, no. 1 (1984): 81–96.

Scanlon, Thomas M. "Rawls' Theory of Justice." *University of Pennsylvania Law Review* 121, no. 5 (1973): 1020–69.

Selznick, Philip. "Foundations of Communitarian Liberalism," in *The Essential Communitarian Reader*. Edited by Amitai Etzioni. Lanham, MD: Rowman & Littlefield, 1998.

———. "The Idea of a Communitarian Morality." *California Law Review* 75, no. 1 (1987): 445–63.

Simmel, George. "The Web of Group Affiliations," in *Conflict and the Web of Group Affiliations*. Translated by R. Benedix. New York: The Free Press, 1955.

Solove, Daniel. *Nothing to Hide: The False Tradeoff Between Privacy and Security*. New Haven, CT: Yale University Press, 2011.

Taylor, Charles. "Cross-Purposes: The Liberal-Communitarian Debate," in *Debates in Contemporary Political Philosophy*. Edited by Derek Matravers and Jon Pike. New York: Routledge, 2003, 195.

———. "The Politics of Recognition," in *Multiculturalism and 'The Politics of Recognition*. Edited by Amy Gutmann. Princeton, NJ: Princeton University Press, 1992.

Toumlin, Stephen. "How Medicine Saved the Life of Ethics," in *Bioethics: An Introduction to the History, Methods, and Practice*, 3rd edn. Edited by Nancy S. Jecker, Albert R. Johnson, and Robert A. Pearlman. Burlington, MA: Jones & Bartlett Learning, 2012, 26–27.

van Seters, Peter. *Communitarianism in Law and Society*. Lanham, MD: Rowman & Littlefield, 2006.

Walzer, Michael. *Spheres of Justice*. Oxford: Basil Blackwell, 1983.

CHAPTER 7: GOOD CITIZENS: GRATITUDE AND HONOR (CUNNINGHAM)

Abu-Lughod, Lila. *Veiled Sentiments: Honor and Poetry in a Bedouin Society*. Berkeley, CA: University of California Press, 1986.

Alexander, Caroline. *The Endurance: Shackleton's Legendary Antarctic Expedition*. New York: Alfred A. Knopf, 1998.

Appiah, Kwame Anthony. *The Honor Code: How Moral Revolutions Happen*. New York: W. W. Norton, 2010.

Barrington, Sir Jonah. *Personal Sketches of His Own Time*. New York: Redfield, 1853.

Benedict, Ruth. *The Chrysanthemum and the Sword: Patterns of Japanese Culture*. Boston: Houghton Mifflin, 1946.

Berlin, Isaiah. *The Proper Study of Mankind*. Edited by Henry Hardy and Roger Hausher. New York: Farrar, Straus and Giroux, 1998.

Cairns, Douglas. *Aidòs: The Psychology and Ethics of Honour and Shame in Ancient Greek Literature*. Oxford: Clarendon, 1993.

Campbell, J. K. *Honour, Family, and Patronage: A Study of Institutions and Moral Values in a Greek Mountain Community*. Oxford: Oxford University Press, 1964.

Cohen, Dov, Richard E. Nisbett, Brian F. Bowdle, and Norbert Schwarz. "Insult, Aggression, and the Southern Culture of Honor: An 'Experimental Ethnography.'" *Journal of Personality and Social Psychology* 70, no. 5 (1996): 945–60.

Egil's Saga, in *The Sagas of the Icelanders*. Translated by Bernard Scudder. New York: Viking, 2000.

El Guindi, Fadwa. *Veil: Modesty, Privacy and Resistance*. New York: Oxford University Press, 1999.

Euripides. *Hecuba*, in *Euripides 1: Medea, Hecuba, Andromache, the Bacchae*. Edited by David Slavitt et al. Philadelphia, PA: University of Pennsylvania Press, 1998, 70–146.

Flanagan, Richard. *The Narrow Road to the Deep North*. New York: Alred A. Knopf, 2014, 329.

Giraud, Léon. "L'Escrime et la femme," *Le Droit des femmes*, June 20, 1886, 143–44.

Goffman, Irving. *The Presentation of Self in Everyday Life*. New York: Anchor Books, 1959.

Greenberg, Kenneth. *Honor and Slavery*. Princeton, NJ: Princeton University Press, 1996.

Gutman, Roy. *A Witness to Genocide: The 1993 Pulitzer Prize-Winning Dispatches on the "Ethnic Cleansing" of Bosnia*. New York: Lisa Drew Books, 1993.

Heath, Jennifer, ed., *The Veil: Women Writers on Its History, Lore, and Politics*. Berkeley, CA: University of California Press, 2008.

Henderson, Frank Stuart. *Honor*. Chicago: University of Chicago Press, 1994.

Homer. *The Iliad*. Translated by Robert Fagles. New York: Penguin Books, 1990.

———. *The Odyssey*. Translated by Robert Fitzgerald. New York: Vintage Books, 1990.

Ikegami, Eiko. *The Taming of the Samurai: Honorific Individualism and the Making of Modern Japan*. Cambridge, MA: Harvard University Press, 1995.
Lansing, Alfred. *South: Shackleton's Incredible Voyage*. New York: Carroll & Graf, 1999.
Lazreg, Marnia. *Questioning the Veil: Open Letters to Muslim Women*. Princeton, NJ: Princeton University Press, 2009.
Lebra, Takie Sugiyama. "Shame and Guilt: A Psycho-cultural View of the Japanese Self." *Ethos* 11, no. 3 (1983): 192–209.
Logan, Harriet. *Unveiled: Voices of Women in Afghanistan*. New York: Regan Books, 2002.
Malouf, David. *Ransom*. New York: Vintage International, 2009.
Marmot, Michael. *The Status Syndrome: How Social Standing Affects Our Health and Longevity*. New York: Henry Holt, 2004.
Miller, William Ian. *Humiliation and Other Essays on Honor, Social Discomfort, and Violence*. Ithaca, NY: Cornell University Press, 1993.
Montaigne, Michel. *The Complete Essays of Montaigne*. Translated by Donald M. Frame. Stanford, CA: Stanford University Press, 1958.
Nisbett, Richard, and Dov Cohen. *Culture of Honor: The Psychology of Violence in the South*. Boulder, CO: Westview Press, 1996.
Njal's Saga. Translated by Magnus Magnusson and Hermann Palsson. Baltimore: Penguin, 1960.
Peristiany, Jean, ed., *Honor and Shame: The Values of a Mediterranean Society*. London: Wiedenfeld & Nicholson, 1992.
Peristiany, Jean, and Julian Pitt-Rivers, eds., *Honor and Grace in Anthropology*. Cambridge: Cambridge University Press, 1992.
Sessions, Lad. *Honor for Us: A Philosophical Analysis, Interpretation and Defense*. London: Continuum, 2010.
Shackleton, Ernest. *South: The Last Antarctic Expedition of Shackleton and the Endurance*. New York: Lyons Press, 2008.
Shakespeare, William. *The Riverside Shakespeare*. Boston: Houghton Mifflin, 1974.
Stevens, William Oliver. *Pistols at Ten Paces: The Code of Honor in America*. Boston: Houghton Mifflin, 1940.
Taylor, Gabrielle. *Pride, Shame and Guilt: Emotions of Self-Assessment*. New York: Oxford University Press, 1985.
Welsh, Alexander. *What Is Honor? A Question of Moral Imperatives*. New Haven, CT: Yale University Press, 2008.
Williams, Bernard. *Shame and Necessity*. Berkeley, CA: University of California Press, 1993.
Wyatt-Brown, Bertram. *Honor and Violence in the Old South*. New York: Oxford University Press, 1986.
———. *The Shaping of Southern Character: Honor, Grace, and War, 1760s–1880s*. Chapel Hill, NC: University of North Carolina Press, 2001.
———. *Southern Honor: Ethics & Behavior in the Old South*. New York: Oxford University Press, 1982.

CHAPTER 8: WINSTON CHURCHILL AND HONOR: THE COMPLEXITY OF HONOR AND STATESMANSHIP (GRIFFITH)

Berlin, Isaiah. *Personal Impressions*. New York: Penguin, 1980.
Cannadine, David ed., *Blood, Toil, Tears and Sweat: The Speeches of Winston Churchill*. Boston: Houghton Mifflin, 1989.
Churchill, Randolph S. *Winston S. Churchill, Vol. 1, Youth, 1874–1900*. Boston: Houghton Mifflin, 1966.
Churchill, Winston S. *My Early Life, 1874–1904*. New York: Touchstone, 1996.
———. *Never Give In! The Best of Winston Churchill's Speeches*. New York: Hyperion, 2003.

———. *Savrola*. London: Octopus Publishing Group, 1990.
———. *The Gathering Storm: The Second World War, Vol. 1*. Boston: Houghton Mifflin, 1948.
———. *Their Finest Hour: The Second World War, Vol. 2*. Boston: Houghton Mifflin, 1949.
———. "The Scaffolding of Rhetoric," *Winston Churchill Centre*, http://www.winstonchurchill.org/images/pdfs/for_educators/THE_SCAFFOLDING_OF_RHETORIC.pdf.
D'Este, Carlo. *Warlord, A Life of Winston Churchill at War, 1874–1945*. New York: Harper, 2008.
Gilbert, Martin. *Churchill: The Power of Words*. Boston: Da Capo Press, 2012.
———. *Prophet of Truth: Winston S. Churchill, 1922–1939*. London: Minerva, 1976.
Hastings, Max. *Winston's War: Churchill 1940–1945*. New York: Alfred A. Knopf, 2011.
Johnson, Paul. *Churchill*. New York: Penguin, 2009.
Stewart, Graham. *Burying Caesar: The Churchill-Chamberlain Rivalry*. New York: Overlook, 1999.

CHAPTER 9: LIFE IN DEATH: DEMOCRACY AND CIVIC HONOR (WINGO)

Arendt, Hannah. *The Human Condition*. Chicago: University of Chicago Press, 1958.
Hobbes, Thomas. *De Cive: The Latin Version*. Edited by Howard Warrender. Oxford: Clarendon, 1983.
Hochschild, Adam. *King Leopold's Ghost: A Story of Greed, Terror, and Heroism in Colonial Africa*. New York: Houghton Mifflin, 1998.
Hurd, Rollin Carlos. *Treatise on the Right of Personal Liberty, and on the Writ of Habeas Corpus and the Practice Connected with it: With a View of the Law of Extradition of Fugitives*. Albany, NY: W. C. Little and Company, 1858.
Krause, Sharon. *Liberalism with Honor*. Cambridge, MA: Harvard University Press, 2002.
Rosen, Michael. "Dignity Past and Present," in *Dignity, Rank, and Rights*. Edited by Jeremy Waldron. New York: Oxford University Press, 2012, 92–93.
Mamdani, Mahmood. *Citizen and Subject*. Princeton, NJ: Princeton University Press, 1996.
Mandela, Nelson. "An Ideal for Which I am Prepared to Die." *Guardian*, April 20, 1964. http://www.theguardian.com/world/2007/apr/23/nelsonmandela.
Mill, John Stuart. *Utilitarianism, On Liberty, Considerations on Representative Government, Remarks on Bentham's Philosophy*. Edited by Geraint Williams. London: J. M. Dent, 1993.
Rousseau, Jean-Jacques. *The Government of Poland*. Translated by Willmoore Kendall. Indianapolis, IN: Hackett, 1985.
Waldron, Jeremy. *Dignity, Rank, and Rights*. New York: Oxford University Press, 2012.
Wingo, Ajume. "Nelson Mandela's Greatness? He Stepped Aside." *Denver Post*, February 8, 2013, http://www.denverpost.com/opinion/ci_24672937/wingo-nelson-mandelas-greatness-he-stepped-aside.
———. "The Aesthetics of Freedom," in *New Waves in Political Philosophy*. Edited by Boudewijn de Bruin and Christopher Zurn. New York: Palgrave Macmillan 2009.
Young, Crawford. *The African Colonial State in Comparative Perspective*. New Haven, CT: Yale University Press, 1994.

CHAPTER 10: THE FEMALE POINT OF HONOR IN POSTREVOLUTIONARY FRANCE (MANSKER)

Andrieu, Gilbert. "A propos d'un livre: 'Pour devenir belle . . . et le rester' ou La culture physique au féminin avant 1914," in *Histoire du sport féminin*, vol. 2. Edited by Pierre Arnaud and Thierry Terret. Paris: L'Harmattan, 1996.

Audouard, Olympe. "La Femme, est-elle individu?" *Revue cosmopolite*, no. 16 (May 2, 1867): 97–103.

———. *Guerre aux hommes*. 2nd edn. Paris: E. Dentu, 1866.

———. *Lettre aux députés*. Paris: E. Dentu, 1867.

———. *Monsieur Barbey d'Aurevilly: Réponse à ses réquisitoires contres les bas-bleus. Conférence du 11 Avril*. Paris: E. Dentu, 1870.

———. *Les Mystères de l'Égypte dévoilés*. Paris: E. Dentu, 1866.

———. *L'Orient et ses peuplades*. Paris: E. Dentu, 1867.

———. *A Travers l'Amérique: Le Far-West*. Paris: E. Dentu, 1869.

———. *A Travers l'Amérique: North America*. Paris: E. Dentu, 1871.

———. *Voyage à travers mes souvenirs*. Paris: E. Dentu, 1884.

Barbey d'Aurevilly, Jules-Amédée. *Les Bas-bleus*. Paris: Palmé, 1878.

———. "Le duel tombé en quenouille," *Le Gaulois*, Sept. 2, 1869.

Bellacois, François. *The Duel: Its Rise and Fall in Early Modern France*. New Haven, CT: Yale University Press, 1990.

Bellanger, Claude, Jacques Godechot, Pierre Guiral, and Fernand Terrou. *Histoire générale de la presse française*, vol. 2. Paris: Presses Universitaires de France, 1972.

Berenson, Edward. *The Trial of Madame Caillaux*. Berkeley, CA: University of California Press, 1992.

Bergès, Alexandre. *L'Escrime et la femme*. Paris: D. Benoist, 1896.

Bibesco, Georges, and Camille Féry d'Esclands, *Conseils pour les duels à l'épée, au fleuret, au sabre et au pistolet*. Paris: A. Lemerre, 1900.

Bird, Dúnlaith. *Travelling in Different Skins: Gender Identity in European Women's Oriental Travelogues, 1850–1950*. Oxford: Oxford University Press, 2012.

Chateauvillard, Comte de. *Essai sur le duel*. Paris: Chez Bohaire, 1836.

Cohen, Elizabeth S. "Honor and Gender in the Streets of Early Modern Rome." *Journal of Interdisciplinary History* 22, no. 4 (1992): 597–625.

Dzeh-Djen, Li. *La Presse féministe en France de 1869 à 1914*. Paris: Rodstein, 1934.

Ferguson, Eliza Earle. *Gender and Justice: Violence, Intimacy, and Community in Fin-de-Siècle Paris*. Baltimore: Johns Hopkins University Press, 2010.

Forth, Christopher E. *The Dreyfus Affair and the Crisis of French Manhood*. Baltimore: Johns Hopkins University Press, 2004.

Frevert, Ute. *Men of Honour: A Social and Cultural History of the Duel*. Translated by Anthony Williams. Cambridge: Polity Press, 1995.

A Nation in Barracks: Modern Germany, Military Conscription and Civil Society. Translated by Andrew Boreham with Daniel Brückenhaus. Oxford: Berg, 2004.

Fuchs, Rachel G. *Contested Paternity: Constructing Families in Modern France*. Baltimore: Johns Hopkins University Press, 2010.

Fuller, Robert Lynn. *The Origins of the French Nationalist Movement, 1886–1914*. London: McFarland & Co., 2012.

Goldberg, Ann. *Honor, Politics, and the Law in Imperial Germany, 1871–1914*. Cambridge: Cambridge University Press, 2010.

Greenberg, Kenneth S. *Honor & Slavery*. Princeton, NJ: Princeton University Press, 1996.

Guillet, François. "La tyrannie de l'honneur: Les usages du duel dans la France du premier XIXe siècle." *Revue historique* 4, no. 640 (2006): 879–99.

Gullace, Nicoletta F. *"The Blood of Our Sons": Men, Women, and the Renegotiation of British Citizenship During the Great War*. New York: Palgrave, 2002.

Honour, Violence, and Emotions in History. Edited by Carolyn Strange, Robert Cribb, and Christopher E. Forth. London: Bloomsbury, 2014.

Jeanneney, Jean Noël. *Le Duel: Une passion française, 1789–1914.* Paris: Seuil, 2004.

Klejman, Laurence, and Florence Rochefort. *L'Egalité en marche: Le féminisme sous la Troisième République.* Paris: des Femmes, 1989.

Laborie, Émile Bruneau de. *Les Lois du duel.* Paris: Manzi, Joyant et Cie, 1906.

"Loi sur la liberté de la Presse," No. 637. *Bulletin des lois de la République française, XII série, deuxième semestre de 1881.* Paris: Imprimerie nationale, 1881.

Madame ou Mademoiselle? Itinéraires de la solitude féminine XVIIe-XXe siècle. Edited by Arlette Farge and Christiane Klapisch-Zuber. Paris: Editions Montalba, 1984.

Mansker, Andrea. *Sex, Honor, and Citizenship in Early Third Republic France.* Houndsmills, Basingstoke, Hampshire: Palgrave, 2011.

Moses, Claire Goldberg. *French Feminism in the 19th Century.* Albany, NY: SUNY Press, 1984.

Nord, Philip. *The Republican Moment: Struggles for Democracy in Nineteenth-Century France.* Cambridge, MA: Harvard University Press, 1995.

Nuñez, Rachel. "Between France and the World: The Gender Politics of Cosmopolitanism, 1835–1914." PhD Dissertation, Stanford University, 2006.

Nye, Robert A. "The End of the Modern French Duel," in *Men and Violence: Gender, Honor, and Rituals in Modern Europe and America.* Edited by Pieter Spierenburg. Columbus, OH: Ohio State University Press, 1998.

———. "Honor and Shame," in *Encyclopedia of European Social History from 1350 to 2000,* vol. 5. Edited by Peter N. Stearns. New York: Charles Scribner's Sons, 2001.

———. *Masculinity and Male Codes of Honor in Modern France.* Berkeley, CA: University of California Press, 1993.

———. "Medicine and Science as Masculine 'Fields of Honor.'" *Osiris* 2nd Series, vol. 12. *Women, Gender, and Science: New Directions* (1997): 60–79.

Offen, Karen. *European Feminisms, 1700–1950.* Stanford, CA: Stanford University Press, 2000.

Palmer, Michael B. *Des petits journaux aux grandes agences: naissance du journalisme moderne.* Paris: Aubier, 1983.

Pateman, Carole. *The Sexual Contract.* Stanford, CA: Stanford University Press, 1988.

Petit, Jacques. *Barbey d'Aurevilly: Critique.* Paris: Les Belles Lettres, 1963.

Pitt-Rivers, Julian. "Honor." In *International Encyclopedia of the Social Sciences.* New York: Macmillan, 1968.

Reddy, William M. "Condottieri of the Pen: Journalists and the Public Sphere in Post-Revolutionary France, 1815–1850." *American Historical Review* 99, no. 5 (1994): 1546–70.

———. *The Invisible Code: Honor and Sentiment in Postrevolutionary France, 1814–1848.* Berkeley, CA: University of California Press, 1997.

———. "Marriage, Honor, and the Public Sphere in Postrevolutionary France: Séparations de Corps, 1815–1848." *Journal of Modern History* 65, no. 3 (September 1993): 437–72.

Roberts, Mary Louise. *Disruptive Acts: The New Woman in Fin-de-Siècle France.* Chicago: University of Chicago Press, 2002.

———. "Subversive Copy: Feminist Journalism in Fin-de-Siècle France," in *Making the News: Modernity and the Mass Press in Nineteenth-Century France.* Edited by Dean de la Motte and Jeannene M. Przyblyski. Amherst, MA: University of Massachusetts Press, 1999.

Salomon, Hélène. "Le corset: entre la beauté et la santé, 1880–1920," in *Histoire du sport féminin,* vol. 2. Edited by Arnaud and Terret. Paris: L'Harmattan, 1996.

Teulet, A. F. *Les Codes de l'Empire Français,* 9th edn. Paris: Librairie Videcoq, 1860.

Thimm, Carl Albert. *A Complete Bibliography of Fencing and Dueling.* Gretna, LA: Pelican Publishing Co., 1896.

Verger de St. Thomas, Charles du. *Nouveau code du duel: histoire, législation, droit contemporain.* Paris: Dentu, 1879.

Vizetelly, Henry. *Glances Back Through Seventy Years,* vol. 2. London: Kegan Paul, Trench, Turner & Co., 1893.

Walton, Whitney. *Eve's Proud Descendants: Four Women Writers and Republican Politics in Nineteenth-Century France*. Stanford, CA: Stanford University Press, 2000.

CHAPTER 11: A WOMAN'S HONOR: PURITY NORMS AND MALE VIOLENCE (VANDELLO AND HETTINGER)

Abbey, Antonia, Catherine Cozzarelli, Kimberly McLaughlin, and Richard Harnish. "The Effects of Clothing and Dyad Sex Composition on Perceptions of Sexual Intent: Do Women and Men Evaluate These Cues Differently?" *Journal of Applied Social Psychology* 17 (1987): 108–26.

Altermatt, T. William, Nathan DeWall and Emily Leskinen. "Agency and Virtue: Dimensions Underlying Subgroups of Women." *Sex Roles* 49 (2003): 631–41.

Baker, Nancy V., Peter R. Gregware and Margery A. Cassidy. "Family Killing Fields: Honor Rationales in the Murder of Women." *Violence Against Women* 5 (1999): 164–84.

Baldry, Anna C., Stefano Pagliaro, and Cesar Procaro. "The Rule of Law at Time of Masculine Honor: Afghan Police Attitudes and Intimate Partner Violence." *Group Processes & Intergroup Relations* 16 (2013): 363–74.

Baumeister, Roy F. and Jean M. Twenge. "Cultural Suppression of Female Sexuality." *Review of General Psychology* 6 (2002): 166–203.

Baumeister, Roy F., and Kathleen D. Vohs. "Sexual Economics: Sex as Female Resource for Social Exchange in Heterosexual Interactions." *Personality and Social Psychology Review* 8 (2004): 339–63.

Berdahl, Jennifer. "The Sexual Harassment of Uppity Women." *Journal of Applied Psychology* 92 (2007): 425–37.

Bordin, Ruth. *Woman and Temperance: The Quest for Power and Liberty, 1873–1900*. Philadelphia, PA: Temple University Press, 1981.

Bowman, James. *Honor: A History*. New York: Encounter Books, 2006.

Brandt, Allan. *The Cigarette Century: The Rise, Fall, and Deadly Persistence of the Product that Defined America*. New York: Basic Books, 2009.

Cahoon, Delwin D. and Ed M. Edmonds. "Male-Female Estimates of Opposite-Sex First Impressions Concerning Females' Clothing Styles." *Bulletin of the Psychonomic Society* 27 (1989): 280–81.

Caulfield, Sueann, Sarah Chambers and Lara Putnam, eds., *Honor, Status, and Law in Modern Latin America*. Durham, NC: Duke University Press, 2005.

Cihangir, S. "Gender Specific Honor Codes and Cultural Change." *Group Processes & Intergroup Relations* 16 (2012): 319–33.

Cooney, Mark. "Death by Family: Honor Violence as Punishment." *Punishment & Society* 16 (2014): 406–27.

Coontz, Stephanie. *Marriage: A History*. New York: Penguin, 2006.

Davis, Kingsley. "Intermarriage in Caste Societies." *American Anthropologist* 43 (1941): 376–95.

Delgado, Anna R., Girardo Prieto, and Roderick Bond. "The Cultural Factor in Lay Perceptions of Jealousy as a Motive for Wife Battery." *Journal of Applied Social Psychology* 27 (1997): 1824–41.

Edlund, Lena. "Son Preference, Sex Ratios, and Marriage Patterns." *Journal of Political Economy* 107 (1999): 1275–1304.

Georgas, James, John W. Berry, Fons J. R. van de Vijver, Cigdem Kagitsibasi, and Ype H. Poortinga, eds., *Families Across Cultures: A 30-nation Psychological Study*. Cambridge: Cambridge University Press, 2006.

Gilmore, David D. *Manhood in the Making*. New Haven, CT: Yale University Press, 1990.

Glenn, Norval D., Adreian Ross, and Judy C. Tully. "Patterns of Intergenerational Mobility of Females Through Marriage." *American Sociological Review* 39 (1974): 683–99.

Glick, Peter and Susan T. Fiske. "The Ambivalent Sexism Inventory: Differentiating Hostile and Benevolent Sexism." *Journal of Personality and Social Psychology* 70 (1996): 491–512.

———. "An Ambivalent Alliance: Hostile and Benevolent Sexism as Justifications for Gender Inequality." *American Psychologist* 56 (2001): 109–118.

Glick, Peter, Susan T. Fiske, Antonio Mladinic, José Saiz, Dominic Abrams, Barbara Masser, Bolanle Adetoun, et al. "Beyond Prejudice as Simple Antipathy: Hostile and Benevolent Sexism Across Cultures." *Journal of Personality and Social Psychology* 79 (2000): 763–75.

Gusfield, Joseph R. "The Social Symbolism of Smoking and Health," in *Smoking Policy: Law, Politics, and Culture*. Edited by Robert L. Rabin & Stephen D. Sugarman. New York: Oxford University Press, 1993,, 49–68

Haidt, Jonathan, Silvia Helena Koller, and Maria Dias. "Affect, Cultures, and Morality, or is it Wrong to Eat Your Dog?" *Journal of Personality and Social Psychology* 65 (1993): 613–28.

Haidt, Jonathan, Paul Rozin, Clark McCauley, and Sumio Imada. "Body, Psyche, and Culture: The Relationship of Disgust to Morality." *Psychology and Developing Societies* 9 (1997): 107–31.

Hausmann, Ricardo, Laura D. Tyson, and Saadia Zahidi. *The Global Gender Gap Report 2011*. Geneva, Switzerland: World Economic Forum, 2011.

Heinrich, Joseph, Robert Boyd, and Peter Richerson. "The Puzzle of Monogamous Marriage." *Philosophical Transactions of the Royal Society* 367 (2012): 657–69.

Hettinger, Vanessa and Joseph A. Vandello. *It's Different for Girls: Purity as a Gendered Moral Code*, 2014.

Infanger, Martina, Laurie A. Rudman, and Sabine Sczesny. "Sex as a Source of Power? Backlash Against Self-Sexualizing Women." *Group Processes and Intergroup Relations* 19, no. 1 (2014): 110–24.

Johnson, Lyman L. and Sonya Lipsett-Rivera, eds., *The Faces of Honor: Sex, Shame, and Violence in Colonial Latin America*. Albuquerque, NM: University of New Mexico Press, 1998.

Keen, Maurice. *Chivalry*. New Haven, CT: Yale University Press, 1984.

Kelley, Harold H. and John Thibaut. *Interpersonal Relations: A Theory of Interdependence*. New York: Wiley, 1978.

Lara-Cantu, Maria A. "A Sex-Role Inventory with Scales for 'Machismo' and 'Self-Sacrificing Woman.'" *Journal of Cross-Cultural Psychology* 20 (1989): 386–98.

Maass, Anne, Mara Cardinu, and Annalisa Grasselli. "Sexual Harassment Under Social Identity Threat: The Computer Harassment Paradigm." *Journal of Personality and Social Psychology* 85 (2003): 853–70.

Mandeville, Elizabeth. "Sexual Pollution in the New Guinea Highlands." *Sociology of Health and Illness* 1 (1979): 226–41.

Merton, Robert K. "Intermarriage and the Social Structure: Fact and Theory." *Psychiatry* 4 (1941): 361–74.

Mintz, Steven. *Moralists and Modernizers: America's Pre-Civil War Reformers*. Baltimore: Johns Hopkins University Press, 1995.

Murdock, George P. *Ethnographic Atlas*. Pittsburgh, PA: University of Pittsburgh Press, 1967.

Nisbett, Richard E. and Dov Cohen. *Culture of Honor: The Psychology of Violence in the South*. Boulder, CO: Westview Press, 1996.

Oishi, Shigehiro. "The Psychology of Residential Mobility: Implications for the Self, Social Relationships, and Well-being." *Perspectives on Psychological Science* 5 (2010): 5–21.

Ortner, Sherry B. "The Virgin and the State." *Feminist Studies* 4 (1978): 19–35.

Pitt-Rivers, Julian. "Honour and Social Status," in *Honour and Shame: The Values of Mediterranean Society*. Edited by Jean Peristiany. London: Weidenfeld & Nicolson, 1965, 19–77.

Posner, Richard. *Sex and Reason*. Cambridge. MA: Harvard, 1991.

Rozin, Paul and April Fallon. "A Perspective on Disgust." *Psychological Review* 94 (1987): 23–41.
Rudman, Laurie A. and Peter Glick. "Prescriptive Gender Stereotypes and Backlash Toward Agentic Women." *Journal of Social Issues* 57 (2001): 743–62.
Schneider, Jane. "Of Vigilance and Virgins." *Ethnology* 9 (1971): 1–24.
Stevens, Evelyn. "Machismo and Marianismo." *Transaction Society* 10 (1973): 57–63.
Tybur, Joshua M., Debra Lieberman, and Vladas Griskevicius. "Microbes, Mating and Morality: Individual Differences in Three Functional Domains of Disgust." *Journal of Personality and Social Psychology* 97 (2009): 103–122.
Vaillancourt, Tracy and Aanchal Sharma. "Intolerance of Sexy Peers: Intrasexual Competition Among Women. *Aggressive Behavior* 37 (2011): 569–77.
Vandello, Joseph A. and Dov Cohen. "Male Honor and Female Fidelity: Implicit Cultural Scripts that Perpetuate Domestic Violence." *Journal of Personality and Social Psychology* 84 (2003): 997–1010.
———. "Gender, Culture, and Men's Intimate Partner Violence." *Social and Personality Psychology Compass* 2 (2008): 652–67.
Vandello, Joseph A., Dov Cohen, Ruth Grandon, and Renae Franiuk. "Stand by Your Man: Indirect Prescriptions for Honorable Violence and Feminine Loyalty in Canada, Chile, and the United States." *Journal of Cross-Cultural Psychology* 40 (2009): 81–104.
Vandello, Joseph A., Vanessa Hettinger, and Dov Cohen, *Female Moral Purity and the Market for Women: A Global Study*. 2015.
Warner, Jessica. "The Naturalization of Beer and Gin in Early Modern England." *Contemporary Drug Problems* 24 (1997): 373–402.
Watson, Lawrence C. "Sexual Socialization in Guajiro Society." *Ethnology* 11 (1972): 150–56.
Welter, Barbara. "The Cult of True Womanhood: 1820–1860." *American Quarterly* 18 (1966): 151–74.
Youssef, Nadia. "Cultural Ideals, Feminine Behavior, and Family Control." *Comparative Studies in Society and History* 13 (1973): 326–47.
Yuki, Masaki and Joanna Schug. "Relational Mobility: A Socio-Ecological Approach to Personal Relationships." In *Relationship Science: Integrating Evolutionary, Neuroscience, and Sociocultural Approaches*. Edited by Omri Gillath, Glenn E. Adams, and Adrianne D. Kunkel. Washington, DC: American Psychological Association, 2012, 137–52.

CHAPTER 12: RESTORING ORDER: THE ANCIENT GREEKS ON TAMING HONOR AND APPETITE (LEBOW)

Aristotle. *The Complete Works of Aristotle*, 2 vols. Edited by Jonathan Barnes. Princeton, NJ: Princeton University Press, 1984.
Diels, Hermann and Walther Kranz. *Die Fragmente der Vorsokratiker*, 7th edn. Berlin: Weidmannsche, 1954.
Herodotus. *The Histories*. Translated by George Rawlinson. New York: Alfred A. Knopf, 1997.
Homer. *Iliad*. Translated by Robert Fagles. New York: Viking, 1990.
Kraut, Richard. *Aristotle: Political Philosophy*. New York: Oxford University Press, 2002.
Lebow, Richard Ned. *The Tragic Vision of Politics*. Cambridge: Cambridge University Press, 2003.
Plato. *The Collected Dialogues*. Translated by Edith Hamilton and Huntington Cairns. Princeton, NJ: Princeton University Press, 1989.
Thucydides. *The Landmark Thucydides: A Comprehensive Guide to the Peloponnesian War*. Edited by Robert B. Strassler. New York: The Free Press, 1996.
Veblen, Thorstein. *The Theory of the Leisure Class: An Economic Study in the Evolution of Institutions*. New York: Modern Library, 1934 [1898].

CHAPTER 13: "THE HONOUR OF THE CROWN": THE STATE AND ITS SOLDIERS (ROBINSON)

Arnot, David. "The Honour of the First Nations—The Honour of the Crown: The Unique Relationship of First Nations with the Crown." In *The Evolving Canadian Crown*. Edited by Jennifer Smith and D. Michael Jones. Montreal: McGill-Queen's University Press, 2012.

Bacevich, Andrew J. *The New American Militarism: How Americans Are Seduced By War*. Oxford: Oxford University Press, 2005.

Bare, Stacy. "On Veterans' Sense of Entitlement: Hey, If Your Country Is Good Enough to Fight for, Then It Is Good Enough to Come Home to," *Foreign Policy*, June 7, 2012. http://foreignpolicy.com/2012/06/07/on-veterans-sense-of-entitlement-hey-if-your-country-is-good-enough-to-fight-for-then-it-is-good-enough-to-come-home-to.

Forster, Anthony. "British Judicial Engagement and the Juridification of the Armed Forces." *International Affairs* 88, no. 2 (2012): 283–300.

Forster, Anthony. "The Military Covenant and British Civil-Military Relations: Letting the Genie out of the Bottle." *Armed Forces & Society* 38, no. 2 (2012): 276.

Gallant v The Queen (1978), 91 DLR (3d) 695, 1978 CarswellNat 560 (WL) (FCTD).

Gross, Michael "Why Treat the Wounded? Warrior Care, Military Salvage, and National Health." *The American Journal of Bioethics* 8, no. 2 (2008): 3–12.

Guerin v The Queen, [1984] 2 SCR 335, 1984 CanLII 25 (SCC).

Ingram, Sarah. *The Military Covenant: Its Impact on Civil-Military Relations in Britain*. Farnham: Ashgate, 2014.

Manuge v Canada, 2008 FC 624.

McCartney, Helen. "The Military Covenant and the Civil-Military Contract in Britain." *International Affairs* 86, no. 2 (2010): 411–28.

McAteer v Canada (Attorney General), 2014 ONCA 578 (CanLII).

McClennan v Canada (Minister of National Defence), 2002 FCT 244.

McMahan, Jeff. *Killing in War*. Oxford: Clarendon, 2009.

Mileham, Patrick. "Unlimited Liability and the Military Covenant." *Journal of Military Ethics* 9, no. 1 (2010): 23–40.

Murrison, Andrew. *Tommy This An' Tommy That: The Military Covenant*. London: Biteback, 2011.

Reynolds, Susan. *Fiefs and Vassals: The Medieval Evidence Reinterpreted*. Oxford: Oxford University Press, 1994.

Ricks, Thomas E. "Sure, You're a Vet, But That Doesn't Mean You Have License to Act Like a Jerk," *Foreign Policy*, June 17, 2011. http://foreignpolicy.com/2011/06/17/sure-youre-a-vet-but-that-doesnt-mean-you-have-license-to-act-like-a-jerk.

Skocpol, Theda. *Protecting Soldiers and Mothers: The Political Origins of Social Policy in the United States*. Cambridge, MA.: Belknap Press, 1992.

Scott v Canada, 2013 BCSC 1651.

Scott v Canada, (2 January 2014), Vancouver, CA041232 (BCCA) (Factum of the Appellant), online: http://equitassociety.ca/11035228_1_Appellant's%20Factum%20.pdf.

The Armed Forces Covenant: Today and Tomorrow. London: Ministry of Defence, 2010.

CHAPTER 14: HONOR IN MILITARY CULTURE: A STANDARD OF INTEGRITY AND FRAMEWORK FOR MORAL RESTRAINT (THOMAS AND FRENCH)

Aurelius, Marcus. *Meditations*. Translated by Maxwell Staniforth. New York: Penguin Books, 1964.

Budoshoshinshu: The Warrior's Primer of Daidoji Yuzan. Translated by William Scott Wilson. Santa Clara, CA: O'Hara Publications, 1984.

French, Shannon E. *The Code of the Warrior: Exploring Warrior Values, Past and Present.* Lanham, MD: Rowman & Littlefield, 2003.
Homer. *Iliad*. Translated by Stanley Lombardo. Indianapolis, IN: Hackett, 1997.
———. *Iliad*. Translated by William Munford. Boston: Little & Brown, 1846.
———. *Iliad*. Translated by E. V. Rieu. Harmondsworth, UK: Penguin Books, 1950.
Morgan, D. O. "The Great Yasa of Chingiz Khan and the Mongol Law in the Ilkhanate." *Bulletin of the School of Oriental and African Studies* 49, no.1 (1986): 163–76.
Spiller, Roger. *An Instinct for War.* Cambridge, MA: Harvard University Press, 2005
Varley, Paul H. *Samurai*. New York: Delacourte Press, 1970.

Index

About the Contributors

Anthony Cunningham is professor of philosophy at St. John's University in Collegeville, Minnesota. He is the author of *Modern Honor: A Philosophical Defense* (Routledge, 2013) and *The Heart of What Matters: The Role for Literature in Moral Philosophy* (California, 2001). His work has appeared in *The Philosopher's Annual, American Philosophical Quarterly, The Journal of Value Inquiry, Dialogue, Mind, Ethics, Philosophy & Phenomenological Research*, and *The Dalhousie Review*.

Dan Demetriou is associate professor of philosophy at the University of Minnesota, Morris. His honor-related publications explain why "honor ethics" is a plausible moral approach that offers a fresh perspective on old debates in metaethics, ethical theory, applied ethics, and (as represented in this volume) political philosophy. His present research contrasts authoritarianism with agonism, and explores the implications of this critical distinction for political and evolutionary psychology.

Amitai Etzioni is university professor and professor of international affairs at The George Washington University. He previously served as a senior advisor at the Carter White House, taught at Columbia University, Harvard, and the University of California at Berkeley, and served as the president of the American Sociological Association. A study by Richard Posner ranked him among the top one hundred American intellectuals. He is the author of numerous books, including *The Moral Dimension, The New Golden Rule*, and *My Brother's Keeper*. His newest book *Privacy in a Cyber Age: Policy and Practice* was published by Palgrave in 2015.

Steven Forde is professor of political science at the University of North Texas. He has published across the history of political thought, including American political thought and international ethics. He has books on Thucydides (*Alcibiades and the Politics of Imperialism in Thucydides*), and John Locke (*Locke, Science, and Politics*). He currently serves as coeditor of the *American Political Science Review*.

Shannon E. French is Inamori professor in ethics, director of the Inamori International Center for Ethics and Excellence, and associate professor in the philosophy department at Case Western Reserve University. She is a senior associate at the Center for Strategic and International Studies in

Washington, DC. Her main area of research is military ethics; especially conduct of war issues, ethical leadership, command climate, sacrifice and responsibility, warrior transitions, ethical responses to terrorism and the future of warfare. She is the author of many scholarly publications, and her 2003 book, *The Code of the Warrior: Exploring Warrior Values, Past and Present,* features a foreword by Senator John McCain. She is editor in chief for the *International Journal of Ethical Leadership* and an associate editor for the *Journal of Military Ethics* and the *Encyclopedia of Global Justice.*

Mark Griffith is professor of political science at the University of West Alabama, Livingston. He lives in Tuscaloosa, Alabama, with his wife and editor Suzette Griffith. He has published articles on John Locke and Winston S. Churchill and is currently working on the historical and fictional writings of Winston Churchill, as well as expanding his chapter "Winston Churchill and Honor: The Complexity of Honor and Statesmanship" into a book.

Vanessa Hettinger is assistant professor of psychology at the University of Wisconsin, Superior. Her research focuses on the sociocultural and social cognitive mechanisms behind attitudes related to gender and sexual orientation. She graduated from Amherst College with a BA in psychology and English in 2004. In 2008 she received a JD from Harvard Law School, and in 2014 she earned her PhD in psychology from the University of South Florida.

Laurie M. Johnson is professor of political science at Kansas State University. She directs K-State's Primary Texts Certificate program. She enjoys teaching undergraduate and graduate students political and social thought, and she is the author of numerous articles and several books, including two on honor: *Thomas Hobbes: Turning Point for Honor* (2009) and *Locke and Rousseau: Two Enlightenment Responses to Honor* (2012), both published by Lexington Books. She is currently working on a book on Alexis de Tocqueville's *Democracy in America* and the question of honor in America.

Sharon Krause is professor of political science at Brown University. She is the author of *Liberalism with Honor* (Harvard University Press, 2002); *Civil Passions: Moral Sentiment and Democratic Deliberation* (Princeton University Press, 2008); and *Freedom Beyond Sovereignty: Reconstructing Liberal Individualism* (University of Chicago Press, 2015). She has also published numerous articles on topics in classical and contemporary liberalism including political agency and civic engagement; freedom and social inequality; emotions and politics; and justice.

Richard Ned Lebow is professor of international political theory in the Department of War Studies at King's College, London. He is James O. Freedman Presidential Professor (Emeritus) of Government, Dartmouth College. He is the author of many influential works on international relations, including *Constructing Cause in International Relations* (Cambridge University Press, 2014) and *Why Nations Fight: Past and Future Motives for War* (Cambridge University Press, 2010). His forthcoming title is *National Identification and International Relations*.

Andrea Mansker is associate professor of history and chair of women's and gender studies at Sewanee: University of the South. She is the author of *Sex, Honor, and Citizenship in Early Third Republic France* (Palgrave Macmillan, 2011) and is currently preparing a book manuscript entitled *Matchmaking and the Marriage Market in Nineteenth-Century France*. Her recent publications include "The Legal Pitfalls of Marriage Brokerage in Nineteenth-Century France," in *Kinship and Community: Social and Cultural History*, eds. Jason Coy, Ben Marschke, Jared Poley, and Claudia Verhoeven (Berghahn, 2014), and "Shaming Men: Feminist Honor and the Sexual Double Standard," in *Confronting Modernity in Fin-de-Siècle France: Bodies, Minds, and Gender*, eds. Christopher Forth and Elinor Accampo (Palgrave Macmillan, 2010).

Ryan Rhodes is a graduate of the University of Oklahoma, where he earned his PhD in philosophy in 2012. In addition to his work on honor, his research interests include philosophy of religion, philosophy of disability, and the philosophy of civil discourse. He sees in honor a valuable conception of morality that is lost to much of modern theory. His other research interests include philosophy of fiction and literature, situationist challenges to virtue ethics, and the problem of evil. He has recently published work in the *International Journal for Philosophy of Religion*. Ryan currently teaches for both Pima Community College and Stephen F. Austin State University.

Paul Robinson is professor in public and international affairs at the University of Ottawa. He is the author and editor of numerous books and articles on various aspects of military and Russian history, military ethics, and international security. His books include *Military Honour and the Conduct of War: From Ancient Greece to Iraq*, published by Routledge in 2006.

Steven Skultety is associate professor of philosophy, and chair of the Department of Philosophy and Religion, at the University of Mississippi. He received his BA from the University of Montana and PhD from Northwestern University. His current research focuses on the way ancient philosophers understood human beings who were at odds with one another, but his interests also include contemporary virtue theory, republicanism, and democratic theory.

Joe Thomas currently serves as the Class of '61 chair and distinguished professor of leadership education at the U.S. Naval Academy and as the academic director, U.S. Customs and Border Protection Leadership Institute, Robert H. Smith School of Business at the University of Maryland. He has also taught at the University of Notre Dame, George Washington University and National Outdoor Leadership School, and is the past Director, John A. Lejeune Leadership Institute at Marine Corps University.

Joe Vandello is professor of psychology at the University of South Florida, where he has been faculty since 2002. His research explores gender and cultural influences on violence and aggression, risk taking, work, and health, and he has published his work in various social psychological and gender-themed journals. He received a BSc in psychology from the University of Iowa and PhD in psychology from the University of Illinois at Urbana-Champaign.

Ajume H. Wingo is associate professor of philosophy and the director of the Center for Values and Social Policies at the University of Colorado at Boulder. He is the author of *Veil Politics in Liberal Democratic States*, published by Cambridge University Press. He is currently working on two book manuscripts, *The Citizen of Africa* and *Civic Immortality: Honoring Liberal Heroics in Africa and Abroad* with Dan Demetriou.